# LETTERS OF THE EMPRESS FREDERICK

# LETTERS OF THE EMPRESS FREDERICK

Edited by Sir Frederick Ponsonby

With a new Foreword by John Van der Kiste

*A & F Reprints*

First published by Macmillan 1928
Published by A & F 2016

Foreword Copyright © John Van der Kiste 2016
All rights reserved

A & F Publications
South Brent, Devon, England TQ10 9AS

Cover: Detail from Crown Princess Frederick William of Prussia, 1880, by Heinrich Joachim von Angeli

ISBN (13-digit) 978-1537313566
ISBN (10-digit) 1537313568

Typeset in Baskerville 11/10.5pt

# Contents

| | |
|---|---|
| Foreword | 2 |
| Preface | 7 |
| Introduction | 9 |
| I: Birth, Education and Marriage | 16 |
| II: Early Years in Prussia | 24 |
| III: The Austrian War | 53 |
| IV: The Franco-Prussian War | 63 |
| V: Bismarck and Russia, 1871-1878 | 106 |
| VI: The Crown Princess and her Family | 133 |
| VII: Foreign Affairs, 1878-1886 | 147 |
| VIII: Prince Alexander of Battenberg | 156 |
| IX: The Illness of the Crown Prince Frederick | 181 |
| X: San Remo | 200 |
| XI: The Reign of the Emperor Frederick | 226 |
| XII: The Emperor William II | 248 |
| XIII: The War Diary of the Emperor Frederick | 263 |
| XIV: The Emperor William's Visit to England | 282 |
| XV: The Fall of Prince Bismarck | 297 |
| XVI: Caprivi's Chancellorship | 318 |
| XVII: Closing Years | 344 |
| Index | 362 |

*Illustrations appear between pages 174 and 181*

# Foreword

(This introduction is based partly on an article by the author which originally appeared in *Royalty Digest*, 21, March 1993)

THE publication of *Letters of The Empress Frederick* in October 1928 was the culmination of an extraordinary series of events. In September 1888, three months after the death of Frederick III, German Emperor, his widow asked for her correspondence with Queen Victoria to be returned from Windsor. Twelve years later, in February 1901, Sir Frederick Ponsonby, equerry and private secretary to King Edward VII, accompanied him on his first visit overseas since succeeding his mother on the throne, to the Empress at Friedrichshof, her country house near Cronberg. Now seriously ill, she had less than six months to live. Anxious that her letters should not fall into the hands of her son, Emperor William II, she asked Ponsonby to take them back to England. His account of how he accomplished this is given in the introduction, and also in his memoirs.[1] The Empress's grandson Wolfgang, Prince of Hesse, later asserted that his story was 'rich in imaginative detail, and much of it is not in accordance with the facts'.[2] Her granddaughter Victoria Louise, Duchess of Brunswick, was even more scathing, writing that 'it reads not only like a crime novel, but has the merit of being one – it is clearly fabricated'.[3]

For over twenty years Ponsonby hesitated to publish the material, but at length a number of biographies and reminiscences, including those of Chancellor Bismarck, two volumes of the former Emperor William's Memoirs, and a biography of the Emperor by Emil Ludwig, based on official German state documents, virtually forced his hand. Ludwig's portrait of the Empress had been particularly damning. Among the letters Ponsonby had in his possession was a memorandum written by the Empress shortly before her husband's death, in which she noted that 'the truth which is being so systematically smothered and twisted must be put down somewhere, no matter whether it be published in my lifetime or no'.[4]

When asked whether publication of the correspondence would meet with court approval, King George V said he was opposed to the idea in principle. He advised Ponsonby to ask the Empress's surviving brother and sisters, Prince Arthur, Duke of Connaught, Princess Louise, Duchess of Argyll, and Princess Beatrice. The latter regarded all family correspondence as for private eyes only, but the others agreed with Ponsonby that their eldest sister had always intended publication in order to set the record straight. At this the King said he neither approved nor disapproved; Ponsonby must act as he thought best. After a year's preparation, the book was published to enthusiastic reviews in the press, and sold very well.

It dispelled several of the myths which had been put about by the Empress's enemies in Germany, namely that she had always despised her handicapped eldest son with his withered arm; that she had ruthlessly dominated her husband, 'poisoning' him with her own liberal hopes and aspirations for a constitutional German monarchy on British lines; and that she had trusted German doctors so little that, against their wishes, she had summoned the British laryngologist, Dr Morell Mackenzie, to take foremost responsibility when Crown Prince Frederick became seriously ill with the cancer of the larynx which ultimately killed him.

The first of the letters, dated 12 February 1859, was written and dictated to Countess Blücher, a lady-in-waiting, while she was recovering from the birth of her eldest son. A second from later that month describes her delight at being a mother, though neither make any reference to his withered arm. Two years later she and her husband became Crown Prince and Princess of Prussia when King Frederick William IV died, and there is a long, particularly moving description of the deathbed scene.

After these family descriptions, the letters become largely political in tone. She describes the 'Danzig incident' in 1863, when the Crown Prince spoke out against Bismarck's muzzling of the press, and the wars in which Bismarck's policy involved the country. There was the shock of Tsar Alexander II's assassination in 1881; her husband's friendship with Crown Prince Rudolf of Austria; and most of all her distress when the Crown Prince became ill early in 1887. He survived his nonagenarian father, William I, to succeed to the imperial throne in March 1888, and Ponsonby was perhaps a little unjust when stating in his commentary that, at this stage, 'the Empress still could not realise that at most her husband could live but a few months'. Otherwise, his selection of letters conveys vividly the battle which the Empress had been fighting to keep her husband's spirits up, while knowing that he was, as some of the more callous conservatives at the Berlin court put it, 'as good as dead'.

Just as moving are the widowed Empress's letters about her eldest son's shameful behaviour and insults to his father's memory, not to mention the witch hunts against Dr (later Sir) Morell Mackenzie and his candid if ill-advised book, *The Fatal Illness of Frederick the Noble*, and her friend Professor Geffcken, who published a series of extracts from the Emperor's war diary, putting a very different perspective on his and Bismarck's roles vis-à-vis the creation of the German Empire in which the then Crown Prince Frederick William had played a more significant role than was generally acknowledged.

To her credit, the Empress defied those whom she maintained were trying to hound her out of her adopted country. She found solace in the building of Friedrichshof, the loyalty of her younger children, and her patronage of numerous charitable societies. Until a riding accident in 1898, and diagnosis of cancer of the spine soon afterwards, her energies were almost undimmed.

Yet during thirteen years of widowhood, she never gave up hope that the true story of her husband and herself would one day be told. As the Duke of Connaught observed in two letters to Ponsonby after the book's publication, he had been right in publishing the letters, more especially as the Emperor had already written and published his side of the controversy; and Ludwig's book would also 'form history unless contradicted.'[5] The former Emperor William, about to enter his eleventh year of exile in the Netherlands, was embarrassed and threatened to sue Ponsonby for theft. On being advised that such a case would be impossible to prove, he purchased the publication rights to the German edition and wrote a preface in which he sought to vindicate his own position and explain his mother's shortcomings of character. He said that she 'was very sensitive and everything wounded her; she saw everything in shadows, everything hostile, saw want of sympathy and coolness where there was only a helpless silence, and her temperament made her use bitter words about everybody. Therefore the reader should not believe implicitly everything she wrote.'[6]

The reactions of other members of the royal family throughout England and Europe were very different. King George, noted Ponsonby, showed initial interest in the book, but after his sharp-tongued sister Princess Victoria denounced it as 'one of the most dreadful books ever published, he joined in the general abuse of it'. Queen Mary said that while he was justified in publishing the book, he should have cut out many of the letters used. Princess Beatrice, who had never approved of the idea, did not read the book but only reviews in the newspapers and condemned it as 'dreadful', while two of the children of the Empress's sister Princess Christian, who had died in 1923, also condemned it.

However the Duchess of Argyll wrote Ponsonby 'a charming letter of approval', as did the Empress's two youngest surviving daughters, the exiled Queen Sophie of Greece and Margaret, Landgravine of Hesse, both of whom had always been very supportive of their mother in her last years and did not always have an easy relationship with their brother William. They did not wish their letters to be quoted, but they thanked him for carrying out their mother's wishes.[7] The Landgravine, who still lived in Germany, also wrote to her friend Lady Corkran that 'you can imagine what it means to me to read my beloved mother's letters & to go through all those times again....Sir F. wrote me a beautiful letter explaining his reasons for publishing the book, & I quite understand. From his point of view he was quite right to do so, but here people of course take a different view. I believe the Emperor is very put out about it.'[8] The Duke of Connaught firmly sided with Ponsonby, writing him two long letters in which he said he had done the right thing, as Ludwig's book 'would form history unless contradicted'.

As for Ludwig himself, he wrote an article in *The Observer* in which he graciously recanted his views of the Empress's character as published in his book. He admitted that had the letters been published earlier, it would have resulted in him making 'substantial changes' in his biography of the Emperor.

The book has since been supplemented by several other volumes of correspondence, including those based on the letters between Queen Victoria and her eldest daughter spanning the years 1858 to 1900 in six volumes, edited by Roger Fulford and then by Agatha Ramm, published between 1964 and 1990,[9] and to an extent the more personal exchanges between the Empress and her third daughter Sophie, Crown Princess of Greece between 1889 and 1901, edited by Arthur Gould Lee and published in 1955.[10] Even so it remains a fascinating, moving document of nineteenth century and biography, and an indispensable source of material for any study of the lives of the last two German Emperors as well as the Empress herself.

Sir Frederick ('Fritz') Ponsonby was born in September 1867, second son of Sir Henry, Queen Victoria's private secretary. He was appointed equerry and assistant private secretary to the Queen after his father's death in 1895 and remained at court for the rest of his life, apart from brief periods of service during the Boer War in 1901-2, and again as a junior officer in the Grenadiers on the Western Front in the First World War. An independently-minded individual and never a fawning 'yes-man', he sometimes incurred the wrath of all three sovereigns whom he served at one time or another, never more so than when he took issue with the social pretensions of Queen Victoria's Indian favourite, the notorious Munshi, with the result that she hardly spoke to him for a year afterwards. (His younger brother Arthur, a radical Liberal Member of Parliament, was once pointedly excluded from an invitation to a garden party at Windsor Castle by King Edward VII after outspoken public criticism of his nephew Tsar Nicholas II). He ended his career as Keeper of the Privy Purse and Treasurer, and was raised to the peerage as 1st Baron Sysonby, shortly before his death in October 1935.

Two years after publishing *Letters of the Empress Frederick*, he produced a volume of court memoirs, *Sidelights on Queen Victoria*. His own autobiography, *Recollections of Three Reigns*, published in 1951, has long been regarded as one of the most lively and even amusing books of its kind. It has been described by one of King Edward's major biographers, Sir Philip Magnus, as 'indiscreet', while a more recent historian, Jane Ridley, calls it 'full and funny (though not always reliable)'[11] and Nancy Mitford wrote to Evelyn Waugh that there was 'a shriek on every page'.[12] Part of one chapter includes a full account of his decision to publish the Empress's letters and the subsequent reaction from those concerned.

This edition contains the full text of the original. The original spacing and paragraphs have been retained, with minor alterations to punctuation, such as the substitution of single for double quotation marks. Footnotes have been moved to the end of each chapter. Additional illustrations have been provided, and a few peripheral non-personal names have been omitted from the index.

John Van der Kiste

## NOTES

1 Ponsonby, Sir Frederick, *Recollections of Three Reigns* (Eyre & Spottiswoode, 1951), p.110.
2 Corti, Egon Caesar Conte, *The English Empress* (Cassell, 1957), p.x.
3 Victoria Louise, Princess, *The Kaiser's Daughter* (W.H. Allen, 1977), p.24.
4 See below, p.14.
5 Ponsonby, *Recollections of Three Reigns*, p.112.
6 *Ibid.* pp.114-15.
7 *Ibid.* pp.112.
8 Van der Kiste, John, *The Prussian Princesses* (Fonthill, 2014), p.115.
9 *Dearest Child* (1964), *Dearest Mama* (1968), *Your Dear Letter* (1971), *Darling Child* (1976), *Beloved Mama* (1981), all edited by Roger Fulford, published by Evans Bros; *Beloved and Darling Child* (Alan Sutton, 1990), edited by Agatha Ramm.
10 *The Empress Frederick writes to Sophie* (Faber, 1955), edited by Arthur Gould Lee.
11 Magnus, Philip, *King Edward the Seventh* (John Murray, 1964), p.xv; Ridley, Jane, *Bertie* (Chatto & Windus, 2012), p.370.
12 *Oxford Dictionary of National Biography*.

# Preface

THE main purpose of this volume of the letters of the Empress Frederick has been to allow the Empress's own words to provide the answer to those cruel and slanderous accusations from which her memory has suffered. For this reason the running commentary necessary to enable the reader to understand the letters has been reduced to the minimum.

These letters, while fairly representing the thoughts and opinions of the Empress, give but a very imperfect picture of her character and personality. An advanced thinker of strong liberal views, she hesitated to express such views freely to Queen Victoria, to whom she knew they would not be acceptable. Moreover, the Empress's many artistic activities had associated her with the world of art, where she had imbibed modern theories which did not appeal to the Queen. Consequently the letters hardly refer to those aesthetic tastes which were an outstanding feature in her life.

The material available not being sufficient for a complete biography, the best course seemed to be to concentrate entirely on the letters. It may be urged that a publication must be premature in which, for judicious reasons, some interesting material has to be suppressed. On the other hand, to delay the production of these letters would be to postpone them for a new generation to whom the Empress Frederick would be unknown except as an historic figure.

The letters speak for themselves. They represent a regular weekly, almost daily, correspondence, characterised by the same dutiful tone on the part of the Empress and the same affectionate wisdom from Queen Victoria.

In this volume of letters reference is made to more recent publications containing allusions to the Empress and in the majority of cases acknowledgment is made in the footnote. This, however, does not apply to several letters from Queen Victoria to the Empress and from the Empress to Queen Victoria which have already appeared in *The Letters of Queen Victoria*, edited by Mr George Earle Buckle, and my thanks are due to Sir John Murray for permission to make use of this material.

The papers of my father, the late Sir Henry Ponsonby, contained letters which, though fragmentary, throw sidelights on the subjects discussed by the Empress: these have also been included.

To the Honourable Mrs Hovell I am indebted for many details connected with her husband's experiences at San Remo and also for allowing me to see the papers and newspaper cuttings she had collected dealing with the

Emperor Frederick's illness.

To many friends I am indebted for advice, but particularly to Sir Rennell Rodd who found time to read through the proofs and make many valuable suggestions. Having been an intimate friend of the Empress Frederick and Secretary of Embassy in Berlin during the most interesting part of her life, there is no one living who has a more intimate knowledge of the history of Germany during that period. I am under a great obligation to Mr S. F. Markham, M.A., for the invaluable assistance he gave me. I have also to thank Mr A. V. Marten for having undertaken the arduous task of transcribing the letters.

F. E. G. PONSONBY

# Introduction

THE circumstances under which the letters of the Empress Frederick came into my possession are so exceptional and even dramatic that I make no apology for giving them in detail.

Soon after King Edward came to the throne in 1901, the accounts of the Empress Frederick's health began to be alarming, and as she was his favourite sister, he decided to go and stay with her for a week at Friedrichshof, near Cronberg. He took with him Sir Francis Laking, his physician in ordinary, and myself as Equerry and Private Secretary. The addition of Sir Francis Laking to his suite was very much resented not only by the German doctors attending the Empress, who rightly thought she was past all medical aid, but also by the Emperor's suite, who considered his presence to be a slur on the German medical profession. It was, however, the King's idea that possibly Sir Francis Laking might do something to mitigate her terrible sufferings by administering narcotics in larger doses than the German doctors were accustomed to give.

After I had been at Friedrichshof for three days, I received a message that the Empress wished to see me in the evening at six o'clock. At the hour named I went upstairs and was shown into her sitting-room where I found her propped up with cushions; she looked as if she had just been taken off the rack after undergoing torture. The nurse signed to me to sit down and whispered that the Empress would be better in a moment as she had been given an injection of morphia. I sat down feeling very helpless in the presence of so much suffering, and waited. Suddenly the Empress opened her eyes and began to speak. How did I like Friedrichshof? What did I think of it? Had I seen all her art treasures? The impression that I was talking to a dying woman vanished and I was suddenly conscious that I had to deal with a person who was very much alive and alert. We talked of the South African War and of the way it was being misrepresented in Europe, and we discussed the political situation in England. She asked searching questions about the King's position as a constitutional monarch and expressed her admiration of our constitution, but after a quarter of an hour this intense conversation and hurricane of questions seemed to tire her and she closed her eyes. I remained silent, uncertain whether I ought not leave the room. Just then the nurse came in and said I had been over twenty minutes and that I really must go. 'A few minutes more', said the Empress, and the nurse apparently consented, for she left the room. After a pause the Empress opened her eyes and said, 'There is something I want you to do for me. I want you to take charge of my letters and take them with you back to England.' When I expressed my readiness to undertake their custody she seemed pleased and went on in a dreamy sort of way: 'I will send them to you at one o'clock tonight and I know I can rely on your discretion, I don't want a soul to know that they have been taken away and certainly Willie [her son, the Emperor William II] must not have them, nor must he ever know you have got them.'

Our conversation was again interrupted by the entrance of the nurse, who explained that the Empress had said 'a few minutes' conversation' and I had been with her for over half an hour. This time there was no doubt I had to go and so I retired to my room wondering if the Empress had said all that there was to be said on the subject.

I dined as usual with King Edward. On this occasion the German Emperor, the Duchess of Sparta (afterwards Queen of the Hellenes), Princess Frederick Charles of Hesse (both daughters of the Empress), Countess Perponcher, Count Eulenburg, General von Kessel, General von Scholl, Rear-Admiral von Müller, Count Hohenau and the German doctors Renvers and Spielhagen were also present. After dinner we talked till about eleven, when everyone went to bed. I went to my bedroom and started work. There was so much to do that the time passed quickly.

This was the first time King Edward had gone abroad since he had ascended the throne. Prior to his accession one Equerry had been able to attend to his correspondence, etc., during his visits abroad, and at first he was under the impression that there would be no necessity to increase the number now that he was king. But, as he found out later, it was a totally different proposition, and the work was really more than one man could do. In addition to his official boxes and letters, the ciphering and deciphering of telegrams, and the arrangement for the Foreign Office King's Messengers, there were the requisition of special trains, instructions to the royal yacht and the escort of cruisers, the ordering of guards of honour and the mass of small detail connected with any continental journey. But what made all this doubly difficult was the fact that I had to accompany the King whenever he went out and that often he was out all the afternoon. I had no shorthand clerk in those days and therefore it meant writing till 2 a.m. every night.

The castle clock boomed one and I waited expectantly, but there was dead silence, and I was coming to the conclusion that I had either misunderstood or that some unforeseen obstacle had prevented the letters reaching me, when I heard a quiet knock on my door. I said 'Herein', and four men came in carrying two boxes about the size of portmanteaux, and covered with black oilcloth. The cords round them were quite new and on each box was a plain white label with neither name nor address. I noticed that the men wore blue serge breeches and long riding boots and I came to the conclusion that they were not trusted retainers but stablemen quite ignorant of what the boxes contained. They put the two boxes down and retired without saying a word.

It now dawned on me that I had undertaken no easy task, and I began to wonder how I was to get such large boxes back to England without anyone suspecting their contents. I had assumed, perhaps not unnaturally, that the expression 'letters' meant a packet of letters that I should have no difficulty in concealing in one of my portmanteaux. But these large corded boxes were quite another matter and the problem of getting them back to England required careful thought. To adopt any method of concealment and to attempt to smuggle them away was to court disaster, as the whole place was full of secret police, but on the other hand, to account for these boxes which had apparently dropped from the skies was no easy matter. I therefore wrote on the label of one 'Books with care' and on the other 'China with care', with my private address, and determined to place them in the passage with my empty boxes without any attempt at concealment.

The next morning my servant was astonished to find this weighty addition to my luggage, but I explained in an offhand way that they were things I had bought in Homburg, and that I wanted them placed in the passage. Perhaps even this was injudicious, as the first thing that happened was a visit from King Edward's courier, M. Fehr, who said that strict instructions had been given to the servants that nothing was to be allowed to come into the castle unless it was passed by himself or the Emperor's Chief of Police; yet in spite of all these precautions he found that two boxes of goods from Homburg had reached me without anyone knowing anything about them! This was very awkward, and I felt I was making a bad start. I told him that Custom House officers were bad enough, but if he began to make trouble before I started I should never get the goods into England. 'It is at the Custom House I want your help, not here,' I said in an aggrieved voice. Under the impression that the boxes contained something contraband and that I intended to invoke his aid to get them through the Custom House he became very confidential and said I could rely on his help. So the boxes remained with my other luggage and were seen by everyone who passed along that passage.

On March 1, 1901, we left Friedrichshof to return to London. That day a party of soldiers from the garrison was employed to carry all the luggage down. I was talking to the Emperor in the hall at the time and out of the corner of my eye I could see the procession of soldiers carrying portmanteaux, suitcases, despatch boxes, etc.; when these two black boxes came past they looked so different from the rest of the luggage that I became nervous lest someone should inquire what they were, but no one appeared to notice them, and the Emperor went on talking. When they disappeared from the hall I breathed again, but not for long because, as ill-luck would have it, they were the last to be placed on the wagon which stood in front of the windows of the great hall, and there seemed something wrong with the tarpaulin cover. The other wagons were covered up, but this particular wagon remained uncovered with these two boxes with their new cords and labels staring at me. The Emperor, however, was holding forth on some subject that interested him, and naturally everyone, including myself, listened attentively. It was a great relief when I at last saw the tarpaulin cover drawn over the luggage and a few minutes later heard the wagon rumble away.

After I arrived in England I took the two boxes to my private house, Cell Farm at Old Windsor, and locked them up.

On August 5, 1901, the Empress Frederick died at Friedrichshof, Cronberg, and the funeral took place on the 13th. It was a long-drawn-out ceremony beginning with a service in the little church at Cronberg, after which the body was taken by train to Potsdam where the final service was held. King Edward this time took with him Lord Clarendon (the Lord Chamberlain), Admiral Sir John Fullerton, Major-General Sir Stanley Clarke, the Honourable Sidney Greville, and myself as Private Secretary.

One evening after dinner Count Eulenburg, the head of the Emperor's household, took me aside and said he wanted to speak to me quite confidentially. He explained that when the Empress Frederick died, no letters or papers had been found, although a thorough search had been made, and the Emperor wished me to ascertain, without making too much of it, whether by chance these letters were in the archives at Windsor. To give some idea of how thorough the search was at Cronberg, Sir Arthur Davidson, who happened to be at Homburg at the time and who drove out to Friedrichshof, told me that the grounds were all surrounded by cavalry and the castle itself by special police, while competent searchers ransacked every room.

I replied that there would be no difficulty about this and that I would write at once to Lord Esher, who was Keeper of the Archives. I accordingly did so, knowing full well that Lord Esher was quite unaware of the existence of these letters, and in due course I received a reply saying that they were certainly not in the archives. This I forwarded to Count Eulenburg, who wrote a short note thanking me for all the trouble I had taken.

Some years later I had another conversation with him on the subject and he seemed then to suspect that I was in some way connected with the disappearance of these letters. He asked me several questions about my visit to Friedrichshof, all of which I was able to answer with candour, although I was conscious at the time that these questions were merely the preliminary overtures to more searching and precise inquiries. Fortunately we were interrupted before we got down to the pith of the matter and I was saved from embarrassing questions.

So the letters have remained undisturbed for the last twenty-seven years, and during all this time the question what the Empress intended me to do with them has constantly occurred to me. Obviously I was not meant to burn them, because she could easily have done this herself had she wanted to do so. With every desire to carry out the wishes of a dying woman, I wanted to make sure that I was rightly interpreting them, but there was no one who could throw any light on the matter; no one to whom the Empress had confided her intentions. There seems no doubt that her letters to Queen Victoria must have been sent out from England to her at Friedrichshof, and the question therefore arises why did she send for these letters when she must have known she had not long to live?

The theory that she intended to look through them and select some for publication is strengthened by the fact that occasionally whole pages are rendered undecipherable with erasures. This must have been her work, and if this is the case it is clear that she wished to erase certain passages from the letters before they were eventually published. The fact that she should have sent for these letters, looked through them, deleted passages, and finally have sent them back to England seems to point to her having contemplated their publication.

Having come to the conclusion that the time had arrived when the letters must be sent away to prevent their being destroyed, she thought she could not do better than entrust them to me. I was not only her godson and the son of one of her greatest friends, but I would have exceptional facilities for taking them to England.

The curious part is that she should not have confided her intention to her brother, King Edward, or given him any hint of what she had in her mind. Presumably the fact that her letters to Queen Victoria had been sent out to her must have been known by King Edward and, therefore, if she merely intended to send them back to the archives, it would only have been natural for her to entrust them to her brother. That she did not do so points to her having wished something more done with them, something which she feared would not meet with his approval. Whether she intended to see me again in order to explain her intentions or whether, if the nurse had not interrupted us, she would have done so at the time, must necessarily remain hypotheses that can never be verified.

The most probable theory is that when Bismarck's *Reminiscences* was published and other contemporary memoirs appeared, she writhed under the criticisms of her conduct and objected to the part she was depicted as having played in German politics. She therefore was determined that her side of the question should at least have a hearing and she intended to select certain letters and edit them for publication, at the same time obliterating any passages that were indiscreet and which time had proved to be inaccurate. Her terrible illness made this impossible, and all she was able to do was to erase certain passages. Finding that her end was approaching, she determined to confide her intentions to me, but circumstances prevented her from doing more than giving me the letters. It seems quite inconceivable that if I was merely to hand them back to the King or put them back in the archives, she should not have said so at once or have spoken to her brother on the subject, more especially as she saw him daily during his visit.

On looking through the letters that had been entrusted to my care I found the following letter or memorandum that had been written to Queen Victoria a few months after the death of the Emperor Frederick.[1]

## MEMORANDUM CONCERNING THE COLLECTING OF MATERIAL FOR A LIFE OF FRITZ

As I have never kept a diary the only documents of the thirty years of our married life that exist are my letters to dear Mama, and my correspondence with Fritz. Dear Mama could do me the most immense service, if she would let someone most trustworthy and discreet (under Sir Th. Martin's supervision) be allowed to make extracts from my letters to her concerning the political events, also matters of the court and our life here, etc., with a view to my having selections made and translated from those extracts later. If dear Mama would allow this to be set about soon, it would be a great service to me. My letters to Stockmar are all burnt, those to Countess Blücher also. I must not let the matter rest, I may die any day, and the truth which is being so systematically smothered and twisted must be put down somewhere, no matter whether it be published in my lifetime or no. I feel that my memory has suffered terribly by the shock I have sustained and by the sorrow which seems to have shaken the very foundations of my being.

I can still remember things which I might not remember later. I ought at least to begin to arrange my material. I should be very thankful if dear Mama could help me in this way.

This seems to confirm the theory that the Empress wished her version of events published and that she even considered the possibility of publication during her lifetime.

After her death in 1901, I came to the conclusion that it was not in her interests that these letters should then be published. Even assuming they had been entrusted to me for this purpose, I felt that these wishes had not been expressed with sufficient clearness to warrant my attempting any immediate publication.

These letters have therefore remained untouched during the last twenty-seven years, and it was only the continual reference to and criticism of the Empress Frederick in recent publications that led me to reconsider my responsibility in the matter. These criticisms have been so bitter and so unjust that in the interests of historic truth, to say nothing of the memory of the Empress Frederick, I came to the conclusion that these letters should now be published.

## NOTE

1 The date would appear to be about September 13, 1888.

# I: Birth, Education, and Marriage

THE Empress Frederick was born at Windsor on November 21, 1840. Although there was naturally disappointment that the first child born to Queen Victoria and Prince Albert should be a daughter and not a son, the British public gave a sigh of relief, since it rendered the possibility of a Cumberland succession still more remote. Hitherto, the next heir to the throne had been the unpopular Ernest, Duke of Cumberland, the 'Hanoverian Ogre', as he was called, whose hideous features, accentuated by a distorted eye, whose vindictive bad temper, reactionary politics and dissolute private life made him feared and hated by the great mass of the people.

The birth of the Princess Royal was welcomed in the illustrated journals of the time with a shower of kindly, if not always refined, caricatures, according to the custom of the period. The infant daughter, Victoria Adelaide Mary Louisa, who now became the next in succession to the throne, was christened at Buckingham Palace on February 10, 1841, The sponsors were Prince Albert's 1841 brother, Ernest, Duke of Saxe-Coburg (represented in his absence by the Duke of Wellington), Leopold, King of the Belgians (who had been the husband of the unfortunate Princess Charlotte), Adelaide, the Queen Dowager, the Duchess of Kent, the Duchess of Gloucester and the Duke of Sussex.

On November 9, 1841, the succession to the British throne was rendered more secure by the birth of an infant Prince, Albert Edward, and in due time there also followed Princess Alice (1843), and six other children to Queen Victoria and Prince Albert.

Very early their father, Prince Albert, who as a cadet of the ducal house of Saxe-Coburg had been very highly educated, busied himself with the education of his children. Especial attention did he give his two eldest, the Princess Royal and the Prince of Wales, and it is interesting to compare the results of his system in the case of the Princess Royal, who responded to it, and the Prince of Wales (afterwards Edward VII), who was in spasmodic rebellion against the unending succession of books, lectures and lessons.

As a child the Princess Royal, who had acquired the pet names of 'Pussy' and 'Vicky', soon began to display those characteristics which formed the keynote to her character. She was only three years old when Prince Albert wrote to the family counsellor, Baron Stockmar, 'Pussy is now quite a little personage. She speaks English and French with great fluency and choice of phrase,'[1] but German was the language she spoke to her parents. Quick, clever, self-willed and high-spirited, she easily outdistanced her brothers and sisters in the rapidity with which she assimilated knowledge, and in the nursery and schoolroom lavished upon them the protecting solicitude of superior years. Acute observers dubbed her over-stimulated and even precocious, but the rapidity of thought was not a passing phase – it remained with her to the end. The exacting mental discipline which her father in her early training enforced upon her – as upon his eldest son - gave her qualities of concentration and assimilation which she never lost.

The young Princess had barely entered her teens before rumour began to be rife about prospective husbands. Early in the field with sound advice on the subject was Leopold I, King of the Belgians, Queen Victoria's trusted uncle, counsellor and friend. The fact, however, that a young Teutonic Prince had already made up his mind to win the Princess rendered King Leopold's dissertations on the advantages to be derived from certain alliances a mere waste of paper.

In fairy stories it is customary for the Prince and Princess of neighbouring kingdoms to meet and fall in love without the knowledge of their subsequently delighted parents, but that a romance of this kind should actually happen in mid-Victorian England seems difficult to believe. The somewhat stilted and artificial romanticism of the fifties hardly prepares the mind for so charming an idyll. It was in the year 1851 that the Princess first met her future husband, Prince Frederick William of Prussia. In that year Europe was ringing with the wonders of the Great Exhibition in Hyde Park, that ironic herald of a decade of war, and the young Prince, sent by his father, the future King William I of Prussia, to study the crowning triumph of Prince Albert's energetic idealism, was the guest of Queen Victoria. Very tall and broad, he was a fine figure of a man to captivate the heart of a young girl, and the touch of austerity imparted by a lonely upbringing may well have been an added charm to the young Princess. At this time he was barely twenty and had seen little of the world, but he was accompanied by a sister a year or two older, Princess Louise of Prussia, who was devoted to him. When this young German Princess became the firm friend of the Princess Royal and went about constantly with her, it followed that the three young people were often thrown together, the Princess Royal's youth protecting her from a vigilance which in those days would have been rigorously opposed to any idea of 'self-determination' in the affairs of the heart.

At the end of August 1855, Queen Victoria and Prince Albert paid a visit to the French Emperor, Napoleon III, in return for the visit he had paid them in the April of that year, and the Queen and her Consort took with them the Princess Royal, now fifteen years of age, and the Prince of Wales. This visit made a lasting impression on the young Princess. The English royal family were received with the greatest magnificence, and many of the beautiful sights of Paris were shown to them. Their imperial host, now at the zenith of his power and popularity, was unremitting in attentive courtesies to his guests. 'To the children, who behaved beautifully and had the most extraordinary success,' Queen Victoria wrote to Baron Stockmar on September 1, 'his goodness, and judicious kindness, were *great*, and they are *excessively* fond of him.' 'Leur séjour en France', she wrote to the Emperor on August 29, 'a été la plus heureuse époque de leur vie, et ils ne cessent d'en parler.' Certainly the youthful Princess did not forget the wonders of the visit, and fifteen years later, when disaster had made the Emperor a fugitive, the Princess recalled, with still vivid remembrance, the happiness of that week in Paris.

It was Princess Augusta of Prussia, the mother of Prince Frederick, who had first suggested the possibility of a marriage, but when she proposed to visit England with the intention of discussing the matter, her uncle, Frederick William IV of Prussia, influenced by his pro-Russian consort, did not look upon the proposal with favour and for the time being it remained in abeyance. At the period the Crimean War was in progress and the Russian leanings of the Prussian court rendered an English alliance uncongenial.

Three weeks after their return home from France, Queen Victoria and Prince Albert welcomed to Balmoral Prince Frederick William, whose determination to marry the Princess Royal had only been strengthened by the opposition of the Prussian court. Prince Frederick, having won over his parents to his wishes, now decided to put his fortune to the test. Exacting as no doubt the Prince Consort was in his demands for an ideal son-in-law, he could find but little fault with this young German Prince, and the only opposition came from the Queen, who pleaded for delay on account of the extreme youth of her daughter. Her counsel of prudence seemed about to prevail when Prince Frederick refused to return home without coming to some understanding, and eventually, in response to his appeals, Queen Victoria gave way and permitted him to pay court to her daughter. The following day, September 21, 1855, Prince Albert wrote to the Earl of Clarendon:

I may tell you in the strictest confidence that Prince Frederick William has yesterday laid before us his wish for an alliance with the Princess Royal, with the full concurrence of his parents, as well as of the King of Prussia. We have accepted his proposal as far as we are personally concerned, but have asked that the child should not be made acquainted with it until after her confirmation, which is to take place next Spring, when he might make it to her himself, and receive from her own lips the answer which is only valuable when flowing from those of the person chiefly concerned. A marriage would not be possible before the completion of the Princess's seventeenth year, which is in two years from this time. The Queen empowers me to say that you may communicate this event to

Lord Palmerston, but we beg that under present circumstances it may be kept a strict secret. What the world may say we cannot help.

The following day Queen Victoria wrote to the King of the Belgians:

MY DEAREST UNCLE - I profit by your own messenger to confide to *you*, and to *you alone*, begging you not to mention it to your children, that *our* wishes on the subject of a future marriage for Vicky *have* been realised in the most *gratifying* and *satisfactory* manner.

On Thursday (20th) after breakfast, Fritz Wilhelm said he was anxious to speak of a subject which *he* knew his parents had never broached to us - which *was to belong to our* Family; that this had long been his wish, that he had the entire concurrence and *approval* not only of his parents but of the King - and that finding Vicky so *allerliebste* he could delay no longer in making this proposal, which, however, I have little - indeed no - doubt that she will gladly accept. He is a dear, excellent, charming young man, whom we shall give our dear child to with perfect confidence. What pleases us so greatly is to see that he is really delighted with Vicky.

Nine days later Queen Victoria noted in her *Journal*: 'Our dear Victoria was this day engaged to Prince Frederick William of Prussia, who had been on a visit to us since the 14th. He had already spoken to us on the 20th of his wishes, but we were uncertain on account of her extreme youth, whether he should speak to her himself or wait till he came back again. However, we felt it was better he should do so, and during our ride up Craig-na-Ban this afternoon, he picked a piece of white heather (the emblem of 'Good luck') which he gave to her; and this enabled him to make an allusion to his hopes and wishes as they rode down Glen Girnoch, which led to this happy conclusion.'[2]

These letters make no reference to the feelings of the Princess, but the assumption is not too far-fetched that far from objecting to the advances of the Prussian Prince she found in them a keen source of happiness. The engagement was kept secret, but rumour soon began to spread, and on March 20, 1856, Mr Cobden wrote to a friend:

... It is generally thought that the young Prince Frederick William of Prussia is to be married to our Princess Royal. I was dining tête-à-tête with Mr Buchanan, the American Minister, a few days ago, who had dined the day before at the Queen's table and sat next to the Princess Royal. He was in raptures about her, and said she was the most charming girl he had ever met: 'All life and spirit, full of frolic and fun, with an excellent head, and a *heart as big as a mountain*' - those were his words. Another friend of mine, Colonel Fitzmayer, dined with the Queen last week, and in writing to me a description of the company he says that when the Princess Royal smiles 'it makes one feel as if additional light were thrown upon the scene' - so I should judge that this said Prince is a lucky fellow and I trust he will make a good husband. If not, although a man of peace, I shall consider it a *casus belli*.

Victorian caution, however, demanded that there should be still no mention of an engagement until the Princess had been confirmed - her confirmation had been fixed for her seventeenth birthday. In point of fact, it took place six months earlier, on March 20, 1856, and a month later, on April 29, after the conclusion of the Crimean War, the happy news was broadcast that the wedding of the Prince Frederick William and the Princess Royal would shortly take place.

That spring, Prince Frederick, or 'Fritz', as he was known in the family circle, paid a long visit to his fiancée. 'The only impression he gave one at that time', noted an acute observer, 'was that of a good-humoured, taking lieutenant, with large hands and feet, but not in the least clever.'[3] Queen Victoria herself played the part of the unsleeping chaperon, a proceeding which, as she wrote to King Leopold, she found very boring, but endured it because she thought it was her duty! 'Every spare moment Vicky has', she wrote on June 3, '(and I have, for I must chaperon this loving couple, which takes so much of my precious time) is devoted to her bridegroom who is *so* much in love that, even if he is out driving or walking with her, he is not satisfied, and says he has not seen her, unless he can have her for an hour to himself, when I am naturally bound to be acting as chaperon.'

At this period, Prussia, having well recovered from the Napoleonic wars and steadily increasing in prestige and commerce, was beginning to feel a little of that acute national pride which was to have such a stimulating effect after the Danish and French wars of the following decades, and the suggestion was made that the heir to the throne of the Hohenzollerns should be married in Berlin. Quick as the rapier thrust came the letter from Queen Victoria to Lord Clarendon (October 25, 1857):

It would be well if Lord Clarendon would tell Lord Bloomfield [the British Minister in Berlin] not to entertain the possibility of such a question as the Princess Royal's marriage taking place at Berlin. The Queen never could consent to it, both for public and private reasons, and the assumption of its being too much for a Prince Royal of Prussia to come over to marry the Princess Royal of Great Britain in England is too absurd, to say the least. The Queen must say that there never was even the shadow of a doubt on Prince Frederick William's part, as to where the marriage should take place, and she suspects this to be mere gossip of the Berlinois....Whatever may be the usual practice of Prussian Princes - it is not every day that one marries the eldest daughter of the Queen of England. The question therefore must be considered as settled and closed.

Against that verdict there was no appeal, and three months later, on January 25, 1858, in the Chapel Royal, at St James's Palace, the Princess Royal, who, as Sarah, Lady Lyttelton, records, displayed 'not a bit of bridal missiness and flutter', was married to Prince Frederick William of Prussia, and thus became the probable co-partner of the Prussian throne.

The honeymoon was but a brief two days at Windsor, as was then the Royal custom. Thirty-six years later the Princess recalled to Bishop Boyd Carpenter her feelings at that time. 'I remember', she said, as she looked around the red brocade drawing-room which overlooks the Long Walk, 'how we sat here - two young innocent things - almost too shy to talk to one another.'[4]

Eight days after the wedding Prince and Princess Frederick of Prussia left London for their new home in Berlin. The parting with her father and mother was an emotional trial for the Princess, who was bitterly sorry to leave England, 'She has had', wrote Queen Victoria to the King of the Belgians on January 12, 1858, 'ever since January 1857, a succession of emotions and leave-takings - most trying to anyone, but particularly to so young a girl with such very powerful feelings.' A month later (February 9) she wrote: 'The separation was awful and the poor child was quite brokenhearted at parting from her dearest beloved papa, whom she *idolises*'. The Prince Consort[5] was no less affected. He was losing not only his favourite child, but also an adoring pupil and companion. There had been an ever-growing intellectual sympathy between them, and the father had communicated to the daughter not only his outlook on life, but also his political liberalism - ma gift which was likely to prove somewhat awkward to the Princess in future years.

On arrival in Berlin, the youth of the Princess, her intelligence and charm, the romantic associations of her courtship, combined with the undoubted popularity of her husband, all found a popular utterance in the vociferous public welcome which greeted her wherever she went during those ensuing weeks. Her manner was singularly quiet and self-possessed, and she seemed to be able to find the right word to say to everyone and to be anxious to appreciate her husband's country. Even so, feeling ran so high in Prussian society against the 'English' marriage, and especially at the court, that Lord and Lady Bloomfield, the then English Minister and his wife, in order to give no cause of offence to the Prussian King and Queen, made a point of avoiding the newly wedded Princess.

A month or two later, Bismarck, then Prussian delegate to the Diet at Frankfort, wrote prophetically to General von Gerlach (April 8, 1858):

You ask me in your letter what I think of the English marriage. I must separate the two words to give you my opinion. The 'English' in it does not please me, the 'marriage' may be quite good, for the Princess has the reputation of a lady of brain and heart. If the Princess can leave the Englishwoman at home and become a Prussian, then she may be a blessing to the country. If our future Queen on the Prussian throne remains the least bit English, then I see our Court surrounded by English influence, and yet us, and the many other future sons-in-law of her gracious Majesty, receiving no notice in England save when the Opposition in Parliament runs down our Royal family and country. On the other hand, with us, British influence will find a fruitful soil in the 1858 noted admiration of the German 'Michael' for lords and guineas, in the Anglomania of papers, sportsmen, country gentlemen, etc. Every Berliner feels exalted when a real English jockey from Hart or Lichtwald speaks to him and gives him an opportunity of breaking the Queen's English on a wheel. What will it be like when the first lady in the land is an Englishwoman?[6]

Walburga, Countess von Hohenthal, who became one of the Princess's ladies-in-waiting, and who later married Sir Augustus Paget, British Ambassador in Rome and Vienna, gives a charming picture in her book of reminiscences, *Scenes and Memories*, of her royal mistress as she looked at the time of her marriage:

The Princess appeared extraordinarily young. All the childish roundness still clung to her and made her look shorter than she really was. She was dressed in a fashion long disused on the continent, in a plum-coloured silk dress fastened at the back. Her hair was drawn off her forehead. Her eyes were what struck me most ; the iris was green like the sea on a sunny day, and the white had a peculiar shimmer which gave them the fascination that, together with a smile that showed her small and beautiful teeth, bewitched those who approached her. The nose was unusually small and turned up slightly, and the complexion was ruddy, perhaps too much so for one thing, but it gave the idea of perfect health and strength. The fault of the face lay in the squareness of the lower features, and there was even a look of determination about the chin, but the very gentle and almost timid manner prevented one realising this at first. The voice was very delightful, never going up to high tones, but lending a peculiar charm to the slight foreign accent with which the Princess spoke both English and German.

Already she possessed an intensely vivid and interesting personality. The restraints of her position had not stunted or crushed her intellectual or spiritual growth, nor her natural enthusiasm and inexhaustible energy. On the contrary, there were those who feared that her manifold interests and activities would result in a dilettantism that would be hard to cure. Such a development, however, was not possible with such a husband - the kind, grave Frederick whose influence upon her was to lead her to the fields of philanthropy and the application of art to industry.

Gradually the enthusiasm subsided - Prussia settled down to its new Princess, and the Princess endeavoured to settle down to Prussia. Here, however, came the first suspicion of a cloud on the horizon. The aristocratic, despotic institutions of Prussia were strangely opposed to the democratic tradition which had sprung up in England since the passing of the first Reform Bill in 1832, and it was the hope of the youthful Princess that she might help her husband to lead the way to democratic reforms on the English lines.

## NOTES

1 *The Empress Frederick: A Memoir*, p.10.
2 *Leaves from Our Journal in the Highlands*, September 29, 1855.
3 *Mary Ponsonby*, edited by Magdalen Ponsonby, p. 241.
4 *The Empress Frederick: A Memoir*, p. 68.
5 Prince Albert had been created Prince Consort on June 25, 1857.
6 *The Empress Frederick: A Memoir*, pp. 41-2.

## II: Early Years in Prussia

THE country that the Princess Frederick now adopted as her own was, in 1858, a second-rate European state. Prussia was in fact not to be compared in power, wealth or security with the Princess's native land. During the Napoleonic wars, Prussia, a shadow of her former self and pushed back behind the Elbe, suffered indignities at the hands of the French which even now have not been forgotten. But the close of the struggle with France found her regenerated and imbued with a strong spirit of nationality and with her territories extended by the addition of the grand-duchy of Posen, Swedish Pomerania, the northern part of Saxony, the duchies of Westphalia and Berg and the Rhine country between Aachen and Mainz. Even then Prussia had a population of only about seventeen millions.

The first step towards German unity was taken a few years later, when Prussia instituted the Zollverein or Customs Union, to which by 1842 all the Germanic States except Mecklenburg, Hanover and Austria acceded. With this statesmanlike step Prussian influence increased enormously and Frederick William IV, who ascended the throne in 1840, made Berlin a centre of learning and natural science. His extravagant views on the subject of royal powers led, however, to the revolutionary movement in 1848 and to the preparation of a new constitution, which endeavoured to combine the French prefect system with Prussian mediaevalism.

Prussia was now fast becoming a 'Prussianised' state whereas England had been becoming more and more liberal and progressive. Further, Germany, as the term was then understood, included an extraordinary number of petty and impotent principalities, dukedoms and other states, each with its ruling family, and for the most part as poor as they were proud. On the borders of Prussia and Denmark were two duchies which were proving an ever-growing source of friction. These two duchies of Schleswig and Holstein had for centuries been deemed indivisible, yet the King of Denmark was Duke of Schleswig and of Holstein, while the population was largely German, and Holstein was a member of the German Federation. Efforts to incorporate these provinces in Denmark led to a revolution in which Prussia successfully took the side of the insurgents, but the result was merely the seven months' truce of **Malmö** which remained unratified by the parliament of Frankfort.

Thus at the time of the Princess Royal's marriage, there were three outstanding questions of importance in Prussia; the first was the leadership of the Germanic states, the second was the question as to whether Prussia was to remain stationary or to advance along liberal lines similar to those which England had adopted, and the third was the future of the duchies of Schleswig and Holstein. From the outset it was evident that with regard to the second question the influence of the Princess would be on the side of the progressive liberal elements.

The German court, of which the Princess was now a leading member, was singularly unlike the English court, which at this period was cheerful and young. Not yet was Queen Victoria overwhelmed by the loss of her husband that plunged the court into a forty years' gloom; it was a happy eager court, high-toned and bright. By contrast, the Prussian court was formal, stiff, and boring: the life was monotonous, the palaces gloomy and uncomfortable and the ceremonies interminable. The honest and sagacious Regent of Prussia, known to history as William I, had begun to feel that he was getting old, and that feeling echoed through the court. In his consort, however, then known as the Princess (Augusta) of Prussia, the Princess Frederick had for many years a true friend and ally, who belonged, in an intellectual sense, to the eighteenth rather than the nineteenth century. **Princess Augusta**[1] knew French as well as she knew German, and among her intimates were many Catholics. As a young woman she was full of heart and warmth of feeling, but she had soon learnt that which her daughter-in-law never entirely succeeded in learning, that circumspection and prudence were essential at the Prussian court, and she took no great part in the affairs of state.

During the Crimean War, when the whole of the Prussian court was pro-Russian, Princess Augusta had been pro-English - a fact which naturally endeared her to Queen Victoria, but which had made her Prussian relatives suspicious and angry. When the Princess Frederick arrived in Berlin as the bride of the King of Prussia's heir-presumptive, the Crimean War was already being forgotten, and the joyous simplicity and youthful charm of the Princess silenced criticism, at any rate for a time.

The Princess Frederick spent her first winter in Berlin in the Old Schloss, which had not been lived in for a considerable time, and was singularly below the Victorian standard of living, hygiene and comfort. The young couple were allotted a suite of ornate but very dark and gloomy rooms; the Princess, who had always been encouraged to turn her quick mind to practical matters, and who delighted in creating and making, found her plans for improvement blocked at every turn owing to the fact that nothing could be done in the Old Schloss - not even a bathroom added - without the direct permission of the insane King.

Not only did the Princess feel uncomfortable in these gloomy and haunted chambers, but she felt 'cribbed, cabined and confined' in the narrow etiquette of the Prussian court. At 'home', as she soon very unwisely began to speak of England, she had been used to say everything she thought from childhood upwards, sure of not being misunderstood, and her habitual honesty and frankness now proved a point of censure to her critical German relatives. Unfortunately this difficulty of restraining her English feelings did not become easier with the passage of years. Small things got on her nerves; German boots, the want of baths, the thin silver plate and the amount of boring etiquette. Although wishing to love her husband's country and to overcome her predilections, she always kept her love for England. In a letter from Potsdam in 1871, she says:

> You cannot think how dull and melancholy and queer I feel away from you all and from beloved England! Each time I get there I feel my attachment to that precious bit of earth grow stronger and stronger....Going away and returning here always causes a commotion in my feelings which wants a little time and reasoning to one's self to get over.[2]

Above all she could not understand the rigid Prussianism of the Prussian reactionary party, and quite early it was noted that 'the very approach of a Tory or a reactionary seemed to freeze her up'.

A few months later, the Prince and Princess set up a modest establishment more on English lines at the Castle of Babelsberg, and here the Princess was much happier in her surroundings. The little Castle, seated on the side of a wooded hill, about three miles from Potsdam, overlooked a fine expanse of water, and commanded a charming view of the surrounding country. 'Everything there', wrote Queen Victoria on her first visit, 'is very small, a Gothic *bijou*, full of furniture, and flowers (creepers), which they arrange very prettily round screens, and lamps and pictures. There are many irregular turrets and towers and steps.'[3]

Early in June Prince Albert visited his daughter and son-in-law at Babelsberg, and wrote to Queen Victoria: 'The relation between the young people is all that can be desired. I have had long talks with them both, singly and together, which gave me the greatest satisfaction.'

Two months later, Queen Victoria and the Prince Consort paid a visit of some length to their daughter. The Queen herself described the visit as 'quite private and unofficial', but she was accompanied by Lord Malmesbury, the Foreign Secretary in Lord Derby's newly formed ministry, and by Lord Clarendon, his predecessor, and Lord Granville, who had been President of the Council in Palmerston's government. Queen Victoria was delighted to meet the gigantic Field-Marshal Wrangel, then seventy-six years of age, who had actually carried the colours of his regiment at Leipzig in 1814, and had, in 1848, as commandant of the troops, dissolved the Berlin assembly by force. 'He was', wrote Queen Victoria, 'full of Vicky and the marriage, and said she was an angel.'

On November 20, 1858, the Prince and Princess Frederick moved from

Babelsberg into the palace in Unter den Linden, which became their Berlin residence. The Princess Frederick was delighted with her new home, but, as in the case of the Old Schloss, the palace required to be brought up to modern standards of comfort, and it was still difficult to get any alterations approved by the old and moody King, who refused one day what he had promised the day before. At last assent was obtained to those alterations which were absolutely urgent, and the Princess spent many happy days in rearranging her new home.

These first years at the Prussian court were spent in the calm routine of home with the periodical public activities that took up such a large proportion of her time. Even manoeuvres, where she appeared on horseback, were within her function, and in November 1858 the Duchess of Manchester, herself an Hanoverian by birth, and who afterwards married the Duke of Devonshire, wrote happily from Hanover to Queen Victoria:

Though Your Majesty has only very lately seen the Princess Royal, I cannot refrain from addressing Your Majesty, as I am sure Your Majesty will be pleased to hear how well Her Royal Highness was looking during the manoeuvres on the Rhine and how much she seems to be beloved not only by all those who know her, but also by those who have only seen and heard of her - the English could not help feeling proud of the way the Princess Royal was spoken of and the high esteem she is held in. For one so young it is a most flattering position, and certainly as the Princess's charm of manner and her kind unaffected words, had in that short time won her the 'hearts of all the officers and strangers present, one is 1858 not astonished at the praise the Prussians themselves bestow on Her Royal Highness. The Royal Family is large and their opinions politically and socially sometimes so different that it must have been very difficult indeed at first for the Princess Royal, and people therefore cannot praise enough the high principles, great discretion, and judgment and cleverness Her Royal Highness has invariably displayed.

Your Majesty would have been amused to hear General Wrangel tell, at the top of his voice, how delighted the soldiers were to see the Princess on horseback and the interest she showed for them - what pleased them especially was to see Her Royal Highness ride without a veil. Such an odd thing in soldiers to remark. The King of Prussia is looking very well, but the Queen, I thought, very much altered. Her Majesty looks very pale and tired and has such a painful drawn look about the mouth....Their Majesties' kindness was very great and the Duke told me of the extreme hospitality with which they were entertained. Everyone high and low were rivalling each other in civility and friendship towards the strangers, especially the English, and one really felt quite ashamed of those wanton attacks the *Times* always makes on Prussia and which are read and copied into all the Prussian papers....

A happy domestic event occurred on January 27, 1859, when a son and heir was born to the Prince and Princess Frederick. Great were the rejoicings, for in the normal run of events the boy would become King of Prussia in succession to his grand-uncle, grandfather and father.

For a time, however, mother and child were in imminent danger, and, as Prince Albert wrote to King Leopold, 'Poor Fritz and the Prince and Princess (of Prussia) must have undergone terrible anxiety, as they had no hope of the birth of a living child'. It was not until the third day that it was perceived that the child's left arm was paralysed, the shoulder-socket injured and the surrounding muscles severely bruised. Medical knowledge was in so elementary a state then that no doctor would venture to attempt the readjustment of the limb, which remained feeble and almost, if not entirely, useless.[4] On this child, her first-born, the Princess lavished all her maternal care, and a fortnight later (February 12) the Princess wrote to her mother:

> I use dear Countess Blücher's hand, by Wegner's[5] permission, to answer your dear letter just arrived, and I cannot describe my pleasure at being again able in a more direct way to convey my thoughts to you, and to be able at last to thank you for all your tenderness and all your love shown to me so unceasingly during this time. How deeply it has touched, cheered and delighted me, and how very grateful I feel to you and papa, I need not say. Your letters have been the greatest comfort to me, and I thank you for them a thousand times. How much I thought of you on the 10th, and wished to have been able to write to you. Fritz conveyed all my wishes I hope....
>
> I fear I may not dictate any more today, dear Mama, and so I will only say that your little grandson is very well.

A further reference to her 'exceedingly lively' son occurs in the letter written by the Princess Frederick to Queen Victoria on February 28:

> Your grandson [she wrote] is exceedingly lively and when awake will not be satisfied unless kept dancing about continually. He scratches his face and tears his caps and makes every sort of extraordinary little noise. I am so thankful, so happy, he is a boy. I longed for one more than I can describe, my whole heart was set upon a boy and therefore I did not expect one. I cannot say I think him like anyone at present, although now and then he reminds me of Bertie and of Leopold, which I fear you won't like. I feel very proud of him and very proud of being a Mama....

The infant prince was christened a week later. Queen Victoria, as she wrote to her 'Dearest Uncle', the King of the Belgians, was almost heartbroken at not being able to witness the christening of her first grandchild, and railed against the '*stupid law* in Prussia' which was 'so particular in having the child christened so soon'. On the day of the christening, March 5, Lady Bloomfield, wife of the British Minister in Berlin, wrote to Queen Victoria:

> I am this instant returned from the christening of His Royal Highness Frederick William Victor Albert, and lose no time in writing a few lines to tell Your Majesty that everything went off as well as possible. I had a very good place close to the door of the Chapel (which only contained the members of the Royal Family) and the dear baby looked so pretty and never cried at all. It seemed very much taken up with the Prince Regent's Orders and kept moving its little hands as if it wanted to play with them. The discourse which was pronounced by Hof Prediger Straus was not too long and very well adapted to the occasion, and I was so happy at last after the ceremony to be allowed to kiss the dear Princess's hand. I have been so longing to see her, if only for a minute. Her Royal Highness looks well, and *not* thin in the face, but she seemed flushed and nervous, and her voice is still weak, so that I am quite sure she still requires considerable care, and I only trust today's fatigue will not have been too much for her. She was sitting close to the baby's bassinet and I so wished your Majesty could have been present. During the whole of this interesting time I have so often felt how very trying it must be for Your Majesty to be absent, but thank God all has prospered and I trust ere long Your Majesty will have the happiness of seeing the dear Princess restored to perfect health and strength. I have no doubt Her Royal Highness will pick up much more rapidly as soon as she begins to go out....

The birth of the Prince resulted in the family moving to Neue Palais at Potsdam, where Prince Frederick had been born, and which became for many years the happy home of the Princess.

In summer of that year Prince and Princess Frederick came to England to spend a holiday at Osborne with the British royal family. The Princess's eldest brother, the Prince of Wales, was at this time nearing his eighteenth birthday, and opinion held that it was high time a suitable princess were found for him. Princess Frederick was at first of opinion that there did not exist in this world anyone good enough to become her brother's wife, but she changed her mind when the beauty and endearing graces of Alexandra, daughter of Prince Christian of Schleswig-Holstein-Sonderburg-Glücksburg,[6] were pressed by her own lady-in-waiting, Countess von Hohenthal (Walburga, Lady Paget), and it was quickly arranged that the Princess Frederick should meet Princess Alexandra informally at Strelitz, and here in the palace of a second cousin on both sides, the Grand Duchess of Mecklenburg-Strelitz, a meeting followed.

The Princess Frederick declared herself to be 'quite enchanted' with 'the most fascinating creature in the world'[7] who, as she wrote to her mother, was bound to succeed in the competition for her brother's hand.[8] But for the moment the project hung fire. All admitted the right of the Prince to make his own choice, and the Princess Frederick returned to Berlin with the consciousness of having done what she could to further an ideal match.

Among the Princess's friends in Germany at this period was an Englishman, Robert Morier, who had held various diplomatic appointments at German courts and had acquired an unrivalled intimacy with German politics. Prince Albert had formed a high opinion of his character and abilities in 1858, and at the time of the Princess's marriage had done everything in his power to have Morier appointed an attaché at the British Embassy at Berlin. Gifted with a rare power for pungency in expression, Morier's frankness quickly won the esteem of the Princess.

Morier had another good friend in the Princess of Prussia, the Princess Frederick's mother-in-law, and it was at her wish, expressed to Lord Clarendon, that the young man was sent to Berlin in order that he might be of use to her son and daughter-in-law. Morier was also on intimate terms with Ernest von Stockmar (son of the redoubtable Baron Stockmar, the counsellor of the Prince Consort), who at the same time was appointed private secretary to the Princess.

Morier's appointment was the beginning of a lifelong intimacy with Prince and Princess Frederick. He became and remained one of their most trusted friends and advisers, a fact which undoubtedly injured his diplomatic career. Probably because Morier had a remarkably strong and original personality, he at once aroused jealousy, dislike and suspicion; he was even said to influence unduly Prince Frederick through the Princess. When, many years later, it was proposed that Sir Robert Morier, as he had then become, should be appointed Ambassador in Berlin, his name was the only one which was absolutely vetoed by the then all-powerful Bismarck.

In June 1859 the war between Austria and the allied French and Sardinian armies broke out, and for the first time the Princess Frederick saw her husband prepare for war. The Prince Regent, while declaring the neutrality of Prussia, cautiously ordered a mobilisation of the Prussian army, and Major-General Prince Frederick William went off to his command over the First Infantry Division of Guards, Fortunately the rapid defeat of the Austrians at Solferino brought the Peace of Villafranca in July, and the Prussian army returned to its peace footing. The defeat of Austria, however, raised anew the question of German hegemony.

In the November of 1859 the Princess came again to England with her husband. 'Vicky', as her father wrote of her to the Dowager Duchess of Coburg, 'has developed greatly of late and yet remains quite a child!' 'She talked', recorded her old governess, Sarah, Lady Lyttelton, 'much of her baby.'[9]

The year 1860 added further happiness to the lot of the Princess Frederick. In the July of that year her eldest daughter, the Princess Charlotte, was born. Late in the September Queen Victoria and Prince Albert were joined at Coburg by the Princess Frederick, and it was on this visit that Queen Victoria first saw her eldest grandchild. Writing on September 25 she says:

> Our darling grandchild was brought Such a little love! He came walking in at Mrs. Hobbs's (his nurse's) hand, in a little white dress with black bows, and was so good. He is a fine, fat child, with a beautiful white soft skin, very fine shoulders and limbs, and a very dear face, like Vicky and Fritz, and also Louise of Baden. He has Fritz's eyes and Vicky's mouth, and very fair curly hair. We felt so happy to see him at last![10]

This was the beginning of an enduring friendship between grandmother and grandson, and in the letters of Queen Victoria there is constant reference to her grandchild; whom she calls 'Dear little William', 'a darling child', and adds that he is a 'dear little boy, is so intelligent and pretty, so good and affectionate'.

In modelling and arranging the nursery for her two children, the Princess Frederick, as was perhaps to be expected, preferred to follow English rather than German lines and ideas - a proceeding that was viewed with disapproval by those ardent innovation-resisting Prussians who constituted the conservative party. The dislike of the high-born Prussian for anything that was English was perhaps only equalled by the dislike of a certain section of the English press for anything that was Prussian. The Prince Consort, who dreamt of a united Germany under Prussian leadership which should guarantee the peace of the world with England, was seriously disturbed by the attacks which *The Times* was constantly making on Prussia and everything Prussian. An article in the *Saturday Review* which he recommended to his daughter to read, said that 'The only reason *The Times* ever gives for its dislike of Prussia, is that the Prussian and English courts are connected by personal ties, and that British independence demands that everything proceeding from the Court should be watched with the most jealous suspicion'. The same argument could have been applied to Prussian opinion. Naturally this animosity materially affected the position of the Princess in Prussia, and she gradually found herself being disliked more and more for two reasons - the first that she was English and could not forget it, and the second that she loved English political and sanitary ideas.

Meanwhile, the Prince Consort, in spite of many political and other anxieties and a sharp attack of illness, continued to instruct his daughter in the art of government, and many and long were the letters he addressed to his still adoring pupil and daughter. These letters, with their liberal ideas, perhaps helped to make the position of the Princess more difficult. The ideal woman in Prussia was then one who, conscious of her intellectual inferiority, contented herself with 'Küche, Kinderstube, Krankenstube und Kirche -

und sonst nichts'. If this view obtained with regard to women in private stations, much more was it considered to be the duty of princesses of the Royal House to abstain from any active interest in public affairs. It is strange that the Prince Consort, with his knowledge of Prussian traditions, did not appreciate this. It is possible that he thought his daughter to be freed by her exceptional ability from the ordinary restrictions and limitations of her rank. Still more, perhaps, he was anxious to give his son-in-law, in the troublous times that seemed impending, an helpmeet who could influence him in the right Coburgian direction. Whatever may have been the reason, the Prince certainly continued to the end of his life to cultivate his daughter's knowledge and grasp of public affairs.

The Princess replied to these learned fatherly epistles at equal length. In the December of 1860 the Prince Consort received from Berlin a long and able memorandum upon the advantages of a law of ministerial responsibility, drafted so as to remove the apprehensions entertained in high quarters at the Prussian court as to the expediency of such a measure. This memorandum was the work of the Princess Frederick, and it is easy to imagine what a storm of indignation would have arisen in Prussia if by any accident or indiscretion the knowledge that the Princess had written such a paper had leaked out. [11]

The preceding months had altered in very few respects the position of the Princess, but an event was now drawing near that was to put her in a position of greater influence. By the end of 1860 it was apparent that the insane King Frederick William IV of Prussia was seriously ill, and with the turn of the year there was a sudden and critical change for the worse, his death following quickly. The event moved the Princess Frederick profoundly, as it was really her first sight of death. After a broken night and day of watching by the bedside of the King, the Princess was awakened at one o'clock on the morning of January 2, but before she could arrive at the King's chamber life had flown. That day the Princess wrote from Potsdam to Queen Victoria:

At last I can find a moment for myself to sit down and collect my thoughts and to write to you an account of these two last dreadful days! My head is in such a state, I do not know where I am hardly - whether I am in a dream or awake, what is yesterday and what today! What we have so long expected has come at last! All the confusion, bustle, excitement, noise, etc., is all swallowed up in the one thought for me.

I have seen death for the first time! It has made an impression upon me that I shall never never forget as long as I live - and I feel so ill, so confused and upset by all that I have gone through in the last forty-eight hours that you must forgive me if I write incoherently and unclearly! But to go back to Monday evening (it seems to me a year now). At a quarter to eight in the evening of Monday the 31st, I took dear darling Affie[12] to the railway station and took leave of him with a heavy heart. You know I love that dear boy distractedly - and that nothing could have given me more pleasure than his dear long-wished-for visit. At 9 o'clock Fritz and I went to tea at the Prince Regent's, we four were alone together. The Princess (of Prussia) was rather low and unwell, the Prince low spirited and I thinking of nothing but Affic and of how dear he is - while we were sitting at tea we received bad news from Sans Souci, but nothing to make us particularly uneasy. Fritz and I went home and to bed - not being in a humour to sit up till 12. About half past one we heard a knock at the door and my wardrobe maid brought in a telegram saying the King was given up, and a note from the Prince Regent, saying he was going immediately. We got up in the greatest hurry and dressed I hardly know how. I put on just what I found and had not time to do my hair or anything. After we had hurried on our clothes we went down stairs and out - for there was no time to get a carriage, or a Footman or anything - it was a splendid night, but 12 degrees of cold (Réaumur). I thought I was in a dream, finding myself alone in the street with Fritz at 2 o'clock at night. We went to the Prince Regent's and then with them in their carriages to the railway station. We four all alone in the train. We arrived at Sans Souci and went directly into the room where the King lay - the stillness of death was in the room - only the light of the fire and of a dim lamp. We approached the bed and stood there at the foot of it, not daring to look at one another, or to say a word. The Queen was sitting in an arm chair at the head of the bed, her arm underneath the King's head, and her head on the same pillow on which he lay - with her other hand she continually wiped the perspiration from his forehead. You might have heard a pin drop - no sound was heard, but the crackling of the fire and the death rattle - that dreadful sound which goes to one's heart and which tells plainly that life is ebbing. This rattling in the throat lasted about an hour longer and then the King lay motionless - the Doctors bent their heads low to hear whether he still breathed and we stood, not even daring to sit down, watching the death struggle. Every now and then the King breathed very fast and loud, but never unclosed his eyes - he was very red in the face and the cold perspiration pouring from his forehead. I never spent such an awful time, and to see the poor Queen sitting there quite rent my heart - 3, 4, 5, 6, 7 struck and we were still standing there - one member of the Royal Family came in after the other and remained motionless in the room, sobs only breaking the stillness. Oh it is dreadful to see a person die, all the thoughts and feelings that crowded on my mind in those hours I cannot describe; they impressed me more than anything in my whole past lifetime! the light of the morning dawned and the lamps were taken away. Oh how sad for the first morning in the year! We all went into the next room, for I assure you, anxiety, watching, standing and crying had quite worn us out. The Princess fell asleep on a chair, I on a sofa, and the rest walked up and down the room, asking one another 'How long will it last?' Towards the middle of the day Marianne and I went into the room alone, as we wished to stay there, we came up and kissed the Queen's hand and knelt down and kissed the King's - it was quite warm still! We stood about and waited till 5 o'clock and then had some dinner, and I felt so sick and faint and unwell, that

Fritz sent me here to bed. At 1 o'clock this morning I got up and dressed and heard that the King had not many minutes more to live, but by the time I had got the carriage I heard all was over. I drove to Sans Souci and saw the King and Queen. May God bless and preserve them and may theirs be a long and happy and blessed reign! Then I went into the room where the King lay, and I could hardly bring myself to go away again. There was so much of comfort in looking there at that quiet peaceful form at rest at last after all he had suffered - gone home at last from this world of suffering - so peaceful and quiet he looked - like a sleeping child - every moment I expected to see him move or breathe - his mouth and eyes closed and such a sweet and happy expression - both his hands were on the coverlet. I kissed them both for the last time - they were quite cold then. Fritz and I stood looking at him for some time. I could hardly bring myself to believe that this was really death, that which I had so often shuddered at and felt afraid of - there was nothing there dreadful or appalling - only a heavenly calm and peace. I felt it did me so much good and was such a comfort. 'Death where is thy sting, grave where is thy Victory?' He was a just and good man and had a heart overflowing with love and kindness, and he has gone to his rest after a long trial which he bore with so much patience! I am not afraid of death now, and when I feel inclined to be so, I shall think of that solemn and comforting sight, and that death is only a change for the better. We went home and to bed and this morning went there at 10. I sat some time with the poor Queen, who is so calm and resigned and touching in her grief. She does not cry, but she looks heartbroken. She said to me, 'I am no longer of any use in this world. I have no longer any vocation, any duties to perform, and only lived for him.' Then she was so kind to me, kinder than she has ever been yet, and said I was like her own child and a comfort to her! I saw the corpse again this morning, he is unaltered, only changed in colour and the hands are stiffened. The funeral will be on Saturday, the King will lie in State till then, his wish was to be buried in Friedens Kirche before the Altar - and his heart at Charlottenburg in the Mausoleum.

When it is remembered that the writer of this letter was only twenty, its poignancy, and the simple, unstudied vividness of the scene in the death-chamber are remarkable. But the letter also shows the nobleness of the Princess's outlook on life. Her sympathy with the bereaved Queen Elizabeth was profound, and their grief brought them together as perhaps nothing else could have done.

Two months later (March 1861) the unexpected death of the Duchess of Kent deprived the Princess of a grandmother with whom were associated many of the happy events of her childhood and girlhood. On receiving the sudden news, the Princess started at once for England, not entirely with the approval of her father-in-law. The Prince Consort, who in this matter of his daughter's relations to her father-in-law always showed exceptional tact, wrote and thanked the King: 'Her stay here has been a great comfort and delight to us in our sorrow and bereavement, and we are truly grateful for it'.[13]

Seven months later the new King of Prussia, William I, and his consort, Queen Augusta, were crowned at Königsberg with fitting ceremonial. The following day (October 19, 1861) the Crown Princess (as the Princess Frederick now became), in a letter to her mother, gave a remarkably vivid and picturesque account of the ceremony, from which humour was not absent. The fact that the day chosen was her husband's birthday gave her great pleasure.

1861

I should like [she wrote] to be able to describe yesterday's ceremony to you, but I cannot find words to tell you how fine and how touching it was, it really was a magnificent sight. The King looked so very handsome and so noble with the crown on - it seemed to suit him so exactly. The Queen too looked beautiful and did all she had to do with such perfect grace, and looked so *vornehm*....The moment when the King put the crown on the Queen's head was so touching that I think there was hardly a dry eye in the church. The Schloss Hof was the finest, I thought - five bands playing 'God save the Queen', banners waving in all directions, cheers so loud that they quite drowned the sound of the music, and the procession moving slowly on, the sky without a cloud, and all the uniforms, and ladies' diamonds glittering in the bright sunlight. I shall never forget it all, it was so very fine.

Dearest Fritz's birthday being chosen for the day made me very happy - he was in a great state of emotion and excitement as you can imagine, as we all were....

The *coup d'oeil* was really beautiful, the Chapel is in itself lovely, with a great deal of gold about it, and all hung with red velvet and gold - the carpet, altar, throne and canopies the same - mthe Knights of the Black Eagle with red velvet cloaks, the Queen's four young ladies all alike in white and gold, the two Palastdamen in crimson velvet and gold, and the Oberhofmeister in gold and white brocade with green velvet, Marianne and Addy in red and gold and red and silver. I in gold with ermine and white satin, my ladies one in blue velvet, the other in red velvet, and Countess Schulenburg together with the two other Oberhofmeisterinnen of the other Princesses in violet velvet and gold. All these colours together looked very beautiful, and the sun shone, or rather poured in at the high windows and gave quite magic tinges. The music was very fine and the chorals were sung so loud and strong that it really quite moved one. The King was immensely cheered wherever he appeared - also the Queen - and even I....

The King and Queen were most kind to me yesterday. The King gave me a lock of his hair in a charming little locket, and, only think, what will sound most extraordinary, absurd and incredible to your ears, made me 2nd *Chef* the 2nd Regt. of Hussars. I laughed so much because I really thought it was a joke - it seems so strange for ladies, but the Regts. like particularly having ladies for their

Chefs. The Queen and the Queen Dowager have Regiments, but I believe I am the first Princess on whom such an honour is conferred....

Half Europe is here and one sees the funniest combinations in the world - it is like a 'happy family'[14] shut up in a cage. The Italian Ambassador sat next Cardinal Geissel, and the French one opposite the Archduke. The Grand Duke Nicholas is here he is so nice. Also the Crown Prince of Wurtemberg, Crown Prince of Saxony, Prince Luitpold of Bavaria, Prince Charles of Hesse (who nearly dies of fright and shyness amongst so many people), Heinrich, Prince Elimar of Oldenburg, Prince Frederick of the Netherlands and the Grand Duke and Grand Duchess of Weimar and wish to be most particularly remembered to you and Papa.

The King and Queen are most kind to Lord Clarendon, and make a marked difference between their cordiality to him and the stiff etiquette with which the other Ambassadors are received. I think he is pleased with what he sees. The King has given the Queen the Order of the Black Eagle in diamonds. I write all these details as you wish them, at the risk of their not interesting you, besides my being, as you know, a very bad hand at descriptions....

The State Dinner last night looked very well. We were waited on by our Kammerherren and Pages - the King being waited on by the Oberhofchargen, our ladies stood behind our chairs - after the first two dishes are round, the King asks to drink, and that is the signal for the ladies and gentlemen to leave the room and go to dinner, while the Pages of Honour continue to serve the whole dinner, really wonderfully well, poor boys - considering it is no easy task....

Fritz would thank you for your dear letters himself, but he is at the University where they have elected him 'Rector Magnificus' and he has to make a speech. We have all got our servants and carriages and horses here - every day - 300 footmen in livery - together with other servants in livery make 400. All the standards and colours of the whole army are here and all the Colonels. Altogether you cannot imagine what a crush and what a scramble there is on every occasion. There was a man crushed to death in the crowd the other day, which is quite dreadful....

Lord Clarendon, who was the British Special Ambassador on the occasion, writing to Queen Victoria on the day after the Coronation, observed that '*the* great feature of the ceremony was the manner in which the Princess Royal did homage to the King. Lord Clarendon is at a loss for words to describe to your Majesty the exquisite grace and the intense emotion with which her Royal Highness gave effect to her feelings on the occasion. Many an older as well as younger man than Lord Clarendon, who had not his interest in the Princess Royal, were quite as unable as himself to repress their emotion at that which was so touching, because so unaffected and sincere....If', Lord Clarendon added, 'his Majesty had the mind, the judgment, and the foresight of the Princess Royal, there would be nothing to fear, and the example and influence of Prussia would soon be marvellously developed. Lord Clarendon has had the honour to hold a very long conversation with her Royal Highness, and has been more than ever astonished at the statesmanlike and comprehensive views which she takes of the policy of Prussia, both internal and foreign, and of the duties of a constitutional King.'

From Lord Clarendon's letter to Queen Victoria it may be gathered that the Crown Princess was much alarmed at the state of affairs in Berlin at this time. The new King saw democracy and revolution in every symptom of opposition to his will. His ministers were merely clerks registering the royal decrees. As yet there was no one from whom he sought advice, or indeed who would have the moral courage to give it. He would never accept the consequences of representative government or allow it to be a reality, though at the same time he would always religiously keep his word. Such was Lord Clarendon's diagnosis of the situation, arrived at after an audience of the Crown Princess.

The Princess celebrated her twenty-first birthday on November 21, 1861, and in the letter which she received from her father, almost the last which he was ever to address to her, he wrote:

May your life, which has begun beautifully, expand still further to the good of others and the contentment of your own mind! True inward happiness is to be sought only in the internal consciousness of effort systematically directed to good and useful ends. Success indeed depends upon the blessing which the Most High sees meet to vouchsafe to our endeavours. May this success not fail you, and may your outward life leave you unhurt by the storms, to which the sad heart so often looks forward with a shrinking dread! Without the basis of health it is impossible to rear anything stable. Therefore see that you spare yourself now, so that at some future time you will be able to do more.[15]

The Crown Princess had barely celebrated her twenty-first birthday when she received from England the sad news of the illness of her father, the Prince Consort. After a short visit to Cambridge the Prince contracted typhoid, and within a few days he was dead. The Crown Princess and her second brother, Alfred, who was then serving at sea, were the only children absent from the death-bed of their beloved father, whose loss the Princess felt acutely, for he had been her guide, philosopher, mentor and friend. It was he who had inculcated liberal doctrines upon her, and who had been responsible for her breadth of vision and delight in learning. The blow fell with stunning effect on both mother and daughter - indeed, it is hard to say which of the two felt more utterly broken-hearted and desolate. Between the Princess and her father there had been ties that were deeper and stronger even than the natural affection of parent and daughter; he had sedulously formed her mind and tastes, and he had become the one counsellor to whom she felt she could ever turn in any perplexity or trouble, sure of his helpful understanding and sympathy. Very soon after her marriage, in a letter to the Prince of Wales, she dwelt on their father as the master and leader ever to be respected: 'You don't know', she wrote, 'how one longs for a word from him when one is distant.'

Nor did the Princess, like many daughters, allow her marriage to weaken this tie; indeed, the thought of the physical distance between them seemed to bring them, if possible, spiritually nearer. For her mother, the Princess felt the tenderest and most filial affection, writing to her every day, sometimes twice a day, but though she and her father only wrote to one another once a week, she poured out to him all her varied interests in politics, literature, science, art and philosophy. It would be difficult to find in history a more touching and beautiful example of spiritual and intellectual communion between father and daughter.

The shock of her grief seemed to strengthen more closely the ties which bound her to the land of her birth and of her father's adoption - an attitude which provoked a good deal of criticism in Berlin. She went to England as often as she could, which was as often as her father-in-law could be induced to give his permission. Such sympathy as the Crown Princess found in Berlin with her father's liberal views came from those who were generally termed 'Coburgers', such as the younger Stockmar, Bunsen and other liberal Germans. The fact that they were 'Coburgers', and not Prussians, discounted with the King of Prussia and his minister any value their influence might have had.

With the accession of William I to the throne of Prussia it must indeed have seemed to the Crown Princess as if some of her own and her husband's hopes and aspirations for a fuller and more useful public life were about to be realised. Both were ardent admirers of English constitutional government, and although here the Prince often sought the opinion of his Princess, his actions were determined by his own breadth of outlook and intellectual gifts. He was nine years her elder, and his character and views had been formed long before their marriage. Both appreciated the characteristics of the other, each adding to the other's store of knowledge, and the true description of their political relationship is that each was influenced by but neither dominated the other. In art and domestic arrangements, however, the Princess was in her own field, as was the Prince with regard to soldiering.

There were many who thought that a year or two at most would be the total term of the new King's sovereignty, for he was sixty-three years of age and himself had the illusion that his life's work was done. But even if a year or two longer had concluded his allotted span, one of his acts alone during that period would have had its effect upon the whole history of Europe and have prevented for the time any further progress of liberal ideas. In 1862 there occurred a bitter dispute between the newly crowned King and his parliament over his resolve to spend an immense sum of money on the reform of the army, and to extricate himself from his grave embarrassments the King summoned Count von Bismarck from the German Embassy in Paris in September to assume supreme power in Berlin as Minister-President and Minister for Foreign Affairs. Bismarck defined the 1862 policy of his life when he inaugurated his long rule at Berlin with a speech to the Prussian Reichstag on September 30 in which he declared: 'It is not with speeches or with parliamentary resolutions that the great questions of the day are decided, as was mistakenly done in 1848 and 1849, but with blood and iron.' For thirty-eight years Bismarck was faithful to this principle of force as the foundation of government, and the majority of his fellow-countrymen wholeheartedly accepted his creed.

Naturally the Crown Prince and Princess regarded this event with dismay, but they were disarmed by the King's threat of abdication and by the opinion urged by the younger Stockmar, who was secretary to the Crown Princess, that they should not intervene in party strife.

The new Minister-President was at this period still under fifty years of age. In his character three dominant traits could be noted pride, fearlessness and secretiveness. Not yet had he acquired that cynical distrust of men nor the fierceness depicted in his determined jaw and angry brooding eyes, such as his later likenesses portray. Taking a strong line with the parliamentary deputies and the press, he rode rough-shod over opposition, dominating his enemies with unconstitutional severity. It was inevitable that neither the Crown Prince nor the Crown Princess, with her father's constitutional teachings deeply ingrained in every fibre, could see eye to eye with this ruthless protagonist of Prussianism, and from the first there were clashes and skirmishes, covert and open hostility. Bismarck regarded the Princess, as he regarded all women, as a *quantité négligeable* in affairs of state, while to the Princess, who had views much in advance of her time, any form of autocratic government was anathema.

Bismarck's own opinion of the Crown Princess is given in his *Reminiscences*.

Even soon after her arrival in Germany [he notes], in February 1858, I became convinced, through members of the Royal House and from my own observations, that the Princess was prejudiced against me personally. The fact did not surprise me so much as the form in which her prejudice against me had been expressed in the narrow family circle - 'she did not trust me'. I was prepared for antipathy on account of my alleged anti-English feelings and by reason of my refusal to obey English influences; but, from a conversation which I had with the Princess after the war of 1866, while sitting next to her at table, I was obliged to conclude that she had subsequently allowed herself to be influenced in her judgment of my character by further-reaching calumnies.

I was ambitious, she said, in a half-jesting tone, to be a king or at least a president of a republic. I replied in the same semi-jocular tone that I was personally spoilt for a Republican; that I had grown up in the Royalist traditions of the family, and had need of a monarchical institution for my earthly wellbeing; I thanked God, however, that I was not destined to live like a king, constantly on show, but to be until death the king's faithful subject. I added that no guarantee could, however, be given that this conviction of mine would be universally inherited, and this not because Royalists would give out, but because perhaps kings might. 'Pour faire un civet, il faut un lièvre, et pour faire une monarchie, il faut un roi.' I could not answer for it that, in thus expressing myself, I was not free from anxiety at the idea of a change in the occupancy of the throne without a transference of the monarchical traditions to the successor. But the Princess avoided every serious turn and kept up the jocular tone, as amiable and entertaining as ever; she rather gave me the impression that she wished to tease a political opponent.

During the first years of my ministry, I frequently remarked in the course of similar conversations that the Princess took pleasure in provoking my patriotic susceptibilities by playful criticism of persons and matters.[16]

This passage, which undoubtedly reflects Bismarck's 1862 real feeling, gives a vivid picture of these two remarkable personalities, each watchful and guarded like two expert duellists who realise the skill of the other. Whatever mistakes Bismarck may have made, he never underrated the Crown Princess's ability.

This critical period in Prussian history made Berlin anything but pleasant for those who refused to swallow Bismarck's potent tonic, and the Crown Prince and Princess accepted an invitation from the Prince of Wales to join him in a Mediterranean and Italian tour. From Coburg the party made a leisurely journey through South Germany and Switzerland to Marseilles where they embarked in the royal yacht *Osborne*. Sicily, Tunis, Malta and Naples were visited in turn. A few days' stay in Rome in mid-November completed the tour and they returned to Berlin in December after an absence of three months. The Crown Princess enjoyed this immensely, and its greatest result was to lay the foundation of that deep love for Italy and Italian art which became one of her strongest characteristics.

It was towards the end of this tour that the Crown Prince and Princess made a short stay in December at Vienna. The American historian, John Lothrop Motley, who was visiting Austria at the time, gives a charming account of his interview with the Crown Princess, who had wished to meet him: 'She is rather *petite*, has a fresh young face with pretty features, fine teeth, and a frank and agreeable smile and an interested, earnest and intelligent manner. Nothing could be simpler or more natural than her style, which I should say was the perfection of good breeding.'

Meanwhile a second son, Prince Henry, destined to become Germany's sailor prince, had been born on August 14, 1862, to the Crown Prince and Princess.

It might have been expected that the Crown Princess's growing family would have disarmed a little of that hostility with which she was regarded by some elements in Prussia. Strangely enough the enmity grew because the arrival of the children, two of whom were boys, naturally strengthened the position of the Princess, and her opponents feared that these young Princes would be brought up in English rather than Prussian ways.

Bismarck, now well in the saddle, soon made it clear that he would not permit the Constitution of 1850 to stand in his way, and he persuaded William I to govern without parliament, and to agree to such an interpretation of the Prussian Constitution as would enable him to muzzle the press. To these autocratic acts both the Crown Prince and Princess were opposed, and decided to make it plain that they were not conniving at such a misinterpretation. The result was a severe estrangement between the King and his son. On June 5, 1863, the Crown Prince wrote to his father, expressing his views, and on the same day, while at Dantzig, during a tour in the performance of his military duties, speaking in public to the chief Burgomaster, von Winter, he declared himself to be opposed to his father's policy. King William at once wrote demanding a public recantation, and threatened to deprive the Prince of his dignities and position. The Crown Prince, in his reply of June 7, declined to retract anything, offered to lay down his command and other offices, and begged to be allowed to retire with his family to some place where he would be under no suspicion of interfering in politics.

The breach between father and son seemed to be complete, and it was with feelings of bewilderment that the Crown Princess wrote to Queen Victoria on June 8:

> I told you, on the 5th, that Fritz had written twice to the King, once, warning him of the consequences that would ensue if the constitution was falsely interpreted in order to take away the liberty of the press. The King did it all the same, and answered Fritz with a very angry letter. Fritz then sent his protest to Bismarck on the 4th, saying he wished to have an answer immediately. *Bismarck has not answered.*
>
> Fritz wrote on the 5th to the King, as I told you. On the same day Mr de Winter, the Oberburgermeister of Danzig, a great friend of ours, a worthy and excellent man, as clever as liberal-minded, told Fritz he would make him a speech at the Rathaus, and begged Fritz to answer him.
>
> I did *all I could* to induce Fritz to do so, knowing how necessary it was that he should once express his sentiments openly and disclaim having any part in the last measures of the Government. He did so accordingly in very mild and

measured terms - you will have no doubt seen it in the newspapers. To this the King answered Fritz a furious letter, treating him quite like a little child; telling him instantly to retract in the newspapers the words he had spoken at Danzig, charging him with disobedience, etc., and telling him that if he said one other word of the kind he would instantly recall him and take his place in the Army and the Council from him.

Fritz sat up till one last night, writing the answer, which Captain von Luccadon has taken to Berlin this morning, and in which Fritz says that he is almost brokenhearted at causing his father so much pain, but that he could *not* retract the words spoken to Winter at Danzig; that he had always hoped the King's Government would not act in a way which should force him to put himself in direct opposition to the King; but now it had come to that, and he (Fritz) would stand by his opinions. He felt that under such circumstances it would be impossible for him to retain any office military or civil, and he laid both at the feet of the King. As he felt that his presence must be disagreeable to the King, he begged him to name a place, or allow us to select one, where he could live in perfect retirement and not mix in politics.

What the upshot of this will be, heaven knows. Fritz has done his duty and has nothing to reproach himself with. But he is in a state of perfect misery, and in consequence not at all well. I hope you will make his conduct known to your Ministers and to all our friends in England. We feel dreadfully alone, having not a soul from whom to ask advice. But Fritz's course of duty is so plain and straightforward, that it requires no explaining or advising.

How unhappy I am to see him so worried, I cannot say; but I shall stand by him as is my duty, and advise him to do his in the face of all the Kings and Emperors of the whole world.

A year of silence and self-denial has brought Fritz no other fruits than that of being considered weak and helpless. The Conservatives fancy he is in Duncker's[17] hands, and that he dictates his every step. The Liberals think he is not sincerely one of them, and those few who do think it, fancy he has not the courage to avow it. He has now given them an opportunity of judging of his way of thinking, and consequently will now again be passive and silent till better days come. The way in which the Government behave, and the way in which they have treated Fritz, rouse my every feeling of *independence*. Thank God I was born in England, where people are not slaves, and too good to allow themselves to be treated as such.

I hope our nation here will soon prove that we come of the same forefathers, and strive for their own lawful independence, to which they have been too long callous.

Queen Victoria did as her daughter wished, and informed one or two of her ministers as to what was happening in Prussia. Lord Russell was shown the Crown Princess's letter by General Grey, who was Private Secretary to the Queen. Lord Russell thought that 'nothing can be more judicious than the course the Crown Prince has adopted - the hope of any good depends on his firm perseverance in it. With the Crown Princess by his side there seems no fear of his not being firm.'

That was the English viewpoint. The Prussian viewpoint was that the Crown Prince and Princess had meddled in matters outside their proper concern - and they lost popularity accordingly. Intimations as to the correspondence between the Crown Prince and King William were published in *The Times*, then in the *Grenzboten* (through Gustav Freytag) and in the *Suddeutsche Zeitung* (through Busch, at Freytag's instance). On June 21 the Crown Princess wrote to Queen Victoria:

> The messenger has just arrived, bringing your dear letter, and the one from General Grey; allow me to answer them both together.
>
> We are well nigh worn out with mental fatigue, anxiety, excitement of the most painful kind. I was ill all yesterday, and feel still very confused! I send you *all the papers* that you may see what Fritz has done, said and written! *He has* done all he could. He has, for the first time in his life, taken up a position decidedly in opposition to his father. His speech in Danzig was intended to convey in a clear and *unzweideutig* way to his hearers, that he had nothing to do with the unconstitutional acts of the Government - that he was not even aware of their being in contemplation! The effect produced on those fifty or sixty who heard it was exactly the one desired, but I know there are many who will not agree. The Conservatives are in a state of indignation and alarm! the King very angry! We are in this critical position without a secretary, without a single person to give advice, to write for us, or to help us; whatever we do one way or the other is abused.
>
> After having read all these papers, you will understand that Fritz can do no more than what he has done! My last letter will explain much of what has happened. We are surrounded with spies, who watch all we do, and most likely report all to Berlin, in a sense to checkmate everything we do.
>
> The Liberal papers are forbidden, so we do not even know what is going on. Fritz's speech was much praised by newspapers in Frankfort-on-the-Main. As for coming to you, dear Mama, you are too kind to say so; at present we can decide nothing, as we have received no answer from the King; our fate is not settled.
>
> If it becomes necessary for us to leave the country, I can hardly say how grateful we shall be to be once again with you, in that blessed country of peace and happiness!
>
> Now good-bye, my dearest Mama, I kiss your hands. I am sure you will think of me in all this trouble. I do not mind any difficulties so long as they end well for Fritz; indeed I enjoy a pitched battle (when it comes to it) exceedingly. Fritz feels his courage rise in every emergency; only the thought of his *father* makes him feel powerless. 'Think if it was your father,' he says to me, 'would you like to disobey him and make him unhappy?'

In a postscript the Princess added:

....The King does not accept Fritz's resignation, and wishes us to continue our journey, forbidding Fritz, however, to say another word openly. We shall therefore carry out our plan of travelling here (at Königsberg) till the 1st of July, when we shall go to the Isle of Rügen. In August I hope to see you, dear Mama, for a day or two; in September are the manoeuvres and a Statistical Congress, which Fritz is to open; therefore I fear Scotland will be quite impossible. Oh dear! what a sad and wretched time we have of it, and no help, no support, surrounded with people determined to put an insurmountable barrier to all we wish to do in a liberal sense, and tormenting the very life out of one! Please send back the enclosed as soon as you can. As soon as the rest of the papers are returned to us, Fritz will send them to you.

M. de Bismarck *has not even* answered Fritz's letter, and the King has forbidden him to give it to the rest of the Ministers!

Bismarck believed that the publication of the letters was due to the Princess, and Busch quotes a memorandum, dated Gastein, August 2, probably dictated by Bismarck, which expressed this view. 'Either', runs the memorandum, 'she has herself attained to definite views of her own as to the form of government most advantageous for Prussia....or she has succumbed to the concerted influences of the Anglo-Coburg combination. However this may be, it is asserted that she has decided upon a course of opposition to the present Government, and has taken advantage of the Dantzig incident and the excitement to which it has given rise in the highest circles, in order to bring her consort more and more into prominence by these revelations, and to acquaint public opinion with the Crown Prince's way of thinking. All this out of anxiety for the future of her consort!' The memorandum went on to state that the Crown Princess's most powerful supporter was Queen Augusta, who was extremely anxious as to her own position towards the country. 'They have had a memorandum drawn up by President Camphausen on the internal situation in Prussia, attacking the present Government, which was laid before the King. In a marginal note the King observes that the principles therein recommended would lead to revolution. Meyer, the Councillor of Embassy, is Augusta's instrument, and it is beyond question that he is associated with the Anglo-Coburg party. The participation of Professor Duncker[18] as also of Baron Stockmar, would appear to be less certain.' The memorandum is accompanied by comments in Bismarck's handwriting, in which the views expressed by the Crown Prince are refuted point by point. In the course of his criticism the writer says, *inter alia*: 'The pretension that a warning from his Royal Highness should outweigh royal decisions, come to after serious and careful consideration, attributes undue importance to his own position and experience as compared to those of his sovereign and father. No one could believe that H.R.H. had any share in these acts of personal authority, as everybody knows that the Prince has no vote in the Ministry....'[19]

A week later (June 30, 1863) the Crown Prince wrote to Bismarck:

> I see from your letter of the 10th instant that at his Majesty's commands you have omitted to communicate officially to the Ministry of State my protest respecting the rescript, restricting the liberty of the press, which I sent to you from Graudenz on the 8th of June. I can easily understand that the opportunity of treating as a personal matter an incident which, as you yourself have acknowledged, might, in its consequences, acquire widespread significance, was not unwelcome to you. It would serve no purpose for me to insist upon that communication being made, as I am justified in inferring from your own words that it will have been done unofficially.
> 
> It is necessary for me, however, to speak plainly to you respecting the alternative which you place before me, namely, to lighten or render more difficult the task which the Ministry has undertaken. I cannot lighten that task, as I find myself opposed to it in principle. A loyal administration of the laws and of the Constitution, respect and goodwill towards an easily led, intelligent and capable people - these are the principles which, in my opinion, should guide every Government in the treatment of the country. I cannot bring the policy which finds expression in the ordinance of the 1st of June into harmony with these principles. It is true you seek to prove to me the constitutional character of that rescript, and you assure me that you and your colleagues remember your oath. I think, however, that the Government requires a stronger basis than very dubious interpretations which do not appeal to the sound common sense of the people. You yourself call attention to the circumstance that even your opponents respect the honesty of your convictions. I will not inquire into that assertion ['Not over courteous', was Bismarck's comment in pencil], but if you attach any importance to the opinions of your opponents, the circumstance that the great majority of the educated classes among our people deny the constitutional character of the ordinance must necessarily awaken scruples in your mind....I will tell you what results I anticipate from your policy. You will go on quibbling with the Constitution until it loses all value in the eyes of the people. In that way you will on the one hand arouse anarchical movements that go beyond the bounds of the Constitution ; while on the other hand, whether you intend it or not, you will pass from one venturesome interpretation to another until you are finally driven into an open breach of the Constitution. ['Perhaps,' was Bismarck's comment.] I regard those who lead his Majesty the King, my most gracious father, into such courses as the most dangerous advisers for Crown and country. ['Youth is hasty with words,' quoted Bismarck.]

To this letter the Crown Prince added the postscript:

Already before the 1st of June of this year I but rarely made use of my right to attend the sittings of the Ministry of State. From the foregoing statement of my convictions you will understand my requesting his Majesty the King to allow me to abstain altogether from attending them at present. A continuous public and personal manifestation of the differences between myself and the Ministry ['Absalom!' was Bismarck's comment in pencil] would be in keeping neither with my position nor my inclination. In every other respect, however, I shall impose no restrictions upon the expression of my views; and the Ministry may rest assured that it will depend upon themselves and their own future action whether, in spite of my own strong reluctance, I find myself forced into further public steps, when duty appears to call for them. ['Come on!' writes Bismarck's undaunted pencil.] [20]

Between the Crown Prince and Bismarck there was now marked hostility, and the Crown Princess naturally sided with her husband in the quarrel. Three months later the Crown Prince communicated to his father the tenor of his letter to Bismarck, and on September 3 wrote to Bismarck:

I have today communicated to his Majesty the views which I set forth to you in my letters from Putbus, and which I begged you not to submit to the King until I myself had done so. A decision which will have serious consequences was yesterday taken in the Council. I did not wish to reply to his Majesty in the presence of the Ministers. I have done so today, and have given expression to my misgivings - my serious misgivings - for the future. The King now knows that I am a decided opponent of the Ministry.

At the end of the letter Bismarck scribbled, apparently as part of a draft reply:

I can only hope that your Royal Highness will one day find servants as faithful as I am to your father. I do not intend to be of the number.[21]

The Crown Princess had now been in Prussia five and a half years, years that, although producing the little series of pinpricks to which everyone is subject, had brought her much happiness. This duel between her husband and Bismarck was the first indication of open hostility. Both the Crown Prince and the Crown Princess had been actuated by the highest motives in their opposition to King William: but Bismarck had won. There could not be two supreme advisers, and the Crown Prince had been dramatically bidden to stand aside. Neither he nor his Princess forgot: nor did Bismarck, who long remembered that here was an opponent who had dared to question his decisions in the secret counsels of the King.

In the Prussian court henceforward there were two main parties. At the head of the reactionary-all-for-Prussia party was Bismarck with the King as his shield. At the head of the liberal-minded 'Anglo-Coburg' party, as Bismarck scathingly referred to it, were the Crown Prince of Prussia and his English-born Princess.

Some of the Prussian dissatisfaction at the views of the Crown Prince and Princess was evinced when, in the following month the Crown Prince, accompanied by his wife, went on a long tour of military inspections in Prussia and Pomerania. In some of the towns they visited en route the municipal authorities ostentatiously refrained from celebrating the occasion; and it was very evident that the official attitude in Prussia was reflecting some wish from a more influential quarter. The result was that in September 1863 there followed a long visit to the English court which lasted until December. The Princess was at home - in England - and tongues began to wag at the incomprehensible preference of the Prussian Crown Princess for a land other than that she had adopted. Meanwhile Queen Victoria had visited Coburg and had had long conversations with Robert Morier, the Crown Princess's friend. Bismarck noted these things carefully, and sedulously fostered the growing disapproval of the mythical English interference in Prussian affairs.

Just prior to Queen Victoria's visit to Coburg, Austria had attempted to take the solution of the German question into her own hands by initiating a scheme for reforming the Federal Constitution, and the Emperor Francis Joseph invited the Princes and the free cities of Germany to a conference in August at Frankfort to discuss the reorganisation of the Germanic Confederation. King William was inclined to accept this proposal, but Bismarck held other views, insisting on complete equality with Austria in Federal affairs. A further invitation from the Emperor suggesting that the King should send the Crown Prince to the Congress of Princes, was also declined.

Nevertheless the Congress was held, and coincided with Queen Victoria's visit to Coburg. Hence there was held a sort of family gathering at Coburg, presided over by Queen Victoria, at which the Crown Prince and Princess were prominent figures. The Congress, owing to King William's absence, was futile; and the well-meant efforts of Queen Victoria, who saw both King William and the Emperor Francis Joseph, failed to bring them into accord. Only a year earlier Bismarck had first made public use of the tremendous phrase that the German question would have to be solved by 'blood and iron'. An opportunity was not long to be delayed of putting this grim policy to the test. In less than a year there was war with Denmark over the duchies of Schleswig and Holstein, and within four years a war with Austria for the leadership of Germany.

The causes that led to the war with Denmark have long been the subject of dispute among historians, and it is perhaps just sufficient to indicate the events prior to the outbreak of war.

On March 30, 1863, a Danish Royal Patent was issued arbitrarily granting to Holstein a new form of government but separating it entirely from Schleswig - which was left under the Danish Rigsraad - and imposing additional financial burdens on both duchies. This was followed up in the late autumn by the incorporation of the duchy of Schleswig in the kingdom of Denmark. The bill for this, passed on November 13, never received the signature of King Frederick VII, who died two days later. He was succeeded by his nephew, King Christian IX, the father of Alexandra, Princess of Wales. Three days after his accession King Christian reluctantly ratified this act.

The position was complicated by the fact that there was a third claimant to the duchy of Schleswig (as well as to that of Holstein) in the person of Duke Frederick of Schleswig-Holstein-Sonderburg-Augustenburg, known familiarly as Fritz Augustenburg, whose partisans included the Crown Prince and Princess, the King of Hanover, the Duke of Coburg and the heads of a few minor German states. Queen Victoria sympathised with the German aspirations and with the claims of the hereditary Prince of Augustenburg, but members of her own family as well as those of the royal families of Prussia and Denmark took various sides with ardent enthusiasm. The question in fact came like a dividing sword between the royal circles of those three countries. The British royal family was connected intimately with both Denmark and Prussia, for two of Queen Victoria's daughters had married German princes, while her eldest son, the Prince of Wales, had married Princess Alexandra (Alix) of Denmark in March 1863. On January 5, 1864, the Crown Princess wrote to Queen Victoria:

....Of politics I can say nothing - only this much which will give you pleasure, which is that the King is much kinder to Fritz and that the Queen is much pleased with him.

My thoughts and wishes are with Fritz Augustenburg, who has embarked on a difficult course, though it was the right one. But I feel much for poor King Christian, with his kind feelings and good heart he must find the position he is in doubly disagreeable. I hope dearest Alix does not fret too much about it all. King Christian has himself to thank for the fix he is in - why did he accept and allow himself to be put in a place not rightfully his own? He might now be living in peace and quiet....

Bismarck now seized the opportunity to his hand, and on January 16, 1864, issued an ultimatum to King Christian to evacuate and abandon Schleswig within twenty-four hours. War resulted.

With the outbreak of war the Crown Princess found herself at odds with her brother and sister-in-law, the Prince and Princess of Wales, who naturally supported Denmark; and with the King and Queen of Prussia, who naturally supported Bismarck.

On the failure of King Christian to abandon Schleswig at Bismarck's bidding, Prussian and Austrian troops invaded the duchy. The gallant but hopeless resistance of the Danes excited tremendous sympathy in England, and Lord Palmerston, the Prime Minister, and Lord Russell, the Foreign Secretary, reflected public opinion in scathing denunciations of the brutal attack. The government, however, stopped short at threats, for Queen Victoria's influence was on the side of neutrality.

The position was now doubly difficult for the Crown Prince and Princess. Whilst regarding 'Fritz Augustenburg' as the rightful claimant, reasons of state compelled their identification with the Prussian policy, to the undisguised impatience of the Prince and Princess of Wales. The Crown Prince, as a Lieutenant-General in the Prussian army, was of course called up for active service, which occasioned further bitterness between the Crown Princess and her brother. 'Vicky little dreamt', wrote the King of the Belgians to Queen Victoria several months later (June 15, 1864), 'in selecting a charming (Danish) Princess (for her brother) that she would become a source of difficulties for England, and perhaps the cause of a popular war against Prussia.'

On January 21 the German troops under Marshal Wrangel entered Holstein, and on February 5 the Danes abandoned their lines of defence - the Dannewerke - in order to save their army. The change in the attitude of the Crown Princess may be gathered from her letter of February 8 to Queen Victoria:

The turn the campaign has taken astonishes us all very much, as we thought the taking of the Dannewerke would be a dreadful business and no one dreamt of the Danes abandoning their position.

I hope and pray that the war may end with honour to our dear troops and attain all the results which Germany expects. You say, dear Mama, that you are glad you have not the blood of so many innocents on your conscience. We have nobody to thank for it but Lord Palmerston and the Emperor Nicholas. If they had not meddled with what did not concern them in the year '48, these sad consequences would not have ensued....

It is impossible to blame an English person for not understanding the Schleswig-Holstein question - after the mess the two *Great Powers of Germany* have made of it, - it remains nevertheless to us Germans plain and simple as daylight and one for which we would gladly bring any sacrifice.

The succeeding weeks saw the continued advance of the Prussian and Austrian troops which culminated in March and April by a fierce attack on the village and fortress of Düppel or Dybböl. The virulent comments in the

British press on the conduct of the allies now turned the opinion of the Crown Princess into even more definite channels, especially when the bombardment of Sonderburg, a town on the island of Alsen covered by the bridgehead of Düppel, was described as brutal and violent.

> If the bombardment [the Crown Princess wrote to Queen Victoria on April 13] of Sonderburg has raised ill feeling towards us in England the most absurd, unjust, rude and violent attacks - in the *Times* and in Parliament - can only increase the irritation or rather more contempt, which is expressed in no measured terms here and generally felt for England's position in the Danish question.
> But even the French see this and defend us against the really childishly indignant attacks upon us - in the *Presse* of the 10th.
> I can see nothing inhuman or improper in any way in the bombardment of Sonderburg - it was necessary and we hope it has been useful. 'What would Lord Russell say if we were every instant to make enquiries about what is going on in Japan - where Admiral Kuper was not so intensely scrupulous as to bombardments.
> I quite agree with Mr Bernal Osborne who calls in his most excellent speech in the *Times* of the 9th the perpetual unnecessary questions which are asked of us here and at Vienna 'Hysteric fussiness'. The continual meddling and interfering of England in other people's affairs has become so ridiculous abroad that it almost ceases to annoy. But to an English heart it is no pleasant sight to see the dignity of one's country so compromised and let down - its influence so completely lost.
> The highly pathetic, philanthropic and virtuous tone in which all the attacks against Prussia are made, has something intensely ridiculous about it. The English would not like it if they were engaged in a war, to be dictated to in a pompous style, how they were to conduct it, indeed I am sure they would not stand such interference. Why should we then be supposed to submit to it?

In May a truce was arranged, but hostilities broke out afresh in June. The Danes, however, were in no condition to continue the struggle and quickly sued for peace. The peace which followed secured Prussia and Austria in the joint occupation of the two duchies. On May 26 the Crown Princess wrote:

> ... I really do begin to think politics are taking a more favourable turn and do not despair of things ending pretty well *now*! What a blessing! Furious as everyone is here about England, the King never misses an opportunity of saying how much he owes you, and how grateful he is to you for your endeavours to keep peace, etc., etc., which he feels certain would not have been preserved but for you. I hope and trust a peace will be made on a basis which will for ever prevent the recurrence of hostilities on the subject of the duchies, and which will bring them and their duke to their lawful rights.
> One thing I own torments me much, it is the feeling of animosity between

our two countries; it is so dangerous and productive of such harm! It is kept up too by such foolish trifles, which might be so well avoided. Prussia has gained unpopularity for itself since some time, on account of the King's illiberal government, but the feeling against us now in England is *most* unjust! Now dear Papa is no longer here I live in continual dread that the bonds which united our two countries for their mutual good are being so loosened that they may in time be quite severed! A great deal depends on who is Minister, that is Ambassador, here. Sir A. Buchanan, who is an excellent man, whom I honour and like personally, is quite unfit for the place and has made himself a very bad position here. He knows no German and understands nothing whatever of German affairs, nor of the position Prussia holds in the different questions which arise. He does not listen to those who do know, and is consequently continually misinformed and 1864 misrepresents things totally, as I saw out of the blue book. He is very unpopular here and has no sort of influence. He picks up his information from bad sources, such as other silly diplomatists who understand nothing at all (the Brazilian, for instance). Sir Andrew is a high Tory and dislikes everything Liberal, the consequence of which is that he totally misunderstands the positions of our political parties; our Conservative party in England cannot be compared with the *Kreuz Zeitung* it is quite a different thing. Strange to say, in spite of all the ill-treatment he has received at his hands, Sir A has a secret liking for Bismarck.

With the end of the Danish War it seemed as if the interrupted cordialities between the Princess Frederick and her brother, the Prince of Wales, might be renewed, but the embers of distrust smouldered for a few months longer. In October the Prince and Princess of Wales, after visiting Denmark, proceeded to Germany and at Cologne had a brief meeting with the Crown Prince (fresh from the battlefield) and Princess. The family differences flamed up afresh.

'I can assure you', the Prince of Wales wrote to Lord Spencer on November 7, 'it was not pleasant to see him (the Crown Prince) and his A.D.C. always in Prussian uniform, flaunting before our eyes a most objectionable ribbon which he received for his *deeds of valour???* against the unhappy Danes.'

## NOTES

1 The fact that Jules Laforgue, the French poet, was appointed reader to her shows that she had literary tastes.
2 *Mary Ponsonby*, p. 242.
3 *The Empress Frederick: A Memoir*, pp. 91-2.
4 Lucien von Balhausen, *Bismarcks Erinnerungen*, p. 74.
5 One of the German doctors in attendance on the Princess.

6 Later King Christian IX of Denmark.
7 Walburga, Lady Paget, *Embassies of other Days*, i. 328 *seq*.
8 Sir Sidney Lee, *Life of King Edward VII*, vol. i. p. 120.
9 *The Empress Frederick: A Memoir*, p. 115.
10 *Ibid*. p. 123.
11 *The Empress Frederick: A Memoir*, p. 127.
12 Prince Alfred, later Duke of Edinburgh.
13 *The Empress Frederick: A Memoir*, p. 138.
14 Alfred, later Duke of Edinburgh. A 'happy family' is a cage at a fair in which animals naturally hostile to one another live apparently in peace and harmony.
15 *The Empress Frederick: A Memoir*, p. 149-51.
16 *Bismarck's Reminiscences*, vol. i. pp. 190-1.
17 Professor Duncker, a Prussian deputy who had been attached to the Crown Prince on King William's accession as a channel of communication in state matters. Both the Crown Prince and Princess trusted him implicitly.
18 As a matter of fact he was not concerned in it. See Haym's work, *Das Leben Max Dunckers*, pp. 294, 295.
19 *Bismarck*, Busch, p. 289.
20 *Ibid*. pp. 235-7.
21 *Ibid*. p. 238.
22 Sir Sidney Lee, *Life of King Edward VII*, vol. I p. 256.

## III: The Austrian War

THE Danish War was only a rung in Bismarck's tall ladder of Prussian aggrandisement and German unity. In those days the rights of small nations were an unknown quantity, but even if the defence of the weak against the strong had been a European aphorism then, it is doubtful whether this solicitude for the smaller countries would have found any place in Bismarck's theories. 'Within two years the alliance with Austria had served its turn. It was Queen Victoria who had expressed the view that it was 'a sacred duty' to strengthen Prussia's prestige - an opinion warmly held by the Crown Princess, but now war between Prussia and Austria almost meant civil war within her family circle. The Crown Princess's brother- in-law, the Grand Duke of Hesse, her cousin the King of Hanover, her uncle Ernest, Duke of Saxe-Coburg, and many others of her German kinsfolk were ranging themselves on Austria's side. The Crown Prince Frederick, however, no matter on which side his relations might be, was bound to fight at the head of a Prussian army against his wife's German relatives.

Meanwhile Bismarck was in no temper to conciliate either the Crown Princess or her mother, Queen Victoria, for several events of minor importance had occurred during the preceding year which tended to widen the breach between them. Early that year it became evident that Prince Christian of Schleswig-Holstein-Sonderburg-Augustenburg, the younger brother of that Duke Frederick ('Fritz Augustenburg' as the Crown Princess called him) whose claim to the duchies of Schleswig and Holstein, although supported by the Crown Prince and Princess, had been so contemptuously dismissed by Bismarck, was eager to win the hand of Queen Victoria's daughter. Princess Helena. When the Danish War ended, Bismarck had shown the force of his mailed fist by depriving Duke Frederick and Prince Christian of their property, commissions and standing. It was obvious that those who endeavoured to thwart the Iron Chancellor must take the consequences.

Queen Victoria, however, had preserved an open mind, and when rumour began to spread as to Prince Christian's admiration of her daughter, she wrote, early in April 1865, to the Crown Princess asking for her opinion of the Prince, and the Crown Princess replied (April 18):

You ask about Christian. You know he is our *Hausfreund.* He comes and goes when he likes, walks and breakfasts and dines with us, when he is here and we are alone. He is the best creature in the world; not as clever as Fritz (Augustenburg), but certainly not wanting in any way. He is very amusing when he chooses. We like him very much. He is almost bald; is not like Fritz, more like his father and eldest sister. He has a much better figure than his brother, and quite a military tournure. Nor is he so distinguished as Fritz, of whom I have the highest possible opinion as regards his character and intellect.

Christian is very fond of children and speaks English. I send you a photograph of him which he gave me. He has not the fine eyes of his brother, but a better mouth and chin. He has the same way of speaking as they all have.

His position here is not an easy or an agreeable one; but he manages to get on very well....

When this favourable opinion of the Crown Princess's was supported by one of the ladies of the Queen of Prussia, Countess Blücher, who was, as Queen Victoria wrote to King Leopold, 'most favourable to the idea', Queen Victoria at once began to consider 'how by degrees it could naturally be brought about'.

In the summer of 1865 Queen Victoria journeyed to Coburg to unveil, on August 26, a statue to the Prince Consort, and thither she summoned the Prince of Wales and the Crown Prince and Princess. Altogether twenty-four of the Queen's near kinsfolk - the majority of them German - attended the ceremony, and among the visitors was (as she wrote) the 'extremely pleasing, gentleman-like, quiet and distinguished' Prince Christian. Queen Victoria took advantage of the occasion to publish her approval of Princess Helena's engagement to him. Bismarck was furious at this implied rebuke of his treatment of Duke Frederick and Prince Christian. That Queen Victoria should publish in such circumstances her assent to an engagement which would obviously offend Prussian susceptibilities, was interpreted by him to be a demonstration of defiance not only on her part, but on the part of the Crown Prince and Princess, and he was slow to forget it.

The following year the tension between Prussia and Austria grew. The Danish War had resulted in Prussia and Austria being co-occupants of the duchies of Schleswig and Holstein: by now Bismarck regarded Austria as an encumbrance and early in 1866 it was evident that the issue of peace or war between the ci-devant allies was hanging by a thread.

We are still [wrote the Crown Princess to Queen Victoria on April 4, 1866] suspended midway between peace and war; not a day passes without some little incident which might be easily laid 1866 hold of to turn the scales on the side of peace, and not a day passes that the wicked man does not with the greatest ability counteract and thwart what is good, and drive on towards war, turning and twisting everything to serve his own purpose.

As often as we are a little hopeful again and see a means of getting out of the fix, we hear shortly after that the means have been rendered unavailable; the tissue of untruths is such that one gets quite perplexed with only listening to them, but the net is cleverly made, and the King (of Prussia), in spite of all his reluctance, gets more and more entangled in it without perceiving it....

It was as the German Crown Princess said - Bismarck had so complicated the issues that war was inevitable. Every effort, however, was made, not only by the Crown Princess, but also by Queen Victoria, to find some means of averting the conflict. Queen Victoria herself tried to moderate Prussian aggressiveness by appealing to the King of Prussia on April 10, to avoid war. She again wrote early in May, this time through the Crown Prince, suggesting a European Conference. A few days later (May 19) the Crown Princess wrote dolefully from Potsdam to the Queen:

....I have hardly courage to write, I can do nothing but harp on that one unfortunate theme. Fritz gave your letter to the King, but he has not said anything about it. Fritz does not think the King will accept the proposal, and thinks that the Congress could only propose solutions which either Prussia or Austria would not agree to. I do not despair, but I think the chances of peace become smaller every day! Heaven help us! It is a most miserable, wretched time.

Our christening[1] will be such a sad one; the day after, my Fritz leaves and joins his troops, taking the command of the Silesian Army; when and where I shall see him again I do not know; what I feel I cannot tell you. I think my heart will break. All is uncertain, and ruin and misfortune of every kind likely.

We hear nothing talked of all day but war and preparations for it. The command which Fritz has received is very fine and very honourable, but a most difficult one; he will have almost exclusively Poles under him, which you know are not so pleasant as Germans. He is busy forming his staff and has been lucky enough to get some very good officers....

In June war broke out, and there followed that short, brilliant Seven Weeks' War which resulted in the humiliation of Austria and gave Prussia the hegemony of Germany.

The distress of the Crown Princess at seeing her husband depart on another campaign against an apparently much more formidable foe than the Danes was now intensified by the loss of her youngest boy, Prince Sigismund, who died on June 18, at the age of twenty-one months. On June 19 she wrote to Queen Victoria:

Your suffering child turns to you in her grief, sure to find sympathy from so tender a heart, so versed in sorrow. The hand of Providence is heavy upon me. I have to bear this awful trial alone, without my poor Fritz. My little darling graciously lent me for a short time, to be my pride, my joy, my hope, is gone,

gone, where my passionate devotion cannot follow, from where my love cannot recall him! Oh spare me telling you how, and when, and where my heart was rent and broken, let me only say that I do not murmur or repine, God's Will be done.

What I suffer none can know, few knew how I loved. It was my own happy secret, the long cry of agony which rises from the inmost depth of my soul, reaches Heaven alone.

I wish you to know all, you are so kind, darling Mama, that you will wish to hear all about the last terrible days. I cannot describe them. I am calm now, for Fritz's sake and my little one's, but oh how bitter is this cup....

Queen Victoria's sympathetic reply brought the following letter from the Princess (June 26, 1866):

A thousand thanks for your dear lines - and the poems - they touched and soothed me. In moments of extreme grief - when one seems unable to realise what has happened, or how one can still 1866 be living at all, one's thoughts naturally turn to those who have gone through the ordeal of such suffering - and is thankful for kindness and sympathizing words! So my thoughts turned to you! Our afflictions cannot be compared, they are too different, but each heart knoweth its own bitterness. A little child does not seem a great loss to other people - but none know but God how I suffer. Oh how I loved that little thing, from the first moments of its birth, it was more to me than its brothers and sisters, it was so fair, so loving, so bright and merry, how proud I was of my little one; and just this one my heart's best treasure was taken, and the sorrow seems greater than I can bear. Oh, to see it suffer so cruelly, to see it die and hear its last piteous cry - was an agony I cannot describe, it haunts me night and day! The last few months my little Sigie had grown so wonderfully forward and intelligent, he was so clever, much more than either of the others, and I thought he was going to be like Papa. Fritz and I idolized him - he had such dear, sweet, winning little ways, and was like a little sunbeam in the house.

Now to see his little empty bed - his clothes, his toys lying about, to miss him every hour and long - oh so bitterly, so fondly and deeply to fold him once more to my heart - it is such cruel suffering. My child, my child, is all I can say! I shall never see it more. I know he is spared sin and suffering. I know that his life was bright and happy as it was short. I feel that I left nothing undone which could have given him joy or comfort. I do not repine or refuse to take the comfort which God had mercifully granted, but I grieve even unto death.

Thanks for thinking of me on Thursday. Yes it was trying and awful, but only for the nerves and the imagination, the blow had fallen, and what is the rest to be compared to it. For two days I could not shed a tear - at the sad solemn ceremony mine were the only dry eyes. I could not cry! My poor Fritz away and at so difficult and dangerous a post. It is a blessing for him that his mind must be occupied with other things. I will not give way. I mean to do my duty and neglect nothing - work and occupation are the only things which can restore balance to my mind, not drown my grief or fill the blank in my heart. Oh no, no time can do that, that sweet little face will ever be there and the yearning for it, but I have many and sacred duties to live for - and I will do them to the utmost of my power - for those other dear children, for my poor dear Fritz!

What our future may be is now very uncertain, when I doubted of that formerly, I used to think earthly goods were so unimportant - as long as we had our little family circle unbroken, and I looked with pride and gratitude on our little flock of five....

Four days later, the Princess again wrote from the Neue Palais:

You have written me three such dear letters, so kind, comforting and soothing. Many many thanks for them. If I ever anxiously expected your letters, it is now when all around share the violent excitement of the awful events passing around, and I alone feel that they cannot drive away my grief. My darling little Love is ever in my thoughts, dulling my sense to other things. A little child is no loss to the rest of the world, none miss it, but to me it is a part of myself, one of my chief interests in life. My little Sigie's loss has cast a gloom over this house and over my whole existence which will never quite wear off. My dear dear little boy. I keep saying that all day. Yesterday I packed up all the clothes I had worked for him all the winter with such pleasure, and that he looked so sweet and pretty in. Tomorrow morning we leave this place where I have been since the night in which Victoria was born - it seems so strange to me to leave one of my little ones here.

My Fritz writes to me very often, he has been in a battle, Heaven protect him. Everyone joins in his praise, which of course is very gratifying to me, his heart is sad and heavy, but he thinks of his duty before all - he is so good - oh, when shall I see him again, and when I do, what a meeting that will be. What have we both gone through since we parted. I know you think of us and feel for your children, dearest Mama, and that is most comforting to us. I say nothing about the war - you know what I think, my head is too weak now to put my idea into a reasonable form. You will not think it unnatural, I know, that my feelings are on the side of my country and husband, though of course one can feel nothing but despair at being obliged to consider other Germans as one's enemies - and wish for their destruction....I cannot describe what a cruel contradiction of feelings one has to pass through, but over all sounds my darling's last cry, and the tears 1866 that I shed for all the poor fallen and wounded and their afflicted families flow over his little grave....

The Princess, putting her own sorrows aside, now turned her energies to the urgent and necessary work of aiding the war hospital service, and in her letter of July 5 begged her mother to send some hospital supplies for the sufferers:

What will you say [she wrote from Heringsdorf] to all that is going on? How terrible is this loss of life....I work very hard to scrape together necessaries for the hospitals, but one finds all exertions cannot supply the wants which are so fearful and so immense. If you can send me something I should be so glad - in our hospitals Austrians, Saxons and Prussians are all taken care of together - therefore what you send will be for all the poor victims. Heaven grant it may soon be at an end. Sponges and old linen are most wanted.

I am so overburdened with writing that I have not been able to answer any letters of condolence yet; all my time is devoted to what I can do to be of any use to Fritz. He is well, I am thankful to say; but to know his precious life is exposed keeps me in such a tremble. He writes to me often and such kind beautiful letters.

My little people are quite well and send you their love little Victoria is very fat and healthy. Will you say all that is tender and affectionate to dear good Lenchen[2] from me - she knows that I think of her and how truly I love her - and wish her every happiness.

The brilliant rapidity with which the well-trained Prussian armies overwhelmed their Austrian opponents now brought in its train the lists of the slain and honours for the living. To the Crown Prince fell the glory of winning the battles of Nachod (June 27), Skalicz (June 28) and Schweinschädel (June 29), and on July 3 came the battle of Sadowa, or Königgrätz, with the total defeat of the Austrians.

....What do you say [wrote the Crown Princess on July 9, 1866] to all these dreadful battles? Are you not a little pleased that it is our Fritz alone who has won all these victories? You know how hard I tried to help in preventing the calamity of war, and how Fritz [did] too, but now it is there I am thankful to think that our cause under Fritz's leadership has been victorious.

You cannot think how modest he is about it never seeking praise, always doing his duty. The soldiers adore him. I am told that when they get sight of him there is always a perfect burst of enthusiasm amongst them. He is leading a dreadfully hard life, but never complains. But the bodily fatigue of being seldom in bed, sometimes thirteen hours on horseback, is nothing, he says, to the exertion of directing so dangerous an undertaking and to all the violent emotions of the contest and the awful impressions of the horrors on the field of battle. To one so kind I know what the shock to his nerves must be.

You know I am not blind or prejudiced, but I must say I have the greatest respect and admiration for our soldiers. I think they behave wonderfully. I hope you will read some of our papers to have an idea of what they have gone through.

A week later she sent some details of the war, gathered from the impressions of eye-witnesses. However proud the Princess might be of the valour of the Prussian troops, there was one thing she could not forget, and that was that the war had been forced by Bismarck.

....There is a good deal [she wrote on July 16] that will interest you, I think - will you please send the papers back when you have done with them. Louise, Arthur, Major Elphinstone and Mr Sahl and Fraulein Bauer may like to see them. I would rather Bertie did not, please, or that they did not go any further as they are not written for other people, but merely what is natural that a Prussian officer should write to his wife.

You know I consider the war a mistake caused by the uncontrolled power of an unprincipled man - that I have no dislike to the poor Austrians in general and that therefore I really can speak impartially. I assure you that if the rest of Europe did but 1866 know the details of this war - the light in which our officers and men - and our public at large have shown themselves - the Prussian people would stand high in the eyes of everyone, and I feel that I am now every bit as proud of being a Prussian as I am of being an Englishwoman and that is saying a very great deal, as you know what a 'John Bull' I am and how enthusiastic about my home. I must say the Prussians are a superior race, as regards intelligence and humanity, education and kindheartedness - and therefore I hate the people all the more who by their ill-government and mismanagement, etc., rob the nation of the sympathies it ought to have. My affection to it is not blind - but sincere for I respect and admire their valuable and sterling good qualities.

I know quite well that they can be unamiable - and make themselves distasteful (there is no disputing tastes), that they have their little absurdities, etc., but at heart they are excellent. And the amiable engaging Austrians commit cruelties and barbarities which make one's hair stand on end. Fritz says he never could have credited it had he not been a witness to it himself. It is their bad education and their religion, I suppose. Oh, may the war soon cease, it is so horrible. I have lost so many acquaintances!

I send you a photo of Miss Victoria - it is not at all favourable - she is such a dear pretty little thing and so lively - she crows and laughs and jumps and begins to sit up and has short petticoats. If I was no continually reminded of what we have lost I should enjoy her so much - and be proud of her too....Henry and Willy are very good and do not give any trouble, they are very happy here.

A few days later peace seemed probable between the belligerents, but the Crown Princess was not over-optimistic.

.... Peace [she wrote on July 27] seems to be doubtful again and I tremble lest the war should be taken up again as I feel certain there would be some more dreadful battles like the day of Königgrätz. Poor Uncle Alexander how I pity him - to be minister at a time when all goes so ill. I am sure it is not his fault.

The war with the minor states[3] seems sadder than that with Austria - it is so much more trying to one's feelings that are all conflicting. 'We have to thank no one but Bismarck for all this. If Germany arises more united, powerful, free and happy from this calamity, one may in time forget the wounds under which one now suffers, but it will never make the war appear justified in my eyes!

I rejoice as a Prussian at the heroic conduct of our troops - but my joy is damped with the fear that they have shed their blood in vain. With such a man and such principles at the head of our Government how can I look forward to satisfactory results for Germany, or for us!

What with the cholera and the battles how many poor families are plunged into grief and distress. It is so sad! No heart can feel more for others than mine which is so heavy and sore....

The campaign proved, as the Danish campaign had proved, the soldier-like qualities of the Crown Prince, and it was with no little relief and pride that the Crown Princess welcomed him back again. On August 10 she wrote to her mother from Heringsdorf:

The day after I wrote to you darling Fritz arrived. I drove into a wood with the children and met him there. We were much overcome and our feelings were of a most mingled nature, as you can easily understand. He is looking well, only thinner and perhaps a little older; at least his beard and his serious expression made him appear so. He has gone through a *great* deal, but is as humble and modest about all he has done as possible, which all really good and right-minded men must be....

About the King of Hanover, he has received a letter from Uncle George, and the Grand Duke of Oldenburg comes here today to express the same wish. At this sad time one *must* separate one's *feelings* for one's relations quite from one's *judgment* of political necessities, or one would be swayed to and fro on all sides by the hopes, wishes and desires expressed by those one would be sorry to grieve; it is one of the consequences resulting from this war. Nothing will or can ever shake Fritz's principles of sound liberalism and justice, but you know by experience that one must proceed in the direction given by the political events which have come to pass. Those who are now in such precarious positions might have *quite well* foreseen what danger they were running into; *they were told beforehand what they would have to expect*; they chose to go with Austria and they now share the sad fate she confers on her Allies. Those who have taken our side or remained neutral are quite unharmed, for example Uncle Ernest, the Duke of Anhalt, the Grand Dukes of Mecklenburg, etc....They all [*i.e.* those states which had sided with Austria] believed the untrue statement of Austria about the strength of her own forces, and would not see that Prussia was likely to be victorious, and so the poor things have broken their own necks. Oh, how cruel it is to have one's heart and one's head thus set at right angles!

A *liberal German-feeling* reasonable Prussian Government would have prevented it all! But as it was not to be decided *à l'amiable*, as rivers of blood have flowed, and the sword decided this contest, the victor must make his own terms and they must be hard ones for many!

I cannot and will not forget that I am a Prussian, but as such I know it is very difficult to make you, or any other non-German, see how our case lies. We have made enormous sacrifices, and the nation expects them not to be in vain....

Twelve days later (August 22) the treaty of peace was signed at Prague, and on January 24, 1867, Schleswig and Holstein were formally incorporated with Prussia. One of the terms of peace, however, was to be the occasion of much bitterness between the Crown Princess and Bismarck. As a punishment for the action of Hanover in siding with Austria that state was annexed to Prussia (September 1866), and eighteen months later part of the private property of the King of Hanover was sequestrated.

In the following years, in spite of the manifold activities of state, the Princess devoted the greater part of her time to the education and upbringing of her sons, and it must have been with keen interest that she read such letters as the following from their tutor, Mr Thomas Dealtry, on April 30, 1870, relative to their progress:

As my readings with Prince William and Prince Henry of Prussia are about to close, I venture to represent to Your Royal Highness the impression I have received of your Royal sons and the gratification I have derived from assisting in their studies.

After having enjoyed many opportunities of watching their characters and dispositions, I can truly say that one seldom meets with boys more engaging or of greater promise.

Prince William has read with me, besides English history, most of Sir Walter Scott's and Macaulay's poetical works, Bishop Heber's *Palestine*, and many of his minor poems, and selections from Tennyson and other English authors. Many pieces he has committed to memory. His Royal Highness has, I think, advanced satisfactorily in his knowledge of the English language, and has evinced a real love for English literature. His interest in his studies has added much to the enjoyment of the hours I have passed with him. His pronunciation and accent still need cultivation.

I have been greatly struck with his generous and manly instincts. Indeed both the Princes are remarkable for their gentlemanly tone of thought and feeling. Prince Henry is as far advanced as most boys of his age.

I do not think they could be better trained than they are, and I am sure their progress and growing intelligence will repay the unceasing and devoted care of their excellent Governor.

A little later, on May 28, 1870, the Princess herself wrote from Bornstaedt to Queen Victoria on the subject of her eldest son:

The poor arm is no better, and William begins to feel being behind much smaller boys in every exercise of the body - he cannot run fast, because he has no balance, nor ride, nor climb, nor cut his food, etc. ... I wonder he is as good-tempered about it. His tutor thinks he will feel it much more, and be much unhappier about it as he grows older, and feels himself debarred from everything which others enjoy, and particularly so as he is so strong and lively and healthy. It is a hard trial for him and for us. Nothing is neglected that can be done for it, but there is so little to be done. Whenever we have the good fortune of going to England again, Mr Paget and the first surgeons must see it, although I know that it is but little use. We have Langenbeck's advice, and he is one of the best surgeons of the day.

Every possible avenue was explored by the Crown Princess to secure for her eldest son the full employment of his injured arm, but all proved unavailing. From time to time she would alternate between hope and fear; hoping passionately that fresh treatment might cure the ill, and then again reduced to despair by the failure of each successive effort.

### NOTES

1 The Princess Victoria was born on April 12, 1866.
2 Princess Helena.
3 Hanover, Saxony, Hesse-Cassel and other minor German states were on the side of the Austrians.

# IV: The Franco-Prussian War

SCARCELY had Europe recovered from the Danish and Austrian wars of 1864 and 1866 when, in the summer of 1870, the tocsin of war was again sounded.

Bismarck wanted war. Napoleon III wanted war. History teaches that there has never been the slightest difficulty in finding a pretext for war when one is wanted, but while Napoleon's object was to retain his throne, Bismarck thought that by war and war alone could the unity of Germany be achieved. Napoleon III *thought* his army was ready, while Bismarck *knew* the Prussian war machine was in perfect working order.

It was the domestic difficulties of Spain that gave them the opportunity they wanted, each being under the delusion that he could cloud the issue and put the other in the wrong. The Spaniards, having driven Queen Isabella from the throne in September 1868 under the false impression that they were cleansing the country from corruption, became hopelessly divided when it came to choosing a new form of government and proved themselves wholly incapable of settling their own domestic troubles. Bismarck, realising that France would or must in certain eventualities intervene, manoeuvred to make what would appear to the world to be the free choice of a ruler by the Spaniards an occasion for such intervention. Marshal Prim, who was virtually the dictator of Spain, although a puppet of Bismarck, was encouraged to ask for the 1870 Roman Catholic Prince Leopold, the eldest son of Prince Anthony of Hohenzollern-Sigmaringen. After protracted negotiations lasting several months this German Prince declined, but at Bismarck's instigation Marshal Prim renewed his offer.

On March 12, 1870, the Crown Princess wrote to Queen Victoria, begging her advice in the intricate matter:

> ... Now I must give a message from Fritz, in fact it is no business of mine, but he wishes me to write it to you in his name, and to consider it *most profoundly secret*.
>
> General Prim has sent a Spaniard here with several autograph letters from himself to Leopold Hohenzollern, urging him most earnestly to accept the crown of Spain, saying he would be elected by two-thirds of the Cortes. They do *not* wish the French to know it, but the King, Prince Hohenzollern, Leopold and Fritz, wish to know your opinion in private....
>
> Neither the King, nor Prince Hohenzollern, nor Antoinette (Princess Leopold), nor Leopold, nor Fritz are in favour of the idea, thinking it painful

and unpleasant to accept a position which has legitimate claimants. General Prim makes it *very pressing*, and that is the reason why they want a little time to consider whether it be right or no to give a refusal. Here no one as yet knows anything about it. Will you please let me have an answer which I can show the persons mentioned? Perhaps you would write it in German to Fritz, as it is particularly disagreeable to me to be a medium of communication in things so important and serious.

It seems the Spaniards are determined to have no agnate of the *Bourbon* family.

In the following months there appeared to be every possibility of the negotiations being successful in solving the difficulty. On July 4, 1870, however, Prince Leopold accepted the Prussian nomination, and King William accorded his permission.

The news of the Hohenzollern candidature came like a bombshell and startled Europe. The Emperor Napoleon and M. Ollivier, the virtual head of the French Ministry, hesitated before taking any step, but the Due de Gramont, the French Minister for Foreign Affairs, declared at once that the candidature could not be tolerated; the Paris press took up the cry, and the Chamber supported the Due de Gramont in his vehement protest. The British Government, Queen Victoria, the King of the Belgians and other friends of peace concentrated upon persuading Prince Leopold to withdraw his candidature. The Crown Princess, now recovering from the birth of her third daughter, the Princess Sophie, who was born on June 14, was bewildered by the sudden changes in the European kaleidoscope, and wrote on July 6 to Queen Victoria:

After the Spanish crown had been *decidedly refused* by the Hohenzollerns and the King, the *former* have been applied to again, and, having changed their minds meanwhile, seem likely to accept it - much to the King's and Queen's annoyance who wisely keep out of the matter and have nothing more to do with it, dreading, as we do, that complications may arise for Prussia, as it is easy more or less to identify the Hohenzollerns with us and with our government. I fear it is a sad mistake on the part of the Hohenzollerns, though I have no doubt that Leopold and Antoinette are as fitted for such a place as the young Duke of Genoa, or many of the others who have been named. Still I cannot but regret their decision, not for Spain but for themselves and us. Fritz will send you a little memorandum on the subject by messenger; he wishes you should know his opinion on this vexed subject.[1]

At the moment there took place a change in the British Foreign Secretaryship. On the death of Lord Clarendon, Lord Granville was appointed Secretary of State for Foreign Affairs. Lord Granville had no sooner entered upon his new duties than he committed himself to the 1870 unguarded statement that no cloud obscured the peace of Europe. Almost the first business, however, with which he was called upon to deal, was Prince Leopold's candidature for the Spanish crown, but fortunately in July he was able to announce that this provocative nomination had been withdrawn by Prussia. The Crown Princess, under the imminent dread of another war, hailed the news with relief.

As you may suppose [she wrote to her mother on July 13], the agitation and suspense of the last few days have upset me terribly....But thank goodness there seems more chance of a good turn in affairs, since we learn that Leopold Hohenzollern has resigned of his own accord - of course the best thing he could do under the circumstances. Here everyone preaches peace and wishes for peace, and I have not heard one imprudent retort to the insulting language of France, which is enough to try one's patience. But if the French are determined to pick a quarrel with us, knowing (as they must) that they are well prepared and we not at all - they cannot choose a better moment for themselves, nor a worse one for us, and I feel sure they will push their audacity further and want the Rhine - only England can prevent that. It was a great comfort to read in your dear letter of the 9th, which I received on Monday and for which many thanks, that you also disapprove of the conduct of France. My horror at the thoughts of a war in our own beloved country you can well imagine. War is horrible enough at all times - for everyone - but what the prospect of it is to wives and mothers is not to be described. Though I would not eat humble pie for the French on any account, I trust it may blow over. Fritz has been distracted - he wrote to the King and to Bismarck and tried to do what he could at Berlin, but there is hardly a soul left there - everyone is away at this time of the year and no one dreamt of complications of any kind.

The danger, however, was far from dispelled. The Emperor of the French unwisely asked for a guarantee that Prussia would not repeat the offence. M. Benedetti, the French Ambassador in Berlin, pressed the demand upon the King of Prussia, who was then taking the waters at Ems, but received the reply that while the King approved of Prince Leopold's withdrawal, he could give no guarantees for the future; beyond that he had nothing to say. To Bismarck such a tame ending to an international incident which had been so promising as a possible impasse was most disappointing, and he resolved to make one more effort to render war inevitable. Napoleon III had put himself hopelessly in the wrong and such an opportunity as this might not occur again. Bismarck 'edited' the official telegram from Ems, describing these events, in such a way as to inflame opinion both in France and Germany, and to make war certain. France walked into the trap and declared war on July 15. Great Britain immediately proclaimed her neutrality, although public opinion was generally on the side of Prussia and most people thought that Napoleon III. and the French Government had no right to attempt to dictate to Germany.

The certainty of war was a cruel shock to the Crown Princess, who, with many others, thought that France was the aggressor and harboured the fear that within a few months Hesse and the Rhine provinces would be overrun by the French. If the cry in Paris was 'to Berlin', that in Berlin was the far more moderate one of 'to the Rhine'

Whilst public opinion in England at first veered strongly to Germany's side, feeling in Germany towards England alternated between extremes of warmth and cold. Later on Germany had reason to complain of British 'neutrality'. 'We sit by', wrote Sir Robert Morier, 'like a bloated Quaker, too holy to fight, but rubbing our hands at the roaring trade we are doing in cartridges 1870 and ammunition.'[2]

It was perhaps inevitable that the war should cause friction between the Crown Princess and the English Royal Family, although Queen Victoria made no secret of her sympathies for Germany. The Crown Princess, in ignorance of Bismarck's 'editing' of the Ems telegram, and feeling that Germany had been wantonly attacked, took up the German cause with chauvinist enthusiasm, while her brother the Prince of Wales, still smarting from the behaviour of Germany to Denmark, was credited with French sympathies. At a dinner at the French Embassy in London he was reported to have expressed to the Austrian Ambassador, Count Apponyi, his hopes of Prussia's defeat and his anxiety that Austria might join France. The story, no doubt with embellishments, was embodied in a despatch from the Prussian Ambassador in London to Count von Bernstorff in Berlin. Its repetition in Prussian court circles soon reached the ear of the Crown Princess, who wrote to her mother from the Neue Palais on July 16, 1870:

You must forgive me if my letter is rambling and incoherent, for my head is completely gone - fright, agitation and sorrow have shaken my nerves very much. All hope is now at an end, and we have the horrible prospect of the most terrible war Europe has yet known before us, bringing desolation and ruin, perhaps annihilation. You would pity me if you knew what my moral and mental suffering is today, and yet the only way to go through such a trial is to keep cool brains and a stout heart - and the latter I have.

We have been shamefully forced into this war, and the feeling of indignation against an act of such crying injustice has risen in two days here to such a pitch that you would hardly believe it; there is a universal cry 'To arms' to resist an enemy who so wantonly insults us.

We are grateful indeed to Providence that you are on the throne of England and that your Government has again so wisely and zealously advocated peace, and tried to call the French to their senses. The British sense of justice will I am sure not be blinded by the French press. Bernstorff writes that Bertie had expressed his delight to Count Apponyi that the Austrians were going to join the French and his hope that we should fare ill. This he is said to have loudly expressed at a dinner of the French Ambassador's. Perhaps it is exaggerated, but of course it is a story related everywhere.

As soon as the rumour of the alleged indiscretion reached the ears of the Prince of Wales, he at once denied that he had made any such statement, and wrote to Mr Gladstone that the story lacked any foundation in truth. So the incident ended officially, but there were many people in Berlin who continued to believe that the Prince of Wales was in sympathy with French aspirations and that the Crown Princess, his sister, was tainted in like manner.

In the meantime, however, the Crown Princess wrote to her mother from the Neue Palais on July 18, 1870:

... In the midst of sorrow, distress and trouble, the thought of you is always a comforting and a cheering one. I saw the King yesterday. I never felt so much for anyone - he was very calm, but the load of anxiety seemed to make him ten years older - he had a quiet dignity about him which could only increase one's love and respect. If you could but see Fritz, how you would admire him. He thinks so little of himself and only of others. It is a dreadful trial for us - enough to strike terror into stronger hearts than mine, but the enthusiasm which seems to be the same with young and old, poor and rich, high and low, men and women, is so affecting and beautiful that one must forget oneself. The odds are fearfully against us in the awful struggle which is about to commence and which we are forced into against our will, knowing that our existence is at stake. In a week the flower of the nation will be under arms, the best blood of the country. I cannot think of the lives that will be lost, the thought maddens me - how willingly would I give mine to save theirs. There is not a family not torn asunder, not a woman's heart that is not near to breaking, and for what? Oh that England could help us. I wish no ill to France, nor to anyone, but I wish Europe could unite, once for all to stop her ever again having it in her power to force a war upon another nation. Think of Hesse, of our lovely Rhine, think of our ports and sea towns. The harvest lost and thousands of poor creatures without work or bread. It seems all a horrid dream to me. Forgive my bad writing, my hand trembles so, and I cannot collect my thoughts. The parting from Fritz I shudder at.

Alice and Louise of Baden must come to us - the King offers Alice this Palace, and I am preparing all for her in case she should come. The future is a perfect blank. What suffering may be in store for us we do not know, but one thing we all know - that as our honour and the safety of our country are at stake, no sacrifice must be shunned. Our feelings are best expressed by altering Lord Nelson's words to 'Germany expects every man to do his duty'....

What a sad Christmas it will be! I am as well as can be expected and try very hard not to make a fool of myself, which is difficult, as my nerves are shaky. I have just this moment received your dear letter of the 16th for which many thanks. It is a great satisfaction to us that you are angry with the French for their behaviour. The King and everyone are horrified at Bertie's speech which is quoted everywhere. I wish I might say it is not true....

To this Queen Victoria replied from Osborne on July 20:

Words are too weak to say *all* I feel for you or what I think of my neighbours! We must be neutral *as long as* we can, but no one here conceals their opinion as to the extreme *iniquity* of the war, and the unjustifiable conduct of the French! Still *more, publicly*, we cannot say; but the feeling of the people and the country here is all with you, which it was not *before*. And need I say what I *feel*? . . .

My heart bleeds for you *all*! The awful suddenness of the thing is so dreadful. Do not overworry yourself, not to make yourself ill. Poor Alice makes us all very anxious, and she seems anxious not to leave Darmstadt. I have no doubt that you will both advise her for the best. My thoughts are constantly with you, wishing your two daughters could be safe here. These divided interests in royal families are quite unbearable. Human nature is not made for such fearful trials, especially not mothers' and wives' hearts. But God will watch over you all, I doubt not. You have the warmest sympathy of all, and all the people in the house take the deepest interest in you....

Before the end of the first month of the war France lost battle after battle and the success of the Germans foretold the ultimate result. There were three armies of invasion under the supreme command of the King of Prussia, on whose staff were Moltke, Bismarck and Roon (the War Minister). The first army was under the King's personal direction, and the second under Prince Frederick Charles, the King's brother. The third, consisting of the South German troops, together with the XIth and Vth Prussian Army Corps, was under the command of the Crown Prince, whose Chief of Staff was his 'old and trusty friend' Lieut-General von Blumenthal. Amongst the officers appointed to the staff of this army was Count Seckendorff, who afterwards became the Chamberlain and the trusted friend and adviser of the Crown Princess. The anxiety of the Crown Princess was acute, and all her fears were poured out to her mother, to whom, on July 22, she wrote:

Your very dear and kind letter was indeed a sunbeam in the darkness of this sad time, for which I thank you from my heart. The days seem like years, with this awful calamity hanging over us - not one passes without many many tears being shed. Today I parted from dear Uncle Ernest (who had only reached Berlin the previous day from Fiume). We both broke down. Dearest Papa's only brother. It seemed so dreadful. But one must not think of this now. All one's energies and all one's courage are wanted to meet the future and the worst that it may bring. All is still undecided as to our plans. Fritz commands the South Germans, the armies of the Kings of Wurtemberg and Bavaria, besides the troops of Baden, and a Prussian Army Corps (his own from Stettin). It is a dreadful position for him, as the Bavarian and Swabian troops are so inefficient and undisciplined that they are of very little use - their leaders are more a hindrance than otherwise, but the King and the Generals could entrust this most difficult task to no one but Fritz. He is looking ill, and the wear on his nerves is very great; at times he is quite overwhelmed and sheds bitter tears, but on the whole he has a clear idea of what he intends and the greatest confidence in the feeling of the people.

I contradicted Bertie's speech energetically and was so glad to do so.

I am very busy indeed, but feel pretty well - of course my nerves excepted, which will not recover from such an upset in a hurry. Pray read the *Folks Zeltung* and the *Kölnische Zeltung* - they will give you all the news.

Dear Uncle Ernest goes with Fritz.

I trust dear Alice will come here later. I think it would be better. I have had no time to write to her. The enthusiasm is grand and imposing. There is something so pure and elevated about it - so sacred and calm and serious - that when I see our finest and noblest men all joining and collecting round their aged Sovereign, they seem to me to be indeed 'The noble army of Martyrs'. How many will return? I am not afraid nor cast down, for I cannot but think that this feeling must give an almost invincible force to our arms. We are prepared for all sorts of reverses and misfortunes and to meet them with courage and patience and try not to give way. Could you and would you send me some old linen, lint and coarse poor men's shirts, also some oiled silk? Perhaps the sisters would collect some and send it to me - it will be used alike for friend and foe - so it will in no way interfere with your neutrality.

I hope that I shall always be able to hear from you and write to you, but of course I do not know. Could you not keep a special messenger going between us and you? England's position on the continent and her continental trade will suffer from her neutrality, but I suppose you cannot help it. The French have really behaved too ill, and surely they are playing a desperate game....

Baby (the Princess Sophie) is to be christened on Sunday at i o'clock. How it makes me think of my darling Sigie, and long for him back, and how I tremble for fear anything should happen to one of the others in this fearful time. Pray thank dear Arthur, dear Lenchen, Bertie and Louise for their kind letters - it was so comforting and soothing to me to read them.

Wegner, Count Eulenberg, Count Seckendorff, M. Schleinitz and Major Mischke go with Fritz. His Staff is composed of General Blumenthal, Colonel Gatberg, Majors Lenke and Hahnke and a lot of South Germans - he will most likely go on Monday or Tuesday. I dare not think of it.....

The following day the Crown Prince returned to the Neue Palais for the baptism of his 'engaging little daughter Sophie', which took place on the 24th 'with the traditional ceremonial and the utmost display of pomp and parade'.[3] On the 25th the Crown Princess wrote to Queen Victoria:

....The Christening went off well, but was sad and serious; anxious faces and tearful eyes, and a gloom and foreshadowing of all the misery in store spread a cloud over the ceremony, which should have been one of gladness and thanksgiving.

My sweet little Sophie was very good and only cried a little bit, but Waldy and Vicky cried and did not like it at all; they were frightened at the clergyman's voice and energetic gesticulations, and Vicky kept sobbing, 'Don't let the man hurt baby'. The King said he could not hold the child, he felt too weak, so the Queen had to hold her; it was a general leave-taking, as I shall see none of the family any more before they leave. Poor little Sophie's first step in this world is not ushered in with any bright omens, and her Mama's heart was heavy and weary in spite of the beauty of the day, the sunshine and the flowers without.

The feeling is very general here that England would have had it in her power to prevent this awful war, had she in concert with Russia, Austria and Italy, declared she would take arms against the aggressor, and that her neutrality afforded France advantages and us disadvantages.

France can buy English horses as her ships can reach England, whereas ours cannot on account of the French fleet. Lord Granville is supposed to take sides decidedly with the Emperor. God knows how it all may end!

Fritz and I took the Sacrament this morning; he does not leave today, but expects to do so tomorrow or the day after. I cannot bear to think of it....

Early next morning, at half-past five, the Crown Prince left the Neue Palais. That day he wrote in his Diary:

....As my wife and I had agreed that, whenever my departure was settled we would bid one another no formal farewell, I had told her nothing yesterday of my start being suddenly fixed for this morning and so spared her the actual final good-bye before the war by giving her no explicit reason for my leaving at such an early hour. Only when I was already on my way did my little daughter Victoria, who saw me off crying and sobbing and would *not* let me go, convey a line or two from me that told her how things stood. My children, on the contrary, knew that I was bound for the scene of action but I must not let my thoughts dwell on those moments.

To her letter to Queen Victoria, written the previous evening, the Crown Princess now added the postscript (July 26):

I sat up till late last night waiting for Fritz's return, and went to sleep before he came. This morning before I woke he got up, and when I asked where he was I was told he had gone back to Berlin, and I found a slip of paper from him saying that he was gone to the Army and had wished to spare me a leave-taking. The thought was *so* kind, and yet now I feel as if my heart would break; he is gone without a kiss or a word of farewell, and I do not know whether I shall ever see him again! I hardly know what I am writing, as my head aches with crying and I cannot stop my tears. My own darling Fritz - Heaven protect and watch over his precious life! Oh that I could be with him and share all dangers, fatigues and anxieties with him. How willingly would I change places with any of his servants!....

To the Crown Princess's appeal in her letter of July 22 'for some old linen, lint and coarse poor men's shirts, also some oiled silk' for the wounded, Queen Victoria, with constitutional correctness, pointed out that it would be difficult to send them ostensibly as it might be interpreted in an unfriendly light by France. On August 4 the Crown Princess replied:

I have just received your dear letter of the 1st. I know how difficult your position must be - you the Sovereign of a constitutional country and a neutral power, I can quite understand that it may be awkward for you to send me things for the wounded *ostensibly* - though I should have imagined you could have sent either to the Empress of the French, or to me - without appearing partial. A wounded man has ceased to be an enemy, and only a suffering human creature, entitled to everyone's help. I think the International Society to which we belong holds this doctrine. I hope I am only doing what you wish - in writing openly what I hear and see and think. I only write as a private individual to you as my dear Mama - at the same time thinking it may be agreeable and useful to you to hear what is thought and said on this side of the water from an unofficial source. I am looked upon with suspicious eyes, as England is supposed to lean to the other side, and Lord Granville and Mr Cardwell looked upon as French. All this is indeed most trying to you, but your long routine, your firmness and political experience will carry you through it all, I hope and trust to the honour and glory of yourself and beloved England. I see so much in the English press which confirms me. The French have begun war in a very ugly way - bombarding an open town (Saarbrück) - and bringing up three Divisions against a Battalion of Infantry and a Cavalry Regiment, seventy of our men and two of our officers are killed. This I suppose you know already.

I have a sprained hand (or rather wrist) so I write with considerable difficulty and you must excuse my scrawl. I must end in a great hurry. I have letters from my darling Fritz from Stuttgart and Carlsruhe and Speyer. He says that the feeling among the South Germans is so cordial that he finds no difference with the Prussians, indeed feels quite at home with them; his reception was something quite extraordinary. Pray read Freiligrath's beautiful Poem in the *Volks Zeitung* of yesterday.

Two days later, on August 6, a decisive German victory was won at Wörth by the army commanded by the 1870 Crown Prince, who defeated the French army of the Rhine under Marshal MacMahon. The victory followed closely upon the first success of Weissenburg which, as the Crown Prince noted in his Diary on August 9,

made much more impression on men's minds than that of the second success reported immediately after the other. But Wörth is a victory of historical significance, for, apart from its importance as a military triumph, it is notable for the French having been beaten for the first time since 1815 in a pitched battle. How wonderful that of all others it was given to me, who could never have looked for such a thing, to go straight into action in the first line.

The victory of Wörth delighted the Crown Princess, who wrote to Queen Victoria on August 11:

You will I know not be angry with me for availing myself of dear Marie Goltz's kindly lent hand to write you this letter, as I am lying down to take a little rest, of which I feel the need. I have this moment received your dear and kind letter of the 8th, for which I hasten to send my tenderest thanks. I am touched and delighted at seeing your true joy at my beloved Fritz's victory! The children's Governor, Lieutenant O'Danne, has arrived here this morning, despatched by Fritz, and bringing me the enclosed, which I beg you to return to me. I am sure the description of the Battle of Worth in Fritz's own hand will interest you; it is so modest and like his own dear self. Lt O'Danne was present at the battle and was full of admiration of Fritz's calmness during the long hours that he commanded, for this fearful battle lasted twelve hours. Lt O'Danne says Fritz is well, and of course very busy indeed.

You ask whether I have lost any friends or acquaintances. Alas! one hears everyday of new ones! An old friend of Christian's, Major Senff, formerly in the same regiment as Christian, was torn to pieces by a shell. Poor man, he was always full of joke and fun.

Then last night I went to see poor old General Esebeck and his wife, who have lost their second son, who leaves a wife just going to be confined and a little child. They have just been married two years and were very happy. The poor mother's grief was heartrending to see. Then a brother-in-law of Herr von Schweinitz's has been badly wounded and also Lt Müller, my former Page. General Bose, one of our ablest officers, is badly wounded in the foot.

We are hourly expecting to hear of another great and awful battle, most likely not far from Metz, as the French seem to be collecting all their forces for a great effort. The eagerness and trembling with which we devour the telegrams is not to be told! How thankful we shall be when this dreadful time is over and one can once more live in peace.

260 wounded Prussians arrived at Berlin yesterday; today a train of wounded French has arrived. I must tell you, and you will be glad to hear, that the captured and wounded French are everywhere treated with great kindness and consideration.

When I said the odds were fearfully against us, when the war first broke out, I was of the opinion of most people, that the French would have overran the Rhine before we could get our troops ready. Fritz never expected he would be able to get his Army together, as he thought the French would occupy the Palatinate, Darmstadt and Baden, and prevent the troops from concentrating. What their treatment of our towns would have been, we have seen by their barbarous bombardment and burning of the inoffensive town of Saarbrücken. We feared that our fertile provinces of the Rhine would be devastated and the battles fought on the German side. This was the pleasant prospect we contemplated three weeks ago, but I never doubted what our success would be if we had the chance of having our forces assembled. I was in Berlin yesterday and visited the temporary hospital camp of wooden huts which is being built with marvellous rapidity on the Kreuzberg, a very healthy situation. The undertaking is directed by our best scientific heads, and will I am sure be a success. They are draining the ground, digging wells, making a temporary railway, laying on gas and telegraph. It will be for the accommodation of 1600. It is being done by the State, and the town, and a Committee to which I contribute.

I afterwards went to the Town Hall to see the depot of linen and hospital requisites, such as bandages, bedding and cloth. The stuffs are bought by the afore-named Committee and made up, either by a quantity of ladies who assemble there daily, or by the wives of soldiers who receive payment for what they do. In the 1870 afternoon I visited my Victoria Bazaar, which is employed in the same way and which will provide Darmstadt and Carlsruhe with hospital linen. Each mark of sympathy on the part of England gives pleasure and is thankfully acknowledged. Kind donations of Manchester and Liverpool have been gratefully received and joyously hailed. The misery and the suffering is immense, and will be greater, but I must say, I do not think there is a female in the country of whatever class she may be who does not do her utmost to alleviate the sufferings of friend and foe, and contribute her last penny towards doing so. It is a great labour of love which comforts many an anxious and aching heart, while it occupies the fevered brain.

I hope and trust to get permission to go and settle at Homburg and get up a small hospital at my own expense. I have got a good many things together for this purpose already, and different kinds of gifts, which go a little way towards fitting up.

I was still very tired from yesterday's exertions and my sleep and appetite are not always of the best, but on the whole I get on very well, and my sweet little Sophie grows and improves and is my comfort and pleasure.

The elder children do not understand much of what is going on in spite of seeing and hearing. Willy and Vicky, each in their way, show much interest in the events of the day....

The victory of Wörth brought the Crown Prince showers of congratulatory messages. On August 19 he noted in his Diary:

....An extraordinary amount of praise has been lavished on me, far more than I deserve. But is it not a strange thing that I, who much preferred to earn recognition in works of peace, am called upon to win such blood-stained laurels? In time to come may the peaceful part of my efforts be all the more beneficent. Even from England come tokens of appreciation for my victory, a thing that pleases me infinitely. Thus, for instance, Lord Granville, in a private letter to my wife, has strongly repudiated the notion that his policy was guided by sympathy for France.[4]

In her letter dated August 4 to Queen Victoria, the Crown Princess had warmly applauded 'Freiligrath's beautiful poem', and she was pleased and complimented to learn from Queen Victoria, who wrote on August 17, that it had been translated into English by Mr Theodore Martin. Three days later the Crown Princess, still immersed in hospital duties, replied:

How beautifully Mr Martin has translated Freiligrath's poem. The article of the *Daily Telegraph* for which I thank you very much is very nice indeed. I am so glad to think our papers do Fritz justice as he deserves. I send you some photographs of the boys which have just been done. I saw some more wounded this morning. Fritz and the Queen are both for my going to Homburg, therefore if the King allows, I shall go there soon....

The excitement here yesterday in consequence of the news of the battle on the i8th was very great, and most anxiously are we expecting details, but I hear that Louis and his brothers are safe, and I suppose the rest of our Princes are so. We are anxiously expecting tidings from Paris. A revolution there does not seem so imminent as it was, but I am very glad I am not in the Empress's position; the Emperor's, too, must be a dreadful one. How well I remember this time 15 years ago; who would have thought then that the Emperor would take such an end! But how is a government to be carried on for the good of a nation, when there is such awful corruption and bribery amongst all the servants of State, for the Emperor has hardly a person about him, who is respectable. How ill Benedetti, Gramont, Ollivier and Leboeuf have served him, for it is mainly owing to them that he has got into this scrape. Ever since the Emperor's health has been failing, the prestige of his genius has been waning and he has made one blunder after another. It is a melancholy history.

All attention was now concentrated upon the two French armies under Marshal Bazaine and Marshal MacMahon respectively. The first, beleaguered in Metz, was now surrounded by the Germans, and the second, which the Emperor Napoleon had joined, had an army of a quarter of a million on its track. Much controversy meanwhile had raged over the question as to which of the armies - the French or the German - was the better armed. The Germans were armed, as in the campaigns of 1864 and 1866, with the needle-gun, but the French were armed with the breech-loading Chassepot rifle. The Crown Princess's views on this and on other war items may be gathered from her letter to Queen Victoria on August 26:

We hear fresh distressing news every day; it would be no use my telling you the names of all the unhappy victims as you do not know them. To us all it is most melancholy as they were our friends, and we are surrounded by their mourning relatives. The one that is the greatest loss personally to us, is Herr von Jasmund, Fritz's former Aide-de-Camp, with whom he was very intimate. He has left his poor little wife behind with a child of two years old. He was a most devoted, attached, trustworthy and excellent creature. It is too sad. Langenbeck, whom you remember, has also lost his eldest son. Countess Alvensleben, Marianne's Grande Maîtresse, has lost both her sons. I could tell you endless tidings of woe! The exasperation against the French grows with every day, which is but natural, seeing that it is they who brought on this war, and not we who would have it, that we are obliged to sacrifice almost all the most valuable lives in the country to resist their overbearing and unjust interference. That they feel this themselves I had a new proof of today. Baron Perglas, the Bavarian Minister, told me that upon the Duke of Gramont being interpellated about bringing on the war so unjustifiably, and getting the French into such a scrape, said: 'La guerre n'était pas inevitable, il y avait vingt manières d'arranger cette affaire. Mais j'ai demandé a Leboeuf êtes-vous prêt? il m'a répondu archiprêt.' How doubly wrong it was of the Ministers to push the Emperor into such a disaster. Of course I feel the greatest pity for thousands of innocent French who are of course not answerable for their Government. I think that Fritz and I feel heartily sorry for them; but in the public at large there is very little commiseration of course. They will never own themselves in the wrong, and go on making the most outrageous inventions.

I had a letter today from Fritz dated the 18th, and yesterday one of his servants arrived. Fritz had been to see the King at Pont-à-Mousson and is now continuing his march on the route to Paris. I have not the slightest idea whether there will be another bloody battle or not. I should fear there would be one more before Paris, and perhaps another desperate attempt of the French to leave Metz. Their far-famed Army is no doubt very good, but their men not to be compared to ours. Their Chassepots are far better than our needle-guns and give them an advantage; their mitrailleuses are very destructive, but are unable to dismay our brave soldiers....

We are all well, and of course my nerves often feel very shaken, as everyone's must, particularly when I have been seeing the unfortunate mourners and sufferers. It is so kind of you all to work so much for the wounded and take so much interest in them. I think there is no one that would not wish to help them. In Berlin and Potsdam they are really very well off, but all along the Rhine we hear very different accounts. Alas! dear Marie Goltz is not going with me. How much I shall miss her! Her husband and brothers are well however. I trust the neutral Powers will not interfere with us as to the terms of peace; they did not prevent the war, nor help us to fight it, so I trust they will let us make our own terms, and not intercede in favour of the aggressor. This would be a great misfortune in more than one point of view, and we are delighted to see by the *Times* that it is not likely.

I must end here, my beloved Mama, kissing your dear hand many times and thanking you most tenderly for your dear letter which was such a pleasure to receive. On this dear day I think of former happy years when all was unbroken and unclouded peace and happiness - and none of us knew what sorrows, trials and anxieties were in store for us! How the world has changed since then! - and yet if one examines carefully one can trace the threads of present evils far back, and many words of dear Papa's come back to me now, and I see how right he was and how true all he said. Darling Papa, I think of him with greater yearning as the time goes on. Oh, why cannot he be here to help us all on - often one feels weary and tired, and I suppose he felt so too sometimes - so we dare not grudge him the blessed rest of the just that have run their course and fought a good fight, but remember him with loving, grateful, yet aching hearts, as he has left a blank, never, never to be filled up in this life.

Will you please give my love to all the dear Geschwister, in particular Bertie and Alix. I am sure dear Bertie must envy Fritz who has such a trying, but such a useful life. I had rather see him serve his country than sit by my side, though Heaven knows how wretched it is to be so much alone as I am and to be in perpetual anxiety. I hope you are well and that all this agitation does not affect you too much.

Meanwhile, the Crown Princess's efforts to render the German hospital system more efficient had met with little support, or even approval, from the authorities. 'My wife', wrote the Crown Prince in his Diary on August 23, 'is going to Homburg with the object of establishing a model hospital there and inspecting those on the Rhine, which are in a sad state. In Berlin and Potsdam all her endeavours and offers of help in the matter of tending the sick were contemptuously rejected, presumably on account of the anti-British feeling!' Such was the opposition with which the Princess had to contend even in so necessary a matter as the provision of adequate nursing services for the wounded!

On September 1 there came for Prussia the crowning victory of Sedan, where the Emperor Napoleon and MacMahon's army of 120,000 men were surrounded and defeated. The Emperor surrendered next day and was sent to Wilhelmshöhe in Cassel. In Paris the news brought about a revolution, which replaced the imperial regime by a Republic, and compelled the Empress Eugénie to fly to England. The news surprised and excited the Princess, who wrote to Queen Victoria on September 6.

....What astounding news! really I could hardly believe my ears when I heard it - here the excitement and delight of the people knew no bounds.

Poor Emperor, his career has ended, and he brought his fall upon himself, and one cannot but pity him, especially for having been the unhappy cause of so much bloodshed and so much woe which never never can be cured! So many hearths made dismal, so many happy homes miserable, so many hearts broken, and above all so many unfortunate men groaning in untold suffering! Unhappy Emperor, he has all this to answer for, and yet he is a kind-hearted and feeling man! He has done the best thing he could for himself under the circumstances; he is sure of the most chivalrous and generous treatment at the hands of the King, and he has of his own free-will surrendered to his equal, which is not so humiliating as being driven from throne and country by an infuriated populace. Such a downfall is a melancholy thing, but it is meant to teach deep lessons. May we all learn what frivolity, conceit and immorality lead to! The French people have trusted in their own excellence, have completely deceived themselves. Where is their army? Where are their statesmen? They despised and hated the Germans, whom they considered it quite lawful to insult. How they have been punished! Whether the war be at an end, or no, we do not know, having had no letters or details since these last events, but as there is no French Army left I do not see with whom we are to fight? The march to Paris is continued, and what difficulties our Army will have to encounter there I do not the least know. It would be grievous for Art's sake for that beautiful capital to suffer. I trust it will not come to that. Whether the Republic will be inclined to make peace who can tell? I fear not. What has become of the Empress and Prince Imperial we have not heard, poor things! I hope they are in safety - they will most likely never see their lovely Paris again! When I think of '48 and '55, and even of last December, when I last saw the Emperor and Empress, it seems like a dream. But even then everyone felt that the Empire was standing as it were on a barrel of gunpowder, and that the least spark would set fire to the whole thing, and no wonder that with such triflers as the Duc de Gramont and MM. Ollivier and Benedetti the conflagration soon began. Had the Emperor been his former self and held the reins of Government tightly it would perhaps not have happened; but his health and energy are gone - he had grown apathetic and incapable of directing matters himself, and as despotism always falls his reign has ended - more like the bursting of a soap bubble than the fall of a mighty monument, which buries all beneath its ruins! What a retribution it seems for the bloody drama of Mexico and for the treatment of the Orleans! These latter have lost all sympathy in 1870 Germany since the abominable letter of Prince de Joinville exciting the populace to defend themselves and get rid of the enemy - by murdering the German soldiers in cold blood! I think it too bad! Voices are heard everywhere in all classes - in defence of Germany regaining her old provinces of Elsass and Lothringen. I cannot say I think it a good thing, but I do not see how the Government are to resist the resolute determination of the German nation to wrest them back at all hazards 1 I have been to Frankfurt today, over the hospitals and seeing the different notabilities - everybody is most patriotic.

We have now no less than 120,000 French prisoners in Germany! Is it not marvellous? Add to that more than fifty Generals and the Sovereign himself! And even now the French will not believe that they have been really and fairly defeated. They attribute it all to chance and accident, and denied each of our victories.

Dear Alice was with me for a day. I think she is really very well and strong on the whole and does a great deal. I do hope Louis will soon be able to return to her! I think my being here is of some slight use and does good. I am able to set much to rights, but it is hard work for her, with the darling baby to care for; however, I manage to get on very well on the whole - not staying too long in the bad air of the hospitals. I am having a hut built at my own expense and the large barracks done up, also at my expense and by my directions. It was in too disgraceful a state to remain as it was. The hospitals in the villages around which I visit of an afternoon are very bad - mostly the people are so tenderly kind to the wounded, but do not understand how to take care of them and are dirty beyond description. I often feel quite sick with disgust, and yet looking after it is the only way to improve an establishment of this kind....

*Sept. 7th*

During these last days I have so often felt reminded of passages in Shakespeare in Henry V and Richard II. There are passages which apply wonderfully to the present extraordinary state of things.

I am sorry for poor General Failly, whom I knew, and who was one of the better sort of French Generals. As for Bazaine and Palikao, I think them wretches, but Bazaine is a capital soldier. Metz and Strassburg are too dreadful to think of. The Germans grieve at having to bombard Strassburg, but it cannot be avoided. Metz cannot hold out very long and the conditions within its walls must be too awful. Our wounded who have come from there say they have been very kindly treated. Poor Lothar Hohenthal, Valerie's youngest brother is also killed! Poor young man, he was hardly twenty, very handsome and full of promise. I have known him ever since he was a little boy. You are very kind to express your sympathy for all the poor bereaved families of my acquaintance. Whenever I have an opportunity I will say so. All this misery draws hearts closer together and brings together those who in happy and quiet days would have passed one another by without taking any notice. The feeling of belonging to one great nation for the first time obliterates all feeling of north, south, high and low - all particularism - this I must say is very delicious to experience - simplifies all things and gives a new impetus to all exertions - poor Germany, she has dearly bought her unity and independence with the blood of her sons. It is a great satisfaction to me to see how Prussian *Wesen*, discipline, habits, etc., is now appreciated and seen in its true light, its superiority acknowledged with pleasure and pride, instead of jealousy, fear, scorn, and hatred. We owe to Frederick the Great and his father, to Scharnhorst, Stein and Hardenberg, what we are, and we say it with gratitude and not vainglory or conceit. We are worthy of England's sympathy and approbation and feel sure that it will not long be withheld from us.

Fritz writes that he has seen many letters which have been seized - from one French officer to another, giving the most awful description of the French Army as regards honesty and morality. The stealing and plundering that goes on is incredible, not only among the Turkos. The Empress did well and rightly in giving up the Crown Jewels of her own accord before there was any necessity. Queen Isabella behaved very differently.

What will Bertie and Alix say to all these marvellous events! When I think of the Emperor and Empress in the zenith of their glory - in '55 - and at the time of the Exhibition when all the Sovereigns of Europe paid them their Court, and they were so amiable and courteous to all. It seems a curious contrast! Gay and charming Paris! Our poverty, our dull towns, our plodding, hardworking, serious life has made us strong and determined - is wholesome for us. I should grieve were we to imitate Paris and be so taken up with pleasure that no time was left for self-examination and serious thought. Ancient history teaches the same lesson as modern history - a hard and stern one for those who have to learn it by sad experience. The poor Emperor has leisure now to study it.

This letter reflects to a singular degree the German opinion of the time - the lack of sympathy with Napoleon, the probability of a rapid end to the war and, as a condition of peace, the restitution to Germany of the provinces of Alsace and Lorraine. Above all, there was the desire that German unity should be proclaimed in no uncertain manner, an opinion which the Crown Prince was urging vigorously in the King's Council. Bismarck's own opinion of the Crown Prince's activity at this period may be gauged from the following extracts:

The initiative for any change in the conduct of the war did not as a rule emanate from the King, but from the staff of the army or from that of the Crown Prince, who was the general in command. That this circle was open to English views if presented in a friendly manner was only natural; the Crown Princess, Moltke's late wife, the wife of Count Blumenthal, chief of the staff, and afterwards Field-Marshal, and the wife of von Gottberg, the staff officer next in influence, were all Englishwomen.[5]

With regard to Alsace and Lorraine the Crown Prince's opinion was most definite.

The annexation of Alsace [he wrote in his Diary on September 12-14] and perhaps of a part of Lorraine, is surely well earned by the sacrifices Germany has made. I would have these provinces administered separately, simply as Imperial territories, in the name of the Empire, by that time we hope restored, and eventually in that of the Bund, without giving them a dynasty and placing them under any reigning house....The immediate concern is to detach Alsace from the great corporate body of France, yet at the same time to make the country feel that it is becoming a member of another equally great state, and is not condemned to have to make one of the little petty states of Germany. Count Bismarck seems to me to entertain so far no specially wild-cat plans; on the contrary, he expressed himself, while we were still at Rheims, in answer to my leading questions, rather cautiously than otherwise.

Meanwhile, in spite of all opposition, the Crown Princess had been successful in organising better hospital conditions at Homburg, and it was from here that she wrote to Queen Victoria on September 17:

....The army is marching onward towards Paris. I hope and trust there will be nothing very awful. I do not think they apprehend very formidable resistance, but I live in dread of something happening as at Laon....

Our hospital arrangements are getting on now nicely, and in another fortnight I trust the place will look very different and the poor creatures be far more comfortable. To overcome the prejudice of doctors and patients against fresh air is really almost impossible. We have not one nurse or dresser here yet, only people from the town, who are dirty, ignorant and useless in the extreme, but we have sent for some better help which we shall have soon. Dr Schröder and Dr Doetz are excellent - but the other doctors are really only mischievous, stupid, old things - many a poor wretch might have been saved if they had understood their work. Prof Schillbach - from Jena - we got over and he has performed many operations, also General Arzt Koch, from Cassel, who tried to set things right a little, as the organisation was really too lamentable.

The Crown Prince's view of his wife's activities is recorded in his Diary for September 10 and 11.

Captain von Dresky [he noted] arrived with letters from my wife at Homburg and other news from home. It is with unfeigned pleasure that I learn from various sources that my wife's presence in the hospitals at Homburg, Frankfort and in the Rhine province is properly appreciated, and also that officials and physicians declare that they are astonished at the wide range of her knowledge. Certainly I would have looked for nothing else, yet it is with unspeakable satisfaction that I hear the facts acknowledged, for it is high time my wife should win the grateful recognition she has long deserved. At this moment she is building a hospital at Homburg at 1870 her own expense, in order to see her own special principles brought into operation.

After the crowning French disaster at Sedan the German armies had little resistance to contend with in the open field and on September 19 they completely surrounded Paris, which prepared for a stubborn defence. Meanwhile, the Empress Eugénie had arrived in England as a refugee. The news of her arrival awoke in the Crown Princess vivid memories of her own visit to France in 1855.

All you say [she wrote from Homburg on September 24, 1870] in your letter is so true. Dear Papa was so right about the Emperor Napoleon. Now he is in sorrow I do not like to abuse him, he has reaped what he has sown, he was the corrupter of all Europe all Europe paid him their court, were dazzled by the splendour of his capital, and his own magnificence, his politics were bad, dishonest and dangerous, and yet he was not a wicked man - like the old King of Hanover, or the late King of Naples. He did many a kind and generous action, and the Empress even more than he did, so that one is disgusted at the violence and spite of the Parisians who seem hardly to be able to find indignities enough to heap on the heads of this luckless pair. The Imperial regime has enough to answer for, besides all the blood that has now been spilt, and this must be so miserable a feeling for the Emperor and Empress that I pity them. Besides they seem to be deprived of means (to their honour be it said).

The letter you sent me about the escape of the poor Empress was very interesting. What a shame that no French gentleman accompanied her! Is it not a sign of how the French have degenerated that now in the hour of danger and tribulation they go on fabricating lies, which they believe in - a French victory at Toul, another before the walls of Paris, etc.? Not until Paris is taken will they see how matters stand and come to reasonable terms, and I do not see how the King can think of peace before.

A most unpleasant piece of intelligence has reached me. Fritz's letters to me of the 1st and 2nd (which I always wondered at not receiving) have fallen into the hands of the French, so that I may have the pleasure of seeing them in some distorted form in the French newspapers. He is much annoyed, as he wrote down the conversation of the King and the Emperor, and different other most interesting details. Another thing also puts me out immensely, that the King after having approved my coming here, now is angry and wishes me to go back to Berlin, which I cannot do, as all the hospital arrangements depend on my being here - and are just beginning to do nicely. Is it not annoying and provoking? I never make a plan that is not crossed by the King or Queen, and they invariably disapprove of what I do - it is very disheartening.

On the previous day, September 23, the French army at Toul had surrendered, and on the 27th Strassburg followed suit. The Crown Princess, meanwhile, had been as active as ever to alleviate the suffering of the wounded and to improve the hospital service, and on September 30 she wrote to Queen Victoria:

....I returned yesterday evening from a most fatiguing tournée to Wiesbaden, Bieberich, Bingen, Bingerbrück, Rüdesheim and Mayence. At all these places I went over the hospitals, which is as trying to one's nerves as possible, besides seeing the authorities, etc. The weather was beautiful, the lovely Rhine looked its best, and had not one such a load of anxiety and worry, and so much business, I should have really enjoyed the tour through this enchanting country. Some hospital arrangements were good, but very few, others tolerable and the rest wretched, dirty and ill managed. Everywhere the population is doing to the utmost of its power and abilities and means to tend the sick and wounded and give them every comfort, but it is often very ill done, and one has many a painful impression. I saw many wounded French officers at Mayence. I went to see the French prisoners, 5,000 of them in a Camp together, a curious sight. They express themselves very gratefully and seem to like being well cared for and not having any more fighting to do.

I have letters from Fritz up to the 23rd. He is well and at Versailles. Paris will keep them some time yet, I fear.

Four days later (October 5) the Crown Prince noted in his Diary:

With regard to the hospital establishments on the Rhine and at Frankfort-on-the-Main, to which my wife devotes especial attention, I hear these spoken of with grateful appreciation. It gives me infinite pleasure to hear in all quarters repeated expressions of the high respect my wife's quiet but strong and efficient activity evokes. In Homburg she has created a perfect model hospital, which it is to be hoped will soon find imitations. I communicated to His Majesty much of what I had learned, but without hearing one word of commendation in reply.

His last sentence gives a little idea of the opposition even in the highest quarters to the philanthropic services of the Crown Princess.

On October 27, the fortress of Metz and Marshal Bazaine's whole army of over 170,000 men capitulated, after a seventy days' siege. This was the fourth French army to be captured in two months, and a German force of 200,000 was thus set free to cope effectively with the new French armies which were being raised by the energy of Gambetta to relieve Paris. The German victories brought deserved honours to many in the higher commands, and the Crown Prince was rewarded for his services by being created a Field-Marshal, an honour which was also conferred upon Prince Frederick Charles. Four days later (October 31) the Crown Princess wrote:

I have not written since the great news of the capitulation of Metz. If one could only hope that Paris would surrender before the awful alternative of a bombardment or famine is forced upon us! There is no use in holding out any longer - it will not give France back her military glory that has faded away - it will only bring endless and horrible misery on many thousands of innocent beings. I believe it is principally owing to General Trochu that they will not give in, and he is sacrificing the inhabitants to his own personal vanity. The Empress is at Wilhelmshöhe, but returns to England today or tomorrow, I hear. Fritz has received the rank of Field-Marshal, and Fritz Carl also - it is the first time that a Prince of this House has ever received this title! I think it is well deserved, I must say. The Queen is gone to Frankfort today to visit the Grand Duke of Hesse and all the family, also the Duchess of Hamilton....I hear nearly every day from Fritz - he is well but much distressed at the thought of the war being prolonged and of the siege of Paris.

Waldy has quite recovered from his illness and is looking very well again, though thin. The others are all well. How is dear Leopold? I have heard nothing about him for so long?

The three captive Marshals are going to be sent to Cassel - so the Emperor at least will have company. It does seem so extraordinary to think of our having taken the French Army wholesale!

The *Times* is so interesting that we are always impatient for it to arrive! The irritation against England is still very great and people are very ungracious to all English. I think it so unjust and it makes me very unhappy. I cannot help getting violent on the subject and, when I hear disparaging remarks made, giving them back with a vehemence not altogether wise. It makes me feel spiteful and savage and upsets me altogether. I am obliged to comfort myself with the reflection that it is but legitimate for the Germans to be in a state of excitement unlike themselves, which makes them a little unfair, considering how their existence was at stake when the war was so wrongly forced upon them. Of course all this is more unpleasant for me than for anyone.

German irritation with England's neutrality indeed continued to grow, and a week later, on November 7, the Crown Princess again voiced her distress at the Anglo-German tension.

....What you say about the feeling between Germany and England [she wrote to her mother] is but too true! It makes my heart sick! There is nothing for it but patience. I know it will not last. In Germany as soon as people's passions and nerves settle and calm down a bit and they have time, which at present they have not, to examine what their imaginary grievance against England is, they will see how puerile are the reasons which have made them so angry and how small are the facts which, so greatly exaggerated, exasperated them so much. I am sure they will be heartily ashamed of their injustice, and grateful for England's kind and cordial sympathy - her grand and magnificent charity - and her masterly descriptions of our deeds in her incomparable press, the first press of the world. Much can be done even now, I am sure, to clear up misunderstandings and explain away difficulties. It will never do to blunder away at one another till we have got either into a serious quarrel, or a settled dislike for which the whole world will suffer. Those, as you so justly and truly say, who are devoted as I am heart and soul to both beloved countries - to the cause of liberty and culture - of which they are the two main supports - have many a bitter moment to go through at present. But the case is not hopeless. If England will be forbearing with her excited sister who has no time to think while she is fighting, I know she will see reason and good feeling return. The cause of anger is really this: when the war broke out Germany, who had to rush into armour unprepared, of course thought herself in the greatest danger, and turned to England, her only friend, for help. England had other considerations - preferred being a spectator to an actor, probably did not think the danger so imminent for Germany as the latter did herself - in short determined to remain neutral. A cry of disappointment and indignation burst forth from Germany - and people said 'If we are annihilated England will be the cause. She knows and acknowledges that we have been unfairly and unjustly attacked, and yet she will quietly see us go to the bottom without stirring a little finger to help us! If she had but spoken out loud - to our neighbour who has so suddenly turned our enemy - if she had but lifted up her voice - and threatened to strike him that disturbed the peace of Europe, France would never have dared to make war and all these lives would have been saved. England hat die Fettsucht - ist zu faul um sich zu rühren und lasst uns lieber zu Grunde gehen als Frankreich ein ernstes Wort zu sagen.'[6] This is the grievance, and it must take time before the feeling of anger will wear out, and the kindly offices England has unceasingly offered since be acknowledged and appreciated.

I think in the main grievance Germany is right and her feeling legitimate, for in my mind I cannot help thinking England could have and should have prevented the war - by a rebuke and a threat - to the party who was the aggressor. But where Germany is altogether wrong is in supposing England hung back from a love of the French and jealousy of ourselves - that Lord Granville was French, and the laws of neutrality interpreted to our detriment and France's advantage; and many minor facts brought up against England were exaggerated and distorted so as to create spite and suspicion and all manner of unkindly feelings - now vented on inoffensive and kindly intentioned Englishmen wherever they appear. The misfortune is that our official representatives are neither of them quite fitted for, nor up to, their position, viz. Bernstorff and Lord Augustus (Loftus). Each though well intentioned has bungled and made *bévues* with mischievous consequences. *If* a great German Empire does come out of the present war, then neither of these persons ought to remain. A charge of such immense importance ought to be confided to the very best heads and hands both countries can produce, so that both be worthily represented. I am sure nothing would set matters straight sooner. Pray excuse my openness.

I find I have not yet thanked you for the pretty and interesting letter from Mr. Haig! What a contrast in the lives your children have been leading during the last three months! The anxiety, excitement and business Alice and I have been in - and Affie - over the sea - in utter ignorance of what is going on in the old world! I hope and trust we shall all meet next year!

In the meantime, two great questions were perturbing the King of Prussia and his military advisers, among whom were pre-eminent the Crown Prince, Prince Frederick Charles, and Bismarck. The most immediate question was the problem of how the war might be most quickly finished; the second, and perhaps a not less important question, was the future of Germany. With regard to the first, although the regular French armies had been decisively beaten, Paris, the heart of France, still successfully resisted the siege which had already been in operation a month. Elsewhere in France new levies were being raised under the inspiration of Gambetta, and 1870 many were the French hopes that soon these armies might combine to raise the siege of Paris. Hence, all the efforts of the German high command were now directed to the speedy reduction of Paris and to the smashing of the new armies as and when they were ready. From the first, however, there appeared to be some dissension among the German staff as to the means by which Paris should be subdued. Bismarck and many of the older soldiers, such as Roon, favoured a bombardment. Others, thinking possibly of the artistic glories of Paris and the lives of the innocent caged within its gates, opposed a bombardment as inhuman, and preferred the weapons of starvation and disease. The Crown Prince's attitude is expressed in his Diary, where on October 22 he notes:

Today the first works were begun for building the siege batteries. Though I have ordered the preparations for a siege to be carried out with the greatest energy and all possible judgment, I am still in hopes that Paris will be forced simply and solely by hunger to open her gates to us, and that many lives will thus be spared to us.[7]

Four days later he noted (October 26):

All persons in authority, I at the head of them, are at one in this, that we must use every endeavour to force Paris to surrender by hunger alone; General von Moltke is in full agreement with me as to this.[8]

Efforts were now made to secure an armistice, but the mission of M Thiers to the German headquarters proved a complete failure.

So now [as the Crown Prince recorded on November 6] no choice is left to us but to take Paris; all the same I still hold by my policy of starving the city out, for this procedure, cruel though it seems, will spare more lives than a regular siege and storming of the city would cost us....[9]

Bismarck, however, was 'extremely desirous of seeing the bombardment begin immediately, in order to hasten the capitulation',[10] and in this view he was supported by public opinion in Berlin.

The Crown Princess naturally echoed her husband's views, and wrote to her mother on November 26, 1870:

Many most affectionate thanks for your dear letter of the 21st, and for the kind and affectionate words you write, which are very precious to me! Fritz writes from Versailles that he does see a chance of the Russian question being settled amicably and satisfactorily.[11] What a blessing it would be. Fritz gets abused here for not hastening the bombardment, but he does all he can to put it off, hoping it will become unnecessary. Moltke and Blumenthal are of his opinion, also General v. Falkenstein whom I saw yesterday, but the public want the excitement of hearing of a bombardment.

In Berlin the cry for the bombardment now grew fiercer, and on all sides the Crown Prince and Princess were attacked and abused as interfering with the just conduct of the war.

Apparently [recorded the Crown Prince on November 28][12] it is becoming a perfect mania in Berlin, this eagerness for the bombardment of Paris, and I even hear that Countess Bismarck-Schonhausen points me out to all and sundry as more particularly the guilty cause of its postponement. And she is quite right, for above all things I do not wish fire to be opened till in the opinion of professional gunners and experts the necessary ammunition each single siege gun requires for an effective uninterrupted bombardment is there on the spot. If that were all, we could have begun firing long ago, but we should very soon have had to stop and have gained nothing by it but a ludicrous failure....To my great satisfaction I hear from home that General of Infantry von Falkenstein shares my views on this question.

For the time being the Crown Prince won his point, and it was not until another month had passed that Paris was subjected to the torture of bombardment.

Meanwhile, a second great question had been troubling the leaders of Germany - the question of the future constitution of their state. All the eminent leaders, including Bismarck and the Crown Prince, were agreed that this was the moment in which to forge the new Germany; one man alone dissented - he who was to become the first Emperor of the new state, the veteran King William. He, as King of Prussia, was content with the *status quo*. German unity, he agreed, demanded something more, but he could think of no title more dignified than that of King, while the Crown Prince, Bismarck and the others favoured the creation of an Empire with William, of course, as its Emperor. On October 13 the Crown Prince recorded in his Diary:

The imperial question is now given serious prominence by Count Bismarck; in fact he told me himself that in 1866 it was a mistake on his part to have treated the idea with indifference; at the same time he had never dreamt the desire for the Imperial Crown would be so strong as it is now among the German people.....Count Bismarck raises the difficulty that supposing the Imperial dignity - which I should like to see made hereditary - transferred to our House, the style of our Court would likewise be changed and the development of greater splendour of circumstance follow as a necessary consequence. However, it greatly relieved his mind when I explained to him how in my opinion that was the very time when the old Brandenburg simplicity must be more thoroughly observed than is the case at the Royal Court of today.[13]

Eleven days later he notes:[14]

I cannot help myself at this crisis from thinking a great deal of the plans my late father-in-law (the Prince Consort) as also the late King (Leopold I) of the Belgians, in conjunction with old Baron von Stockmar, entertained for a united Germany under a monarchical head. God so willed that those men should conceive the notion of a free German Imperial State, that in the true sense of the word should march at the forefront of civilisation and be in a position to develop and bring to bear all noble ideals of the modern world, so that through German influence the rest of the world should be humanised, manners ennobled and people diverted from those frivolous French tendencies....Once we Germans were recognised as honest champions of such convictions an alliance might well be attained with England, Belgium, Holland, Denmark and Switzerland against Russia and France, and thereby peace be assured for many a day. Then in course of time the way would be paved for an understanding with France and thus bring about the utilisation of rich resources in the domain of Science, Art and Commerce, to the reciprocal advantage of both nations.

Great was the joy of the Crown Prince when he learnt on December 2 that the youthful King Ludwig of Bavaria at Bismarck's suggestion had written to King William begging him to assume the Imperial title. The next day the Crown Prince noted in his Diary:

Today, one I have for so many years held in honour and affection as my sister's birthday, has acquired a special importance for our House and country from the fact that the King of Bavaria, in an official communication in his own hand to our King, has begged him to assume the Imperial dignity....The gist was something to this effect, that now the German Confederation had been restored, it seemed to King Ludwig to be only right that it in turn should further develop into the old-time Empire with the Emperor at its head, and that, if His Majesty showed himself disposed to adopt the idea, he was ready to invite the German Princes and Free Cities, whom he had informed of this step, to offer him the Imperial Crown. The contents of this letter put His Majesty quite beside himself with displeasure and took him altogether aback; so he seems to have no inkling that the draft of it went from here to Munich. The King held that the matter came just at the most inopportune time possible, as he looked upon our prospects at the moment as very black and our position highly perilous. Count Bismarck replied that the election of the Emperor had nothing to do with the fighting now going on, but was rather a victory in itself and a consequence of the victories won up to the present, and that, even if we were driven back to the Meuse, the question was distinct from military incidents and a matter of simple right. But the King was not going to change his mind today and saw in 'Emperor and Empire' simply a cross for himself to bear and for the Prussian Kingdom generally! After leaving the King's room, Count Bismarck and I wrung each other's hand, without saying much - for we felt that the decision was made and that from today 'Emperor and Empire' were restored beyond possibility of recall.

Only for the evening of his days will my father probably enjoy its honours; but on me and mine devolves the task of setting our hands in true German fashion to the completion of the mighty edifice, and that on principles consonant with these modern times and free from prejudice and prepossessions.[15]

On December 10 the Reichstag included the words 'Emperor' and 'Empire' in the text of the new German Constitution. The German Empire was in being. How much of the credit for this should be attributed to the Crown Prince and how much to Bismarck is a point that will no doubt be eventually decided by history, but there is no doubt that it was the Crown Prince who persuaded Bismarck to take the decisive step. Prince Bülow, in a book on German politics published in 1913, confesses 1870 that the idea of a united Germany emanated originally from the Liberal party, but adds that it required the Conservative party, or rather Bismarck, to carry it out. It was not, however, from the Liberal party alone that the Crown Prince derived his ideas, because the Prince Consort had often explained to him his conception of a German Empire. On December 14 the Crown Prince noted in his Diary:

My thoughts are busied in a very special way today with my beloved, never-to-be-forgotten father-in-law, who this day nine years ago was taken from us. Had he lived, much would have gone differently and turned out differently in the development of the world's history, above all it would have been a subject of congratulation in his case if only he could have witnessed the restoration of the Empire, the complicated questions involved in which so often formed the subject of his talks with me. In particular, I recall perfectly a conversation we had during a stroll in the gardens of Buckingham Palace, in which he more especially stressed the point that we Prussians would have to give up this idea of playing a decisive role without assistance from Germany. His notion was not that of gaining by force of arms the ends the attainment of which was hindered by the stupidity of the Princes and the narrow-mindedness of the nation; but indeed no one in the year 1856, when peace at any price was in fashion, could have imagined that a time would ever come for such a magnificent and puissant revival of the manly spirit of Germany as we witness at the present moment. What a great mind like that of the enlightened Prince Consort wished and worked for can only gradually come to maturity; his blessing will not fail to be upon the building up of the new Empire.[16]

In the meantime opinion at the German Headquarters had hardened steadily in favour of the bombardment of Paris, whilst in Berlin the demand for this measure became a shrill hysterical clamour. The Crown Prince, however, still maintained the opinion that 'a bombardment would be no good, strong as is the tide of opinion at home in the opposite direction ', and he was warmly supported in his objection by General von Blumenthal and Count Moltke. That same day, December 14, he noted in his Diary:

In Berlin it is now the order of the day to vilify my wife as being mainly responsible for the postponement of the bombardment of Paris and to accuse her of acting under the direction of the Queen of England; all this exasperates me beyond measure. Countess Bismarck-Schönhausen and the Countess Amélie Dönhoff, a lady of the court of the Dowager Queen Elizabeth,[17] have repeated the scandal quite openly. But who in Berlin can judge what is best to do before Paris? Did we by any chance consult these wiseacres about Weissenberg, 'Worth and Sedan? And yet our exploits at that time have been deemed quite exemplary. But now in this case, where the bombardment calls for the most thorough preparations, especially so because of grave sins of omission on the part of the War Ministry, and in which we are faced with a siege on an utterly unprecedented scale, for which the necessary material has not been got ready, we should, of course, without more ado just loose off our guns, simply because the laity are of the opinion that Paris must then quite obviously capitulate! Yet, if only one of these clever people would be so good as just take the trouble to get a pair of compasses and measure how far our batteries, armed with the heaviest cannon, can actually reach, and if folks at Berlin would only realise that though shells may fall in the forts, the houses of the city itself are far out of range, so that the inhabitants would not be in the slightest degree incommoded by the firing, then perhaps they would understand that we are not the dolts they take us for at home. If we did proceed to a regular siege, the storming of the fortifications that must inevitably accompany any such operation, would cost us a frightful toll of men. I should just like to see the outcry that would then be raised at home! No, we shall not allow ourselves to be moved one hair's-breadth from our conviction just to please these gentlemen sitting at home in comfortable, cosy rooms. I should like these experts to come along here, take matters in their own hands, and show whether they understand the job better than we do![18]

Here surely was the *reductio ad absurdum* of the notion that the Crown Princess dominated her husband. In the first place, a soldier like the Crown Prince was certainly not likely to consult his wife on questions relating to the prosecution of the war when it was as much as he could do to keep her informed of what had happened the week before. Had the Crown Prince been the weak man he is often depicted as, he would have been far more easily influenced and dominated by the other generals who were constantly with him, but from all accounts he took a line of his own and constantly advocated a course of action that was by no means popular with the army. The theory that he was overridden by his wife therefore rests on no foundation whatever. Whenever any Queen or Princess interests herself in politics and repeats the views of her husband, it is invariably said that the wife dominates, and in this case there is small doubt that the Crown Princess not only took a most intelligent interest in politics, but also probably repeated, perhaps a little tactlessly, the views she had heard her husband express or that she read in his Diary, which he continued to send her. Later, when he became a sick man and relied on her in a thousand and one ways, there was, of course, every excuse for the people in Germany to rush to the conclusion that she was the one that counted, but at that time of the war of 1870-71 this slander can only have been invented by people who were looking for a pretext to depreciate her.

It is curious to note that while in England Queen Victoria was accused of sympathising with the Germans, the Crown Princess was said to be scheming with her 1870 mother to prevent Paris from being bombarded, and it was Bismarck himself who in later years said to his creature Busch: 'Perhaps I may be allowed to mention the influence brought to bear by the English ladies against the bombardment of Paris. You remember, "Schurze und Schtirzen" (aprons and petticoats), that is to say, freemasons and women.'[19]

Meanwhile, the fighting still continued, and on December 4, after a series of sanguinary engagements, Orleans surrendered to Prince Frederick Charles. Two days later the Crown Princess wrote to Queen Victoria:

Many affectionate thanks for your dear letter received yesterday. Meanwhile we are trembling with anxiety and excitement, as righting has been going on every day. Orleans having been retaken is of great importance and perhaps may bring this cruel bloodshed to an end sooner. Everyone is firmly convinced that the French will wish to begin another war again as soon as they possibly can to wipe out the stain of 1870 on their military glory. For this reason it is argued we must take a part of Lorraine and Alsace, so that when they do begin again our frontier may be a better protection to us, since we are never safe from being overrun by the French whenever their Government thinks it necessary to begin a fresh quarrel with us. I own I share this opinion and I find it universal both among soldiers, statesmen and the public at large.

The funds for the sick and wounded are very low - things and money are sadly wanted!

How is the Wolsey Chapel getting on? I am so glad to hear the Albert Hall pleases you and that the monument looks fine. How I long to see all these things again, but make plans one cannot! And as our visit may be unwelcome and a *gêne*, of course the chances of my being once more at home get rarer year by year. It makes me very sad....

The title of Emperor of Germany has been proposed to the King by the King of Bavaria. I think he will accept it, though I am not sure. How strange it seems!

Five days later (December 11) she wrote:

....The fighting that goes on daily distracts us. The French are determined to go on and we shall have to go on likewise. About Alsace and Lorraine there is but one voice all over Germany, that, if we do not keep them (or part of them), we shall be doing a wrong thing, as we shall be exposing ourselves to the same calamity as threatened us in July - being attacked and overrun by the French, whenever it suits them, as our frontiers are too weak to keep them out. Our only chance for a long era of peace, which Germany is burning and thirsting for, is by so subduing the French, that they will not wish to be at us again (at present they are not subdued and do not own themselves to be beaten), and making our frontier so formidable, that we *are* protected from the dangers of an attack....

The Crown Princess's efforts at alleviating the condition of the wounded now began to secure some measure of approval, and the Crown Prince in his Diary (December 21) noted that

It was a more cheerful piece of news for me to learn that my wife's doings as an expert in matters of nursing and tending the sick are rightly appreciated. Thus a detailed report from the Consulting Surgeon to the Hospitals of the XIth Army Corps, Professor Schillbach of Jena, has appeared, which describes the results achieved in the Homburg Hospital, in which my wife never ceased to take an active interest, as the best of all those connected with the Corps.

As if to emphasise Germany's intention to crush France, the order for the bombardment of Paris was given on December 30, Bismarck at length having prevailed over the humanitarian protests of the Crown Prince who, therefore, 'fixed the 4th January as the day for the opening of this wretched bombardment....Bismarck', he added, 'has made us great and powerful, but he has robbed us of our friends, the sympathies of the world and - our conscience.'[20] The effect, as the Crown Prince said, of this drastic step on the part of Germany was to alienate what little sympathy there now was in England for the triumphant German cause, and the tension between the two countries became evident in many little incidents which the Crown Princess did her best to smooth over. As she wrote to Queen Victoria on December 30:

> It is so kind of you to break lances for the Germans in England; this mutual distrust is too dreadful. It must be the aim of our statesmen to dispel these feelings, so unjust, unnecessary, and injurious to all that is useful. Here, the feeling is getting much better....
>
> That the Prussian officers should be rude to the English ones is too bad; but I fear our dear countrymen are a little awkward and ignorant of the forms which Germans are accustomed to. I know they quite neglect to have themselves named, and this the Prussians misunderstand and take for intentional rudeness, which they then fancy it is their duty to return; this is too stupid, but *I know* it is the case. It all comes from an imperfect knowledge of one another's national habits, for I have found those Englishmen and Germans who have lived much in both countries get on particularly well together, and are the best of friends. Prussians are really very civil, but they expect this *Vorstellen* introducing and presenting; and if it is forgotten they are offended. I do not think *half* the English that go abroad have an idea of this being necessary; on the other hand the Germans do not know that it is not the custom in England and this always creates little disagreeables, and when there is so much excitable matter in the air, and feelings are so irritated, every trifle is taken at more than it is worth. Hence these eternal squabbles and misunderstandings which make *me* utterly wretched.

A few days later General Kirchbach, with the approval of the Emperor of Germany, sent to the Crown Princess a screen that had been taken from the boudoir of the Empress Eugénie at St Cloud. The Crown Princess was anxious that it should be restored to its rightful owner, who was now a refugee in England, and promptly sent it to Queen Victoria. Her accompanying letter (January 4, 1871) ran:

> I have sent off a large parcel to you, containing a screen. This screen stood in the Empress's boudoir at St Cloud. When the French shells set fire to the house, the Prussian soldiers, as you know, tried to extinguish the fire and save the valuable things. A Prussian soldier made his way through smoke and flames at great risk of his own life, and carried off this screen, which he delivered up to General Kirchbach (a few minutes later it would have been burnt). General Kirchbach asked the King's leave to send me this screen, and obtained it. Although St Cloud is *not* the private property of the Emperor and Empress, and the *mobilier* belongs to the State - consequently is no longer theirs, yet *I* consider

this, and everything else saved, not a trophy of war, and do not see what *right* I have to keep it. Moreover, I would not wish to have anything in my possession which had belonged to the Empress, who has always been *so kind* to me, and on different occasions made me such handsome presents. I have said nothing to anyone at Versailles, neither to the King nor Fritz, as I can do what I like with a thing that has been sent to me, but I would ask you, dearest Mama, to restore this screen to the poor Empress when you think fit; you can tell her its history and how I came by it. Of course I *cannot offer* it *as a present*, whilst we are at war - that would not do; besides, I consider it simply restoring a piece of property to its rightful owner, which please must be YOUR *doing*. I trust in this way no one can blame me, whilst I am doing what I simply consider my duty.

I do not approve of war trophies, at least of *ladies* possessing them; for soldiers they are lawful, of course, and every army in the world considers them so. Perhaps you will kindly tell me when the parcel arrives, and when it has through your kindness reached its destination....

The arrival of the screen placed Queen Victoria in a predicament. To restore the screen to the Empress might give the French proof that the Germans had been guilty of plunder, and her opinion was supported by Earl Granville, who wrote to her on January 7:

In this country war trophies mean flags and guns, etc., etc.; the presents taken from palaces and country houses, which are said to have been sent in great quantities from France to Germany, would be called here acts of plunder, or looting. There may be a slight distinction in an article taken from a palace belonging to the State, which had been destroyed by the fire of the French; but in English ideas it would have been better if the Crown Prince had abstained from anything that looked like a sanction to the habit of the German Army. It would be difficult for your Majesty to receive as a present something which is known to have been taken from the palace of a State with which your Majesty is in friendly alliance; and there is something awkward in restoring, to the Empress here, that which belongs to the State in France. The offer might be refused, and the French entourage might make much of this proof of plunder.

The screen was, therefore, packed up again and returned to the Crown Princess. When the Empress Eugénie settled down with her husband at Chislehurst it was sent to her from Germany and so finally reached its rightful owners.

Meanwhile, the war dragged on. Paris, heroically suffering the greatest hardships, was still withstanding all German efforts to reduce it. The steady influx of wounded into Germany increased, and the indignation of the Crown Princess at the appalling conditions of some of the Berlin hospitals is well evidenced in the following letters:

I go into the hospitals every day [she wrote to Queen Victoria on January 7], What an effort it costs me I cannot tell you, as I have nothing to do in them and I see how badly managed they are without being able to improve them. The stifling atmosphere is enough to knock one down - and the dirt too repulsive - but the managing ladies seem quite satisfied - the poor victims are so touchingly contented, patient and grateful in their untold sufferings! My spirits are very low and bad the thought of all the misery, woe and suffering of both countries weighs day and night upon me. After Paris is taken perhaps there may be a chance of peace. I honour the French for not giving in, though I think they are exhausting their country and pushing their *point d'honneur* too far. I think that those who did not wish for war should openly say so now; the consequences of war are not their doing and they are not responsible for it, therefore they should try to stop the mischief it is doing. Our army is straining every nerve in this sad contest. The bombardment of Paris is a grievous necessity and felt to be so by everyone engaged in it.

These times are more trying than I can describe - one's feelings are lacerated on all sides - the most cruel impressions crowd upon one - and the horizon seems hopelessly dark and dreary.

You cannot think [she wrote again on January 11] how wretchedly unhappy I am about the war. The bombardment is too dreadful to be thought of, and yet I know it cannot be helped. The French should have thought of all the risks they were running in case theirs should not be the winning side when they forced the war!

The position and task of our troops is too arduous and perilous - the hardships and dangers they have to go through are too great for there to be much pity left for our enemies in the public at large, whose feelings are of course so harassed and worked up - by all they have to endure in many ways, by the absence of their relations and by our losses, and the sad and cruel sight of the crowded hospitals! But I cannot help feeling the deepest pity for our unfortunate enemy - though I attribute to them alone the blame, and the responsibility for all the endless misery daily incurred. I suffer more at present from the thought of all this than from my personal anxiety for Fritz and the long trying separation. I would gladly bear my share and much more if I could but save the lives of the poor creatures, victims of the war!

Three days later she again wrote:

As the messenger has only this minute arrived, I have hardly a minute's time left to answer your dear and kind letter - which was balm to my harassed feelings! I cannot describe the soreness and anxiety, the mental sufferings I go through daily on so many scores. The Queen and Fritz share all these feelings - their sentiments are just and elevated - the future weighs on them as it does on me they know all the dangers and difficulties before us! I have had two beautiful letters from dear Fritz, which do his kind and noble heart such honour! What our army has to go through is really dreadful, and the esprit de corps is really magnificent, fills me with admiration and respect. But the public at large are excited, irritable, etc., and do not show themselves to advantage.

The poor Queen is not so popular as she deserves! She is perhaps not always happy in the things she does, and her feelings for French and Catholics are slightly different from mine - -you know she displeases people. But she strives hard to fulfil all her duties, and has a really *vornehme Gesinnung* as a lady, a Queen and a Christian ought to have, and at these times which are so hard and trying deserves gratitude and sympathy and respect.

I send you a statuette of Fritz in plaster of Paris which is very like, till I can get you a better one in bronze. I am sure he will be so much pleased to stand in effigy on your table. I have received no photos by this messenger.

You ask why Fritz Carl is called 'the Red Prince'. He always wears the uniform of the Red Hussars of the Guards, or the Ziethen Husaren, of which he is Colonel, who have red coats with silver - and a red Kolpack.

I think the protest of the French against the bombardment foolish and undignified. They have bombarded us night and day for two months, why should our batteries not answer? They refused to listen when England tried to mediate at the beginning of the war, and would not brook interference. I do not see why they should cry out for help now, merely because they over-rated their own forces and under-estimated Germany's power. My grief for the sufferings they have to endure is unbounded, but how can we as a nation help it? And how immense is the loss entailed upon us by the continuation of the war....

Meanwhile, the German victories had smoothed the path for German unity. The princes, headed by the King of Bavaria, now invited King William to assume the leadership of Germany; and on January 18, in the Palace of Versailles, he was proclaimed, with imposing ceremony, German Emperor. The change of title was by no means warmly welcomed by the Prussian royal family. On January 20 the Crown Princess wrote to Queen Victoria a letter which shows how difficult was at times the position of the Princess in the German court:

I was going to tell you by the Empress's (Queen's) own desire that she knew nothing whatever of the adoption of the Imperial title on the 18th, nor of the Proclamation. The Emperor is so averse to the whole change that he did not like it spoken of beforehand, and no one else took the initiative of informing us here of what was going to be done! Of course this was an embarrassing and awkward position for my mother-in-law - who resented the proceeding very much. I had a deal of difficulty in calming her down. She calls me to witness her having known nothing until the day came. I own it is wrong, but I do not think it strange. At Versailles everyone is wrapt up in military things, and the anxiety, uncertainty and responsibility are so great that all other considerations seem to be forgotten or at least treated hurriedly.

You say you are glad that my Mama-in-law and I get on well now together. The wretchedness of my life when we do not, you do not know. I am only too glad when she will let me be on a comfortable footing with her. No one knows her really good and great qualities better than I do, or is happier to see her in a good humour. What I am going to say may sound presumptuous, but I do not think the Empress could have a daughter-in-law who better appreciated the good she has in her - who is more devoted heart and soul to the cause she has served, who can enter into her interests more thoroughly, or is more ready to catch up the thread where she has left it and work in the same direction. I have fought her battles and smoothed her path wherever I could. I bear no malice or resentment, though she has made me suffer much (more than you perhaps can imagine). I am glad to forget it, and remember only her better moods and her acts of kindness. I feel a deep pity for her as nature has given her a character and temper which must tend to unhappiness and *Unbefriedigung* wherever she be, and she has had many a sore and bitter hour to go through during her life. I shall feel happy and thankful if I can in any way contribute to make 1871 this and the later period of her existence more peaceful and happy.

I have not a minute to myself, not even to rest of an evening, as I either go to the Queen, or she comes to me. I can do this now (though it is a great sacrifice), but when Fritz comes home I shall not be able, and I fear she will not understand this.

I will prepare some little extracts from Fritz's letters for you, which I am sure you will like. Dear Fritz, the long separation seems very hard sometimes, but I have no right to complain.

The defeats of General Bourbaki [at Belfort by General von Werder] and General Chanzy [near Le Mans on January 11 by Prince Frederick Charles] are a great thing and I trust will bring this horrible war to an end sooner.

Five days later, January 25, 1871, the Crown Princess remembered with pathetic sentiment the occasion of her wedding thirteen years earlier.

I waited till this day so dear to me had come round to thank you for your dear letter of the 21st. How much my thoughts are with you today and darling Papa! How I cling to all the precious recollections of you both and your love - my home and friends - so fast receding into the past!

I little thought then [she wrote] that this day would find Fritz where he is now and engaged in so awful a task! And yet I am so proud of him and every day more grateful that I am his - there lives no kinder, purer, nobler, better man than he is, and is not that the greatest praise one can bestow and worth all military glory twice over? These six months' separation are very hard, but his love and kindness make me happy from afar and I am touched at his finding time to write every day to me in spite of all he has to do! His letters are a great comfort!

The awful sufferings of the French move one to the greatest pity, but of course my feelings are specially harassed by thinking of all our poor men have to go through! Blessed will the day be when we have peace - and all man's ingenuity, all the powers of head, heart and hands can be devoted to efface the sad trace of all these horrors I I am sure much can be done, and that is at this sad time the thought from which I derive most comfort.

The sentimentality for France - so apparent in England - is sad for us - though it can be easily explained. I think that people will acknowledge that it has more to do with the feelings than with reason, and therefore I trust it will pass over - when unlucky France gives up her resistance.

Two days later the eldest son of the Crown Princess celebrated his thirteenth birthday. That day the Crown Prince echoed the thoughts of the Princess as he noted in his Diary:

Today is Wilhelm's thirteenth birthday. May he grow up a good upright, true and trusty man, one who delights in all that is good and beautiful, a thorough German who will one day learn to advance further in the paths laid down by his grandfather and father for the good governance of our noble Fatherland, working without fear or favour for the true good of his country. Thank God there is between him and us, his parents, a simple, natural, cordial relation, to preserve which is our constant endeavour, that he may always look upon us as his true, his best friends. It is truly a disquieting thought to realise how many hopes are even now set on this boy's head and how great a responsibility to the Fatherland we have to bear in the conduct of his education, while outside considerations of family and rank, court life in Berlin and many other things make his upbringing so much harder. God grant we may guard him suitably against whatever is base, petty, trivial, and by good guidance train him for the difficult office he is to fill![21]

It was now beginning to dawn on the French, or rather the Government in Paris, that further resistance was hopeless, as their supplies must give out in a week's time. In Germany everyone was tired of the war and wanted peace. The Crown Princess echoed the feelings of the majority when she wrote on January 28:

A thousand thanks for your dear letter by messenger which gave me so much pleasure with all its kind wishes for the 25th, and yesterday our dear Willie's birthday. He was so delighted with your presents. I had arranged a little surprise for him and the others, allowing them to go to the Schauspielhaus and see a Panorama, which amused them very much. We are trembling and hoping for peace! This wish or passionate prayer of two whole nations must be granted - it would be a disappointment too dreadful to bear, if peace did not come. Everyone is worn out with the strain on all one's feelings - on the one side, patriotism and the pride which looks upon one's troops, and on the other the pity for the poor French, the grief at the death of so many of our dear soldiers, and the anxiety, which never leaves one day or night, about those still in the field.

I telegraphed our title to you yesterday. We are called Kaiserliche und Königliche Hoheit Kronprinz des Deutschen Reichs und von Preussen. The King is called Deutscher Kaiser, König von Preussen, but usually Kaiser und König; the Empress, of course, 'die Kaiserin-Königin'. She is beyond measure delighted at your kind words to her and those to me about her. I am always spoken to as Imperial Highness (I own I liked the other better), but as it reminds one of the great political fact of Germany's being gathered under one head, I am proud to bear this title. I send you today the extracts from Fritz's letters. Pray let them remain unknown to anyone except just Lenchen and Christian. I have not even told Fritz that they are copied and sent to you.

Dear Aunt Clementine's letter I have sent as you wished to Alice, without letting anyone else see it. You can surely answer her that if the French Government had listened to yours in this month of July, they would never have exposed their beautiful capital to the unavoidable horrors of war, siege and bombardment! They were warned, but would not listen.

I am sure you would be pleased with William if you were to see him - he has Bertie's pleasant, amiable ways - and can be very winning. He is not possessed of brilliant abilities, nor of any strength of character or talents, but he is a dear boy, and I hope and trust will grow up a useful man. He has an excellent tutor, I never saw or knew a better, and all the care that can be bestowed on mind and body is taken of him. I watch over him myself, over each detail, even the minutest, of his education, as his Papa had never had the time to occupy himself with the children. These next few years will be very critical and important for him, as they are the passage from childhood to manhood, I am happy to say that between him and me there is a bond of love and confidence, which I feel sure nothing can destroy. He has very strong health and would be a very pretty boy were it not for that wretched unhappy arm which shows more and more, spoils his face (for it is on one side), his carriage, walk and figure, makes him awkward in all his movements, and gives him a feeling of shyness, as he feels his complete dependence, not being able to do a single thing for himself. It is a great additional difficulty in his education, and is not without its effect on his character. To me it remains an inexpressible source of sorrow! I think he will be very good-looking when he grows up, and he is already a universal favourite, as he is so lively and generally intelligent. He is a mixture of all our brothers - there is very little of his Papa, or the family of Prussia about him.

The intense desire of the Crown Princess for peace was now gratified. The steady bombardment of Paris, coupled with starvation within its gates and the failure of all efforts at relief, compelled the Parisians to sue for terms. On January 28 Paris capitulated, and an armistice of three weeks was agreed upon between Bismarck and Jules Favre, the French Minister for Foreign Affairs. The Crown Princess was relieved, but by no means jubilant. As she wrote to Queen Victoria on February 4:

> Many most affectionate thanks for your dear letter by messenger. I was sure you would feel as thankful for the Armistice as we do! Fritz praises Monsieur Jules Favre. I pity the luckless man to have to be the bearer of tidings which must irritate the Parisians and provincial war party to the extreme; but I trust that party is losing ground. They seem to have totally miscalculated the amount of food contained in Paris and were therefore obliged to capitulate. What an intense relief it is to know that the sufferings of those poor creatures are at an end!
>
> We know nothing about the Emperor's return, but he cannot leave his Army before Peace or (what would be too awful and seems most unlikely) a recommencement of hostilities is decided upon. Just fancy in these six months we have lost (the Prussian Army) 1100 Officers alone! Does it not seem too dreadful! Half our acquaintances and friends are gone! It makes me quite ill to read the newspapers and all the accounts of the destruction and 1871 ruin in France. It is the retaliation for the way in which the French treated Germany in 1806-1809 - from which we are still suffering. The town of Königsberg had not finished paying off the contribution levied by Napoleon I last year!
>
> Perhaps the Emperor and Fritz will return for the opening of the Reichstag, which is to be on the 9th March.
>
> I go to the hospitals whenever I can spare an hour and many are the sad and heartrending sights I have seen. The cold causes such dreadful frostbites. Yesterday I was told of five unlucky wretches whose feet were frozen on the railway and who will have to have their feet taken off. All these horrors make me too miserable, the thought of what so many poor unfortunate human beings have to endure haunts me day and night.

The proposed terms of peace were hard. There was magnanimity, even chivalry, in Prussian treatment of Denmark in 1864 and Austria and Saxony in 1866; neither was shown to France in 1871. The greater part of Alsace and Lorraine, a huge indemnity and other crushing spoils were demanded. In vain did the Crown Prince and even Bismarck seek to relinquish the claim to Metz; Moltke and the generals were resolute. The spirit of France had to be broken, and it could only be broken, they urged, by the rod of humiliation. English opinion now veered over entirely in favour of France, and the Crown Princess, in her letter of February 7, 1871, when these terms of peace were rumoured, dismissed them as preposterous.

> Many most affectionate thanks for your dear letter of the 4th. I cannot think how mine could have been such a long while on the road! Meanwhile you will have the report about the most exorbitant conditions of peace contradicted; it

seems it was invented by a German newspaper correspondent. I never believed it for a moment. At such a moment as this, a report of this kind is enough to make everyone cry out. No one seems to doubt of the possibility of peace being soon concluded at Versailles, in spite of Gambetta's efforts to 1871 the contrary. It is too ardently desired by both sides not to succeed in the end, though I am sure we shall be worried and excited by all sorts of fluctuating reports, difficulties, etc., before the final settlement.

The British Government possibly held the same views, for two days later, at the formal opening of Parliament, the speech from the throne seemed to express sympathy with France, an event which gave great annoyance to the German Empress. The following day (February 10) the Crown Princess wrote to Queen Victoria:

I saw the Queen-Empress, who was irate about your speech in Parliament, saying that it flattered the French unnecessarily and expressed unconcealed sympathy with their cause, that it omitted saying a word about the origin of the war, or even expressing again what everyone had admitted, that Germany was attacked and not attacking, that the passage about Germany was more than cold and decidedly the reverse of civil. The Empress went on to add that it had made the same impression upon everyone here, that it would create a very bad feeling, etc. In short, she was very angry. As I could not go her length about it, we could not agree. Alas, it is true that the excitement against England is very great just at this moment. It was not so a fortnight ago, but now people are frantic at the anti-German feeling in England, which reveals itself more every day. They think it unjust and unfair! How I suffer from all this I cannot say, as of course I cannot hear a word said against England - and I give it back (I fear not always gently) when I hear sharp words. Popular opinion is like the sea - it is easily lashed up into fury - and the waves calm down by degrees when the wind ceases blowing - and so it will be with these storms of indignation in both our countries, there is injustice in the feeling of both. I must own the speech did not strike me in the sense which is attached to it here, and I fancy it was well adapted for England, which of course is the proper criterion.

In reply to a further letter from the Crown Princess,[22] Queen Victoria, whose affection for her eldest grandson had been long remarked, made reply:

I will finish today [she wrote on February 11, 1871], and wish just to touch on your answer to my observations and hopes respecting Willie. The vehemence with which you speak of 'the horror of low company' would make it appear as though I had advocated it! The low company you speak of consisting of actors, actresses, musicians, barbers (in one case at least), etc. are the very reverse of what I suggested, for those sorts of people are the proudest and unkindest to those below them and to the poor. What I meant (but what I fear your position in Prussia, living always in a Palace with the ideas of immense position of Kings and Princes, etc.) is: that the Princes and Princesses should be thoroughly kind, *menschlich*, should not feel that they were of a different flesh and blood to the poor, the peasants and working classes and servants, and that going amongst them, as we always did and do, and as every respectable lady and gentleman does here – was of such immense benefit to the character of those who have to reign hereafter. To hear of their wants and troubles, to minister to them, to look after them and be kind to them (as you and your sisters were accustomed to be by good old Tilla) does immense good to the character of children and grown-up people. It is there that you learn lessons of kindness to one another, of patience, endurance and resignation which cannot be found elsewhere. The mere contact with soldiers never can do that, or rather the reverse, for they are bound to obey and no *independence of character* can be expected in the ranks.

The Germans must be very different from the English and above all from the Scotch - if they are not fit to be visited in this way. But I fear they are, from what dear Papa often said, and the English even are in that respect, especially in the South - for in the North they possess a good deal of that great independence of character, determination, coupled with real high noble feelings, which will not brook being treated with haughtiness. The Germans have less of this.

Dear Papa knew how to value and appreciate this, and so do our children as much as I do and all reflecting minds here. This is what I meant and maintained is essential for a Prince or Princess of our times. Regarding the higher classes, the way in which their sins and immoralities are overlooked, indulged, forgiven - when the third part in lower orders would be highly punished, is enough to cause democratic feelings and resentment. I am sure you watch over your dear boy with the greatest care, but I often think too great care, too much constant watching, leads to the very dangers hereafter which one wishes to avoid.

It is a terrible difficulty and a terrible trial to be a Prince. No one having the courage to tell them the truth or accustom them to those rubs and knocks which are so necessary to boys and young men.

That your dear boys may grow up all that you can wish and desire and be good men and Christians and beloved and looked up to - is my earnest prayer![23]

To this letter the Crown Princess made reply (February 15):

Many affectionate thanks for your dear, long and interesting letter which I received the day before yesterday and am distressed not to be able to answer as fully as I should like. But it does not seem to me as if I had misunderstood your first letter. I think in the main as you do - though I suppose I expressed myself differently. You wish the same results as I do. But my children see more beyond the walls of a Palace than you think, although we are so much more in town than you and dear Papa used to be. Our farm and the village at Darmstadt, where the children are with me every day, gives them an opportunity of going in and out of the cottages - though the inhabitants are not all so nice and simple as one could wish. The German *Bauer* is not a very amiable individual and is distinguished by his obstinacy and hardness. Country life affords a thousand opportunities for a natural *Verkehr* with the people of hamlets and villages - which of course those who live in a town are debarred from. Our little school is an interest which the children share, and the more independent we become the more we shall be able to procure for our children all that is healthy, simple, natural and good for their minds and character. So I think you will see I do understand what you mean.

Meanwhile, the latent irritation between England and Germany seemed to be growing, and the position of the Crown Princess had become more difficult. Moreover, now that British public opinion had become anti-German, those whose sympathies were with the French did not hesitate to accuse Queen Victoria and her family of a breach of neutrality in sending messages of congratulation to the German royal family. These accusations became so serious that the matter was brought up in the House of Commons, but Mr. Gladstone poured what oil he could on these troubled waters, and the matter was eventually dropped.

The Crown Princess was full of sympathy for the difficult part her mother had to play and viewed with intense regret the growing animosity between England and Germany. On March 4 she wrote:

A thousand most tender thanks for your dear and kind letter by messenger. I am sure it must give you who are so generous, kind and just, pain to think of the animosity growing in England against Germany, but it is no use shutting our eyes against facts, and that it is one I do not doubt. It makes your position often trying, I am sure; but I can understand what that position is; you must not in any way allow yourself to be separated from your own people - the first people in the world, for I may say so to you, and it is every day more my conviction. How much I have suffered from the feeling between the two nations I cannot say! How at times unkindly and unjustly I have been used! And how many tears I have shed! But one must learn to look at things philosophically. Peoples are like individuals in many things. One knows what a quarrel is between friends or relations, one can trace the reasons small or great, and can calculate their effects on an excited brain. Time cures this. Now we have peace at last, the news of our doings in France will no longer exasperate the English by working up their pity for the most unfortunate but guilty French.

Peace too will put an end to the part of a neutral, which is a most difficult part; and though I regretted England should have played it, still I think the Government has done it admirably; that it should have been taken at all, exasperated Germany; now that reason is removed I am sure it will calm down. If angry words, scoffs and taunts, thrown backwards and forwards like a shuttlecock, conjure up mischief and ill-will, so must kind acts and words, and the rightly expressed sentiments of sensible men, reproduce the feelings which ought to exist between Germany and England. Count Bismarck is not eternal, he will be as quickly forgotten as the poor Emperor Napoleon, who is now scarcely remembered....

A fortnight later the victorious Crown Prince returned to Berlin - and once again the Crown Prince and Princess and their family of six were reunited. The Crown Princess's cup of happiness was full. Her work in the hospitals had at length received some little recognition, her husband had returned covered with glory from an arduous war, her family appeared to be growing up well and strong, and Germany had taken her place in the front rank of the Great Powers. For the third time in seven years a war had been brought to a successful conclusion, each time with increased prestige and territory for the conqueror. Germany was *en fête*, and the Crown Princess was now unknowingly at her zenith. On March 28, 1871, she wrote to Queen Victoria:

Many thanks for your dear letter received yesterday. By Louise's telegram I see the Emperor Napoleon [who had been released from Germany and, for the third time in his career, had taken up his residence in England] has been to see you. I am sure this visit must have been a painful one to both! We hear from different sides well acquainted with his doings that he has great hopes of regaining his throne since this dreadful revolution in Paris. I wonder he can wish it - and is not too proud to entertain any such idea after all that has been said and written in public about his Government by the French....

We are quite exhausted by the fatigue of these continued fêtes, for I suppose there will be a repetition when the troops return and the statue of Frederick William will be unveiled. How the Emperor and Empress can stand it and like it all is beyond my comprehension - all other mortals get knocked up. The state of France makes it impossible to tell when our troops will be home. The middle of May, most people say.

Even after the peace of Frankfort, however, Anglo-German animosity did not appear to undergo any alleviation, and when it was rumoured that a statue of King Frederick William III was to be unveiled at Berlin on June 16 with all the pomp of the return of the victorious German army, but in the absence of the British Ambassador (Lord Augustus Loftus, who was on leave in Baden), The Crown Princess telegraphed to Lord Granville, the British Foreign Secretary, to ask if this slight could not be avoided. Lord Granville's reply (June 14) ran:

I have had the honour of receiving your Royal Highness's telegram of today and I gladly avail myself of an opportunity of writing a few lines to your Royal Highness.

There is a series of circulars to our Ambassadors abroad, regulating their conduct when this country has been a neutral during the time of a European war, on the occasion of rejoicings at the victories which have been gained.

I am afraid if our Ambassador was at Berlin at a moment when German enthusiasm must, as at the present moment, be raised to the highest point after the glorious and extraordinary achievements of the last year, the observance by him of the rules, which have been laid down and acted upon on former occasions, would create some comment and disappointment among those who were not aware of our rules. Lord A. Loftus having taken two months' leave, it is perfectly natural he should not be at his post. The embassy will be illuminated, and I have received the Queen's permission to write a letter instructing Mr Petre to congratulate the Emperor warmly in Her Majesty's name on the inauguration of the statue of Frederick William the Third....

On June 16 the statue was formally unveiled after a march past of the triumphant returning troops and the presentation to the Crown Prince of his Field-Marshal's baton, but the absence of the British Ambassador was remarked.

Queen Victoria was now anxious to restore harmony between the Crown Princess and her brother, the Prince of Wales, whose French leanings during the war had caused much heartburning in Berlin. With this end in view the Queen invited the Crown Prince and Princess and their family to London in July, when a happy reconciliation was made, the Prince of Wales showing all his old cordiality. At the outset, the Crown Prince and Princess stayed (from July 3 to 13) at the German Embassy, where the Prince and Princess of Wales often visited them. The four were in agreement on many points, notably in their joint 'horror' of Bismarck, whose unprincipled 'driving power' was, the Crown Prince deplored, 'omnipotent'.[24] The Crown Prince returned to Germany on the 13th, but the Princess remained to spend the summer and early autumn with the Queen at Osborne or Balmoral. At both places she had many opportunities of renewing that cordial relationship with her brother which had been somewhat interrupted by the war.

## NOTES

1 The Crown Prince's memorandum is given on pp. 22-4 of vol. ii. of *Queen Victoria's Letters*.
2 *The German Empire*, W. H. Dawson, i. 346.
3 *The War Diary of the Emperor Frederick*, p. 10.
4 *Ibid.* p. 63.
5 Butler's *Bismarck*, p. 124.

6 England is growing fat is too lazy to stir herself and prefers to let us be ruined rather than say a stern word to France.
7 *The War Diary of the Emperor Frederick*, p. 165.
8 *Ibid*. p. 169.
9 *Ibid*. p. 181.
10 *Ibid*. pp. 200-1
11 On October 31 Russia repudiated the clauses of the Treaty of 1856 which ensured the neutralisation of the Black Sea. The Conference of London which followed in January 1871 ratified the abrogation.
12 *The War Diary of the Emperor Frederick*, pp. 202-3.
13 *Ibid*. pp. 155-6.
14 *Ibid*. p. 168.
15 *Ibid*. p. 210.
16 *Ibid*. p. 222.
17 Widow of King Frederick William IV.
18 *The War Diary of the Emperor Frederick*, pp. 222-3.
19 Busch's *Bismarck*, p, 185
20 *The War Diary of the Emperor Frederick*, p. 238.
21 *Ibid*. p. 285.
22 Which is unfortunately not available.
23 Both this letter and the following one refer to other letters which are unfortunately missing.
24 Extract from Queen Victoria's Diary, cited in article entitled 'Queen Victoria and France', by R. S. Rait in *Quarterly Review*, July 1919, pp. 10, 11.

# V: Bismarck and Russia, 1871-1878

THE startling and overwhelming German victories in the field during the Franco-German War had now placed Germany upon a pinnacle of military glory. Her mercury had risen rapidly, and Bismarck, prudent, watchful and ambitious, early realised that the first essential to the security of the new German Empire was the continuance of benevolent friendliness on the part of Russia. Germany, no longer a fortuitous concourse of antagonistic states, was now a power to be reckoned with. In alliance with Russia, Austria and Italy she would be the dominating factor in Europe - the goal to which Bismarck was driving. Hence in the following year Bismarck arranged a meeting between the Emperors of Germany, Russia and Austria, and there resulted that vague friendly *Dreikaiserbund* which was presumed to be the forerunner of alliances.[1]

One of the diplomatic changes following the Franco-German War was the translation of Lord Augustus Loftus, the British Ambassador at Berlin, to St Petersburg, and his replacement by Mr Odo Russell (afterwards Lord Ampthill). The Crown Princess had never been on terms of more than social acquaintance with Lord Augustus Loftus, whose Danish sympathies during the war of 1864 had antagonised her, but with the new Ambassador there sprang up at once a keen, delightful and lasting friendship. At Vienna Russell had begun his diplomatic career, and after short periods at the Paris, Constantinople and Washington embassies, he was appointed, in 1858, to the British Legation at Florence whence he was detached to reside in Rome. At the end of 1870, his tact and ability were recognised when he was sent on a special mission to the headquarters of the German army at Versailles, where he became the trusted friend of the Crown Prince. In 1871 he was appointed Ambassador to Berlin. He had scarcely entered upon his duties when he received instructions from the Foreign Office to intimate to Bismarck (now Chancellor of the German Empire) that Great Britain was in danger of being involved in war with Russia.

In the preceding year the rivalry between Great Britain and Russia in Central Asia and the Near East had become more and more acute, and Bismarck had carefully fostered a growing friendship that had sprung up between the Emperors of Russia and Germany. In the October of 1870, the Emperor of Russia, feeling that while Germany and France were locked in a death struggle there was small chance of their intervening in outside affairs, determined to rid Russia of an irksome article in the Treaty of Paris of 1856 which prohibited her using the Black Sea for warships. Lord Granville, the

British Foreign Secretary, immediately threatened war as the consequence of this cynical disregard of the Treaty. Bismarck suggested a conference, which eventually took place in London in March 1071, when a new treaty was signed by which the neutralisation of the Black Sea was annulled. The British diplomatic defeat was complete, and neither Germany nor Russia forgot that at this juncture their mutual support had been too much for Great Britain.

Not unnaturally Bismarck's policy ran counter to the aspirations of those who sought a closer understanding between the new Germany and England - of whom the Crown Princess, rightly or wrongly, was assumed to be the leader. In addition to the international questions which threatened European complications, there were no less difficult problems due to dissensions within the German court. The imperious and vindictive Bismarck was by no means friendly to the Empress Augusta, whom he conceived to be opposed to his policy of limiting the powers of the Catholic Church in Prussia, nor indeed were his relations with the Crown Princess any better: and he frequently complained to the British Ambassador in the bluntest language of the lack of harmony between them. Lady Emily Russell, wife of Mr Odo Russell, writing to Queen Victoria on March 15, 1873, after an official dinner at the British Embassy which had been attended by the German Emperor and Empress, gives an indication of the tension which then existed:

I avail myself of Your Majesty's gracious permission to write, to say how deeply gratified we have been by the visit their Majesties the Emperor and Empress have deigned to pay us, and by the exceptional favour conferred upon us, by their Majesties being pleased to accept a dinner at the Embassy.

This high distinction, which no other Embassy has ever yet enjoyed in Berlin, is due to those deep feelings of devoted admiration which Her Imperial Majesty the Empress Augusta never ceases to express in eloquent and glowing terms, when speaking of her friendship and sympathy for Your Majesty. My husband says that this gracious demonstration of goodwill towards Your Majesty's Embassy reported by all the press of Germany, will do more towards improving the friendly relations of England and Germany, he has so much at heart, than a thousand despatches and blue books. The Empress whose conversation is so brilliantly clever, as Your Majesty knows, was more so than ever throughout the evening. Her Majesty repeatedly said 'I fancy myself in dear England', and before rising from dinner drank Your Majesty's health in terms of affectionate respect and with all sincere good wishes for Your Majesty's welfare and happiness. Their Imperial Majesties were immensely cheered by the crowd in the street both on coming to, and leaving the Embassy.

Your Majesty is aware of the political jealousy of Prince Bismarck about the Empress Augusta's influence over the Emperor, which he thinks stands in the way of his anti-Clerical and National policy, and prevents the formation of responsible ministries as in England. The Empress told my husband he [Bismarck] has only twice spoken to Her Majesty since the war, and [she] expressed a wish that he should dine with us also. According to etiquette he would have had to sit on the left side of the Empress, and Her Majesty would then have had an hour during which he could not have escaped conversing. Prince Bismarck accepted our invitation but said he would prefer to set aside etiquette, and cede the 'pas' to the Austrian Ambassador. However, on the day of the dinner and a short time before the hour appointed, Prince Bismarck sent an excuse saying he was ill with lumbago. The diplomatists look mysterious and hint at his illness being a diplomatic one.

Prince Bismarck often expresses his hatred for the Empress in such strong language that my husband is placed in a very difficult position and still more so, when he complains of the want of harmony existing between Her Royal and Imperial Highness the Crown Princess and himself. He says he is able to agree with the Crown Prince, but he fears that will never be possible with the Crown Princess.

This state of things is very distressing and my husband is more unhappy about it than he can ever say, because he foresees difficulties in the future that will be quite beyond the influence of diplomacy, Prince Bismarck being so unscrupulous in his use of the press to undermine his political enemies - as his letter insinuating that the Empress was sending money to the refractory Catholic priests through the Chamberlain Count Schaffgotsch proves.

My husband fears that Prince Bismarck will seek to make the 1873 position of the Crown Princess with the public a very difficult one, in order to have his own way about the administration of Germany, which he wants to unify altogether, as Cavour unified Italy - by mediatising the reigning Princes.

The Emperor expressed in the warmest terms his high sense of honour conferred on Countess Bernstorff by Your Majesty's visit and said how much touched he and the Empress had been by it Their Majesties do not yet know whom Prince Bismarck intends to propose as successor to poor Count Bernstorff.

We had the honour of a visit, a week ago, from Prince William and Prince Henry accompanied by Herr Hintzpeter, Their Royal Highness' Preceptor. Everyone who has the gratification of speaking to Prince William is struck by his naturally charming and amiable qualities, his great intelligence and his admirable education. The return of Their Imperial Highnesses the Crown Prince and Princess has been a great joy and gratification and also to witness the perfect restoration to health of the Crown Prince. We had the honour of dining alone with Their Imperial Highnesses the day before yesterday and we were delighted to see how well His Imperial Highness looked, and seemed, and that with the exception of being a little paler his illness had left no traces. Her Imperial Highness was looking very well.

Ever since the Franco-German War the relations between the Crown Princess and the Prince of Wales had known no cloud, and brother and sister repeatedly exchanged visits. When, in July 1874, the Crown Prince and Princess visited London, where they stayed at the German Embassy, *The Times*, in a burst of good feeling, described the Crown Prince as 'the consistent friend in Prussia of all mild and liberal administration', and predicted that when the liberal-minded Crown Prince ascended the German throne the main obstacles to friendship between the two countries would disappear.

At the end of August 1874 the Prince and Princess of Wales came to Berlin to attend the confirmation of Prince William of Prussia - the Crown Princess's eldest son - and after the boy's confirmation his uncle, the Prince of Wales, wrote on September 1, 1874, to Queen Victoria from the Neue Palais:

I was much struck with the solemnity and simplicity of the service. Willy went through his examination admirably, and the questions he had to answer must have lasted half an hour. It was a great ordeal for him to go through before the Emperor and Empress and all his family. I was only too glad to take the Sacrament with Vicky and Fritz and Willy, after the ceremony, and the service is almost the same as ours. Willy was much pleased with your presents which were laid out in my sitting-room. Your letter to him and the inscription you wrote in the Bible I thought beautiful, and I read them to him. All you said I thought so very true.[2]

The Crown Princess's own letter to her mother (September 1) ran:

It is a difficult task to give you a description of today, as my heart is so filled with emotion that I do not know where to begin. But first of all let me thank you most tenderly for all your kind and touching marks of sympathy. The kind letter you wrote me arrived this morning before the ceremony began, which was of course a great comfort, as I feel your absence very much on this occasion. Your letter to William and especially what you wrote into his Bible was beautiful and touched Fritz very much indeed. We thank you a thousand times for it! Willy was delighted and surprised at suddenly becoming the possessor of so large and beautiful a picture of dear Papa! Dear Bertie is *all* kindness, so considerate, so amiable and affectionate - so kindly accepting all that we can do for his comfort or entertainment, which alas is not much. He is as amiable a guest as he is a host, and this is saying a *great* deal! It is a *great* comfort and happiness to have him here, as I should have felt rather low at having no one of our family present.

The ceremony took place at 11. Fritz and I drove with Willy and took him into the vestry to wait until the company had assembled and taken their seats in the church! We received the Emperor and Empress and the few members of the Prussian family who were here outside the Friedenskirche in the cloisters you may remember, and then all went in. The church was prettily decorated with wreaths of green and green plants, a low platform had been erected in the middle with two steps, on which the temporary altar stood, and a chair and a little desk were placed for Willy. A carpet of my own working covered the steps, and the pall which once covered my darling Sigie's coffin, and which I gave to the church as an *Altardecke*, covered the Communion Table; it is all of white satin with S and a crown in gold in the corners.

For the members of the royal family there were two rows of chairs. The rest of the company in the nave stood (I fear they must have been very tired, as the ceremony *was* very long). William behaved very well, and was not at all either shy or upset - and showed the greatest *sang-froid*. He read his *Glaulensbekenntniss* off in a loud and steady voice - and answered the forty questions which the clergyman put to him without hesitation or embarrassment. The Emperor's interest is warm, but alas his influence on the child's education whenever he enforces it is *very hurtful*! The Empress means most kindly. She was deeply moved and so was the Emperor. Charlotte, Henry and Vicky cried the whole time. The clergyman's three *long* addresses might have been better and shorter, still they did not spoil the ceremony! The communion followed directly after - dearest Bertie took it with us and Willy, no one else receiving it except three ladies and two gentlemen of our household. The Emperor and Empress remained as *spectators*.

As you like to hear little details I will add that I was in black with a plain white crepelissa bonnet, and Willy in uniform. Sometimes I feel too young for a mother of a son already confirmed, and then at times so old! Another thought grieves me - though one ought not to shrink from a sacrifice! Today is a sort of break up - in two days the boys leave us for school where they will stay three years - only returning for the holidays - then Willy will go into the army and Henry to a naval school! I feel giving them up like this very much!

Tomorrow is the parade at Berlin, and then the day after dear Bertie leaves in the early morning. Tomorrow Charlotte, Vicky and Waldie leave for Aussen for three or four weeks, so I am rather in low spirits, but it will do them good. Sandown has done worlds for them already and I trust this will brace them up for the winter.

May I beg *one* favour - you have conferred so many on us that I hardly like to ask, still I will venture - will you send some mark of your approbation to Willie's excellent tutor Dr Hintzpeter, to whom the boy owes everything. You know it has not always been very easy for me, nor have I always been in the Dr.'s good graces, but he has bravely done his duty by the boys and devoted himself *heart and soul* to their education. A mark of encouragement would, I am sure, give the greatest pleasure such as a few words written, and a print of yourself!

I hope you will not think me too *unbescheiden*.

I must end now, dearest Mama, being in great haste and already late; will you impart a little extract of this to the Geschwister who may like to know how this first Confirmation in the younger generation has gone off! 'With renewed tenderest thanks for all your kindness - for the splendid gifts and the dear and memorable words to Willy.

In the few years that had elapsed since the end of the Franco-Prussian War the resilience of the French temperament had been evident in the dispatch with which France set about healing her wounds. Before the end of 1873 the whole of the indemnity had been paid off, German troops had evacuated her territory, and France was on the road to recovery from her military humiliation. Bismarck watched the French rebound with suspicion, and rumours about the increase of the French army and the importation of horses into France on a huge scale led him to fear a surprise attack, and the German press was mobilised to call attention to this menace.

Queen Victoria now appealed in an autograph letter to the German Emperor William I to do all he could to prevent another war breaking out, and asked the Tsar Alexander II, who was in Berlin at the time, to help with his influence. Her timely interference was fully justified, for the Tsar's opposition had the effect of frustrating Bismarck's plans.

Meanwhile, the Chancellor had directed his energies to reducing the power of the Roman Catholic priesthood in Prussia and had come into collision with the Pope, who expostulated against the drastic measures that were being adopted to bring the Roman Catholic Church under state control. King William, on Bismarck's advice, replied with a stern rebuke to the Pope, and even France and Belgium were made to disavow all sympathy with the Catholic Bishops who had protested against Bismarck's persecution of their Prussian co-religionists.

The relations between the Crown Princess and Bismarck at this period were almost at their worst. Since he had become Chancellor his attitude in general had become much more intractable, much more ruthless. To his rivals, potential or active, he adopted the attitude that Rome adopted towards Carthage. Germany must go on, juggernaut-like, to its great destiny as arbiter of Europe, and if a few individuals were so inconsiderate as to stand in the way of the German machine, they must be crushed. The Crown Princess, however, was not one of the rabble who crowded the streets - she sat at the foot of the throne - and a slight turn in fortune's wheel would give her the right to be co-occupant of that throne. Bismarck could not crush her. But her liberal leanings, her democratic sympathies, her abhorrence of the mailed fist and the policy of blood and iron, created in him a resentment and bitter fury that echoed through the courts of Europe. The Crown Princess saw that Germany required 'rest, peace and quiet' and resented the hostility which Bismarck was stirring up within and without the state. Her attitude may be gauged from her letter to Queen Victoria of June 5, 1875 - the day following a long interview between the Crown Prince and Bismarck. Her letter runs:

Fritz saw the great man yesterday evening, who is going away into the country for some time! He assured him that he sees no cause anywhere for alarm on the political horizon, that he had never wished for war nor intended it, that it was all the fault of the Berlin press, etc. He said he deeply regretted England being so unfriendly towards us, and the violent articles in the *Times* against us. He could not imagine why England suddenly took up a position against us. He added that you had been much excited and worked upon against us, etc., and even named the Empress Eugénie, etc.!!! This seems so foolish to me! Certain it is that he did not intend (as you will read in the little German *aperçu*) to alarm the world to the extent he has done, and is now very much annoyed at the consequences. He also fancies that in England there is great anxiety about India, and that England must therefore try to make friends with Russia (*à nos dépens*). Bertie's journey to India is mentioned as a symptom! This seems to *me* very absurd - but that is what he thinks. Lord Derby's speech has also offended him, which I cannot understand. I feel sure all this irritation will blow over. But to us and to many quiet and reflecting Germans it is *very sad*, and appears *very* hard - to be made an object of universal distrust and suspicion, which we *naturally* are as long as Prince Bismarck remains the *sole* and *omnipotent* ruler of our destinies. His will alone is law here, and on his good or bad humour depend our chances of safety and peace. To the great majority of Germans and to most Prussians, this is a satisfactory state! He possesses a prestige unequalled by anything and is *all powerful*! To me this state is simply *intolerable* and seems *very dangerous*! Germany wants rest, peace and quiet - her commerce and the development of her inner resources are not progressing as they should! Our riches do not increase and we are in a most uncomfortable and crippled state which will so remain as long as the sword of war hangs over our heads.

The Great Man does *not quite* shut his eyes to this - and that makes me hopeful. But as long as he lives we cannot ever feel safe or comfortable - and who knows what it will be like when he has gone! He fancies the conflict with the Roman Catholic church will be quite over by next spring; and I know many who share this opinion. At present Prince Bismarck is bent on being as well as possible with France, England, Austria, Russia and Italy and all other states. He knows very little about foreign countries, and about England nothing at all, so he is often wrong in his surmises and believes any nonsense his favourites tell him. His ideas about the press are very mediaeval - in fact he is mediaeval altogether and the true theories of liberty and of modern government are Hebrew to him, though he adopts and admits a democratic idea or measure now and then when he thinks they will serve his purpose; and his power is unlimited.[3]

Queen Victoria replied on June 8:

I have just received your dear long letter with the enclosure which I have not had time to read properly, but I wish just to answer those principal points in your letter, though of course you know *how* absurd these ideas and notions of Bismarck's are.

First, as regards my being irritated against Germany, or *anybody else* working upon me! It was I ALONE who, on hearing from ALL sides from our Ministers abroad of the danger of war, told my Ministers that *everything* MUST be done to prevent it, that it was too intolerable that a war should be *got up* and brought about by mutual reports between Germany and France, that each intended to *attack* the *other*, that we must prevent this and join with other Powers in strong remonstrances and warnings as it was *not* to be *tolerated*. No one wishes more, as you know, than I do for England and Germany to go well together; but Bismarck is so overbearing, violent, grasping and unprincipled that *no one* can stand it, and *all* agreed that he was becoming like the first Napoleon whom Europe had to join in PUTTING down. This was the feeling, and we were determined to prevent another war. At the same time I said France must be told she must give *no* cause of anger or suspicion to Germany, and must *not* let them have any pretext to attack her. France will for many years be quite incapable of going to war and is terrified at the idea of it; I *know* this to be a fact. The Duc Decazes is a sensible prudent man, fully aware of this, and one who is doing all he can to act according to this advice.

I wrote at that moment a private letter to the Emperor Alexander urging him to *do* all he could in a pacific sense at Berlin, knowing the anxiety he had to prevent war, and how much he loved his uncle and he him.

As for anyone working upon me in the sense Bismarck thinks, it is too absurd. I am not worked upon by anyone; and though I am very intimate with the dear Empress,[4] her letters hardly ever contain any allusion to politics, certainly never anything which could be turned against her or me, and she sends her letters either by messenger or in indirect ways, and I mine the same.

You know *how* I dislike political letters and politics in *general*, and therefore that it is not *very likely* that I should write to her on them! and the Empress Eugénie I only see once or twice a year and she never writes to me!! and never speaks politics to me. So then you see what nonsense that is!....

But Bismarck is a terrible man, and he makes Germany greatly disliked; indeed *no one* will stand the overbearing insolent way in which he acts and treats other nations, Belgium for instance.

You know the Prussians are not popular unfortunately, and no one will tolerate any Power wishing to dictate to all Europe. This country, with the greatest wish to go hand in hand with Germany, cannot and WILL *not stand it*.[5]

Even in those days the Balkans never failed to provide a spark for any conflagration that was impending in Europe, and when the Christians in Bosnia and Herzegovina broke into rebellion against Turkey in 1875 both Russia and England urged the Porte to grant adequate reforms. But the confusion grew worse, and when, in July 1876, Montenegro and Servia declared war on their suzerain, Turkey, the Balkans were aflame from coast to coast. Mr Gladstone, who had always concentrated his rhetorical powers on the atrocities committed by the Turks, now emerged from his retirement and headed a violent agitation against Turkey that had sprung up in Great Britain. Regardless of British treaty obligations, he demanded that the traditional policy of supporting Turkey should be abandoned, and that the Turks should be expelled 'bag and baggage' from the Slav provinces, if not from Europe altogether.

The situation was complicated by the successes of the Turkish armies, which threatened the existence of Servia so far as to bring about the possibility of Russia's intervention. On September 16, 1876, the Crown Princess wrote to Queen Victoria:

.... What you say about the Oriental question seems very true to me! The difficulty surely is that there are *many different* questions which have to be settled which are then collectively called the 'Eastern Question', and thus confuse the public. Mr Gladstone seems to have proposed so enormous a change that I cannot imagine it could have another effect than that of unsettling everything and putting nothing safe or durable in its stead. It must be very difficult for your Government to steer clear of all these dangers; on the one side to promote peace, on the other to keep an *ever-watchful eye* on Russia, which is now more than ever necessary, and lastly to come to some radical cure and final settlement of a question which has so long been an open sore to Europe. The Russians *can not* be trusted! It is they who urged on the Serbs, they who fought, and they who, it seems to me, are responsible for giving the Turks an opportunity of displaying their barbarity towards the so-called Christians who, I fear, only differ from the Turks in name - though I am very sorry for them. Would it not be wise to settle beforehand how far we intend to allow the Russians to approach our frontier in India, and while we are on the best terms with them, declare *once and for all* that one stage further in that direction would be *war*? Would it not prevent their attempting to annoy us in those quarters? and would it not be a very harmless measure?

A month later (October 23, 1876) she wrote:

There seems to be a little pause in the state of Eastern affairs. What alarms me sometimes is the vague fear or feeling that Russia may get the better of everyone, and manage to get her own way in everything! Her own way in all things is not good for England's interests. Are people in England quite alive to all the danger?....Would Russia attack the Turks if the English fleet were in the Black Sea and Austria and Germany stood aside?....Is there no fear of making it impossible to stop the Russians later if they are allowed to fight and conquer the Turks just as they please? Do you not think that a great decision on the part of the English would stop their beginning a war, the end of which is impossible to foresee? Though one may heartily desire to see Turkish misrule cease in Europe and wish both the Christians and the Mussulmans a better Government than heretofore, one cannot wish to see Russia simply in possession of the country and Constantinople after a bloody war, and free to make difficulties for England whenever she chooses.

One cannot defend the Turkish cause as a cause, or wish blood and money to be spent in supporting a Government alike so corrupt and inhumane, and which offers no guarantee of being able or willing to carry out reform. If the matter could be settled for the good of the Turkish population and those of the Principalities against the Turkish and Russian Governments, surely it would be the right thing; but how?

Has Morier ever been heard on the subject? He was very strong on it in '53 and '54, when his excellent reports struck dear Papa so much!

Bismarck's policy of conciliating Russia had undergone no change since the Franco-German War, and Queen Victoria, writing to the Crown Princess on October 21, expressed the shrewd opinion that Russia's policy in the Near East, which aimed finally at the overlordship of the Balkans and the occupation of Constantinople, was due in no little measure to the support and tacit approval of Bismarck. On October 25, 1876, the Crown Princess, who appears to have misconceived Bismarck's policy, replied:

I have just received your dear letter of the 21st with many thanks. I have shewn it to Fritz and am to tell you from *him* what he thinks, as he supposes you will prefer having an English letter to a German one and I write our own dear honest language to you better than he can. You say Germany is with Russia. What does all this mean after Prince Bismarck's offers, messages and promises? We have no *precise* information as to how Germany is supporting Russia, but from what we can *gather* from different well-informed sources we have perceived the German Government gradually leaning towards Russia and not towards England and Austria! It is sorely *against* Prince Bismarck's will and liking, I am sure, as he does not care for a Russian alliance; but an alliance he must have, being in the disagreeable position of having *always* to be on his guard against France. This spring he would have given anything for a hearty response to his overtures! He wanted to know *what* British policy was going to be and he would have backed it up - he got no answer, or only what was *very vague* - so that he said to himself, as indeed all Germany does, 'Oh! there is no use in reckoning on England or going with her; she has no policy, will do nothing and will always hang back, so there is no help for it but to turn to Russia, though it be only a *pis-aller* for a better alliance, and one more congenial to us and more in harmony with our interests! Austria is too weak, too unsettled, in too shattered and precarious a state to be any use as an ally. The only strong Power willing to stand by Germany when she is in a pinch is Russia, therefore we must, whether we like it or no, keep on the best terms with her and serve her, so that she may serve us, as in 1870.' Surely Prince Bismarck is not to be blamed for this; it is only common prudence and good sense to make sure of having a strong friend when one is liable to be attacked any day! If Lord Derby had spoken out in the spring, and if the Berlin Memorandum had been accepted, matters would now stand differently. Bismarck wanted *England* alone to decide the Eastern Question, play the first part and have the *beau rôle* now taken by Russia, to my intense disgust. I think it is not too late now, to come to a *satisfactory* and close understanding with Prince Bismarck, as at any moment Russia may go even a step further than Germany can quietly agree to.

I hope that if no peace is come to satisfactorily now, and the Russians occupy Servia and Montenegro, that then England will persuade Austria to occupy Bosnia, and England herself send Lord Napier at the head of the troops to occupy Constantinople, and the British fleet into the Black Sea. I am certain this would be the very best thing. There would be no war. Turkey would carry out the reforms which were enforced; Germany could, I am sure, back up Austria and England, and Roumania, which is dying to be supported by England and Austria, would aid to counterbalance any overweight of Russia. At last some arrangement could be come to which would be satisfactory and lasting! Fritz is so very strong on the matter, that he wished me to say *all* I could in support of this view. He has not seen Prince Bismarck lately. Could not a special letter, message, or person, though none could be so good as Lord Odo Russell, be despatched to Prince Bismarck?

It is a signal proof of the innate generosity of the Crown Princess that in spite of her previous suspicion of Bismarck she was now inclined to credit him with the highest motives. She believed that they were 'simple and honest', and on October 28 again wrote to her mother:

Many thanks for your dear letters by messenger as to the Eastern question. I can only repeat what I said last time of Bismarck's calculations and motives, as far as we are acquainted with them and can judge of them. I think they are quite simple and honest. I do not think that one can exactly say that Germany is assisting Russia, as we know for certain (*i.e.* through what Field-Marshal Manteuffel says) that the Emperor Alexander would make war tomorrow if he could be certain that Germany would 'ihm den Sieg sichern'. This he will not obtain from Germany as far as we can learn.

We saw a very nice and intelligent officer yesterday (our Military Attaché at Vienna) who has been to Belgrade and in Servia lately. He gave us most interesting accounts. He says there was not an atom of enthusiasm for the war in Servia, that the people and their Sovereign were driven to it against their will, that the plan originated with Russia, and the party which pushed on the war, in Russia, was so strong that he did not think the Emperor Alexander could resist or follow his own inspirations, and thus the Russians could *not* stop the movement which has been so long fermenting and preparing.

It would appear that the chief objection the Austrians have to occupying Bosnia is that, as they have a profound distrust of Russia, they do not like acting in common with the Russians for fear of being afterwards asked by them to give up some Austrian territory to them, whereas in this respect they have nothing to fear from England or Germany.

Oh dear what a complicated question it is, and how many new ones it raises on all sides! One does not see the end of it all! This same gentleman says that the Turkish infantry is very good, very well disciplined, brave and enduring - excellent soldiers who do not even murmur at being kept five months without their pay. Their artillery and cavalry are said to be very bad indeed, and their fortresses not worth much.

The British Government now pressed for an armistice, and put forward a policy of local self-government for the Turkish provinces in the Balkans. There was much negotiation about the duration of the armistice, and finally Russia, by a sudden ultimatum to the Porte on October 31, enforced its limitation to two months, though it was subsequently extended to March 1877, when peace was signed between Servia and Turkey.

Meanwhile, the situation had undergone two important changes. The Sultan Murad had proved incompetent, if not insane; and a palace revolution had deposed him in favour of his brother Abdul Hamid. Moreover, in England, the force of the 'Bulgarian atrocities' agitation had largely spent itself, and the danger of bringing Russia into the field was being realised. Russia now suggested that she should occupy Bulgaria and that Austria should occupy Bosnia, while the British fleet should come up to Constantinople in order to bring further pressure on the Porte. The scheme was rejected by Britain, but it was agreed that a conference of the powers should be held at Constantinople to seek a settlement of the question. Lord Salisbury, no friend to Turkey, was appointed the representative of Great Britain. The acute differences between Great Britain and Russia were emphasised by Lord Beaconsfield's pronouncement at the Guildhall on Lord Mayor's Day, 1876, that, while England was essentially a non-aggressive power, yet her resources were such that 'in a righteous cause England will commence a fight that will not end until right is done'; while the Emperor Alexander stated at Moscow on the following day that, if he could not obtain the necessary guarantees from the Porte, he was determined to act independently.

The Crown Princess, on this occasion an enthusiastic supporter of Bismarck, was eager to give the German point of view to her mother, to whom she wrote on November 11:

> I really do not think it is fair to say 'the great man' has behaved very badly.

At least I see no proofs of it, or of an undue, or unfair, favouring of the Russians, and I see no obstacle, in him, to England's and Germany's going together, nor, I am sure, does he wish for one.

The duplicity of the Russians increases from day to day, and no one can be a match for them, because no one possesses the art of saying a thing with so much aplomb and doing the very reverse. General Werder, who arrived two or three days ago with an autograph letter to the Emperor from the Emperor of Russia, said, quite simply and openly, that the Court were now going for five days to Moscow, that it was a most unusual and demonstrative measure; but that Moscow was now the centre of the agitation for war, and that there would be *great* demonstrations there, to show the Emperor that he *must still* adopt more energetic measures. General Werder, who is Russian to the backbone, made no secret of it that the Russians had no intention of having peace, that they *could* not *stop* where the matter now was, and that the warlike preparations were going on with great energy and rapidity.

What can it all mean? Evidently they *now* say, and personages even *think*, that is to say, the Emperor does, that they do *not* want Constantinople, but perhaps in a few weeks they will say 'Circumstances have been stronger than we thought, and have forced us, etc. etc.'

I am certain they want to make tributary states of Roumania and Bulgaria, which will be as good as Russian, then they can cook up a fresh question whenever it suits them, as they raised this one, and wantonly pushed the Servians into a war. The *next* time, perhaps the Russians will find the opportunity for taking Constantinople better. The choice of Lord Salisbury seems to be an excellent one, as he is a clever, quick and energetic man....

On his way to the Conference, which began on December 12, 1876, Lord Salisbury visited in succession Paris, Berlin, Vienna and Rome. At Berlin he was welcomed by the Emperor, the Crown Prince and Princess and Bismarck. In course of an interview with Bismarck Lord Salisbury learnt that the German Chancellor intended Germany to be neutral between Turkey and Russia. 'Another argument in the same sense', wrote Lord Salisbury to Lord Derby on November 25, 1876, 'I draw from the assertions of the Crown Princess. She is shrewd, behind the scenes, and hates Bismarck like poison: and she said several times with much energy, 'You may be quite sure that it is true that Bismarck wishes for peace'. Both she and the Crown Prince expressed themselves anti-Russian.'[6] From these interviews Lord Salisbury came to the conclusion that while Bismarck wished for war between Russia and Turkey, which would diminish the fighting power of Russia, he dreaded a war between England and Russia because German neutrality would be difficult.

The Conference met on December 23. Simultaneously the new Sultan promulgated a liberal constitution. Relying on this gesture and on the divisions between the powers, he successfully resisted their demands. A month later, on January 20, 1877, this impotent Conference was dissolved.

Russia's action immediately after the abortive conference was puzzling. Whilst preparations were being made for war on Turkey, she professed to maintain the European concert, and in March, General Ignatieff, the Russian delegate at the Conference and Ambassador in Constantinople, began a series of visits to the capitals of Europe to explain the Tsar's readiness to continue his co-operation with the other powers. From Paris the Russian general and diplomatist proceeded on March 14 to London, where he was hospitably received during his week's stay. Whilst Ignatieff was in Paris, the Crown Princess, unaware of his plans, wrote to her mother (March 10):

I am rather sorry Ignatieff did not go to England; it would perhaps have taken his vanity down a little and it is always good and useful to hear what he has to say. If only all the Governments together would agree to what the Russians now want! It would not be a dangerous or compromising thing and would satisfy the Russians and in their eyes save their honour, so that they need not go to war - it would save so many poor innocent creatures on both sides from being killed, *and certainly* [be] the best thing for the Christians in Turkey. The war once begun, no one can tell where it would stop, and who might not be drawn into it. I am so convinced that the fate of the world is *now* in the hands of Europe and that the guarantee asked for by the Russians could so easily be given, as it would be more or less a matter of form, an *Ehrenrettung* for the Russians who have got into a scrape, and no one acts contrary to their own interests in this case by helping them out. It would also be the best thing for the Turks, as it would save them from a ruinous war, and make them set about their reforms in good earnest, which of course they never will do unless they see that they *must*. This is also the Emperor's opinion and that of a distinguished Frenchman whom we saw the other day.

England was now quite willing to act with the other powers in their endeavour to reform Turkey, provided that Russia and Turkey, between whom war seemed probable, agreed to disarm. If that guarantee were forthcoming, England was prepared to urge anew on the Porte a joint protocol of domestic reform.

Meanwhile, the British Ambassador at Constantinople had found himself in disagreement with the British Government, and Lord Beaconsfield's choice for a successor fell on Austen Henry Layard, who had every sympathy with the government's vigorous policy.

At this period Bismarck was ill, and deeply mortified by the decreasing support afforded in Germany to his domestic policy. Up to then the Chancellor's resignations had not been numerous, and the cry of 'Wolf' still created alarm. On April 7, 1877, Lord Odo Russell wrote to Lord Derby:

DEAR LORD DERBY - I have told you in a despatch all about the crisis, which is simply that Bismarck is *really nervous* and in want of rest - and the Emperor reluctant to part with him altogether. Besides physical ill-health, Bismarck is morally upset by the decreasing support his policy suffers from, on the part of the Emperor and of Parliament, which he attributes to the Empress's hostile influence on his Majesty, and to the Pope's influence on the Catholic Party in Parliament, instead of simply attributing it to his very disagreeable manner of dealing with his Sovereign and his supporters, and to the violence of his dealing with his opponents. 'What he wants is the power to turn out his colleagues from the new Cabinet at his pleasure - a power this Emperor will never concede to his Chancellor. At Court on Thursday last the Emperor told me he would give him as much leave as he pleased, but would not let him resign. The Empress told me Bismarck must be taught to obey his Sovereign. The *Crown Prince* told me he deplored the situation, but could not venture to interfere since his father never consulted him. The *Crown Princess* told me she could settle it all in five minutes if she had her own way. The *Grand Duchess of Baden* told me she could cry to see her father so worried at eighty. The *Grand Duke of Baden* told me he found Bismarck intractable. *Princess Bismarck* told me her husband's health was more precious to her than his post, and the Emperor could not expect him to commit suicide by working himself to death. Other well-informed people told me that Bismarck would probably accept leave and return to his office next winter as usual. No one will know much more about it until the German Parliament meets again, I imagine. The final signature of the Protocol has given great satisfaction to everyone at Berlin from the Emperor downwards. Peace is believed to be possible as far as Russia is concerned, but the attitude of Turkey does not yet inspire confidence, and the departure of the Turkish Envoy for Russia to settle about demobilisation is anxiously looked forward to. The Emperor told me on Thursday that he hoped Mr Layard would soon be at Constantinople, as England alone could persuade the Porte to be reasonable and peaceful. I always thought Layard the right man for Turkey and am delighted at his appointment. I hope he will advise the Porte to pay their debts out of the money saved by demobilisation and persuade them to mend their ways, moral and material.

The signature of the Protocol has placed us en règle with Europe and we can no longer be held responsible for the coming war, if the Turks will not accept the friendly counsels of the Powers, although I confess I do not see how any Government can stand the permanent moral interference of six well-meaning friends without going mad! Job found *three* too many.

All hopes of accommodation on such lines as these, however, were dispelled by Russia's declaration of war on Turkey on April 24, 1877. A week later (May 3) the Crown Princess wrote to Queen Victoria:

....I can well imagine how very anxious you must be about the *Oriental* question. That Russia has a purpose and makes the protection of the Christians her pretext is certain. Some very well-informed people, who know a great deal about the Russians, have told me that the Russians *wanted the Dardanelles* and nothing else - upon which I replied 'It is the very thing they will never get.'

Whether the Emperor Alexander has been *forced* into this war by a party, as Napoleon III was into the last war, I cannot quite make out. I am only so afraid that Gortchakoff, Ignatieff, and other candid statesmen of this kind, are urging King Victor Emanuel to try and get a part of the Italian Tyrol from the Austrians, and the Austrians would fight for that to the last.

I do trust this would not be; the bulk of the Italians would much dislike this, as they have so many interests in the East, commerce, etc....and their merchants are important people in Turkey, and in all the East and the Levant, where their tongue is spoken! If there be a means of preventing the Russians from taking what they *must not have*, by the combination of all the other Powers together, and without the other Powers fighting, it would be the best thing. If France, Germany, Austria, England and Italy were to say *together*: you *shall not have the Dardanelles*! But, of course, I do not know how that could be done.

There seems to be no other preventive to a great conflagration than a firm combination of the other Powers, and that is quite easy for England to obtain.

Poor Marie,[7] how *wretched* for her all that is! I feel so sorry for her; and poor Affie[8] must be very unhappy too.

During Lord Salisbury's visit to Berlin in November 1876 Bismarck had suggested to him that England should occupy Egypt, but the proposal met with short shrift from Disraeli, who 'didn't see how it would benefit us', especially 'if Russia possessed Constantinople'. Bismarck, still keen to embroil England with France, now made the same suggestion to the Crown Princess, who promptly wrote to her mother (July 11, 1877):

The Oriental war is much talked of everywhere; all *lovers* of England are so anxious that this opportunity should not pass by, of gaining a firm footing in Egypt! It would be such an essential, wise, useful thing. Perhaps you remember how pleased all who wish England well were, when the shares of the Suez Canal were bought, because everybody thought it was the first step towards what appears the *wisest* policy in the *real* interest of England, and her rule in India. No one can understand why the present Cabinet hesitate so long to take a step which seems so evident an advantage, and which England would often regret later, should the present opportunity be missed....I must say I devoutly hope and pray that Egypt may be ours, as I foresee so much good from such a change, both for the unhappy ill-used population who deserve better government, better masters and better treatment, and for the development of agriculture, of trade; commerce then will open up many a new source of riches, and the land is so fertile. I think England has a *great* mission there, and a *firm* future would be secured to Egypt itself. How I wish this could be done in your reign! Who can it harm?

I hear some people in England think that Prince Bismarck has an *arrière-pensee* when he expresses his conviction that England ought to take Egypt He has no other *arrière-pensee*, but that he considers a *strong* England of great use in Europe, and one can only rejoice that he thinks and feels so. As to a wish to annex Holland, and let France take Belgium, I assure you that it is nothing but a *myth*, and a very ridiculous one. Everybody who knows the state of things here thoroughly, knows that nobody of importance ever entertained so wild and crazy an idea....

Queen Victoria, before replying, sent the letter on to Lord Beaconsfield, who commented (July 16) that the letter 'might have been dictated by Prince Bismarck. If the Queen of England wishes to undertake the government of Egypt, Her Majesty does not require the suggestion, or permission, of Prince Bismarck. At this moment Lord Beaconsfield understands that there is an offer from the Porte to sell its suzerainty of Egypt, Crete and Cyprus to Your Majesty. It has not been formally placed before the Foreign Office, but of the fact there is no doubt.'

The following day Queen Victoria replied to the Crown Princess:

....I will now answer your letter of the 11th, relative to Egypt, the proposal about which *coming from you* has indeed surprised me very much, and seems to me Bismarck's view. Neither *Turkey* or *Egypt* have done *anything* to *offend us*. Why should we make a *wanton* aggression, such as the taking of Egypt would be? It is not our custom to *annex countries* (as it is in *some others*) unless we are obliged, and forced to do so, as in the case of the Transvaal Republic. Prince Bismarck would probably like us to seize Egypt, as it would be giving a great slap in the face of France, and be taking a mean advantage of her inability to protest. It would be a *most greedy* action. I own I *can't* for a moment understand *your* suggesting it. What we intend to do we shall do *without* Prince Bismarck's permission, for he has repeatedly mentioned it to Lord Odo Russell. Buying the Suez shares is quite another thing. That was *more or less a commercial transaction*. How can *we* protest against *Russia's* doings, if we do the same ourselves?

Four days later the Crown Princess replied:

....I am very sorry I was so misunderstood about Egypt. Of course I did not mean that a 'wanton aggression' on an unoffending friend should be made, nor an annexation; but that virtually England's influence should be paramount there (under one form or another) both for the benefit of England's interests and for the happiness of an oppressed and unfortunate people. This wish has been one which many many English, both military men and others, have entertained *before this war* was thought of, and I think that they certainly did not think so because it was a 'view of Bismarck's', any more than *I* did! How and when such a thing could come to pass, is, of course, quite another thing. That English influence should be stronger in the East than Russian seems to me desirable in more than one way, and any distrust of Prince Bismarck (should he share this opinion) would not make me change my view of the subject....

Events in the Balkans now again claimed all attention. The dramatic progress of the Russian troops towards Constantinople received in July an almost miraculous check by the heroic resistance at Plevna of a Turkish army under Osman Pasha. The world was astounded at this sudden recovering of 'the sick man of Europe', and Russia was now in a dilemma. To go forward was impossible whilst Osman Pasha stood barring the way, and honour would not permit a retreat On October 19, 1877, the Crown Prince wrote to Queen Victoria:

....It is with a feeling of horror that I notice the approach of winter - whilst the thinned armies of Russia and Turkey are still opposed to each other, looking forward with eagerness to a decisive battle.
This dreadful war, planned in a spirit of haughtiness and decided upon for a long time, impresses everyone with the importance of two failings, i.e. *to be in the wrong* and *to underrate the strength of one's adversary*.
The Russians would not forgive Germany the successes in great wars and the re-establishment of our national power; they looked out therefore for an opportunity to gain easy victories and to revive the belief in the 'nimbus' of Russian strength. This was - to my fullest belief - the chief motive which led to the sowing of so much mischief that at length the war, for which long preparations had been made, became inevitable in spite of the Emperor's own will. 'Slavs' and 'Christians' are in this question only the means to serve a totally different end and object.
And now the poor Czar, who is in truth a lover of peace, is placed in the midst of his troops, without commanding them; he must witness, for months, the most dreadful carnage without obtaining success; he is unable to conclude peace, because the honour of the Russian arms will not allow it.
It may be assumed that quite in the end the Russian superiority of numbers and resources generally will enable them to get the better of the Turks, but I am at a loss to think what sort of compensation they may find for their horrible losses.
Since I have been fated to witness three wars, I feel myself a real horror whenever I hear of fresh campaigns, and it requires truly an effort on my part to hear, and study, the details of the war reports. When we ourselves had to fight, our enemies were, to the greatest part, civilised people who - in spite of wild passions being let loose - were always anxious to observe the precepts of humanity, but here in the East, the contending forces are led by fanaticism and love of destruction combined with religious infatuation.

The Turks - it must be said - stand up for the defence of their own homes; and this fact enlists for their cause a good deal of sympathy which otherwise they would not deserve. Having looked forward, with perfect resignation, to the collapse of their domination in Europe - the Turks themselves are struck by their unforeseen successes, as well as the rest of the world.

Osman Pasha's brilliant resistance of five months came to an end on December 10, and with the fall of Plevna the Russians had a clear road to Constantinople with scarcely a barrier in the way. British feeling against Russia now rose to fever heat, and the 'Jingo' cry for war rang through the country.

Servia, elated at the Russian success, again declared war on Turkey (December 14, 1877), and it seemed as if Gladstone's fiery demand that the Turk should be swept 'bag and baggage' from Europe was like to be accomplished by Russia. On December 17 the Crown Princess wrote to Queen Victoria:

....What do you say to the Servians rising *now* that Turkey is in such distress! The very thought of the cruel way in which Turkey has been fallen upon, forced into war and half crushed, for no other purpose and no other reason than the Russian jealousy of German military success during the last war, and to gratify Russian ambition and vanity, makes one quite ill! It seems so unjust! I wonder whether poor Osman Pasha is taken great care of and has all his wants; he behaved so heroically. The Turkish government seem as unwise as possible and hamper the army in every way.

The prospect of Constantinople being occupied by the Russians was one that caused alarm on many sides, and to the demand that England should intervene the Crown Princess added her voice. On December 19 she wrote to Queen Victoria:

....As regards politics - *what can* one say! Oh! if I could only see you for one half-hour to say what fills my heart and soul! *If* England does *not* assert herself *powerfully* - she will do herself a harm which perhaps people living in happy England hardly can realise! Ridicule and contempt England can very well stand and laugh at the ignorance of the benighted people that know no better; but England cannot afford, or rather ought not, to lose her position in Europe. The feeling is so strong now abroad that England is quite powerless, has no army, a fleet that is no use, because naval battles are past, has no statesmen, and cares for nothing more than making money, because she is *too* weak to have a will, and if she *had* one, she has no power of enforcing it! *How* I do long for one good roar of the British Lion from the housetops and for the *thunder* of a British broadside! God knows I have seen *enough* of war, to know *how horrible*, how wicked, how shocking it is, and how worse than sinful those who *bring it on* without a reason, and plunge thousands into misery and despair! But are not *dignity*, *Honour*, and one's *reputation* things for which a nation, like an individual, must be ready to sacrifice *ease*, *wealth*, and even blood and life itself!

My experience of politics and things in general on the continent, and a *careful* observation of them, has *led* me to the firm conviction that *England* is *far* in advance of all other countries in the scale of civilisation and progress, the *only* one that understands Liberty and *possesses* Liberty, the *only one* that understands *true progress*, that can civilise and colonise far distant lands, that can develop commerce and consequently prosperity, the *only* really happy, the *only* really free, and, above all, the *only really humane* country, that will give *so* readily, *so* generously, and *so* wisely to alleviate suffering, be it ever so far off from sight! *Surely then* for the good of us *all*, for the *good* of the *world*, and *not* only of Europe, England should *assert herself*, make herself be listened to!

In this Turkish and Russian war, of course there are two opinions *everywhere*! One wishes Turkey to disappear and therefore will let Russia do the work of annihilation; the *other* thinks a nation, *however* corruptly and badly governed, *ought* not to be wiped out by one power, without the others being heard! To invite Turkey to reform her ways, and force her to do so, would have been better than making war in this shameful way. But *now* for Russia and Turkey to make a separate peace, without England being even consulted - I should think a downright insult and a fatal blow to English interests! If England suffer in her prestige, *vis-à-vis* of Europe, *what* does she in the eyes of Oriental nations!! and what will the 80 millions of fighting *men* - England's subjects in India - think, if the Mother country stirs not a finger now!!

There is a school in England that thinks she should not pretend to be a great Power, but subside into one of a *second* order and interfere no more in wars, etc. This may be true, but then England ought not to possess *half* the world, as she does *now*! and *woe* to the world when England abdicates the *leadership* and the pre-eminence as the champion of *Liberty* and progress!

England can surely have troops enough from India that can fight better than the Turks even, and are a match for any number of Russians!

If *Russia* be allowed, she will become the *bane* of the world! She must have *some* one Power to keep her in check, she does not represent Liberty, progress, enlightenment, humaneness and civilisation, but if she got *too* strong, and a man like the old Napoleon ever were born there, she would indeed be a terrible danger. That is the only power to fear, not poor Germany that *can never*, or *ought* never to grow out of her own confines.

We hear that the Servians have been pressed very hard by the Russians to assist, and that Charles of Roumania does not wish to carry on the war any farther!

I suppose British ships could prevent Batoum being taken. I hope, dearest Mama, you will burn this immediately and not be angry with me for saying all this so openly; I can say it to no one else!

I hear *everybody* here is *very Russian*; we did not find it so on the Rhine. I avoid the subject here with everyone! I cannot help feeling so much for Alfred and Marie, it must be so painful for them!

I *cannot* understand the *Times*; it seems to me to take a strange view of things. How much I think of you and what your feelings must be throughout!

Prince Bismarck has become a *myth*, he is neither seen nor heard of.

The fortunes of Turkey had now become a matter of party politics in England, and Lord Beaconsfield, whose sympathy with the Turks was no secret, decided that England should come to Turkey's rescue: a policy that by no means pleased the whole of the conservative party. The division of opinion in the Cabinet was notorious, and when it was decided to send the British fleet to protect Constantinople, the order was cancelled the following day. Lord Derby disliked the whole policy, and it was said that he and Lord Carnarvon intended to resign. On January 25 the Princess wrote to Queen Victoria:

....As to politics, was ever anything more distressing! The Russians - I have no fit word for them - are using every endeavour to make the world believe that the armistice has only been prevented by the English intervention, and that England is responsible for all the bloodshed. They are evidently pushing on to Constantinople as hard as they can. The leading article in the *Daily Telegraph* of the 21st I think exactly hit upon the truth! What terrible complications! We know for certain that the Greeks have had direct and peremptory orders to rise and fight those unhappy Turks - these wretched Servians the same.

My Father-in-law is more Russian than can be described, and though the generality of the officers of the Guard are so too, there are many in Germany and even here, who dislike and distrust the Russians with all their heart and grieve at the success of their false lying policy and their ambitions and violent schemes. The Empress and I often sit and lament. The accusations of the Russian press against England are really in language of a violence which is beyond all bounds....If *only* the British fleet went to Constantinople, and an armed force were sent to Gallipoli and Constantinople and ships to the Dardanelles, it would stop the Russians, who seem to reckon on England's doing nothing, and who grow more daring and insolent day by day! I am almost certain that in this way they would be obliged to desist from going to Constantinople, which they at present intend to do. We (England) have still time to get there before them, still in our hands to enforce a fair peace, but it is the very last hour, and in a few days it will be too late, and ever will England regret it when Russia has completely absorbed Turkey, and then at any moment can make an alliance with the French and seize upon the Suez Canal and stop our road to India!

I feel sure that if the fleet had only been sent to Constantinople directly after Plevna, the Russians would have stopped short and many a poor wretch be still alive, who has died a cruel death. If a force under Lord Napier were landed in

Constantinople in a short while we could settle the terms of peace much easier, and I think that not a drop of English blood would be shed, nor one precious life lost, because our presence and our firmness would bring the Russians to their senses.

We have just heard a report that Lord Derby and Lord Carnarvon are going to resign, but of course we do not know whether it is founded! Anything that means action and decided and prompt action is good at this present critical time, and anything that is the reverse I cannot but regret, as we shall be damaging our interests in a terrible way. Here I suppose they will do nothing whatever happens. I feel so much for you in this time of anxiety without dear Papa at your side to share the work and the responsibility and help you in every way! But you have clearly seen where the danger was from the beginning, and I hope will have the satisfaction of seeing the right course taken and Europe freed from the illusion that England will not and cannot stir a finger in any question, any more, but has abdicated her former position altogether.

Five days later the Princess, now, as she wrote, 'in a perpetually pugilistic frame of mind', heard of the counter order to the British fleet at Malta, and promptly wrote (January 30):

....As to politics I am in horror and despair! The counter order to the fleet has had such a *deplorable* effect - and all the enemies of England laugh and rub their hands and are delighted, whereas the friends of England are convinced that Russia is telling fresh lies and playing fresh tricks, that the armistice is all humbug, that they are pressing on to Constantinople and not telling England the truth about the terms of peace! I am afraid this is very likely. Ignatieff, of course, behaves as badly as possible, Prince Reuss, in his way, also. Count Schuvaloff appears to be anxious to conciliate and do his best. Lord Augustus Loftus seems to be alive to Russia's designs, and Count Münster uses every endeavour to make English policy appear in its very best light, at which the Emperor is very very angry (and many others) and think him 'zu Englisch' and anti-Russian. Austria's game I cannot penetrate. The Austrian press has been very rude and bitter against England and the Russian press knows no bounds in its abuse of England.

Here there is a story that the British fleet turned back from the Dardanelles, because one Turkish gun was fired, and the Turks will not have the English! Of course we know how false that is.

Poor Sadullah Bey said to me last night, at the Court Ball - when I could not help telling him how *sorry* I felt for him and his countrymen - 'Notre seul espoir est l'Angleterre'. The more I hear and the more time passes, the more I regret the English fleet and British troops not being at Constantinople and Gallipoli and the Dardanelles long before this! I feel sure it would have frightened the Russians into their senses, and made them amenable, if not to reason - yet to the demand of fairer terms of peace; whereas *now* - they will please themselves.

I do not like to reproach the peace party in England with want of patriotism and with great selfishness - and I am *certain* they have not an idea of the harm they are doing their country abroad. It is not only that they cause British policy to be called weak, vacillating and bungling, but it gives a totally wrong impression of England's power and England's regard for her own dignity and interests!

I hope I am not very wrong in saying all this, but as a devoted and loyal British heart, mine feels bitterly the taunts and sneers and the tone which people dare to assume about a country so vastly superior to all others in every sense, and which consequently ought to take the lead and *make itself listened to*.

I know you feel all this and must be troubled and anxious beyond measure.

I am perpetually in a pugilistic frame of mind, as I have to hear and read so much which is hardly bearable, because one cannot have the satisfaction of knocking somebody down.

Three weeks later, in February 1878, the Crown Princess wrote to Queen Victoria:

.... Things look very bad indeed in politics. Alas! the Russians think themselves a match for the English twice over, but not for England and an ally, and to get this ally seems to me so important! Whether the Austrians are to be relied on is so doubtful and difficult to know! Prince Bismarck has, however, no wish whatever to see everyone quarrelling as you say, and on the contrary he must not quarrel with Russia, but can only regret anything that strengthens her or weakens England's power. This is self-evident and needs no explanation, he would be a madman to wish anything else. I fancy he is of opinion that it is the worst moment for England to go to war, and that the time is past, when it would have been useful and likely to lead to a result, *i.e.* to stop Russia's proceedings, which Austria and England might have done some time ago!....

Meanwhile, on February 13, the order to the British fleet at Malta to proceed to Constantinople was repeated, and this time carried into effect, but five days later it was ordered to leave Constantinople for a station thirty-five miles south of the city. The Treaty of San Stefano was signed on March 3, 1878, after an armistice had been concluded, and by its articles Servia was declared independent and Bulgaria created an autonomous principality under the sphere of Russian influence.

Three weeks later Lord Derby, who had always been out of sympathy with the Government policy, resigned, and was succeeded by Lord Salisbury. British policy, no longer directed by a divided Cabinet, was galvanised into strong action, and Lord Salisbury not only demanded in a masterly circular that the Treaty of San Stefano should be submitted to the judgment of Europe, but showed he was in earnest by announcing that 7000 Indian troops were under orders for Malta. Although naturally Russia strongly objected, the other European powers supported Lord Salisbury's proposal and after much negotiation a conference was agreed to. The news of Lord Derby's resignation and the terms of Lord Salisbury's circular to the powers elated the Crown Princess, and to her mother she wrote on April 5:

> Indeed since Lord Derby's resignation and Lord Salisbury's Circular, one can hold up one's head again, and no longer feel oppressed by the weight of anxiety and misgiving about what may be coming! Now we know that England has a policy, and that it is a clear and right one, and this has already changed the aspect of the whole question.
>
> Except amongst the sworn friends of Russia, I think there is universal approval of England's step and England's views, and *everywhere* a feeling of relief that at last England should have come forward and spoken up. In Austria they are delighted, and what the unfortunate Turks and other principalities must feel, I can well imagine! What a blessing for them all to feel that their fates are not to be settled by Russia *alone*, whose treacherous behaviour to them all has opened their eyes as to the nature of Russia's aims. Neither England nor Austria can be bent on war; but they must not shrink from it, if it be forced upon them.
>
> I cannot help thinking that the Russians will draw back and give way, and that the whole may yet be satisfactorily settled without a war.
>
> I cannot help congratulating you on the turn affairs have taken. How much easier you must feel now. Poor Lord Derby seems to have been treated with so much kindness and consideration, that one cannot pity him! Oh, how *much* he has to answer for, and how vast is the harm his indecision did!....
>
> I wish you could see the articles of the *Augsburger Allgemeine Zeitung* the *Kölnische Zeitung* and the *Journal des Débats* just now, as it is interesting to see how *good* and beneficial an effect Lord Salisbury's Circular has had....

In May the Powers accepted Bismarck's offer to act as 'honest broker', and preparations were made to summon the Congress of Berlin.

During the preliminary discussions that took place before the Congress met, the main points were agreed to. Russia consented to divide the big Bulgaria of the San Stefano Treaty into two provinces, and Austria gave 1878 her consent on the condition she should be allowed to occupy Bosnia and Herzegovina. The way was now clear for Bismarck to issue the formal invitations for the Congress of Berlin, and on Sunday, June 2, 1878, the German Ambassador in London, Count Münster, handed to the Foreign Secretary, Lord Salisbury, at the latter's house at Hatfield, Prince Bismarck's official invitation to Great Britain to take part in the Berlin Congress on June 13. The chief guests under the Foreign Secretary's roof at that moment happened to be the Crown Prince and Princess of Germany, who had come over from Marlborough House, where they were returning the visit which the Prince and Princess of Wales had paid them at Potsdam earlier in the year. The tranquil feeling which the invitation evoked was, however, rudely shattered within a few hours by the arrival of news of the attempted assassination of the Crown Prince's father, Emperor William I. The Crown Prince and Princess at once left for Germany. The Emperor proved to be severely, though not fatally, wounded, and the Crown Prince on reaching Berlin was invested with the Regency of the German Empire. It was while the Crown Prince exercised this responsibility that the Congress of Berlin performed its work. The Crown Prince's liberal aspirations had little opportunity of practical exercise during his short term of power, and the potent will of Prince Bismarck, who resolutely clung to office, remained in the ascendant.

By July 13 the Congress of Berlin had concluded its labours. Heavy work had fallen on the shoulders of Lord Beaconsfield, England's chief envoy, who had many opportunities of meeting the Crown Princess. On the day 1878 on which the Congress dissolved, the Crown Princess wrote to Queen Victoria:

The Congress has ended its labours! I am only so afraid that the hurry to get over the work has been *too* great, and that the durability may suffer; it has been driven on with such desperate haste by Prince Bismarck, and that is not good! These matters are too serious to stand a hasty treatment. Nobody can rejoice more heartily and sincerely than I do at the Treaty with Turkey, and the occupation of the Isle of Cyprus! Amongst all friends of England this has produced the very *best* impression, and many of the German newspapers have praised the measure very much.

I think it will be excellent, and trust the once so flourishing island will become so again, and that it may be a means of making the poor Turks govern better and get their unhappy devastated country into better order, and be a wholesome check to the Russians who will feel that they are *watched*, and cannot '*get up*' another war - as they have done this.

I am sure you too must feel happy and relieved that it has all ended so; if England is known to be ever vigilant and ever on the alert, and determined NOT to be trifled with, and has all her means ready at hand, her forces, etc., the peace of Europe will *not*, and *cannot* be disturbed again so soon! It has been a capital thing that the Foreign Ministers of different nations have made each other's acquaintance, it will make written communication a very different thing in future! Prince Bismarck is much struck and pleased with Lord Beaconsfield.

Just before the Congress dissolved, Lord Beaconsfield wrote and told the Prince of Wales of the secret arrangement by which Britain undertook the defence of the remaining Asiatic dominions of the Porte and was allowed to occupy Cyprus, while the Sultan promised to give effect to the necessary reforms for the protection of Christians. 'England', the Prime Minister wrote, 'enters into a defensive alliance with Turkey as respects all her Asiatic dominions, and with the consent of the Sultan we occupy the island of Cyprus. It is the key of Asia, and is near to Egypt. Malta is too far for a military base for 1878 these purposes.'[9]

The Anglo-Turkish Convention - details of which were published two days after Lord Beaconsfield sent the Prince of Wales the news of it - although it disconcerted the friends of France, was warmly welcomed by the Crown Princess, who wrote to her mother on July 16:

> I am all impatience to hear from you after the event of the Turko-English Convention and the occupation of Cyprus. I think it such a great event, and as I already wrote, one which must give pleasure to all friends of England I Lord Beaconsfield has indeed won laurels, made himself a name, and before all restored to his country the prestige of power and dignity it had so lost on the continent, thanks to Lord Derby and Mr Gladstone. You must feel *intense gratification* after all the anxiety and worry you went through! I was very sorry to take leave of Lord Beaconsfield, who certainly has a great charm when one sees more of him, and of Lord Salisbury, who is such a truly amiable man! The others, alas, - I saw little or nothing of! Schuvaloff is much pleased at the result of the Congress. Prince Gortschakoff *not at all*. The Roumanians went away deeply disappointed and dejected - but I do not see how anything else could have been obtained for them after they had once placed their fate in Russia's hands! I was very glad to see Sir Henry Elliot, whom I had not seen since 1857.
>
> The Emperor looks very well, but he is still weak and the doctors will not fix a day for letting him go out - or move here, etc....They leave it to him, and I think it such a pity, for he is not the least inclined to leave Berlin, and his strength will never increase here.
>
> I think the Empress looking well; but I hope she will be able to return to Baden and her cure soon![10]

Within a few months the Emperor was well enough to resume the duties of his office, and on December 5, 1878, the Crown Prince relinquished the Regency. Nine years later he was to take up the full burden of sovereignty on the death of his veteran father, but it was during these short six months alone that the Crown Prince really tasted the joys of ruling.

### NOTES

1 In 1879 the Austro-German Alliance was formed, which was joined in 1882 by Italy, thus creating the Triple Alliance.
2 Sir Sidney Lee, *King Edward VII*, vol. i. p. 430.
3 Partly published in Buckle and Monypenny's *Life of Disraeli*, vol. v. pp. 424-425.

4 The German Empress Augusta.
5 Cited in the *Quarterly Review*, July 1919, in article entitled 'Queen Victoria and France', by Sir S. Lee.
6 *Life of Robert, Marquis of Salisbury*, by Lady Gwendolen Cecil, vol. ii. p. 99.
7 The Duchess of Edinburgh.
8 The Duke of Edinburgh.
9 Sir Sidney Lee, *King Edward VII*. vol. i. p. 437.
10 Partly published in Buckle and Monypenny's *Life of Disraeli*, vol. vi. pp. 344-5.

# VI: The Crown Princess and her Family

HOWEVER pressing affairs of state may be, however dramatic and enthralling the events through which a nation is passing, the main interests of a wife and mother are the affairs of her family, and to this rule the Crown Princess was no exception. Not only towards her husband and children did she show every sign of loving affection, but towards her brothers and sisters and their children she displayed an equal depth of feeling. Her letters are full of tender references to this or that niece or nephew, and nothing interested her so much as the love affair or wedding of any one of her numerous relatives. It was thus with peculiar happiness that she welcomed to Berlin, in the February of 1878, her brothers, the Prince of Wales and the Duke of Connaught, on the occasion of a double marriage in the German royal family. The first was that of the second daughter of the Emperor's nephew, Prince Frederick Charles of Prussia, to Frederick Augustus, the heir to the Grand Duke of Oldenburg. But even more interesting to the Crown Princess and her brothers and sisters was the marriage of the Princess's eldest daughter, the Princess Charlotte of Prussia, to the hereditary Prince Bernhard of Saxe-Meiningen. The double wedding was celebrated on February 18, 1878, with an exhausting ceremonial that lasted more than six hours.

The Emperor [wrote the Prince of Wales to Queen Victoria on February 20] is looking wonderfully well, and in a few days he will be eighty-two. Vicky and Fritz are most blooming. It is impossible to find two nicer boys than William and Henry, and they are continually with us, for Fritz and Vicky have so much to do. Dear little Charlotte looked charming at the wedding, like a fresh little rose.[1]

That same day the Crown Princess wrote to Queen Victoria:

I begin my letter this morning to finish it tomorrow morning, if I possibly can! I have just received your very dear letter, for which so many thanks, as well as the beautiful locket, which will be so very precious to me, especially as a sign of your being here with us in thought today. I feel very low, as you can imagine, and try not to think of it all! Charlotte is quite unconcerned, and very happy, especially delighted to see Bertie and Arthur. How lovely the locket is, and the Angel on it, and how nice to have their two photos inside! This kind and charming gift gives me so much pleasure! You asked yesterday by telegraph whether the young people go to Potsdam tonight. It is impossible and would be too fatiguing for them, as the wedding is so late in the evening, and the Fêtes begin tomorrow and continue till Saturday, so they will live at the Schloss in an apartment prepared for them, which is very handsome, and which I have tried to make as comfortable as possible! Yesterday there were a great many arrivals, and there was also the signing of the wedding contract. The other *Brautpaar* are not looking at all well, Elizabeth[2] is so thin and pale and feels leaving her home very much, though it was a wretchedly uncomfortable one. Still the idea of going off to Oldenburg seems to make her very sad. I believe it is a very ugly and very dull place, and neither the Grand Duke nor the Grand Duchess is very attractive.

To this letter the Princess added a long postscript the next morning, which ran:

I have got up, beloved Mama, to finish my letter to you, as last night at 12 when I reached my room I felt so upset and miserable that I should only have written nonsense. How your dear telegrams touched me I cannot say! I knew your thoughts would be with us....At 4 in the afternoon the dressing began, and as I dressed Charlotte while I was dressing myself it was rather a long and rambling business. She really looked very pretty - in the silver moiré train, the lace, the orange and myrtle and the veil (dangerous innovations for here) - but they were all very well taken by the Emperor and Empress! For the *mariage civil* which took place in our drawing room there were heaps of people, such as did not wish to go to the Schloss. Herr von Schleinitz's address to the young couple was very fine, touching and impressive! After this the signing was done and they were married. Charlotte said she felt quite light and happy now it was over and would not mind the rest of the ceremonies at the Schloss! I then led her downstairs - and drove off with her - in a carriage with eight horses and all the grooms carrying torches! At the Schloss all the ceremonies went off according to the programme you have seen! It was very very long, very hot, very tiring, and almost too serious, solemn and heavy for a wedding, but so it always is here. After the *Fackeltanz*[3] I took her to her room after the Crown had been taken off, I helped her to undress and get ready for going to bed, and with an aching heart left her, no more mine now, to care for and watch and take care of, but another's, and that is a hard wrench for a mother. With pangs of pain we bring them into this world, with bitter pain we resign them to others for life, to independence - and to shift for themselves. We bore the one for their sakes and with pleasure and so must we the other.

When I came back last night and looked into her little empty room - and empty bed - where every night I have kissed her before lying down myself - I felt very miserable. However it must be so - and she looks very happy and shed not a tear yesterday, and Bernhard dotes upon her....I am sure she is thankful the wedding ceremony is over! It all went off very well we may say, and that is a thing to be thankful for. How we missed you and how I thought of adored Papa and Grandmama and Aunt Feodor and all beloved ones whose race is won and who rest in peace and who will be missing to the end of our days! 'What a happiness that Bertie and Arthur were here! and how glad I am that Leopold of Belgium and Marie, Uncle Ernest and Philippe Coburg were there....

I have thought more of you than ever in my life and more than of anyone else! Mothers do not lose their daughters if all love their mothers as much as I do you.

Three days later (February 22) the Crown Princess wrote to Queen Victoria:

I am really half dead with fatigue and feel most wretched, but am beyond measure distressed at not having written to you every day, as I ought to have done, but which was perfectly impossible!

The first few days were terrible, when I saw Charlotte come in with Bernhard, and no longer stand by me, but take her place by the side of all the married Princesses and leave again with him - without hardly being able to say Good-night to me! Then going home from parties without her, and not knowing what she is about...is a dreadful thing to get accustomed to, but now that I see her so happy and merry and gay, and looking blooming and enjoying herself, that feeling is beginning to wear off with me. I think it is inhuman to give all these fêtes for the poor young people - and the exhausted and agitated Mamas. But, however, this evening is the last, thank God. Charlotte has been looking very pretty in all her new things, and Bernhard seems so happy. The Duke of Meiningen has quite softened and has become very amiable, and delighted with Charlotte who is quite taken with his goodness, while Bernhard's kind heart has melted towards his Papa - which I am very glad of! Charlotte, though looking very well and looking blooming, has fainted three times from the heat of the rooms, to which she has never been accustomed. Tomorrow our dear young people move off to Potsdam and into their sweet little house in which I trust they will be very happy! It seems so funny to me when people talk of my *Frau Tochter*. To think of my becoming so venerable!

The Emperor and Empress are looking particularly well and are most kind and sympathising! All the guests are in the highest good humour, and I never saw an assembly of Princes and Princesses and relations go off so well and harmoniously. The public too are in the best of humour and most civil to Bertie and to Leopold and Marie! Bertie and Arthur have the greatest 'success' and are thought so charming and amiable by everyone. Your not being here is universally regretted! I made Count Seckendorff write about the wedding and told him also to say that Bertie's visit to Prince Bismarck, who is unable to go out or attend the fêtes, has given great pleasure here.

The genial atmosphere created by these two marriages led to a further marriage, for the sister of one of the brides. Princess Louise Margaret, the third daughter of Prince Frederick Charles of Prussia, now became engaged to the Duke of Connaught. But before the marriage could take place the whole court was plunged into mourning by a series of tragic happenings at Darmstadt, where the family of Princess Alice, the Crown Princess's favourite sister, were stricken with diphtheria. On November 16, 1878, the youngest child died from the disease that during the previous fortnight had prostrated nearly every member of the grand-ducal family. The mother, Princess Alice, had the dreadful task of breaking this sad piece of news to her only surviving son, and his distress was such that the mother, disregarding all the physicians' injunctions not to embrace her children, clasped him in her arms, and thus received the kiss of death. In spite of all medical efforts, Princess Alice died on December 14, 1878, the same day on which the Prince Consort had died seventeen years earlier. Between Princess Alice and the Crown Princess there had always been sympathy and devotion, which increased in later years owing to the fact that both of them, having married German princes, were resident in Germany. The blow was most distressing for the Crown Princess, who wrote to Queen Victoria on December 15, 1878:

.....I am in an agony of mind I cannot describe - my thoughts fly backwards and forwards from you to poor unhappy Louis in his loneliness and bereavement, then to those poor darling children whose fates are more deeply affected than any by the perfect destruction that has come over their happy home!
Sweet darling Alice - is she really gone? So good, and dear - so much admired. I cannot realise it, it is too awful, too cruel, too terrible. - One can only hold fast to the belief that resignation and gratitude are the never dying principles with which we must accept what life brings, the blessings and the trials, the grief and the happiness, the sunshine and the darkness which are inseparable....Oh that God would give wings to our souls to soar into the regions of calmness and peace above, where the grace of charity shines and the agonising details of ruin and destruction disappear from our frail eyes. - Dead, dear darling! Blessed peace is hers and all suffering is over: but you, dear Mama, I know and feel what you are going through and I suffer for you from the inmost depths of my heart. - I feel as if sorrow had made me quite old in two days. Our darling! I can hardly bear to write her dear name: she was my particular sister, the nearest in age, the only one living in the same country with me! We had so many interests in common and all our children were so near of an age! A peculiar tenderness for her was always in my heart, which perhaps she herself did not know or feel, and which no little difference or misunderstanding (of which, thank God, there were but few) ever lessened. We had been through so much together, had been through the same trials, till those came that lately overwhelmed her! I had always thought her fate fraught with many a difficulty, in spite of her dear and sweet husband, and of her charming home. These last

years have been particularly trying for all who belong to Germany, and both she and I felt greatly, each in a different way. How anxious I have felt about her dear health I cannot tell you. It often tormented me to see her so frail, so white, and her nerves so unstrung, though it only added additional charm and grace to her dear person and seemed to envelop her with something sad and touching that always drew me to her all the more, and made me feel a wish to help her and take care of her, poor dear!...Her last letter to me, a little pencil note, which, alas, I did not keep, was a cry of anguish for her sweet little flower, so rudely torn from its stem. I never heard from her again....

But now those unfortunate children! I have no words to describe what I feel for them. A life without a mother's love is no life....How can a man, even the kindest and best as dear Louis is, know all that is required for the bringing up of girls? But you, dear Mama, will always take an interest in them and give them your support and advice and all that is in my power I shall do for them!....

Three months later, on March 13, 1879, the Duke of Connaught, the Crown Princess's second brother, was married to Princess Louise Margaret, but even this happy event had barely occurred when a further tragedy happened in the Crown Princess's own family. Of all her children, the one whose health gave her the most anxiety, and who in turn perhaps received the greatest amount of maternal love, was her fourth son, the little Prince Waldemar. In spite of all her devotion, the little ten-year-old Prince sickened and died in the closing days of March. It was on the morning of March 27 that Queen Victoria, then in Paris on her way to Lake Maggiore, received a telegram from her daughter which ran: 'Have just taken a last look at the beloved child. He expired at half-past three this morning from paralysis of the heart. Your brokenhearted daughter, Victoria.'

The blow was a severe one, but good news followed ill, for two months later there came the glad tidings that the Crown Princess's eldest daughter, Charlotte, had been safely delivered of a baby girl. Thus, at the age of thirty-nine, the Crown Princess was a grandmother - an event which closely approximated to Queen Victoria's own history, for she had become a grandmother at the age of thirty-eight.

To all her surviving children the Crown Princess displayed to the full that tender maternal consideration which was one of her most marked characteristics, but with regard to her attitude towards her eldest son, Prince William, many bitter, ill-informed and even malicious attacks have been made upon her. One recent biographer, for instance,[4] speaks of 'the cold-heartedness of a despotic mother', who 'could not forgive the imperfection of her eldest child' and 'cherished in her heart a secret grudge against her misshapen son'. Such words as those have no foundation in fact and would seem attributable to a presumption derived from the divergencies which manifested themselves in later years. It is perhaps well to recall an earlier letter of the Crown Princess's of January 28, 1871,[5] in which she states, 'I am happy to say that between him and me there is a bond of love and confidence that I feel nothing can destroy'. In the years that followed none was more eager to fight battles on her son's behalf than the Princess, and one such incident may be mentioned. On January 27, 1877, Prince William came of age on his eighteenth birthday. Queen Victoria, his grandmother, offered the young Prince the Grand Commandership of the Bath. Prince William, however, held that he was worthy of a higher distinction, and his mother promptly wrote to Queen Victoria pointing out that the Emperors of Russia and of Austria, and the King of Italy had already sent the Prince the highest orders at their disposal, and that the German Emperor himself had in earlier years bestowed not only on the Prince of Wales, but also on his brothers Alfred and Arthur, the highest order in his power to give - the decoration of the Black Eagle. The Order of the Garter, she urged, was the only one that would suffice. 'Willy', she added, 'would be satisfied with the Bath, but the nation would not.' Queen Victoria yielded to the Crown Princess's pleading on her son's behalf, and on his eighteenth birthday the future Emperor William II received the Order of the Garter.

Most particularly was the Crown Princess anxious that her eldest son should receive the education and fall under the influences which would fit him to lead his country forward in the paths of peace and progress as a liberal broad-minded monarch. When the young Prince was but a schoolboy she had been eager to break through the stiff traditional educational regime of the Prussian court and, after much debate, had won her point, with the result that her two eldest sons were sent from their military school at Wilhelmshöhe to the Lyceum at Cassel, where they were treated as civilians. The intoxicating events of three brilliant wars exercised, however, an influence which so liberal a curriculum was ineffectual to counteract, and there developed early in Prince William indications of a wish for independence that marked the beginning of the differences of opinion between mother and son. Whilst the Prince was in his teens he naturally had to defer to the opinions of his parents, but when, in 1880, at twenty-one years of age, he returned to his parental home from the Potsdam garrison where he had discharged the duties of a first lieutenant in the regiment of guards, it became evident that the military clique which surrounded him had exercised influences which caused grave apprehensions in the minds of his parents. In his character there was indeed much mingling of good and ill. From his mother he had inherited an intellectual quickness and ability which for a century had been rare among the Hohenzollerns, but with it was combined a sensibility which made him particularly susceptible to flattery and resentful of anything that tended to detract from his own importance. As a result, mother and son were now frequently estranged. The story is by no means an unusual one: in fact it happens every day where mother and son, both having similar personalities, hold diametrically opposed views on life. Up to the time that Prince William left home, all the Princess's letters show that she was devoted to him and thought of nothing but his happiness and his future success. Possibly the mistake she made was to try and make him as like his father as possible, and to this mould the future Emperor, conscious of powers in other directions, could not be forced or persuaded to conform. In his outlook on the world he saw before him two obstacles to complete power. The first was his octogenarian grandfather, the Emperor William I, who, however, could not be expected to live much longer; the second was his father, the Crown Prince, now fifty years of age, whom he regarded as a powerless heir-apparent with little control over his time or finances, and checked continually by the Emperor and the powerful Bismarck. To the young Prince, the liberal opinions of his father were anathema, and the evident English sympathies of his mother he deemed unpatriotic. Both parents, although they saw with dismay these new tendencies, regarded them with a parental love that overlooked their worst manifestations, and in all the letters of the Crown Princess to Queen Victoria at this period it is noteworthy that he is mentioned proudly, fondly and indulgently.[6]

Early in 1880 Prince William became secretly engaged to Princess Augusta Victoria of Schleswig-Holstein-Sonderburg-Augustenburg, daughter of that Duke Frederick who sixteen years previously had laid claim to the Duchy of Holstein, and niece of Prince Christian who had married the Crown Princess's sister Helena.

Four days after the secret engagement, the Crown Princess, who had a fear that the betrothal might not meet with the approval of the Berlin court party, owing to the bride not being one of the inner circle, wrote to Queen Victoria (February 18):

Willy has written most touching letters (in his own funny style) about his great happiness. He engaged himself to dear Victoria on the 14th, and had to leave again on the next day so as not to attract attention, as it is all yet to be kept a secret. 'We received the letters yesterday and the news caused us great emotion as you can imagine, but we also feel very thankful and much relieved. You will perhaps see our dear future daughter-in-law before we see her ourselves, as there is a chance of her going to England and we should hardly see her before June.

Fritz wishes me to say that he recommends her to your kindness. As your dear sister's grand-daughter and your grandson's bride, we feel sure you will have a little place in your heart for her.

What a very horrid thing has happened at St. Petersburg![7] It makes one's blood run cold, to think of what might have been, and of the danger that may still surround the unfortunate Emperor. How can human beings be so cruel! and yet I am afraid the deeds committed by the authorities, police, etc., on Russian subjects have been no less cruel, and Siberia with all its horrors, the awful treatment of the Poles, are terrible things which cry for vengeance. But really to have the last Act of the Prophets in one's dining room in good earnest is too dreadful. Guy Fawkes and Gunpowder Treason one had thought were things of the past. Luckily these horrid attempts hardly ever succeed, but it is all a chance; they might fail nine times and succeed on the tenth. The poor delicate Empress, what a shock to her nerves! And poor Marie, what a fright for her and for them all. This Emperor is such a kind and humane man that one feels doubly for him. This must make a dreadful sensation everywhere.

To Queen Victoria's sympathetic answer, the Crown Princess replied on February 21:

What, indeed, has not happened! Fritz makes me laugh with his dismal forebodings, but he is convinced that some day or other the Russian attempt will be copied at Berlin, and that these horrors only excite imitation.

Of course, the science of destruction has been carried to a great perfection by dynamite, nitro-glycerine, torpedo, Thomas watches, etc. These are horrible engines of death which have been thought charmingly useful in time of war, but when accessible to wicked people, or even to excited maniacs, may deal most frightful damage - still I am inclined to think that in spite of all this human life has become more sacred than it was. Formerly Emperors of Russia who were in anyone's way were throttled, poisoned or assassinated in one fashion or another. 'Le despotisme tempéré par l'assassination', as Voltaire called the Russian form of Government, whereas now assassins are no longer to be found among the officers of the Imperial Guard and nobility, etc., but are confined to a band of reckless, lawless men, who are for the moment dreadfully dangerous. How far spread this conspiracy is, is of course most difficult to guess. What connection with the 'Internationale and Communists' of other countries the Nihilists have, is not known, but in Russia there is so little honesty, truth and justice, that it will be very difficult to find out the real criminals, and any amount of innocent people may be suspected and even punished. It is a horrible thought. How horrified poor Marie must have been, and Affie too. It is too shocking an event....

About Willy I will only add that I do think it will be a very unpopular match at Berlin, because the poor Holsteins are *mal vu*, and there is a widespread, though very false, idea that they are not *ebenbürtig*. But I am sure this prejudice will wear off very quickly.

Early in March Prince William's fiancée arrived in England on a visit to Queen Victoria. The Queen was at once attracted to her prospective granddaughter-in-law (who became 'Dona' to the family circle), and wrote cordially of her to the Crown Princess. On March 26 the Crown Princess replied:

I am so delighted that you think Victoria so gentle and amiable and sweet. She always struck me as such. I am sure she must win all hearts. Her smile and her manners and expression must disarm even the bristly, thorny people of Berlin with their sharp tongues, their cutting sarcasms about everybody and everything. The announcement has been much better taken than I had dared to hope. There are of course many who are dissatisfied, but they are in society and court circles; in the public at large the news has been received with pleasure, as is proved to me by the many letters I receive. If I have been remiss in writing lately, it is because I have so much to do in the way of writing an account of the *Verlobung*.

My wishes are exactly the same as yours about Willy. I much wish he should see a little of the world before marrying, though all the time he was here it was the same as in Belgium and in Holland and in London - he does not care to look at anything, took no interest whatever in works of art, did not in the least admire beautiful scenery and would not look at a Guide Book, or any other book which would give him information about the places to be seen. In this way you will admit that travelling is not of much use, it is decidedly not his turn.

I also much wish that the marriage should take place in the course of next year. I think it is a great blessing that Victoria is 22, and not 17, for in a place so difficult to get on in that is a great advantage.

On the following day she wrote:

Congratulations on William's engagement come to me now on all sides - it is often a sore trial to speak of joy, happiness and festivities and receive congratulations, when one has an aching void at heart. But such is life: while some are looking eagerly forward, others feel that they must ever be casting longing looks backwards to the time that was, and there is a melancholy jealous feeling of consolation in the feeling that we remember, when all 1880 others forget, the beloved ones that once brightened our home with their dear presence. But I am very, very grateful for Willie's happiness and sure dear Victoria will be a blessing to everyone because she is so gentle and good.

Nor did the elation show any signs of diminution during succeeding months.

Willy [wrote the Crown Princess on May 24] looks so happy and I must say I think people have come round wonderfully. Everyone seems disposed to like Dona, and what feeling there was against the marriage has almost disappeared. I am very, very thankful for this, for their dear sakes, and for the future.

The Crown Princess was now to learn of a love-story which, to one of her upbringing and rigid sense of right and wrong, must have appeared particularly lacking in the pleasing features usually associated with a wedding. Into her world of decorum, where the diversities of fortune and happiness had shown themselves in familiar guise, a tragedy of passion and tears obtruded itself.

On June 3, 1880, the Princess was disturbed to learn of the death of the Empress Marie of Russia, mother of the Duchess of Edinburgh (the Crown Princess's sister-in-law), and hastened to express her sympathy with the bereaved Emperor Alexander II and his daughter. Within a few months, however, she was scandalised to learn that the Emperor had married again within six weeks of his wife's death. The circumstances certainly were unusual, and there were many who looked with tolerant eye upon the Emperor's hasty remarriage. Although ostensibly the Emperor's first marriage had been a happy one, he had some years previously fallen madly in love with one of the most beautiful women in Russia, the Countess Dolgoroukova, the daughter of a wealthy nobleman. Her parents, realising the turn events had taken, sent their daughter away to Naples for two years, but the separation only served to strengthen the love affair, and when the Emperor went to Paris on a visit, the Countess fled from Naples to join him and returned with him to St. Petersburg. In order to throw a cloak over this illicit love affair, she was appointed Lady-in-waiting to the Empress, and lived in the Winter Palace in apartments to which a secret entrance had been added.

During the twelve years that she lived in the Palace, four children were born to her, and her position, difficult as it was, was to some extent made possible by her great beauty, her charm and her unfailing tact. When the Empress died, it was generally supposed that the Emperor would marry her, and although six weeks was certainly a shorter period of mourning than either court or nation expected, yet society at St. Petersburg made allowance for this lack of convention. The marriage being morganatic, the Emperor now bestowed upon his bride the title of Her Serene Highness Princess Yourievsky.

To the Crown Princess this story of passion and intrigue, culminating in tragedy, appeared as a horrifying irruption into the placid stream of her well-ordered life. It was as if a reader of Schiller were to be unexpectedly confronted with a telling page from one of Dostoievsky's works. With an effort she adjusted herself to the new situation, and on hearing of the Emperor's marriage wrote to Queen Victoria on November 12, 1880:

Fritz wishes me to tell you that on Monday he had a letter from General Schweinitz enclosing one from St. Petersburg from our Military Attaché, General Werder (the intimate friend of the Emperor Alexander) saying: The Emperor was married to Princess Dolgoroukova on the 26th July in presence of General Adlerberg and General Rilésef. He has given the name of Yourievsky to his wife and children. It is not to be made known until the 2nd or 3rd December. The Emperor Alexander has desired a letter to be written to my father-in-law informing him of the fact. The Emperor (my father-in-law) wrote this to Fritz two days ago. We knew from another source that after the marriage ceremony the Emperor sent for Minny and the Cesarewitsch and presented his wife to them and asked them to be kind to her. The unbecoming haste with which the Emperor had the marriage rite performed while the mourning for the poor Empress was yet so fresh, I think can be accounted for and to a certain extent be justified by his desire to do his duty as a man of honour by a lady and his children whom he had placed in so painful a position. He feels his health breaking and his life very uncertain in the condition Russia now is in, and most likely wishes to legalise the ties he has formed before a sudden death might prevent him from making this reparation. What one must feel bitterly is the want of respect to the poor Empress's memory, so devoted and virtuous a wife and loving a mother. General Schwemitz says that anything is better, however, than the former state of things, which was a crying scandal. The poor Empress's feelings were not considered while she lived, therefore what can be put straight in such lamentable *Verhältnisse* should be done without delay, and I am sure you will agree with me that it is better so. Much as the children feel their father's marrying again, yet it must be preferable for them to feeling ashamed of the life he was leading.

I am more shocked than I can say at the whole business, it reminds one of Louis XIV and XV, and I feel very sorry for the Emperor, as I am sure he is much too kindhearted a man not to feel into what a fix he has got himself. On the other hand, in Russia morality stands so low, and people are so lax and so indifferent that they do not care what happens. Please do not say you have heard all this from me. No doubt the Emperor Alexander will have sent you word in some way - perhaps through Alfred?

In the same autumn Prince William spent a month in England as the guest of Prince Christian, his bride's uncle, at Cumberland Lodge, Windsor, and on his return to Berlin at the end of November preparations were made for his approaching wedding. The Crown Princess, while welcoming her eldest son's marriage, could not but feel a pang at the coming separation from her son, and wrote to her mother on January 1, 1881:

It is the last time we have Willy unmarried, in the same house, in his old rooms with us. He thinks me absurdly sentimental to observe this and says it is all the same to him in what place, or house, or room he lives. I hate saying the words 'last time' to anything, as much as I do the words 'Good Bye'. Being soft-hearted is very inconvenient it is true, but we cannot help it; those who are not, feel much more comfortable.

The letter seems to emphasise the difference in temperament between mother and son - a difference that was to be so acutely accentuated during the next few years. It was during the early 'eighties that Prince William seemed to become more and more imbued with the idea that his mother was pro-English and worked against German interests.

The wedding festivities took place on February 27, 1881, and were the occasion for the promotion to the peerage as Lord Ampthill of Odo Russell, the intimate friend of both the Crown Princess and the Prince of Wales. On the day of the wedding the Crown Princess wrote to her mother:

All has gone off very well till now. The *Einzug* was really fine. Dear Dona looked charming and everyone was taken with her sweetness and grace. Her face wore a look of innocent happiness, which did one good to see. Her toilette was very becoming - a light blue and gold brocade, with pink and white China asters, and her pearls and your beautiful pendant round her neck.

The weather was fine and everyone in a good humour. The crowd cheered and seemed pleased, and the decorations were really very pretty indeed.

I was quite exhausted yesterday evening, or I would have written directly. I had a diadem on, which pressed my head a great deal, and did not take it off for six hours and a half. The reception in the Schloss also went off very well, and even Prince Bismarck appeared.

Today will be very trying and I wish it were over.

My parents-in-law are wonderful and never tired, standing, heat, toilettes, talking, nothing seems to knock them up.

I thought so much of you, dearest Mama, and of the days when I arrived here. It is made far easier to Victoria than it was to me, and I hope she will never suffer from *Heimweh* as I do to this day.

Scarcely a fortnight after the echoes of the wedding bells had died away there came the tragic news that the Emperor Alexander II of Russia had been assassinated by a bomb on his way from a military review at St Petersburg. The first bomb which was thrown exploded in the rear of the carriage. The Emperor at once alighted, when a second bomb was thrown which inflicted frightful injuries. He died two hours later. One of the dramatic incidents connected with his death was that only a few days before he had given instructions for a will to be prepared in favour of his morganatic wife, Princess Yourievsky. The will was brought to him to sign on the same day as an important ukase granting various reforms, the signing of which was a lengthy matter. He therefore postponed signing until his return from the military review, but from that function he never returned. The news of the Emperor's death was a terrible shock for the Crown Princess, who wrote to her mother on March 14:

One is so horror-struck, that one really does not know what to say! Poor dear

Emperor Alexander! To die a shocking death - it is too awful! For with his faults and failings he was so amiable and charming and lovable, so kind-hearted and well-meaning. To be destroyed in so horrible a manner; it makes one shudder and tremble, and fills one with pity, grief and sorrow! Thank God the dreadful telegram said 'Il n'a pas repris connaissance', so that one may hope the fearful injuries had deprived him of all pain and consciousness, which is merciful. Poor darling Marie!! How will she stand so terrible a shock? To lose both parents within a year and her Father, whom she doted on, in such a manner!! I suppose I shall see her this evening at the railway station!

All the circumstances are so terrible! This new marriage had cast such a chill over all *relations de famille*; and had done him much harm with the public! They say he was so very happy!! I pity the poor woman now for she loved him very much, - though she had no business to be where she was yet. I am sure the poor creature must be in an agony!

My father-in-law shed many tears, and is most deeply grieved, but I am happy to say it did not give him a sudden shock, which it might have done had he been younger! At his age impressions are not so violent. He was so fond of his nephew! I shall never forget how kind and nice the poor Emperor Alexander always was to me. As for the Nihilists *not* being destroyed - I am quite sure of that, and could not share dear Affie's sanguine views on the subject!

Too many cruelties, too much severity had been shown by the Government for a long period of years - for a spirit of revenge not to spring up, which is then too difficult to quell. The saddest part is that it should be wreaked out on so well intentioned and kind hearted a Sovereign - who was not the tyrant the others had been before him, though he had a *little* of it in him at times, as mostly all Czars must have! The state of *all* grades of Society there is too *bad* and too sad! How will they get into a civilised State of Liberty and order where all that cruel oppression, that sending to Siberia and slowly killing families wholesale, - will cease, and the life and freedom of the subject be protected by wise and humane laws conscientiously carried out! Despotism is a demon - that has all savage crimes and cruelties in his train, and must sooner or later lead to such terrible things, which then usually fall on the innocent.

> Vor dem Sklaven wenn er die Kette bricht,
> Vor dem freien Menschen zitt're nicht.[8]

I am so sorry for Sacha[9] and Minny,[10] to take up a murdered father's Crown is *too* dreadful. I know what we felt when we were so nearly in the same position!

I have not closed my eyes all night, I was so shaken with horror! Thank God the poor Empress was spared this. The poor Emperor always expected such a death, and for years has felt like a hunted hare - safe nowhere. What a life at such a price! I must own I always dreaded it - and thought that if those attacks on his life continued, one would be successful.

Fancy the confusion at Petersburg, the terror, and all the horrible reprisals they will resort to! As dangerous in my eyes as the rest of the state of things!

Bloodshed and cruelty all round - it makes one shudder and creep! I must end, dearest Mama, in a hurry. We go to the Greek Mass at half past 11 - to the Russian Embassy, and whether Fritz has to go off to St. Petersburg or not, I don't know.

Already much of the beauty of life had vanished for the Empress. In Germany she had not won that love and veneration which her mother now commanded in England; always there were those who were willing to place the worst constructions upon her most innocent and well-meant acts. She was misunderstood but one person at least understood her her husband whom she loved and adored with all her heart. Never once had the idyllic promise of those early days of marriage been broken never once had the finger of disillusion destroyed the gossamer beauty of a perfect marriage. However trying and difficult affairs might be, two things as yet she felt she could count on with unerring trust the love and affection of her children and the unchanging, unceasing loyalty and love of the husband she adored.

## NOTES

1 Sir Sidney Lee, *Life of King Edward VII*, vol. i. pp. 431-2.
2 Daughter of Prince Frederick Charles of Prussiam
3 Torchdance in which the Bride and Bridegroom dance with every member of the Royal Family in turn.
4 Emil Ludwig, *Kaiser Wilhelm II*, p. 6.
5 Quoted on pp. 97-8, supra.
6 To say as Ludwig says (*Kaiser Wilhelm II*, p. 13), 'When his father's long life exacerbated him (the Crown Prince) beyond endurance, he revenged himself on his son', is a statement that lacks foundation.
7 On February 17 there was an attempt to assassinate the Tsar. At seven o'clock in the evening a mine exploded under the dining-room as the Imperial family were descending the stairs to go to dinner.
8 Before the Slave when he breaks his chain, Before the Freeman tremble not.
9 The Czarewitch.
10 Married daughter of the King of Denmark, sister of Queen Alexandra.

## VII: Foreign Affairs, 1878-1886

THE decade following the Treaty of Berlin had shown a gradual increase of German influence in world affairs, but at the same time a somewhat remarkable decline of British prestige. In these years Bismarck definitely made new departures in domestic and foreign policy. In home affairs he continued negotiations with the Vatican over the anti-clerical May Laws, whose author. Dr Falk, resigned office; and he abandoned free trade and began to build up a constructive system of protection. In foreign policy he risked strained relations with Russia by signing a defensive alliance with Austria, and even made tentative overtures towards a rapprochement with Great Britain although no definite offer of an alliance was made till ten years later. On November 3, 1879, Queen Victoria wrote to the Crown Princess:

> What Fritz said about the alliance or good understanding between Germany and Austria is not new to me. It came in a secret form two months ago to my ears; but only now have I heard it from Lord Salisbury who heard it from Count Karolyi. I am naturally pleased at the prospect which a cordial defensive alliance between Germany and Austria offers in the interest of peace. The value of such an alliance, however, would be greatly diminished in my eyes if it gave umbrage to France. Fritz seems to think our influence might be used in deterring France from opposing herself to such a league, but how far or under what conditions our influence can be exerted beneficially is a question involving a great many considerations, and I know not yet what Lord Beaconsfield's and Lord Salisbury's views are. But I am certain that any league against France would never be tolerated by this country.
>
> Fritz's name shall not be mentioned, and I am very grateful for his giving me the important information he has done. If he hears more I trust he will let me know. And I may soon be able to say more.

In the years that followed the Eastern question came up again and again. Turkey, the sick man of Europe, seemed to recover after the drastic surgical operation which the Congress had decided would be the solution of his troubles, and two years later Ottoman sovereignty and Ottoman misrule were again defying the doctors. In the meantime the great opponent of Lord Beaconsfield's Eastern policy, Mr Gladstone, had his turn at the Eastern problem. His Cabinet, with Lord Granville as Foreign Secretary, entered office in April 1880, just in time, as Lord Dufferin said, to prevent England from coming into conflict with all the world.

Bismarck was determined that the terms of the Treaty of Berlin should be adhered to, and pointedly said (December 5, 1879) that 'the sound bones of a single Pomeranian grenadier' would not be sacrificed to solve a Balkan wrangle. Yet neither Montenegro nor Greece would be satisfied until those rectifications of frontiers promised in the Treaty had been carried out by Turkey, and Turkey, recovering, felt sufficiently well not to respect her obligations.

With a view to the adjustment of these claims, a European Conference met in London in June 1880. Turkey, however, objected to the decision of the Conference that she should cede the port and littoral of Dulcigno to Montenegro. On July 10 the Crown Princess wrote:

The present moment seems to me a *most critical* one, and one that demands prompt and energetic action on the part of England. The Turks will not give way to European advice alone; the Russians *encourage* their resistance and also further the demands of *all* those interested in taking a portion of Turkey for themselves, knowing that they can in that way obtain their Constantinople. Until they have it they will never *rest*, nor will the 'Eastern question' ever be terminated; they will work at bringing it up again under every possible shape and form with their own peculiar cleverness and astuteness. They know full well, that no other European Power has a very great interest to prevent their having Constantinople and they reckon on England's inability to prevent it. England *must* and can prevent it, but *only now*, in a few weeks it would be *too* late. Torpedoes will be placed to prevent English ships coming up, and the partition of Turkey will be effected with much cruelty and bloodshed.

Why can our ships not come into the Dardanelles? Why cannot England who has been obliged to do *so* much for the Turks, and has spent money and life *enough* to prevent Russia from taking possession of Constantinople, not *prevent* it to the end! Mr Gladstone's policy has, of course, hastened on the crisis which would have taken years to come to its present state. The Turks have had *every* chance of reforming and mending their ways - they are incapable of doing so, and even their best friends must allow that they can remain in Europe no more - Why not use *douce violence*, *i.e.*, go in and *oblige* them as friends to carry out what they *cannot* do themselves! Why not send Sir Lintorn Simmons to make a military convention with them and some ships to the Golden Horn! Why not leave Mr Goschen[1] there and send more people to take in hand Turkish finance and administration? It is the *only way* to prevent cruel bloodshed and war! The other European Powers would, I *am certain, not oppose* such a plan! If later the Sultan would take up his abode at Smyrna and even move down to Asia Minor, and Constantinople remain under English administration till an independent State, guaranteed by the European Powers, and an independent Sovereign at its head can be established, so much the better! The danger of a State which would be Russia's vassal, to be absorbed by her at a convenient moment, would be averted!

Roumania, Bosnia and Bulgaria, now so afraid of Russia, would have someone to *lean on*, and in that part of the world it would be *English* influence and not Russian influence that would reign and govern! What a benefit to the world in general that would be!

I trust there may be *energy* and *decision* enough at the Foreign Office to *take* the right step and *not* to wait or hesitate; in a fortnight it would be too late. The Russians will be into Constantinople like a shot on the first opportunity! Of this we have plenty of evidence.

They think the English Liberal Government are determined to do nothing, and this makes them very confident of success. I am not Russophobe and think it very unjust, but I know what the Russians think and intend! I am Turcophile, *i.e.*, I wish to see the Turkish population, instead of being *massacred* and obliged to *fight* again, enjoying a Government such as the one under which our Mussulman population in India prosper and not the cruel and barbarous rule of Russian officials inspired by the fanaticism of the Greek religion!! As we *cannot* keep up the Sultan's rule, surely we ought by every means in our power to prevent him and his people being swallowed up by the very Power we resisted in 1854.

You know I have always put forward this view and hold it!! If Alfred be not the proper Sovereign for an independent State (which would develop out of a British occupation) there is Arthur and Leopold, or the Duke of Genoa, or other Princes might be found in Germany who could undertake such a task - Prince Waldemar of Denmark!! There are *many* Prussians who think it would be very good to have the Russians at Constantinople. Prince Bismarck does not exactly wish it, and would *prefer English* influence to another, but of course to have the Russians busied in the East makes him feel less threatened at home; they are such very unsafe neighbours and slippery friends, and Germany is so uncomfortably placed between France and Russia, that one is always on the 'qui vive'.

I hope you will not mind my having spoken out so plainly, but my convictions are *so very strong* on the subject and time is *so very* precious - not another moment should be lost, and a bold 'coup' made - The details of *how*, I am sure there are clever heads in the Cabinet enough to make out!

*P.S.* - On this subject the interests of England, Europe and the world at large seem to me quite identical - *not* so the interests of Russia, which are purely selfish and *not* humane, or civilizatory or for the honour and glory of liberty and progress!

In the October of 1881 the general elections in Germany resulted in a large Liberal majority, an event which pleased the Crown Princess, who wrote to Queen Victoria on November 5:

....I am very glad the German elections have returned so many liberals, and I hope it will show Prince Bismarck that the Germans are not all delighted with his government, though I do not think he cares a bit! I wonder why he does not say straight out 'As long as I live both the constitution and the crown are suspended'; because that is the exact state of the matter. No doubt he is quite patriotic and sincere, and thinks it is for the good of Germany! He thinks a great central power is necessary and that one will must decide and the state be everything and do everything like one vast set of machinery, say the 'Inflexible', for instance, where the captain alone works everything by electricity and directs the ship....so Prince Bismarck wishes with the pressure of his little finger to direct the whole, and thinks it doubly necessary for safety's sake in case of being attacked by France or Russia.

I do not like this state of things, but most Prussians and Conservatives do....

The Princess was not long left in doubt as to Bismarck's determination to be the sole controller of the German ship of state, for three weeks later, on November 29, he bluntly declared that in spite of the liberal majority he did not intend Germany to be ruled after the English fashion, and on January 7, 1882, an Imperial rescript was issued against parliamentary government. Once again Bismarck was supreme.

One result of these political changes in England and Germany was a steadily increasing tension between the two countries, which was not minimised by Bismarck's insistence on the impossibility of any alliance with England owing to her parliamentary control of foreign policy. A general election bringing in a new ministry might, he thought, overturn any foreign understanding made by its predecessors, and his policy was accordingly one of deep distrust of England, particularly during the Gladstone regime. This distrust extended to those in Germany who were known to be of English sympathies, and even the Crown Princess found herself surrounded by a network of espionage. It was about this period that there was attached to the Crown Prince's suite by Bismarck a Count Radolin-Radolinsky, who had orders to watch the activities of the Princess's Court Chamberlain, Count Seckendorff. Not unnaturally Radolinsky's domineering attitude gave considerable cause for trouble, for while he appeared to support the Crown Princess's views and opinions, his presence was a thorn in the flesh to the more loyal members of her suite. It was in 1882 or 1883 that the Crown Princess's friend, Lady Ponsonby, wrote to her husband, who was secretary to Queen Victoria:

I don't think the Queen realises what an extraordinary state of things exists in Germany in the way of espionage and intrigue. They, the Foreign Office, which means Bismarck, wanted to put a man of their own about the Crown Princess so as more effectually to control the Crown Prince when he became Emperor. Seckendorff refused to play the spy, and, although being opposed to the Crown Princess in politics, would not lend himself to this intrigue. They began by dismissing his brother, after twenty years' service, from the Foreign Office without any reason being given. Then they appointed Radolinsky (Court Marshal to the Crown Prince) with orders to get rid of Seckendorff. Radolinsky furthered, or appeared to further, the Crown Princess's views about Bulgaria, and ingratiated himself into her good graces and then began the undermining of Seckendorff. I think Seckendorff is to blame for his dictatorial manner, and she may have made him, as is the wont of the family, too much 'the indispensable one', but I feel convinced on the whole that he is being got rid of under false pretences, for Radolinsky's manner of defending the Crown Princess simply consists of spreading these reports and in trying to detach her family from her.

In the following years this rivalry between Radolinsky and Seckendorff, inspired by Bismarck, was to reach proportions that gravely perturbed the Crown Princess, but for the moment the espionage and intrigue was hidden from her eyes.

One of the most trusted friends of the Crown Prince and Princess now died at Potsdam. The death of Lord Ampthill (Odo Russell) was a sad blow for them both, for even though the able Ambassador's successor was Sir Edward Malet, whose staff included Colonel L.V. Swaine as Military Attaché, no one could quite replace the gifted Lord Ampthill, who had been their friend for over twenty years. On August 30, 1884, the Crown Princess, who was then on holiday in England, wrote to Queen Victoria, who was at Osborne.

I feel I have not *half* thanked you for the charming stay you allowed us to have in this sweet, peaceful little cottage which I love so much! It was indeed delightful in every way and I know not how to express all my gratitude, also for letting my little people stay here while I am away. I shall feel they are all so safe, and well cared for.

The *more* I think of Berlin, and the poor dear Lord Odo's successor, the more I fear that amongst the diplomatists the *right* person *does* not seem to be at the present forthcoming. The next few years are the most important; later, who could be better than Morier, but just now I really *only* see TWO *men*, the one, Lord Acton, and the other Lord Arthur Russell! Whether Lord Granville *could* do it, whether they would be willing, are questions of course I know nothing about.

My opinion you must take at what it is worth, but it is the only conclusion I can come to after my reflections and I sadly fear it will be disagreeable to poor Lord Granville, who is already so much worried and troubled....(Lord Arthur has had some diplomatic training and was the secretary of his uncle, Lord John.)

In that year the Crown Princess again met Mr Gladstone, and to an inquiry from Lady Ponsonby as to what she thought of the Liberal leader she replied (October 17, 1884):

....You asked me what I thought of Mr. Gladstone when I saw him at Balmoral? I thought him, as I always do, a wonderful man for whom I have the greatest respect and admiration, and who interests me deeply, and whose society I think perfectly charming! Such knowledge, such culture, such a memory, such earnestness of purpose, and such simplicity. Alas! I fear not the right man to solve the knotty questions which, as an Empire, England has to deal with, but invaluable in stemming the tide of democracy, because, as a true Liberal, he has the confidence of so many thousands and is the only one who can form a bridge between the old and the new. Whether he has the keen sight, the eagle eye of the statesman, I do not know. I fear not. Whether the measures he has adopted, Land Bill, etc., were right, I dare not say. I do not feel sure. The conscientiousness, the high and lofty aims he certainly has; but at this present moment he seems so absorbed by the wants of the lower classes and middle class, and with the task of giving them all they can and may safely have, that the other great problems that hurry on are scarcely treated with the care and ability they require. The East, our Colonies, our Army and our Navy must not be neglected. France and Germany are allowed to be wanting in respect, and this *never*, never ought to be. It is well not to be too thin-skinned, but we ought not to allow others to trifle with us!

If there is a conference at Berlin to settle, as they say, what is to become of Africa, ought England not to make the proposals and to insist on what decisions are to be taken? England is a great deal too humble to foreign Powers! They only misunderstand her. We get no thanks for our modesty and moderation. The tone of the German press towards England, with few exceptions, is execrable, but as it is as stupid as it is insolent one had better pay no attention to it.

The Germans are always reproaching the English for having prejudices against Germany, and forget that *they* have many more and much more deeply-seated ones about other countries, especially England! They imagine England is jealous of Germany's attempting to have colonies. I am almost certain that the whole agitation about colonial enterprise would not have been cooked up so much by the German government if it were not a useful handle for the elections and for securing the measure of the foundation of a line of German steam-packets which the Chancellor wants to carry. The nation is really like a child, delighted with a new toy or dainty morsel held out to it - a sugar plum - greedily trying to snatch it and furious with anybody or anything that seems to put difficulties in the way! This colonial sugar plum may easily turn into a bitter almond, and the beginning seems to me sad enough if it cannot be obtained without an estrangement between England and Germany.

In the following year, 1885, Mr Gladstone's government received a new lease of life, but it then became dependent upon the Irish nationalist vote for its parliamentary majority. In the Liberal ministry which was formed in

February 1886, Mr Gladstone willingly admitted Mr John Morley as Chief Secretary for Ireland, but it was with great reluctance that he included the Radical leader, Mr Joseph Chamberlain, as President of the Local Government Board. One striking omission was that of Sir Charles Dilke. All these statesmen were well known to the Crown Princess, but the appointment which gave her the greatest pleasure was that of Lord Rosebery to the Foreign Office, a promotion which also delighted Bismarck and his son, Count Herbert Bismarck. On February 5, 1886, the Crown Princess wrote to Queen Victoria:

I am very glad indeed that Lord Rosebery is appointed to the Foreign Office. I saw Herbert Bismarck yesterday evening at a party and he was quite delighted and said his father was immensely pleased, and hoped and trusted Lord Rosebery would walk in Lord Salisbury's footsteps; also that his father had great confidence in Lord Rosebery's abilities, intentions and energy. This was *quite sincere*, and it was not difficult to see that Prince Bismarck really desires to be *well* with England and really approved Lord S.'s Eastern policy.

Mr. Gladstone now made it clear that he intended to go through with his policy of Home Rule for Ireland, and in his first interview with Queen Victoria early in February he outlined his scheme. To Queen Victoria's letter giving this news, the Crown Princess replied (February 5):

So many thanks for your dear letter of the 3rd and for the memorandum, *i.e.* the notes you made of your first interview with Mr Gladstone, which interested us extremely. I think your conversation was very satisfactory. I, too, am afraid that he will fail and that the scheme is impossible, but there is no doubt that he is most thoroughly in earnest and that he knows the immense responsibility he has taken upon himself and does not conceal any of the difficulties from himself, I am glad Lord Harrington spoke so plainly to him. It is strange Lord Spencer should have changed his views so much since May. Mr J. Morley I know, and he always struck me as a clever, learned, cultivated man, decidedly quiet and serious and without vanity. That Mr Gladstone should not be blind about Mr Chamberlain and Sir C. Dilke is also a good thing.

In short from the paper you so kindly sent, and which I much admire, the lookout seems a little better than I feared. 'To examine' the wishes of the Irish people is no doubt a sacred duty. But the two millions that clamour and that are in a state of organised revolt, and under the tyranny of Mr. Parnell and his followers are *not* all Ireland! and I am sadly afraid that there is no satisfying these, and if they were satisfied it would be mischief, misery, rum and injustice to all the others! The Irish-Americans, the Fenians, the irreconcilable 'invincibles', etc., are not to be won over by mere legislation, distribution of land, etc. The Irish question seems to me to be composed of two elements. The one, that of evils that can be remedied and of reforms which are just and in accordance with the times, and would work well and be a benefit to the country. The other element is an evil which only force can overcome. Lawlessness and violence is a form of war and only can be met by taking up the quarrel, but the strife is not one with all Ireland, or with the Irish people it is with that portion or faction who will not keep the peace and who force war upon England with or without reason. The less reason they have, the more justifiable is force in putting them down. Therefore the Government can solve the problem by conscientiously sifting the question to the bottom and seeing where still an evil remains which can be remedied by peaceful methods. It will strengthen England's hands for the struggle if there is to be one.

War with America was once prevented and dear Papa worked harder than anyone to stop it, and war with the disaffected part of the Irish population may be avoided by striking a blow at the terrorism, which enthralls so many who are powerless to resist. A more difficult problem was never put before a nation! It puts to the test our constitutionalism, our national temper, common sense and energy, our political understanding and our statesmen! But no question was ever so bad that there was not some road out of it, and I trust it will be found. Is Mr. Gladstone the genius to find it or is he not? - there is the question. I do not dare give an opinion on this as I really do not know! The will, the earnestness of purpose, the readiness, the sacrifice, yes! but he has taken some steps and expressed some views where one feels one cannot agree, nor see the wisdom of them, and where one can only share Mr Goschen's, Lord Harrington's, the Dukes of Bedford's, Argyll's and Westminster's objections.

You must indeed feel the keenest anxiety, but you have done all you could, all that was fair and right and wise, and must now trust that good will come out of it! I cannot say how much I feel for you and share all your doubts and fears and anxieties, but being sanguine by nature I am never without hopes and the composition of the Cabinet certainly offers many a comforting feature. You will miss Lord Salisbury much, I am sure. I hope Lord Rosebery will prove a good Foreign Secretary, and his nomination is a thing to be thankful for....

A fortnight later (February 19, 1886) the Crown Princess wrote to Queen Victoria:

....I wonder why a special commission of inquiry on Irish affairs - composed of a junction of Liberals and Conservatives of course with the *exclusion* of the Parnellites could not be called to examine thoroughly all that is so dark and complex still in the question, and propose to the Government means of reform and pacification with the *fixed* and *decided* intention of never giving way to Parnell, Fenians, Socialists, Anarchists, Americans and priests and Home Rulers, etc., and of restoring law and order and respect for authority.

One does not feel confidence in Mr Gladstone being perfectly certain as to what he *may* and will *not* do; in so knotty a question if one is already determined as to what *cannot* be done it clears up the problem, and it is easier then to find what *is* and ought to be done. If the advanced Radicals contemplate the possibility of an alliance with anarchists, to carry measures of reform, *all* other parties should combine against them.

I also admire many of Mr Gladstone's great qualities very much, but should be utterly unable to follow him blindly, as the stable and steady elements seem so wanting in his composition, and just at present these qualities are so indispensable if one is to feel confidence in his policy. I own mine is very small.[2]

In the following July Mr Gladstone, faced with overwhelming parliamentary difficulties, resigned. Lord Salisbury for the second time took the helm of the vessel of state to steer a course vastly different from that of his democratic predecessor.

## NOTES

1 *Mary Ponsonby*, p. 252.
2 Mr. J. G. Goschen, MP (afterwards Viscount Goschen) who was temporary Ambassador at Constantinople.

# VIII: Prince Alexander of Battenberg

MARRIAGES, especially love matches, are a constant source of trouble to parents. Difficulties may and do arise because of differences in temperament, family feuds, or even financial settlements, and with a royal family not only are these risks multiplied, but there is the added terror of international politics and diplomatic considerations to complicate matters. The Machiavellis of Europe see in an apparently normal betrothal a golden opportunity of grinding a political axe or of carrying out some coup that may alter the whole trend of politics. Under such circumstances, princes or princesses who have become engaged find themselves converted into pawns on the international chess-board and made instruments of political intrigue. It was such a series of events that converted the happy engagement of Prince Alexander of Battenberg with Princess Victoria, the daughter of the Crown Princess, into a European complication which threatened at one time to involve the resignation of Prince Bismarck, and had the disastrous consequence of widening the breach that had unfortunately appeared between the Crown Princess and her eldest son.

It was in the May of 1886, when Prince William was suffering from an inflammation of the ear, that for the first time the Crown Princess complained to her mother of his distant behaviour:

....Dr Bergmann [she wrote on May 25] thinks Willy will go on all right, and is quite content. Dr Trautmann continues to make out that it is most serious and that two or three days ago it was even very dangerous, and both agree that great care must be taken to get the ear thoroughly well. Bergmann does not think the inflammation need ever return, and could find nothing amiss with the drum; he says there is no need for any operation whatever, that the inflammation had gone down and there was no more matter or discharge, pressure on the brain or any other uncomfortable symptoms. Willy is allowed to be out and to walk in the garden, but is ordered to keep very quiet. We met him in the garden and I thought him looking all right. He did not condescend to remember that he had not seen me for two months, or that I had been to England and to Homburg, or that his sisters had the measles. He never asked after them or you, or any of my relations in England, so that I felt hurt and disappointed as I had been tormenting myself so much about him. He is a curious creature! A little civility, kindness and *empressement* go a long way, but I never get them from him. However, now he is not well I will certainly take no notice of his strange want of thoughtfulness. Still, it is very painful to a soft-hearted Mama to feel so plainly that her own child does not care whether he sees her or no, whether she is well or ill, or away, etc. Dona is most devoted to him and never leaves him for one minute; they seem very happy and contented together.

This letter emphasises the fact that in the years since Prince William's marriage there had been a cooling-off of affection and even a growing antipathy between the son and the mother. Prince William, whose political tendencies led him into paths unfrequented by his mother, had now cut himself adrift from all parental authority and was beginning to show an increasing disrespect for his mother which hurt her as only a son can wound a parent. Before long the seeds of an open quarrel were only too manifest even to outsiders. The immediate cause of the difference was the Crown Princess's desire that her daughters should marry, as Prince William had done, for love rather than for reasons of state, and when it became evident that she favoured Prince Alexander of Battenberg's desire to marry her daughter Victoria, the views of mother and son conflicted. Not only the Crown Prince and Princess, but also Queen Victoria viewed with approval the Prince's suit; on the other hand, there was an early undercurrent of opposition which both Prince Bismarck and the Tsar of Russia encouraged. The reason was not far to seek.

The Treaty of Berlin had created a new state, that of Bulgaria, which, while still under the nominal suzerainty of the Sultan, was regarded by Russia as being bound to her by ties of race and religion. The choice of a first ruler for the infant state awakened bitter animosities, and it was the Tsar's nominee, Prince Alexander, who was finally elected in April 1879. Prince Alexander, then a handsome and attractive youth of twenty-two, was the second son of the Prince Alexander of Hesse and intimately known to the Crown Princess. His eldest brother, Prince Louis of Battenberg, was a great friend of the Prince of Wales, and married in 1884 Princess Victoria of Hesse, the daughter of the Crown Princess's sister Alice. Another brother, Prince Henry, also became related to the Crown Princess later, for, in 1885, he married Princess Beatrice.

Immediately after his election to the Bulgarian throne Prince Alexander paid a series of visits to the various European courts. At Berlin he found Bismarck 'very kind', and in London (June 1879) he found a firm friend in Queen Victoria, who liked him and thought him 'sincere and honest'. It was during this tour that he made the acquaintanceship of the Crown Princess's daughter Victoria, who was then seventeen years of age.

Prince Alexander, who was called in the family 'Sandro', had no sooner taken up the actual burden of sovereignty than he showed that he would be no catspaw of Russia, but would rather encourage Bulgarian aspirations towards complete independence. In the September of 1883, now the virtual dictator of Bulgaria, he definitely opposed Russian influence by dismissing

Colonel Redigher and other Russian officers. The Crown Princess wrote immediately to Queen Victoria, urging that it was most important that England should support and encourage Prince Alexander. Queen Victoria sent the letter to Lord Dufferin (November 18, 1883), the British Ambassador at Constantinople, whose representations resulted in peaceful relations being re-established between Bulgaria and Russia.

Two years later, in 1885, the projected marriage of the Princess Victoria to Prince Alexander was vigorously promoted by the Crown Princess, at first in secret. But the moment the project came to the ears of Bismarck (June or July 1885), who favoured the King of Portugal as the Princess's husband, it was doomed.

As soon as I heard of it [he told Busch three years later] I made representations to the Emperor, verbally and in writing. He allowed himself to be convinced by the reasons I adduced, and refused to give his consent, although she said the Princess loved him. Of course, he is a handsome man, with a fine presence; but I believe her nature is such that she would accept any other suitor, providing he were manly. Moreover, that is entirely beside the question. We must look at the political objections and dangers. The old Queen is fond of matchmaking, like all old women, and she may have selected Prince Alexander for her grand-daughter, because he is a brother of her son-in-law, the husband of her favourite daughter, Beatrice. But obviously her main objects are political a permanent estrangement between ourselves and Russia and if she were to come here for the Princess's birthday, there would be the greatest danger that she would get her way. In family matters she is not accustomed to contradiction, and would immediately bring the parson with her in her travelling bag and the bridegroom in her trunk and the marriage would come off at once.

Prince William took the side of Bismarck, and the first open quarrel between the Empress and her son was kindled by this flame.

It had even come [Ludwig relates] to an exchange of rings between the girl and this Battenberg Prince, when Bismarck interposed on the Tsar's behalf, and instantly found Prince William on his side. A violent scene between mother and son ensued at the beginning of 1885; it was thought desirable to remove him from Potsdam.[1]

For the moment, the opposition of Bismarck and the aged Emperor prevailed; but the Crown Princess did not lightly relinquish her project, and determined to strengthen Prince Alexander's position in Bulgaria. In November 1885 war broke out between Servia and Bulgaria, but in the following month peace seemed probable, and on December 5, 1885, the Crown Princess wrote to Lady Ponsonby:

The Eastern question *does* look a little brighter, I am happy to say. I am heart and soul with the Bulgarians, and hope for an independent, united Bulgaria in the shape of a kingdom, and unshackled by Russians or Turks. The people deserve and the Prince deserves it, and it would be a very good thing for Europe, as it would prevent the Russians from continually meddling and intriguing in this Eastern question and would leave poor old Turkey to die a natural and, I hope, a painless death, without fresh convulsions, horrors and bloodshed. Russia would have to swallow it, and Austria too. German public opinion would highly approve of it in every way. I think England would have cause to rejoice and France and Italy would not mind. These are my *private* opinions. Of course, they cannot be proclaimed on the housetops, as the Government and Diplomacy here are obliged to study Russian susceptibilities and not to oppose her in any way....[2]

Three months later peace was signed between Servia and Bulgaria. Eastern Roumelia was now virtually (though not nominally) joined to Bulgaria, and Prince Alexander was appointed governor of the province for five years. On March 4, 1886, the Crown Princess wrote to Lady Ponsonby:

I am still very, very anxious about Bulgaria. But, thank God! the Peace is now signed. Few people in the world have gone through what Prince Alexander has had to struggle with in *every* shape and form. My admiration for him increases every day. As a patriot, a soldier, and a statesman, he has shown an energy, patience, perseverance, modesty and moderation such as one has rarely seen and which one can only find in the perfect gentleman. And he owes it to *himself* alone, as he has hardly anyone about him with whom he could share the responsibility. He *deserves* to be successful and to be happy. May he be so! I tremble for his safety and for the difficult time he will still have to fight through before his enemies learn to let *him alone* and do him justice, and before his country and his own position are safe from the plots and intrigues which are still so rife against them. He and his cause indeed deserve sympathy and support from all well-minded people, and it is only the wilfully prejudiced who can find anything to blame in his conduct, or those under the direct influence of the lies and calumnies of his bitter enemies.[3]

In the summer of 1886, however, the Tsar's long account with the youthful ruler, who had dared to defy Russian aims, was ready for presentation, and negotiations began between Russia and Turkey for the cession of part of Prince Alexander's territory to Russia. The Crown Princess was full of sympathy for the young ruler, and her attitude is plainly indicated by the following letter to her mother dated May 15, 1886:

We have heard from the F.O. at Berlin today that the news from Bulgaria is bad and that the Russians are agitating most violently and that behind Sandro's back they are treating with the Turks for the cession of the harbour of Burgas to Russia. Perhaps it might be advisable to warn him of this danger. It is a thing which his own country would never forgive, if he allowed the best harbour to be ceded to the Russians. This seems the method they are adopting to upset him and drive him away. Besides it is also said that his Ministers are more or less playing him false and the form in which the union has been obtained is considered by them *ein Misserfolg, eine Niederlage*, and that they wish to make him alone answerable before the country for this. They wish to take away all the Roumelian officers before the elections, as they are also so much for Sandro. This all sounds bad. Most likely you have the same news, but it is worth while being watchful and giving him a friendly hint perhaps, if possible. His position is very difficult, painful and dangerous. Meanwhile the Greeks seem coming to their senses and one hears Alfred spoken of with much praise as understanding his work so well. The blockade is already having a good effect.

Meanwhile, M. de Giers, who had become Gortchakoff's assistant at the Russian Foreign Office in 1875 and was already marked out as his successor, had planned a visit to Franzensbad to see Bismarck. The Crown Princess dreaded such a meeting, and wrote to her mother on May 29, 1886:

All these speeches in Russia, at Sevastopol, Moscow, etc., are very disquieting, I think, and yet if the Emperor of Russia is not prepared to make war, now, and invent a pretext, I do not see what the Russians mean to do. They have evidently tried all the means in their power - the worst and most treacherous - to upset Sandro and make a revolution in Bulgaria, and without obtaining the result they expected! The Greek and Turkish affair seems coming to a peaceable end, though there are no plums for them to pick out of that pie. They say Giers is coming to Franzensbad and will pay a visit to Prince Bismarck at Friedrichsruhe. I sincerely hope nothing will come of this, as it has always made mischief whenever these two have met. Wladimir and Mischka are at Berlin tomorrow, but I shall not see them, as we are obliged to entertain all the gentlemen of the Exhibition Committee here tomorrow.

It interested me very much to hear what Sir W. Jenner said about Willy's ear! I see him every day and he is doing all right, but has been much more amiable, friendly and civil, also more cordial these last days....

On July 6, 1886, Russia suddenly repudiated the clause of the Treaty of Berlin under which Batoum, on the Black Sea, had been declared a free port. Lord Rosebery, the British Foreign Secretary, at once made a protest, but British influence in foreign affairs had reached so low an ebb that the protest was disregarded. A few days later Lord Rosebery and the other members of the Liberal Cabinet resigned, the general election of that month having given Lord Salisbury and the Conservative party a majority over all parties in the

British parliament.

A month later, on August 8, the two Emperors of Austria and Germany met at Gastein. To the amazement of the Crown Princess, the Crown Prince was not invited to be present, but her son William, however, managed to find his way into the conference. Three days later the Crown Princess wrote to Queen Victoria:

I hear from a perfectly undoubted source that my poor fat friend at Petersburg[4] on being asked about Lord Rosebery's note about Batoum said 'Yes, he had received something, *mais rien qui valait la peine d'être communiqué*'. I suppose he did not wish Germans to know what sort of note it was ; but that Germans happened to know, or guess, that an important and decided note was coming or had come.

We are rather horrified at hearing that William was at the interview of the Emperors at Gastein and that he is going to Skerniewski to see the Emperor of Russia I It is perhaps not true, but as such things are always arranged between the Emperor and William without consulting or informing us, it may be, and I need hardly say that it would make endless mischief and do endless harm. William is as blind and green, wrong-headed and violent on politics as can be. He swears by Reuss VII who is such a silly, conceited and false individual - Russian down to his fingers' ends. It is really rather hard upon us, and our position a very painful one. I still hope it may not be.

Lenbach, the celebrated artist, is here and will be in England next month! Will you please allow him to see the pictures at Buckingham Palace? Prince Eugene of Sweden paid us a visit here yesterday. The Emperor arrives tomorrow morning.

*P.S.* Prince Lobanoff told Reuss VII that the Czar was quite tired of the Bulgarian question and that he had said - if the Bulgarians really chose to get on without Russian protection they were welcome to it and had better try. This is not true! The Emperor's animosity is more active and violent than ever! It was only said to take in Reuss VII, which it did.

A fortnight later the animosity between the Tsar and Prince Alexander came to its climax. On August 22 the young ruler was kidnapped at Sofia by Russian officers, carried off to Keni Russi in Russian Bessarabia, and soon afterwards compelled to abdicate at the pistol's point. He was permitted to return to Bulgaria a week later when, broken in health and spirits, he submitted to Russia, and on September 4 announced his intention to abdicate. On the 8th he left Sofia with simple dignity and on the 25th General Kaulbars, the Russian Commissioner, arrived, and began a policy of intimidation. Five days later, M. Tisza, the Hungarian Prime Minister, declared for the maintenance of the Treaty of Berlin and Bulgarian independence, and this declaration stiffened the attitude of the Bulgarian Regents and the premier, M. Radoslavoff, who now began firmly to resist

Kaulbars. Russia's reply was to send warships to Varna and to land soldiers at that port.

Was ever anything so exasperating [wrote the Crown Princess to her mother from Portofino on October 5, 1886] as the way Kaulbars goes on in Bulgaria? One did not give the Russians credit for so much stupidity, in spite of all their slyness and wiliness! They will set the whole population against them, which would be a very good thing! I hope no new Prince will be elected, or, if a candidate of Russia's be chosen, that Europe will not accept or recognise him. I hope the Russians will find themselves in a regular hornets' nest. Their behaviour is too outrageous....

Nor did the attacks on Prince Alexander in the Berlin press give the Crown Princess any occasion for any change of feeling:

The attacks [she wrote on October 23, 1886] of the Berlin official press on Sandro continue - it is mean, and shameful, besides utterly ridiculous. It is, of course, to flatter the Tsar, and the great man (Bismarck), and impress our Emperor, but no one else believes or listens to it in Germany.
To think of poor Sandro being held up as a danger to Germany - an enemy to peace and the *only* cause of disturbance in Europe!! whereas the only disturber is Russia, and Russia alone! Why not admit it, and admit that one is obliged to humour Russia from fear, instead of making such far-fetched inventions to excuse and explain one's policy? I think it shabby and nasty, and so do many others. All this is very tormenting.

The Crown Princess was even more shocked when, on November 1, the Russian officers who had kidnapped the Prince were released, and it became evident to all the world that Russia was acting and had acted with a cynical disregard for treaties or morality. The Crown Princess was roused to anger at these indignities, and wrote to her mother from Portofino on November 8:

....I was sure you would think it monstrous as I do to liberate those treacherous, abominable conspirators in Bulgaria, the Russians having thereby the insolence and barefaced audacity to proclaim to the world what at least one thought they would have wished to conceal, that the shameful dastardly plot against Sandro was of their making and carrying out! So much the better that it was *not* invented by Bulgarians! Russian officials are capable of any infamy, that is not new!
The Hungarian speeches seem very good. Amongst other things, the Czar must be terribly misinformed. I suppose a word of truth never reaches his ears so-called absolute monarchs are always dupes, consequently less free in their actions while yielding to their own caprice without restraint or consideration of

any kind. They are pushed by those who know how to excite them! Tyrannical and violent as he is, I suppose he is the tool of the Panslavists and of all the lying officials in his service. And it is to this that the rest of Europe seems to bow at this moment. It does seem rather humiliating, but I trust it will not last.

What a time of it these unfortunate Regents are having.

In spite of Queen Victoria's indignation at the action of 'the barbaric, Asiatic, tyrannical' Tsar, as she wrote to Prince Alexander,[5] the British Government reached the conclusion that Great Britain had no direct interest in Prince Alexander's misfortunes. The declining influence of Great Britain in Europe at this period was reflected in the Crown Princess's letter to her mother of February 7, 1887:

We have heard from Petersburg, that the Czar speaks with utter contempt of England, saying England had already quite withdrawn from European politics and was too weak to take any part in them, and was not to be feared in any way. Other Russians say there is *not a single gun* on board a British man-of-war that can be fired off, and not a single musket in the British army or navy that had a proper bayonet, that they were all only imitation steel and could not be used; that the English ammunition was useless, as it did not fit the guns, and the whole of the English army administration so bad that it would break down if England dared to go to war; the British lion had no teeth, etc....

The Persian Minister at St Petersburg said that British influence was completely gone in Persia - (this is not quite untrue) - and that India would not be long in British hands; the prestige was gone, the disaffection and discontent great, and the Army not to be relied on. It makes one so furious to hear all this. It is never so dangerous to be underrated as overrated, and perhaps it is not a bad thing that the Russians should underrate us so much.

Yesterday people seemed a little less alarmed about war; but the anxiety is still very great.

The Conservative Government of Lord Salisbury, which had replaced Mr. Gladstone's Liberal ministry in 1886[5] now, however, began to take a great interest in European affairs, which, by March of 1887, became so overcast as to threaten a storm. Austria and Russia were at loggerheads over the question of their respective influence in the Balkans.

It was while this question loomed so threateningly over the European sky that there came to Berlin the Crown Prince Rudolph of Austria, the Emperor Francis Joseph's heir, who had married, in 1881, Princess Stephanie, second daughter of King Leopold II of Belgium. Whilst in the German capital he had a series of conversations with the Crown Prince and Princess of Germany, and it was after one of these that the Crown Princess wrote to Queen Victoria (March 17, 1887):

Today Rudolph had a very interesting long conversation with Fritz and with me! He said that he thought a war was inevitable (which we do not). He spoke of the intense desirability of a close understanding between England, Germany, Austria and Italy. He seemed very anxious about the good understanding between Austria and England, and said that the Austrian government dreaded not being able to secure some sort of useful understanding, as though Lord Salisbury might be willing, yet English cabinets changed so often, and with them the policy of the country, that it made it so difficult to rely on England's help and her word. He repeated that Count Kalnoky (the Austrian Minister of Foreign 1887 Affairs) was most English in his feelings and sympathies that Sir A. Paget (the British Ambassador) had a most excellent position at Vienna and was very much liked there! Rudolf seemed to think Count Karolyi (the Austrian Ambassador in London) so *baissé* that he was of no use at all, and would not be ambassador for many months longer. Rudolf complained that the older official men in Austria had so the habit of being deferential to Russia that they forgot the exigencies of the present moment, and he feared it was so here too, which, of course, we did not deny! In the war, which Rudolf seems to think impending, he said that if England would only assist in the Black Sea and keep the Turks in order, preventing them from joining the Russians, the service they would render would be immense! He very reasonably said that in a war one could not do any serious damage to Russia - provinces could not be taken from her, etc., the only positive result that could be obtained would be to prevent her from gaining her own ends and having her own way. He seems to think that Russia will attack Austria in Galicia, and that it is all-important Italy should promise to keep quiet and not attack or harass Austria, so that the latter need not leave a soldier on the Italian frontier, but take all the men she has to the north. Rudolf thinks England could render inestimable service in keeping Italy in order, *i.e.* seeing that she keeps her promises, as Italy's cabinets also changed very rapidly and policy was very variable.

Rudolf thinks that if Germany helps Austria against Russia, the French will instantly attack Germany and that the coming war will be extremely serious! He thinks France far stronger, better armed, better prepared and more patriotic than she was - Russia also far more fit for fighting than she was during the Turko-Russian war, but so shamefully governed and so fermented with discontent that this alone made the Government anxious for war, in order to create a diversion.

Rudolf says there is no denying that at this present moment Russia played the first fiddle in Europe, and was the strongest power and imposed her will on the rest; and that this would remain a constant danger, as she could get France to join her whenever she liked. The only thing that could keep them in check was the Alliance of the four other powers above mentioned! Rudolf says that the Sultan distrusts England and Austria and is afraid of them, while he has a great leaning to Russia and liking for Russians and the Czar, which Rudolf had plenty of opportunity of noticing while he was at Constantinople.

Rudolf says his father is still perfectly furious with the conduct of the Russians in Bulgaria - he himself thinks as Fritz and I do.

I was unable to perceive anything of his idea of the Donaureich which I have repeatedly heard is his hobby. He spoke with marvellous clearness, intelligence and common sense and is quite au fait of everything and has been entrusted with different messages to Prince Bismarck. He is quite aware that his views tally more with ours than with our Emperor's or Willy's.

Meanwhile, search was being made for a new ruler for the throne of Bulgaria. On April 22, 1887, the Crown Princess wrote to her mother:

Do you think it is true that Ferdinand of Glücksburg has been lighted upon as candidate for the throne of Bulgaria? We hear that it is a close secret, and that a Prince has been found, though it is not known who. So much seems certain, that the poor Bulgarians are in such straits that they will jump at a Prince who is in any degree eligible and then keep him. As Ferdinand is the first cousin of Minny, it might be possible that he has been thought of....

There was an idea of Sandro's marrying Culma![6] and she it was who would not hear of it, because she heard that the children would have to be Greek, which she thinks sinful. William was very cross with her, and called her a goose; he had a great admiration for Sandro in those days. If a Prince is found and accepted, of course, all the Powers will be too glad to approve of him and keep him there I But then, also, the dream of Sandro's returning is over for ever! This is always urged by many who are dying to see him return in triumph and become King, but still I think he was right in refusing to go now. It would have been an awful risk! Goltz Pasha says (but this only in confidence) that the Sultan cannot bear Sandro, distrusts him and considers him the cause of all evils and troubles, expenditure and uncertainty to the Porte and does not wish him to return! How far this is the work of Nelidow, one cannot know! What does Sir William White say on the subject? As Sir W. White and Goltz Pasha are friends, I suppose Sir W. White could only say the same. Prince Bismarck would prefer anyone to Sandro and any lady to a German candidate. He does not scruple to say that his policy is quite changed since the Treaty of Berlin, when he boldly crossed Russia's plans and went in for a Bulgarian principality which he thought would develop into an independent state. He was glad then that it was a German Prince! He advised Sandro to accept! Now, says Prince Bismarck, the situation is entirely changed for Germany. Then, France was nowhere, but now he considers France strong, and very well armed, and he knows how easily a Franco-Russian Alliance could be made!! He is right therefore in not offending Russia, and in humouring her where he can, where he seems to me to be wrong is in thinking that he can buy her friendship by any sacrifice he could make! He is also wrong in allowing her to strengthen herself, which she would if she got Constantinople and the Black Sea *via* Bulgaria.

Europe has been very short-sighted, since she seems to think that by dropping the Bulgarians altogether and leaving them to their fate, she can prevent awkward questions from being raised and can avert war. This seems to me a miscalculation. If Prince B. had been *anständig* he would have let Sandro know (because he was a German) that Germany's position had altered, her policy with regard to Bulgaria would be changed and he and his country abandoned, instead of which Sandro was left to find that out for himself at the risk of losing his life! This was more than nasty in a statesman who had encouraged Sandro to go there! If he had advised Sandro openly and kindly to leave - to return to Germany and throw up the game, as the Russians were determined to crush him, and Germany was determined not to interfere, Sandro could have retired when he pleased, instead of being ruthlessly sacrificed to the treachery and wickedness of the Russians and now ill-treated at home to please them and, as it were, justify Prince Bismarck's conduct in his own eyes - towards his victim! He furthermore tries to justify his conduct by accepting every ridiculous lie and calumny against Sandro! This does not blind impartial people, however, though it pains those who admire and love Sandro very much. Russia, it seems, is turning her eyes towards Egypt and Afghanistan, and seems to think it the best and most promising field for mischief of her own kind and liking. The state Russia is in seems to be a very unsatisfactory one to say the least. I do not know what Morier writes, but we hear people are quite prepared for fresh attempts on the Emperor's life.

We are rather shocked at Kaulbars (the Russian Commissioner in Bulgaria) having received such a mark of favour from the Emperor of Austria. It looks much as if those were right who say that Kalnoky is very Russian and terribly afraid of Russia.

To return to what you said in your letter about Ernst Gunther;[7] it distresses me much that he shows so little gratitude and proper feeling towards Christian and Lenchen who have done so much for him, and that he thinks only of himself and not at all of his cousins. It is not at all nice and so surprising in the son of Fritz Holstein! Not more surprising and painful, though, than that our son should be as he is; forget all love and gratitude and let himself be used as a tool and instrument against his parents! William has more brains than Ernst Gunther and can be very nice and amiable when he likes! Vain and selfish they both are, and they both hold the most superficial rubbishy political views - rank retrograde and chauvinist nonsense in which they, in their childish ignorance, are quite fanatical, and which makes them act as they do, each in his way. It pleases the Emperor, Bismarck and his clique and the Court, so they feel very tall and very grand! Bismarck is a great man, and you know that I am always ready to give him his due in all things and try my best to get on with him in every way, but his system is a pernicious one, which can only do young people harm in every way - to admire his blind followers and admirers and the many who wish to rise by a servile and abject pandering to his every wish and whim. These are all William's friends now, and he is on a footing of the greatest intimacy and familiarity with them! It is easy to see how bad and dangerous this is for him and for us! Exactly what we knew it would be, when the Emperor and Bismarck overrode all Fritz's objections, all his entreaties. William's judgment is being warped, his mind poisoned by this! He is not sharp enough or experienced enough to see through the system, nor through the people, and they do with him what they like. He is so headstrong, so impatient of any control, except the Emperor's, and so suspicious of everyone who might be only a half-hearted admirer of Bismarck's that it is quite useless to attempt to enlighten him, discuss with him, or persuade him to listen to other people, or other opinions! The malady must take its course, and we must trust to later years and changed circumstances to cure him! Fritz takes it profoundly *au tragique*, whilst I try to be patient and do not lose courage! It is after all a very natural consequence of the Emperor having enforced the contrary of all we wished and thought salutary for William, and the natural consequence of Bismarck's omnipotence. I hope you will not take any notice of this when you see William and be as kind to him as usual the reverse would do no good, he would not understand it, and only put his back up. As you live so far away you are not *censée* to know all this. I think and hope his visit to England may do him a deal of good, as he is fond of being there and has been far too little I He would be delighted to travel, see India, America, China and Australia, but the Emperor will not let him. It would be excellent for him.

*April 23.*

I really ought again to apologise for writing so much about ourselves, but one's pen runs on when one thinks of the kind and sympathetic spirit of the one to whom one's words are addressed. The dream of my life was to have a son who should be something of what our beloved Papa was, a real grandson of his, in soul and intellect, a grandson of yours. Waldie gave me hopes of this -his nature was full of promise from the first, and I saw it with such pride and pleasure, and thought I could one day be of use to him I He is gone! and I can be of but limited use to Henry, and of none to William in any way! But one must guard against the fault of being annoyed with one's children for not being what one wished and hoped, what one wanted them to be. One must learn to abandon dreams and to take things as they come and characters as they are - one cannot quarrel with nature, and I suppose it knows best, though to us it seems cruel, perverse and contrary in the extreme. But it ends in one's feeling somewhat solitary at times!

To return to Prince Bismarck, he has so much that is brutal and cynical in his nature, so little that is noble and upright, he is so completely a man of another century than ours, that as an example or an ideal he becomes very dangerous. He is a patriot and is a genius, but as a school there could not be a worse one! Opinions such as William holds are very much the fashion nowadays in Germany - they have half created the immense power Bismarck possesses and he has half created them. But they are only a phase in the development of Germany! I think a dangerous and an unwholesome one, as they are a bad preparation for the solution of all the grave and difficult questions which will have to be the work of the next 20 or 30 years.

Mr Gladstone, the Home Rulers and Parnellites are also a strange spectacle. The Government have a very difficult task before them! Mr Bright wrote an excellent letter a few days ago, I thought.

A week later (April 29) the Crown Princess, who had not abandoned all hope of Prince Alexander regaining his throne, wrote to Queen Victoria:

> If only the Regency could go on governing for a time in Bulgaria, and if only the miscreants could be punished, the Constitution modified and in time the Kingdom be proclaimed, then Sandro could go back. But how can he if he is confronted by difficulties which make it impossible to govern with success and which he has no legal means of overcoming? One could not advise him to begin with a *coup d'état*. Would the Russians swallow this without war? Would the other States hasten to recognise the new state of things and in some sort of way guarantee its not being upset again - or is it impossible? Do you think this will and can develop in the next few months? If he is not interfered with and the inner difficulties are arranged before he returns, by a military dictator or something of the kind, then I am sure he could maintain himself, but not unless. Of course Prince Bismarck will not care for or encourage this solution - as Bulgaria is indifferent to him and he hates Sandro, but for all that, whatever good comes out of such a situation will be reaped by Germany, England, Italy and Austria! They cannot and must not officially suggest further or push such a thing, as it would force Russia for her honour's sake to abandon her present passive attitude, and that would mean general war; but if the Bulgarians could work it out themselves quietly and it then be accepted, it would surely be the best that could be done. Russia would have to digest her disappointment if she would not make war, and all the others would be satisfied. Prince Bismarck's attitude of friendship towards Russia, of course, forbids his even giving this thing so much as a thought. He would never give either official or unofficial advice to the Bulgarians or to Sandro, and on this question keeps completely aloof, as it is the one with which he can easiest oblige the Russians without sacrificing anything he cares about! I only think that all this obliging is no use and of no avail and that the Russians will do just what they please and ally themselves with the French whenever they think convenient. At present the good understanding between the other Powers makes them think the moment inopportune! If ever Russia and Germany become enemies, then Bulgaria becomes of the greatest importance, and it is this eventuality that our best military men always keep more in their mind's eye than Bismarck does they all still look to Sandro and value his military reputation and talents and his Statesmanship and consider him a trump card, for such an opportunity which may however never come.
>
> *April 30.*
>
> I have every reason to believe that there are people at Darmstadt who are very ill disposed towards Sandro and his brothers, and who encouraged Henry

in the *Auffassung* of the Emperor, Empress, William, Louise of Baden and Bismarck, which he has very strongly. This is very tiresome, and a hard trial to poor Moretta.[8]

A postscript which the Princess added sheds a little further light on her opinion of Bismarck. Eight days earlier, M. Schnäbele, the French Commissary at Pagny railway station, was arrested when within a few yards of the German frontier, and imprisoned at Metz. There was at once a great outcry in the French press over this indignity, but the Crown Princess was not apprehensive of any ill results.

In the Schnäbele affair [she wrote] I think Prince Bismarck will be very mild and conciliatory and not irritate the feelings of the French purposely. When he likes to be *versöhnlich* he can, as he was in the affair of the Caroline Islands with Spain, but it simply depends on his own will and caprice.

The Princess was right, for that day (August 29) M. Schnäbele was released, and the affair ended.

In the preceding month, on July 7, Prince Ferdinand, the youngest son of Prince Augustus of Saxe-Coburg and Princess Clementine of Bourbon-Orleans (known to the Princess as 'Aunt Clem'), was elected Prince of Bulgaria by the Bulgarian parliament. The great powers all decided not formally to recognise his sovereignty, and his position from the outset was somewhat difficult.

The Bulgarians [the Crown Princess wrote on September 1] will soon realise that with the best intentions Ferdinand is not like their Hero Prince, to whom they behaved so badly and whom they must ever miss.

Her sympathy with Ferdinand's predecessor had indeed in no wise diminished. On October 17, 1887, she wrote to Queen Victoria:

How I envy your seeing Sandro! I am so glad to think he is with you; I am sure it must do him good *au physique et au moral*. Please tell me how you think him looking and whether he is in good spirits!

In the following month the Tsar visited Berlin, and the subject of Bulgaria came again under discussion. On November 29, 1887, the Crown Princess wrote to Queen Victoria:

What a row there is now at Berlin about the visit of the Czar and Bismarck's conversation, his threats and hits against the court and against the Orleans family! I should not wonder if Bismarck had tried to fling a stone at Sandro to please the Czar. The whole business is neither pretty nor dignified, and I am heartily glad we are not in the midst of it, but it is very bad for Willy.

Bismarck's uncompromising attitude to Prince Alexander did not, however, appease the Tsar and his ministers, who were still determined to bring Bulgaria entirely under Russian influence. In the event it seemed as if war might break out again between Turkey and Russia over the question of the principality, and on January 5, 1888, the Crown Princess wrote:

Politics are not in a very quieting state, but still I hope and think that war will be avoided. I think that Prince Bismarck is at a great deal too much pains to prove to Russia that he has no interest in preventing her from doing what she likes in Bulgaria! Russia might have known that long ago, if she had chosen, and if she does not choose to know it, or believe it now, all the dirt Prince Bismarck is trying to throw at Ferdinand and at the poor Orleans family will be of no use, and is so much pains lost, just as all the infamies and treachery and calumnies, the indignities he allowed to be heaped on poor Sandro's innocent head, have not brought Russia's friendship as they were intended to do!! These 'middle age' fashions of treating politics I cannot admire, and in the 19th century it is hardly the thing to take a leaf out of the book of the Medici. I do love honesty and plain dealing, fairness and simplicity, and one does so sigh and long and pine for it!! One is so sick and weary of a system which stoops to means which are so low, even be it wielded by ever so great a man, and be its success and brilliancy worshipped by a crowd of short-sighted admirers, who, their national vanity being flattered, fancy themselves great patriots, while the standard of national sentiments and aspiration is being lowered and deteriorated. How long, how long, will all this last!!! I suppose it is to outlast us and our lifetime!!! Prince Bismarck's power and prestige are greater than ever, the poor dear Emperor is but a shadow, and Willy is Prince Bismarck's willing tool and follower! 'A quelque chose malheur est bon.'

Russia was now becoming more and more exasperated with Bulgarian nationalist aims, and it was evident that unless the powers signatory to the Treaty of Berlin could bring diplomatic pressure to bear upon Russia, there was risk of a second attempt being made to dominate the Bulgarian ruler. On January 8 the Crown Princess wrote:

I hear from the best sources that Prince Bismarck is doing all he can to prevent war, in every way, and is intensely anxious for England to show her determination actively to support the three allied powers, Germany, Austria and Italy. Prince Bismarck also disapproved of the talk about Fritz's resignation, etc., and equally of William and Dona having attended the Stöcker meeting. I do not believe in a war! I think that if Russia sees so many arrayed against her, she will draw in her horns and not plunge into so unsafe an adventure....

The Emperor is not quite well, having one of his attacks again, which, though not dangerous, are very painful, I fear, and weaken him. Bernhard has returned from Meiningen, where the sorrow for his Grandmama is deep and universal....I wonder whether all those things are in the eyes of B. ridiculous 'quixotry'. What we have suffered under this regime!!! How utterly corrupting has his influence been on his school his employes, on the political life of Germany! It has made Berlin almost intolerable to live in, if one is not his abject slave!! His party, his followers and admirers are fifty times worse than he is! One feels as if one would like to send up one great cry for deliverance and that if it were answered, one great deep sigh of relief would be given. Alas, all the mischief wrought would take years to repair!! Of course those that only look at the outside aspect of things see Germany strong, great and united, with a tremendous army (in time of war near three millions of men!), a Minister who can dictate to the world, a sovereign whose head is crowned with laurels, a trade that is making an effort to outdo all others, the German element making itself remarked everywhere in the world (even if not loved or trusted). They cannot think we have any reason to complain, but only to be thankful. If they did but know at what price all this is bought! Perhaps you will think I am only croaking!

A week later, January 14, she wrote:

....I do hope and trust that Europe will not be so foolish as to try and oblige Ferdinand to leave Bulgaria. It would be only inviting Russia to take possession of the country, which would really be iniquitous. Why should that unfortunate country, which has become emancipated only so lately, be forced back, under the yoke of Russia, by united Europe ? How sad to see the whole work of Sandro's life undone again his heroic efforts to free his people made useless. One cannot have much sympathy with Ferdinand, still if the Bulgarians like to have him and he can manage to maintain himself and is ready to stay, what right has Europe to upset him, and what interest in doing Russia's bidding and fetching the chestnuts out of the fire for her? Russia wants to have Bulgaria, is afraid of getting into a big war, consequently wishes the others to help her! *I.e.*, assist the great and the oppressor against the smaller and the weaker! It would be a real shame. I cannot conceive England or Italy doing such a thing, or Austria either ! Germany's policy has been so mean and so cynical throughout that I should not wonder if she advised putting the country under Russian rule altogether - little she cares for the legitimate aspirations of a small nationality. Still I fancy she would never interfere very actively. Russia has only two ways of possessing herself of Bulgaria, the one is by a military occupation which means war, the other would be the often-tried method of conspiracies and of stirring up risings, etc., through secret agents, and by bands of Montenegrins or Macedonians, as now at Burgas, but the Bulgarians seem well able to cope with these attempts to overthrow their Government!

I wonder what Sir William White says now and what the Turks will do? The Russians have barred their own road to Constantinople by their own bad behaviour to the Bulgarians. It would be strange indeed if some of the Great Powers cleared the way for them again and removed this obstacle. Do you not think so too? Morier is in England now and most likely would not be of my opinion.

I do not think we shall have a war. The Czar does not wish for one and Prince Bismarck is doing all he can to prevent it; the French are also quieter now.

In the early days of 1888, Lord Randolph Churchill, a friend of the Prince of Wales, paid a visit to St. Petersburg with a view to finding some possible means of paving the way to an Anglo-Russian understanding. He went entirely in an unofficial capacity, and his entire visit seemed to the Crown Princess to be somewhat 'ill-advised'. At Berlin en route. Lord Randolph met Sir Robert Morier, the British Ambassador to St. Petersburg, who was then on leave. Sir Robert warned the self-appointed emissary of England against any discussion on the international situation with authorities in Russia. The warning was ignored, and Lord Randolph interviewed not only M. de Giers, the Russian Chancellor, but also the Tsar, and expressed in unequivocal language his opinion that Russian and British interests were identical. His actions, which by no means met with Queen Victoria's approval, were now warmly denounced by the Crown Princess, who wrote on January 31:

I still think Lord Randolph Churchill's visit to Petersburg very mischievous! It is childish of him to speak of England's policy under the Liberal Government being friendly and loyal towards Russia. Russia is never loyal to anyone, and therefore it is impossible to keep to written agreements, or to be friendly; though one need not be the reverse. One can only avoid offending Russia needlessly, never trust or believe her, and be always on the qui vive. I am afraid the loyal and friendly attitude towards Russia was due to weakness and indifference, blindness to real facts and an imperfect knowledge of the whole Eastern question, its direct and indirect bearing on our interests in India. Morier belongs to a school to which Lord R. Churchill evidently leans, who think that India is completely to be severed from the rest of the East and that what happens in the Mahommedan world of Turkey or the Eastern provinces under Russian rule in no way affects India. Such is not the case. I wonder that those who consider themselves the friends of the weak, the oppressed, of liberty and of civilisation, should be so ready to see the people of the Balkans thrust back against their will under Russian tyranny and oppression, should count for so little the danger of seeing Russian power extend over that part of the world to the detriment of Austria, to the detriment of the population of the Balkans and certainly to the detriment of our own power! Why should the rest of civilised Europe give way to Russia in everything? The worst Government in the world and the most corrupt of States! I cannot understand it!! Russia will not go to war if she sees that the rest of Europe (France excepted) mean to resist her.

I hope Morier will do no more harm at Petersburg! It is very likely he might be dangerous with Crispi at this moment; anything which could spoil the good understanding between England and Italy would be a great danger.

Lord Randolph's visit, however, did no great harm, and won the approval of the Prince of Wales. International relations at this period, however, were not of such a nature as to be mollified by courteous phrases, especially with regard to the question of Bulgaria, on which the Crown Princess wrote on February 15:

Of politics I will say nothing - only that Fritz thinks if anything so foolish is done as to attempt to put Bulgaria back under Russia's control against her will, by consent of the Powers, endless trouble will be the consequence. The development of this country's independence did not owe its origin to any initiative, or ambitious personal design on the part of its former Sovereign - it was a thoroughly natural and popular movement (in spite of Prince Bismarck trying to represent it as the reverse in his speech). This movement was caused by the evil proceedings of the Russians and by their attempt to thwart everything that was done to secure a peaceful development of order and prosperity in that country - an incessant war against the Government of that country, which at last exasperated the people, and has made them firmly determined not to be a Russian province any more than Greece, Servia or Roumania. Should the Liberal Powers therefore accede to Russia's demands (which she would make formally as soon as she thought they would be granted) they would be committing an iniquity in the first place and a blunder in the second.

In the event no change was made in the status of Bulgaria for a decade, and then, in March 1896, the great powers, Russia included, formally recognised Prince Ferdinand as Prince of Bulgaria.

## NOTES

1 Ludwig, *Kaiser William II*, p. 15.
2 *Mary Ponsonby*, p. 250, December 5, 1885.
3 *Ibid.* p. 256, March 4, 1886.
4 Sir Robert Morier.
5 E. C. Corti, *Alexander von Battenberg, sein Kampf mit dem Zaren und Bismarck* (Vienna, 1920), p. 267, where Queen Victoria's whole letter is given in a facsimile reproduction.

6 Princess Victoria Frederica Augustine Mary Caroline Matilda, elder of the two younger sisters of Prince William's wife. Princess Victoria married in 1885 Duke Frederick Ferdinand of Schleswig-Holstein.
7 Duke of Schleswig-Holstein.
8 The Princess Victoria.

*Prince Frederick William and Victoria, Princess Royal,
with Queen Victoria, Prince Albert and family, 1855*

*Queen Victoria, the Prince Consort and their children,
with Princess Victoria second from left*

*Prince and Princess Frederick William, 1858*

*Crown Princess Frederick William, 1862*

*Crown Princess Frederick William, c.1870*

*Crown Prince Frederick William, c.1870*

*Crown Prince Frederick William with his two elder sons, Princes William and Henry, c.1874*

*Crown Princess Frederick William with Queen Victoria and Princess Victoria Melita of Edinburgh (front), Princess Victoria of Wales and Princess Victoria of Prussia (back), 1884*

*Empress Victoria, 1888*

*Empress Frederick and Queen Victoria, 1889*

*Emperor William II*

*Empress Frederick, 1900*

# IX. The Illness of the Crown Prince Frederick

THROUGHOUT all the trials and tribulations that disturbed the life of the Crown Princess, there was one thing that she could count upon - the love and sympathy of her husband. Their mutual affection had known no cloud, and it was with pleasant memories that they both looked back on the past, and with confidence and hope that they looked forward to the future. But there now appeared the first indications of those agonising events which were to destroy that beautiful serene happiness. It was in January 1887 that the Crown Prince, then fifty-six years of age, first began to suffer from hoarseness, and his Physician-in-Ordinary, Surgeon-General Wegner, soon realised that it was sufficiently serious to warrant consultation with a specialist, with the result that Dr Gerhardt, Professor of Medicine at the University of Berlin, was called in, and he, on March 6, diagnosed a small growth on the left vocal cord, but was unable to say whether it was of a malignant nature or not. A fortnight later, on March 22, the Crown Prince, in making a speech on the occasion of the Emperor's ninetieth birthday, showed unmistakable signs of hoarseness.

Meanwhile, Dr Gerhardt, uncertain as to the nature of the 'granula', strove to remove it surgically. This treatment, however, failed, and he then burnt it down with the galvano cautery, but while, as the result of this operation or series of operations, the growth disappeared, the hoarseness and some of the pain remained, and the Crown Prince was advised to go to Ems, whither he went with the Crown Princess on April 13. It was from Ems that the Crown Princess wrote to Queen Victoria on April 29:

....So many thanks for your kind enquiries after Fritz. His spirits are far better here than at Berlin, and his throat seems daily improving. All the irritation, swelling and redness is fast subsiding, he never coughs, and has not the feeling of soreness, but part of the little 'granula' which Professor Gerhardt could not take off with the hot wire, because the throat was too much irritated, is still on the surface of one of the *Stimmbänder* and will have to be removed when we go home, then I think the hoarseness will quite disappear. Fritz now eats and sleeps and looks well. Of course he takes no long walks and does not go uphill so as not to fatigue or heat himself, and is asked to talk as little as possible....

On the Crown Prince's return to Berlin early in May, Gerhardt, however, found no signs of improvement: the hoarseness remained, and the wound was not healed. Professor Ernst von Bergmann, an eminent surgeon, a liberal in politics and a friend of the Crown Prince, was now called into consultation, and he expressed the opinion that the growth should be removed by a surgical operation. A day or two later, on May 17, the Crown Princess wrote to Queen Victoria:

....My heart is very heavy since this morning, as I find that the doctors, although satisfied with the general effect of Ems, which has taken all catarrh away, and satisfied with Fritz's health, now discover that the lump in the larynx is not a simple granulation on the surface of the mucous membrane which can be removed by touching with the electric platina wire, but that it is most likely a thing they call 'Epithelion', and that, if it is to be removed, it cannot be got at from inside the throat, as it may also exist under the larynx in a fold, where it cannot be reached. The celebrated surgeon, Professor Bergmann, is for operating from the outside, and you can imagine that this is not an easy operation or a small one. I own I was more dead than alive with horror and distress when I heard this. The idea of a knife touching his dear throat is terrible to me. Of course Fritz is as yet not to know a word about this. He is at times so very depressed....that he now often thinks his father will survive him, and I have fine work to make these passing sad thoughts clear away, which I am happy to say they do after a short while.

Today the gentlemen consult again, and I am going to town to find out from them what more they think and have resolved....

My fear and dread is that a swelling of that kind, if not removed by some means or other, might in time develop into a growth of a malignant and dangerous character. I hope and trust and believe that there is no such danger at present. I do so hope that the views of Bergmann and Gerhardt are exaggerated....

Gerhardt and Bergmann now suggested an operation known as thyrotomy, involving the splitting of the larynx and the removal of the growth, but suddenly Bismarck intervened.

....The doctors [he records in his *Reflections*] determined to make the Crown Prince unconscious, and to carry out the removal of the larynx without having informed him of their intention. I raised objections, and required that they should not proceed without the consent of the Crown Prince....The Emperor, after being informed by me, forbade them to carry out the operation without the consent of his son.'[1]

Bismarck now arranged for a further consultation at which the best specialist advice was to be called in, and this conference was attended not only by Gerhardt, Bergmann and 'Wegner, but also by Dr Schrader, Surgeon-in-Ordinary to the Crown Prince, Dr Lauer, Physician to Emperor William I, and Professor Tobold, a senior Berlin laryngologist. Their opinion, given on May 18, was that cancer was present, and that the surgical operation proposed by Bergmann should be performed. When Bismarck read this report and understood the gravity of the situation, he determined that the best expert in Europe, no matter of what nationality, should at once be summoned. Although strongly opposed to the Crown Prince in politics, and disliking intensely what he regarded as the 'interference' of the Crown Princess in the affairs of state, he felt that all differences of opinion were but petty matters compared with this question of life or death. There were two or three such specialists recommended, one of whom was an Austrian and another was an Englishman - Dr Morell Mackenzie - whose acknowledged eminence in laryngology was recognised by his colleagues. His deftness of touch and his manipulative skill were not the least of his recommendations, but he was, as after-events were to prove, perhaps a little indiscreet, over-sensitive and somewhat polemical.

Much controversy has arisen as to who selected and sent for Mackenzie, and it was commonly supposed that the Crown Princess was responsible for the summons of the English surgeon to the bedside of her stricken husband, and the fatal termination of the disease soon afterwards has been seized upon to place her in a wholly false position before history. 'Her distrust of German therapeutics', to use the words of a recent German historian, Dr Emil Ludwig, 'has come to be regarded as largely responsible for his tragic and untimely end.' The foundation for this erroneous view is to be found in statements circulated in the German press at that period, and in such subsequent testimony as that of Dr Henry Semon, who quotes the private diary of his father, the late Sir Felix Semon. According to this last version, the Crown Princess asked Dr Wegner who he thought was the greatest throat specialist; Dr. Wegner, in reply, pointed to Dr Mackenzie's text-book, which had been translated into German and prefaced by Sir Felix Semon, who paid a great tribute to Mackenzie's skill. The Crown Princess then, according to the Semon version, despatched a telegram to Queen Victoria and requested her to arrange for the attendance of the English surgeon forthwith, and at the Queen's request Sir James Reid, her physician, left Osborne for London to interview Mackenzie. In a letter to *The Times*, dated January 25, 1928, Dr Henry Semon then goes on to relate that his father's unpublished manuscript states that 'when Reid had delivered his message, Mackenzie showed him the cable he had received from the German physicians, which requested him to start immediately for Berlin'. Sir Felix Semon also adds about the Crown Princess that, during her interview with Wegner, 'when she had finished reading my preface to the German translation of Mackenzie's book, she commanded Wegner to press for a consultation with Mackenzie', and the result was the official telegram to Morell Mackenzie from the German doctors.

There is, however, another version which appears to be much nearer the truth. Sir Rennell Rodd, in a review of Emil Ludwig's *Kaiser Wilhelm II*, published in *The Times* of December 1, 1926, questioned the accuracy of several statements in this book. In proof of his contention, Sir Rennell Rodd relates how the Crown Princess had come to luncheon at the British Embassy early in 1887 in order to attend a christening and how, when the conversation turned to the Crown Prince's illness, Sir Edward Malet suggested the possibility of obtaining another opinion and the Crown Princess had in reply expressed her ignorance as to who were the best authorities. Almost immediately after luncheon, however, Bismarck paid a visit to the Ambassador and while conversing about the illness said that arrangements had been made for a British specialist to come to Berlin. There seems, therefore, no possible doubt that at luncheon that day the Crown Princess did not know of the existence of Morell Mackenzie, and further that the British specialist's original summons came from the German doctors at the probable instigation and certainly with the full approval of Bismarck.

Dr Emil Ludwig, however, refused to accept this evidence, which was founded on the recollections of a Secretary of Embassy after forty years had elapsed, and preferred the general consensus of the German medical authorities supported by Bismarck. It happens to few men to be able to refute so completely the misrepresentations of an adversary as Sir Rennell Rodd was able to do, when he published in *The Times* of January 18, 1928, the following letter, written on November 14, 1887, by the British Ambassador to Count Herbert Bismarck in execution of a desire expressed by Queen Victoria that he should counteract the circulation of stories injurious to the Crown Princess by emphasising 'the well-known fact' that it was the German doctors themselves who sent for Mackenzie. Sir Edward Malet's letter ran:

DEAR COUNT BISMARCK - Will you kindly glance your eye at the passage which I have marked in this evening's *Norddeutsche Allgemeine Zeitung*? You will see that to the Queen of England also is to be attributed that the Crown Prince was committed to the care of the English specialist. The context indicates that the word 'also' means that the other person was the Crown Princess. Now as a matter of fact, of which I am sure that you are aware, the Crown Princess had nothing to do with calling in Sir Morell Mackenzie, still less the Queen. The report that the Crown Princess sent for him originally is doing her great injury, and is devoid of truth.

Would it be possible, with reference to this paragraph, which gains credence through appearing in the semi-official paper, to state authoritatively in the same paper, or in the *Reichs Anzeiger*, that Mackenzie was called in by decision of the physicians attending the Crown Prince, and that the Crown Princess was not even consulted, and that certainly the Queen of England had nothing to do with it? I am sure your chivalry will make you feel as I do about these statements.

Believe me to be, etc.,<br>
E.B. MALET.

From a note appended to this draft [continues Sir Rennell Rodd] it appears that Count Bismarck spoke to the Ambassador about the matter the following day. He took the view that it was not certain that the Crown Princess might not have suggested Morell Mackenzie and that there was a danger of making matters worse by publishing a statement which the German doctors might dispute. He undertook, however, to speak to his father to see if anything could be done. The Ambassador's positive statement that the report was devoid of truth was justified not only by his conversation in the previous May with the Crown Princess, when she said that she did not know who were the great throat specialists, but also by what the Chancellor himself had told him at the time. But his appeal to a sense of chivalry for the correction of a statement devoid of truth....remained without effect, and the legend received confirmation without protest....

One further testimony must be considered: in the official report of the illness of the Emperor Frederick published in 1888, it is made clear that the name of Morell Mackenzie was first put forward by Wegner and accepted by Gerhardt and Bergmann.

On the essential point all versions agree, that the first request that Morell Mackenzie received to attend the Crown Prince came to him from the German doctors, *and it was on this request that he acted*.[2]

The next day, May 19, the Crown Princess, who then knew that the German doctors had telegraphed for the English specialist, wrote to Queen Victoria:

....I was over yesterday at Berlin to speak to the doctors, and Bergmann told me that he would not decide on performing the operation before Morell Mackenzie has given his opinion, but that if Morell Mackenzie viewed the case exactly as he did, the operation would take place at once. Fritz will not be told until just before the moment....

I spent a terrible day yesterday; it is so difficult to appear unconcerned when one's heart is so torn, and it is so important he should eat and sleep and feel well up to this moment....

....All the doctors say that Fritz has been quite rightly treated till now, and are satisfied that no time has been lost and that nothing else could have been done, and that Professor Gerhardt was the right authority to go to. I cannot telegraph much, as already the talk and gossip at Berlin is considerable and people are worried at Fritz's not appearing at the parades, etc., and one does not wish to make an unnecessary stir. Of course, if M.M. arrives soon, we will make him write to you and Sir W. Jenner,[3] so that you are kept informed. I am not so frightened about danger to Fritz's life; thank God, I do not apprehend that, nor that this swelling is of a cancerous kind, nor does Bergmann, who says when once it is taken away, he does not think it will return; but I am so distressed to think that his dear voice, which is so necessary to him in his position in the country and army, etc., will be gone, and I know it will be an awful trial to him....

On the evening of the 20th, Morell Mackenzie arrived at Berlin. After a preliminary but careful examination, he announced that he was not sure that an operation was necessary, and asked that a fragment of the larynx should be removed and submitted to microscopic examination by Professor Rudolf Virchow, a man of European reputation as an anthropologist and pathologist. That evening the Crown Princess wrote to Queen Victoria from Berlin:

Dr M. Mackenzie says he cannot advise an operation before being quite sure that this growth in the throat is a malignant one! He still has his doubts. He will not give a decided opinion until he has seen more of Fritz, and thoroughly examined the throat again. He will endeavour to detach the smallest fragment from the growth and will have it examined under the microscope by Professor Virchow, so that its nature may be established from this he will then advise what is to be done! Oh how relieved I am! I shall be able to sleep tonight and look at my darling Fritz without the agonising thought that tomorrow may be the last we have to spend together. I bless Dr M. Mackenzie. Of course I know the operation may yet have to come off!!

Prince Bismarck came to see me this afternoon and was really very nice! He said his wife sent me word I was not to allow such an operation. I said I had nothing to allow what the responsible authorities decided on as the best, we should have to submit to, and we were bound to follow their advice.

The Emperor has sent for the doctors:

1. Prof Bergmann.
2. Prof Gerhardt.
3. Dr Tobold (Specialist for Laryngoscopia).
4. Dr Wegner.
5. Dr Lauer (Emperor's physician).
6. Dr Schrader (Wegner's *remplaçant*).

They are obliged to ask the Emperor's permission for so serious an operation and to tell him the whole, as they cannot tell Fritz. I am sure the Emperor will not take it in, nor understand one word. They have also sent for the Haus Minister and have written to the Empress!

I can say for certain that the German medical gentlemen seemed much less anxious to hurry on the operation after they had talked with Dr M. Mackenzie than before they had seen him! It seems he did not know what he was called for and did not therefore, unfortunately, bring his instruments with him!

We spend the night here and go back tomorrow after Dr M. Mackenzie has tried to obtain a little portion of the growth, which is very difficult and may not succeed until the fourth or fifth trial....

On the following day Mackenzie made another examination; this time removing a tiny portion of the larynx which he submitted to Virchow for investigation. Virchow was unable to discover any sign of cancer, but expressed the opinion that the fragment was too small, and that another should be taken. It was now that the views of Mackenzie and some of the German doctors diverged. Bergmann and Gerhardt maintained that the clinical signs indicated cancer. Mackenzie could not agree until there was proof positive.

The next day, May 22, 1887, the Crown Princess wrote to Queen Victoria:

This morning Wegner brought Virchow's report on the little fragment of the growth. He is unable to discover any sign of cancer, but the fragment was too small and another will have to be taken off tomorrow, which will be much more difficult, as the growth being reduced in size by the little bit taken away, there will be so little to lay hold of, and with the German instruments Dr Morell Mackenzie cannot do it! His own which he has telegraphed for arrive tonight at 10. Tomorrow morning he will try (only in Wegner's and Gerhardt's presence) to obtain the bit wanted. He still fancies that the growth is an innocent one until the reverse is actually proved by Virchow's examination and till then he strongly urges not deciding on this horrid operation! Of course the suspense is very trying to me, but I own the hope held out is a very great relief, and as I am sanguine by nature, I easily cling to it....

I cannot bring myself to believe the worst, it seems too cruel! I fancy all this will come right somehow and only the remembrance of the scare remain, which was bad enough.

This letter, written from a daughter to her mother, brings out clearly the attitude of the Crown Princess, and it may be well here to consider the causes which might have influenced her opinions.

The German Emperor, William I, was already over ninety years of age, and in the natural sequence of life could not for long sustain the burden of sovereignty. The Crown Prince as his heir would, in the normal course of events, succeed him, but if that Prince were suffering from an incurable complaint that would render him incapable of exercising the power of the crown, then, it was argued by many, the Crown Prince should be passed over in favour of his son, Prince William. Already the dread word 'cancer' was being whispered far and wide, and it was certain that if the malady were pronounced to be malignant there would be those who would urge that 'a sovereign who cannot speak should not rule'. Rumours were circulated that the family laws of the Hohenzollerns excluded an heir to the throne who suffered from an incurable physical complaint, but these laws contained nothing of the kind, and the Crown Princess must have known that there was no such bar to her husband's eventual accession. On this point Bismarck spoke later with authority. 'The family laws', he wrote,[4] 'contain no provision on the matter, any more than does the text of the Prussian constitution.'

The Crown Princess had much of her mother's tenacity of royal power, and there were those who afterwards did not scruple to say that during this period the Crown Princess was anxious that for these reasons the illness should not be diagnosed as cancerous, and that she impressed her views on Morell Mackenzie. Such a charge is baseless. There is not one jot or tittle of evidence in favour of such a slander. Mackenzie and the other doctors were given a free hand subject to the wishes of the patient, and their opinions and treatment were unbiassed and uninfluenced by the Crown Princess. All that the Crown Princess did, in fact, was to do what ninety-nine women out of a hundred, German or English, would have done in her place, and that was to place her reliance in the specialist who gave the greatest hope for the complete recovery of the patient. Naturally, she did not want to see the husband she loved subjected to an unnecessary operation, and it was with supreme joy that she received on the following day Morell Mackenzie's and Virchow's report to the effect that the second portion of the larynx removed showed no signs of cancerous growth. Upon this, the proposal to operate was abandoned, not, however, without protests from those who had suggested it - Professors Gerhardt and Bergmann. Gerhardt later alleged that during this operation Mackenzie had injured the healthy right vocal cord, an accusation which Mackenzie strenuously denied. Mackenzie was also accused of purposely taking a portion of the healthy side of the throat and sending it to Virchow, but it is quite inconceivable that a man of Mackenzie's reputation should do such a thing: nor does there appear to be any valid reason why he should thus wish to deceive wilfully Virchow and the Crown Princess. It must be remembered that at this period the incipient stages of cancer were difficult to recognise. Now it is known that there are diseases of a non-malignant nature that so closely resemble cancer that the greatest experts cannot tell the difference. Thus, at the time, even the most skilful specialist in this particular case could prove nothing, he could only maintain or deny that cancer was present. Much of the difference of opinion over the Crown Prince's illness had its basis in the fact that medical science was then in so rudimentary a stage with regard to these particular complaints that diagnoses were often barely more than guesswork based upon assumptions.

In any case, Mackenzie and the two German doctors were now irremediably estranged - and when doctors quarrel, the outlook for the patient is indeed gloomy!

Mackenzie was now anxious that the patient should come to his clinic in England 'like an ordinary mortal'[5] and the Crown Princess approved the idea. On May 24, 1887, she wrote to her mother:

....We are much more hopeful and reassured about Fritz's throat now. His voice is completely gone for the present, and his throat feels sore and uncomfortable, but that is only from the little operation of taking a little bit from the growth, I hope to be able to tell you more in the course of a day, when Wegner, Gerhardt and their colleagues have considered Dr Morell Mackenzie's views and proposals. He thinks he can cure Fritz quite well by treating his throat from the inside, but of course one cannot pull about the throat every day: it would do harm and set up general inflammation, irritation, swelling, etc., and everything must be done to avoid this, and destroy the growth by degrees. If the other doctors come round to this opinion in consequence of Virchow's researches, then I think we need not be anxious any more, and only most careful and conscientious to effect the best cure possible....

Of course the public are very anxious at Berlin, as something of the dread we were in is beginning to transpire.

*Later.*

Gerhardt, Wegner and Dr M. Mackenzie were quite satisfied with Fritz's throat this morning! There is to be one more consultation and then Dr M. M. will go home. Wegner and the others want his advice carried out here and him to leave the treatment to Tobold. This I think will make a muddle, and it would be better for Fritz to go to Brighton, St Leonard's, etc., and to have the treatment carried out by Dr M.M., himself, but I dare not suggest this last, as it would annoy the people here and make them angry with me. If they should propose it, then it would be another thing, but I do not think they will!

Gerhardt says the treatment must be very slow and not hurried in any way; and he would wish that M. M. should carry it out himself. I now leave it to them to settle their minds amongst themselves and shall not interfere with them.

Gerhardt early expressed his opinion to the Crown Princess, who wrote on June 2 to Queen Victoria:

I yesterday evening spoke to Prof Gerhardt and begged him to tell me exactly what he thought! He told me: 'Ich sehe die Sache von Woche zu Woche *ernster* an! Das Stückchen, welches M. Mackenzie fortgenommen, ist wiedergewachsen - die Geschwulst ist in Eiterung übergegangen, &c. - jetzt ist auch die *andere* Seite des Halses, das *andere* bisher freigebliebene Stimmband ergriffen - ein Substanz-Verlust ist schon vorhanden. *Wenn nickt Dr M, Mackenzie helfen* und *heilen kann*, so giebt es keine Rettung ausser die Operation von 'Laryngotomie' - und zwar unter viel *schlechteren* Bedingungen als vor 14 Tagen! Also ist und bleibt meine *einzige* Hofrhung, dass Dr M. Mackenzie *recht* behalten möge in seiner Auffassung, und dass es seiner Behandlung gelingen möge, denn wir haben nichts mehr vorzuschlagen.'⁶

Of course you can understand that this makes me utterly miserable! Thank God, Fritz does not guess it and this will not reach the ears of the public unless the doctors talk, which I have implored them not to do! I keep it quite to myself, but I feel wretched, and my nerves are in a very shaky condition from the constant anxiety and uncertainty and the strain to appear perfectly unconcerned. The doctors wish Dr M. Mackenzie to come here once more and have a consultation with them, and then we shall go to England and take Prof. Gerhardt with us for a short while and then one of the others will come in his stead to report on the course and result of the treatment and state of Fritz's health. I am having enquiries made about small quiet hotels near London, Chislehurst, Richmond, Surbiton, Hampstead, Sydenham, Wimbledon, where we could go, so that Fritz was not in town, but could go daily to Dr M.M., or see him daily. Fritz must not talk, so he must keep out of everyone's way! His one hope and wish is to be at Westminster Abbey on the 21st [for Queen Victoria's Jubilee] and represent the Emperor. I have told the Emperor so yesterday! He agreed to this if the doctors allow it! If M. Mackenzie allows it, we can then go to Norris Castle the beginning, or near the middle of July! ... I hope from there to be able to appear at whatever Fêtes you may wish to have me, but he must not; it is very hard upon him, and he is terribly depressed, as he wanted to go about and see so many people and things in London and had so long been looking forward to your Jubilee! He is also terribly annoyed at William wishing to come forward so much and take his place without asking him, etc. However all this, painful, disagreeable and disappointing as it is, must be borne without a murmur, and so long as his throat gets right, and if Dr Mackenzie's opinion and hopes and the promises he held out gain the day, we must be satisfied!...

People here do not half like Fritz leaving the country on account of the Emperor's age, and yet he clearly ought to go to England and get himself cured by the only person who has said that he thinks he can cure him!!....

Preparations were now being made in England for the celebration of Queen Victoria's Jubilee to commemorate her fifty years' reign. The Crown Prince was determined to represent the German Emperor, although the suggestion had been made that Prince William should do so, and the Crown Prince thought that advantage might be taken of his visit to England to undergo the treatment that Mackenzie had suggested.

Meanwhile, the doctors still disagreed. Bergmann and Gerhardt clung to their opinion, and Mackenzie, supported by Virchow's analysis, clung to his. The Crown Princess, the German Emperor and Empress, and Bismarck himself all knew of this divergence: any one of them, with insistence, might have supported Gerhardt and Bergmann's opinion and have compelled an operation. None insisted. Each of them left it to the doctors to decide what was best. The German doctors produced statistics to prove that the operation they recommended was successful in seven cases out of ten: Mackenzie believed he might be able to effect a cure in two months. With such an alternative before them can anyone blame the Crown Princess, the German Emperor and Empress, or Bismarck, for giving Mackenzie a fair chance? All acted in the best of faith and without *arrière-pensée*. When life is in danger all other interests are subsidiary.

On June 3 the Crown Princess wrote to Queen Victoria:

> I am still struggling between hopes and fears, I cannot bring myself to believe that the German doctors are right! People torment me with questions - some say it would be my fault if anything happened to Fritz in England, etc. Wegner is haunted by the idea that the swelling may suddenly in the course of a few hours grow so large that suffocation may be imminent and tracheotomy have to be performed instantly, that we should therefore not leave home! This fear seems to me exaggerated and the case highly improbable, but I am not a doctor! Others are again tormented by the idea that Fritz may be helpless in bed in England and the Emperor die, when he cannot be had!!! All these things are always possible, and one cannot be kept a prisoner here, or be prevented from following a useful course by the fear of what might happen.
>
> Dear old Roggenbach [Baron von Roggenbach, the Prussian representative in Frankfort] was here for two days and I cannot say with what touching and fatherly care he gave us his advice - really so good and kind! He is most anxious for Fritz to go to England, and also thinks it would frighten and depress Fritz terribly if he were not allowed to go to Westminster Abbey on the 21st. He is full of grave apprehensions, but thinks - happen what may - the awful operation of Laryngotomy ought not to be allowed. It is too dangerous and if it succeeded would leave the patient a broken man! One other older and fatherly friend, to whose devotion I can trust, is excellent General W. von Loë - he is a celebrated and eminent Cavalry General; by a curious coincidence and in spite of William being one of his followers and admirers, he well knows that it would be very dangerous, if such young heads suddenly took up the task left by an aged Sovereign of 90! People are disturbed, nervous and anxious and alarmed, and I shall be glad if Dr. M. Mackenzie comes and again finds it in his power to dispel all these fears! I have one instinctive feeling that they may not be founded on any real facts, but the doubt is very disagreeable and wearing, especially as it must be so carefully concealed from the dear patient, who is oftentimes much depressed....
>
> I must ask a favour of you! Under the present circumstances and for the present, it would be the greatest relief to us if we could bring over all our private papers to England. Would you allow them to be locked up in the iron room leading out of dear Papa's Library at Buckingham Palace? We should feel much happier. I can explain more when we meet.

Mackenzie by now doubted the diagnosis resultant upon his early removals of minute portions of the larynx and now decided, without informing Gerhardt, in order to be perfectly sure one way or the other, that two further particles should be removed. Accordingly, on June 8, another operation was performed. The Crown Prince was now in excellent health and eagerly looking forward to his visit to London to take part in the Jubilee rejoicings. The day following this operation the Crown Princess wrote to Queen Victoria:

> I can write to you today with a much lighter heart, as Dr M. Mackenzie sees no unfavourable symptoms in my darling Fritz's throat since he last examined it. He has removed two tiny particles of the growth and Virchow will again examine them! I hope then the Doctors, who are like St. Thomas the unbeliever, will at last believe that it is of a harmless nature! Of course, Mackenzie cannot swear that this benign growth may not become a malignant one, but he sees no reason to assume this! The only one thing which is in any way against the best prognostication is that Fritz is of an age in which growths are usually not of an innocent nature the harmless ones are pretty common with children and young people....
> One is really driven half distracted with all these things.

Virchow's report upon the particles removed in the second operation corroborated Mackenzie's opinion.

> In spite of the most careful examination [he reported]....no single portion was detected which has been pathologically changed sufficiently to make this worth mentioning....In this operation a more central portion (of the growth) has been gripped....the healthy condition of the tissues close to the cut permits of a very favourable prognostic opinion. But [he added] whether such an opinion would be justified concerning the whole of the malady cannot with certainty be determined from the two extirpated pieces. In any case there is nothing present in them that could arouse the suspicion of further and more serious disease.[7]

The relief of the Crown Princess at the pronouncement may be imagined.

The scene of this tragic drama now moved to England, for it was hither that the Crown Prince and Princess journeyed for the dual purpose of attending Queen Victoria's Jubilee and of having the advantage of the treatment which Mackenzie had prescribed. Wegner and Landgraf (Professor Gerhardt's laryngological assistant) accompanied the royal party, which arrived in England on June 14.

When Queen Victoria passed in procession on June 21 from Buckingham Palace to Westminster Abbey, there rode in the cavalcade of thirty-two princes the towering Lohengrin-like figure in the white uniform, silver breastplate and eagle-crested helmet, of the Crown Prince of Germany a tragic figure, outwardly the embodiment of princely grace and splendour, but inwardly conscious that if it was indeed cancer that had laid its stranglehold upon him, his span of life was drawing to a close.

At the close of the Jubilee festivities, the Crown Prince and Princess spent two months in England first at Norwood, then in the Isle of Wight, then in Scotland. Whilst the Crown Prince was in England another doctor had been called into consultation - Dr Mark Hovell, senior surgeon to the Throat Hospital. Mackenzie was anxious that the Crown Prince's absence from the German court should now be prolonged, but the failing health of the nonagenarian ruler of Germany rendered his return to Berlin imperative unless events were to be left 'en l'air' or in the hands of Prince William. The Crown Princess fought, as she herself expressed it, 'tooth and nail' for the continuance of her husband's stay in England. As she wrote to her mother on August 30:

....I have received letters from influential persons from Berlin saying Fritz must come home, that his health was only the first consideration when it was a question of real danger to life, that he was not a private individual and therefore could not only do what was best for his health, that the Emperor might often be persuaded from attending to business, that affairs could not be left 'en l'air' nor committed to William's hands, and that Fritz must therefore not leave Potsdam and Berlin. I shall have to fight this tooth and nail! It would be madness to spoil Fritz's cure while he is in a fair way to recovery, but not well yet! I know the life there, the fatigues, the constant calls upon us and duties without end!! He would never cure his voice....The Emperor, the Empress and Bismarck wish Fritz to be cured first, but I admit that they do not see or know all the reasons which have been put forward by these other people, the Generals, etc....It is rather hard that because the Emperor has constant little attacks Fritz is not to be allowed to get well in the proper way!! It seems to me sacrificing the future to the present. Fritz writes to me overjoyed that you have so kindly promised to knight Dr Mackenzie - he is especially pleased at this kindness of yours and very grateful.

The fight which the Princess made to prevent the return of her ailing husband to the bustle and activity of Berlin was successful, and when, on September 3, the Crown Prince and Princess left England it was, on Sir Morell Mackenzie's[8] advice, to Toblach in the Tyrol that they went. Dr Hovell alone accompanied them, but he was joined a few days later by Major Schrader, Surgeon-in-Ordinary to the Crown Prince.

The Crown Prince and Princess had been accompanied to England by the principal officers of their suites, and it was unfortunate that at Balmoral a quarrel broke out between the Crown Prince's Court-Marshal, Count Leszczyc de Radolin-Radolinsky and the Crown Princess's private secretary and Court Chamberlain, Count Seckendorff. The quarrel had originated some five years earlier, when Radolinsky had been appointed to the Crown Prince's suite in order to watch Seckendorff.[9] On September 9 the Crown Princess wrote from Toblach to her intimate friend Lady Ponsonby:

....I am *so thankful to you* for having given me this correct information about Ct Radolinsky's conversation at Balmoral. Count R. behaves in the *strangest fashion*; and is more dangerous than I can say. Curiously enough before I got your letter at Munich, I saw an old friend of ours, old Baron v. Roggenbach at Frankfort, and *he* told me that Ct Radolinsky had been at pains to speak to *all* the Emperor's gentlemen at Ems in exactly the same strain, and the same words you write to me! My friend was quite *disgusted*. Of the vox populi *against* Ct S-, which Ct R- is so fond of speaking about, I can find out nothing. My friends say it does not exist, but that of course Ct S- has enemies! It is *these* who have got hold of Ct R- and taken advantage of Ct R's s credulity, of his excitability and of his irritation against Ct S-. The principal person who works in this direction is Ct Eulenburg! You know what a false, unscrupulous, ambitious man he is; he owes Ct Seckendorff a *grudge* and wishes to injure him as he is very jealous of him; and fears Count Seckendorff might prevent the Crown Prince from listening more to him in future. Count Radolinsky is sincerely attached to us, but he quite forgets it is *not* his business to take *our affairs* out of *our* hands and try to settle them as he thinks right and fit (out of devotion) behind our backs and against our will! If he has let himself be *persuaded* that it is for *our* good, he will dash violently into a thing, and use the least *fair* of measures to accomplish his ends without hesitation. How *can* he say 'the *family* had asked him to speak to the Queen'? Who are 'the family'? At Berlin they consist of the Emperor and Empress who are on *our* side and *not* on his, - our three eldest children who are *also* on *our* side - and not his! Therefore that is an *invention*! What business of *his* is Ct. S.'s promotion or non-promotion? He is not his superior!

I had a long conversation on board the yacht with Ct R-. He referred to my letter to him, and said that he thought it very hard and *most cruel*! He said he had *never* spoken to *any members* of the English court on the subject, but *they* had asked him so many questions, and had *forced* the subject upon him. He had found so *great* a dislike and indignation against Ct Seckendorff at the English court that he had not needed to add his own impressions; it had only been a proof more to him of how widely spread Count S's bad reputation was!! I gave Ct Radolinsky a piece of my mind, but whether I shall thereby *stop* him in his insane endeavours to get rid of Count S. I do not know. Ct Radolinsky *has* been to Prince Bismarck about it, and has *also* begged Herbert Bismarck to work on his father and on our son William in this sense!!! Old Prince Bismarck does not go out or mix in the world and is thoroughly dependent on the tales that are carried to him by his satellites, which he always implicitly believes.

You will admit, dearest Mary, that this is not pleasant. It is what is commonly called a very nasty intrigue! Count R is now at Berlin and *here* there is peace and harmony....

I miss beloved England terribly, more and more! the simple truthful ways - the straightforward yet keen-sighted, *manly* men, the *refined* and intelligent women, the pleasant ways and kind hearts, the unchanging friends and dear memories of old! Germany has other charms and other blessings, but I often feel *very* solitary, and rubbed up the wrong way. I plunge into all the serious thoughts, books and pursuits I can, to steel myself with philosophy against the pricks and thorns that *will* make one sore even if one is determined to rise superior to them....

It was at Toblach that the Crown Princess heard more of the intrigue and machinations for setting aside the Crown Prince in favour of Prince William. All these might have been countered and perhaps checked had the Crown Prince and Princess returned to Berlin, where Prince William and Count Herbert Bismarck, the son of the veteran statesman, were gaining in power and influence every day. But her husband's health was the first consideration of the Crown Princess, who wrote to her mother on September 14:

You will remember how earnestly we wished William to leave Potsdam, so as to be out of the Berlin and Potsdam atmosphere, both socially and politically so bad for him, where he is flattered and spoilt, and makes the Emperor do everything he likes! All the older Generals were of our opinion. We hear today that William has frustrated all these attempts and plans and made the Emperor decide that he is to remain at Potsdam (which means spending half the day at the Foreign Office with the great man's son and satellites and the evening with the Empress). Fritz is much annoyed, and people write to him saying how necessary it is for him to be at Berlin, to be some little check on William! But Fritz cannot and must not go to Berlin. His voice is much hoarser again and the throat not so well, but it varies and today it is less red than yesterday!

Whilst at Toblach the health of the Crown Prince appeared to improve, and in many journals, both British and German, Mackenzie was lauded as the man who had saved the Crown Prince from a dangerous and unnecessary operation.

Preparations were now being made in Berlin to celebrate the twenty-fifth anniversary of Prince Bismarck's appointment to the office of first minister. The Crown Princess regarded the 'fuss' as somewhat exaggerated, and on September 27, on the eve of leaving Toblach, which was now proving too wet and cold for the invalid, to proceed to Venice, she wrote to Queen Victoria:

We leave early tomorrow morning. Alas! the weather has quite spoilt this afternoon, so that I fear our long drive tomorrow will not be pleasant and we shall see nothing of the beautiful country between here and Langoram, which is all new to me, and I was so anxious to see! This is very disappointing....From Germany we hear that it is very cold everywhere, so that I am glad we are going south! What a fuss has been made about the 25th anniversary of Prince Bismarck coming into office! More than one sad and bitter thought fills our mind when one thinks of the means he has used to achieve great things and of the havoc he has made of much that was precious, of good and useful men's lives and reputations, etc., and of the evil seeds he has sown, of which we shall some day reap the fruits.

It is perhaps not his fault, he is *un homme du moyen age* - with the opinion and principles of those dark days when *la raison du plus fort était toujours la meilleure* and what was humane, moral, progressive and civilised was considered silly and ridiculous, and a Christian and liberal spirit absurd and *unpraktisch*. The young generation see his prestige and his success and are proud of it and like basking in the sunshine of his fame and celebrity. He has done very grand things and has unequalled power and unrivalled strength at this moment! Oh, if they were but used for the good cause, always one would be ready to admire and to bless him! He has made Germany great, but neither loved, free, happy, nor has he developed her immense resources for good! Despotism is the essence of his being; it cannot be right or good in the long run!

Whilst at Venice the Crown Princess wrote to Lady Ponsonby (October 5):

....I wish you were here with us at Venice! How I should like to go about with you, and we should both never cease *admiring*! I have to bottle up my enthusiasm a good deal so as not to bore my fellow-travellers, who cannot share it. I am not able to enjoy things as usual, nor with as light a heart, as the Crown Prince is, of course, unable to be out much, and may not speak, though, alas! *he will not obey* the strict injunctions of the doctor, and refrain from using his voice more than a very little! It is very difficult in a town, and going about, which, of course, amuses and interests him.

We are going to Baveno tomorrow and trust we may have a fortnight's fine weather. I miss the walks and the pure air, the delicious pine-woods and *splendid* scenery of Toblach, even here, in lovely Venice.

Dr (Morell) Mackenzie is satisfied, *on the whole*, but evidently the tendency to catch cold and the delicacy of the throat are very great. The *slightest* thing causes swelling and congestion, pain and hoarseness, and, of course, retards and impedes progress. This makes the Crown Prince much more depressed, impatient and fidgety than he need be, and incessant letters from Berlin, impressing the 'necessity' of returning to Germany, and the bad impression produced by our absence, are very galling.

Count Radolinsky writes to me that people put the blame on me for keeping my husband away from home. I answered that I thought such criticism was as unjust and ignorant as it was spiteful and impertinent. '*Travailler pour le roi de*

*Prusse*' is a good French saying, for I am weary of being constantly blamed and picked to pieces by people who have no right and no business to meddle in our affairs. Whenever anything is wrong, it does not matter *what* it be, it is put on *my* back. The court and official world find me a very convenient scapegoat. It is rather flattering in one way, as it shows they think me too good-natured to be likely to pay them out one day. Most of these amiable people are not worth knocking down, even if one had the power of distributing a few *coups de poing*. Of kind and good friends I have so many in other circles that I really do not mind; but at times I feel the *ingratitude* I meet with very bitterly, as I am conscious of trying to be as civil and courteous to everyone at Berlin as I can; of trying to do a good turn to people *whenever* I am able, and of trying to please: but there are those who *will not* be pleased. I am an English woman, suspected of Liberal, of free-thinking and artistic tendencies; of cosmopolitan and humanitarian sentiments and the like abominations in the eyes of Bismarck; so I am labelled 'suspicious' and 'dangerous' by the clique who are all-powerful now. I cannot help it. I keep as quiet and make myself as small as I can, but I cannot change my skin to please them, nor shall they tread me underfoot, as they would like to some day.

After all, it is only *sometimes* that I boil over with annoyance, as I usually feel how much greater and better and more useful people than I am have been continually attacked and abused and more from ignorance than evil intention. So one ought to make every allowance for people's different tactics, views and opinions. '*Tout comprendre c'est tout pardonner*', and one must learn the hard lesson of being tolerant to the intolerant, which I try very hard to learn....[10]

On October 6 the Crown Prince and Princess left Venice for a three weeks' stay at Baveno, near Lake Maggiore, where Sir Morell Mackenzie again visited his patient. It was from the 'Villa Clara' at Baveno that the Crown Princess wrote on October 9:

Dr Mackenzie left yesterday morning. He will write to Dr Reid as soon as he gets home. He thinks Fritz getting on very nicely, but says it all depends on him and if he will not talk and avoid cold and damp he may be quite well in three or four months! Whenever Fritz's throat does not hurt him he is very unmanageable and gets very impatient of any restraint, but I hope he will be encouraged by the progress he is making in doing all the doctors beg him....

It was here at Baveno that the Crown Prince and Princess were visited by their son William, who, as the Princess wrote to Queen Victoria on October 17, 'till now is very nice, amiable and friendly'. 'Henry', she added, 'comes tonight, and I hope he will be nice too.' Apparently both sons were considerate and courteous, and refrained from expressing their doubts as to Mackenzie's ability as a doctor.

Fritz [the Crown Princess added] promises to be good and not to speak. He is dreadfully annoyed by all the foolish articles about himself in the German newspapers! They are as tactless as they are impertinent and unfair! Most likely you have read them! He is going on quite nicely. Dr Hovell is very clever and inspires me with the greatest confidence!

The penultimate references were to a series of articles then current in the German press, possibly inspired by Bismarck, which hinted that the Crown Prince knew that his disease was cancer, but that on the ground that he wished to reign, did not want to be pronounced incurable!

The Crown Princess now wrote to her mother (October 25):

There is nothing new to tell you about Fritz beyond that at times his throat is a little more congested than at others! I think his voice has improved, it seems clearer and stronger to me, but he will not believe it!....

Meanwhile the aged Emperor was showing distinct signs of failure, but as yet no serious alarm was expressed as to the state of his health. On October 31 the Crown Princess wrote from the Villa Clara:

Fritz is hoarser again, but not from any cold, or any apparent reason the voice is better at times and then again less well. He is taken the very greatest care of and cannot well catch cold. The Emperor seems no worse, so that we are not alarmed about him....

The continued absence of the Crown Prince from Germany now caused more grumblings at Berlin, and when it became known that he proposed to stay at San Remo for a time, the dissatisfaction increased. On October 27 the Crown Princess wrote to Queen Victoria:

I am driven quite wild with the newspapers of Berlin and dear Ct Radolinsky keeps writing that people are so angry with me for choosing San Remo - and for not calling in another German doctor! Really it is excessively impertinent of these people! The Emperor would not have others forced upon him if he were satisfied; so why should we? It is impossible for Fritz to be better treated and more carefully than he is! To disturb the treatment would be to run the risk of spoiling it. It would be too wrong. Pray say nothing about my having told you what Ct R. wrote! You cannot imagine how spiteful and nasty people are - and how I get teased and tormented! On the other hand there is so much real concern about Fritz's health and real love and devotion to him - then one is glad to see people care so much and take it up so warmly. But there is a clique who are determined to find fault, and to criticise all and every thing - and who are half jealous of his having an English doctor and living in an English house and think it a fine opportunity to have a fling at me! It is so foolish and narrow-minded and unreasonable! When one is only trying one's best to cure Fritz as soon as possible...

We leave on Wednesday, November 3rd, for San Remo and have taken the Villa Zirio belonging to an Italian, and built by him! I am sure Kanne could tell you all about it. It is very expensive but new and clean - and pretty comfortable, I believe, which is so important for Fritz!...

A few days later the Crown Prince and Princess left for San Remo with high hopes. Up to this point, Mackenzie's optimistic prognostications had been almost justified. No further bad symptoms had developed, and there were many hopes that the patient was on the high road to recovery. At San Remo, however, the third phase of the illness was to unfold its tragic events.

## NOTES

1 *Reflections*, p. 331. See also Sir Rennell Rodd's *Social and Diplomatic Memories*, p. 112 *seq*.
2 See Sir Felix Semon's *Memoirs*, p. 148, and Sir Rennell Rodd's *Social and Diplomatic Memories*, vol. i. p. 112 *seq*. Also correspondence in *The Times*, December 1, 1926; January 18, 21, 23, 25, 1928.
3 Queen Victoria's Physician-in-Ordinary.
4 *Reflections*, vol. ii. p. 331.
5 Ballhausen, *Bismarcks Ermnerungen*, p. 390.
6 Translation: 'I regard the matter with increasing anxiety. Where M. Mackenzie removed a small portion it has grown again - the tumour is suppurating, etc., on the other side of the throat, the other vocal cord, which hitherto has remained healthy, is attacked - there is already a considerable amount of damage done. If Dr. M. Mackenzie cannot assist and cure it there is no chance of recovery save in the operation known as 'Laryngotomy'. It would have to be performed under far less favourable conditions than would have been the case fourteen days ago. Therefore my only hope is that Dr Mackenzie may be right in his opinion and that his treatment may be successful, for we have nothing else to suggest.'
7 Sir Felix Semon's *Memoirs*, p. 151.
8 He was knighted by Queen Victoria on September 2 at the request of the Crown Prince.
9 See supra, p. 155.
10 *Mary Ponsonby*, pp. 258-259.

# X. San Remo

THE Crown Prince and Princess had barely been twenty-four hours at the Villa Zirio in San Remo when the most drastic change in the condition of the patient was noticed by Dr Hovell. The Crown Princess at once telegraphed for Sir Morell Mackenzie, who arrived on November 6, and thereafter never left his patient until the end. Mackenzie now at last realised that the disease was more serious than he had thought, and when asked by the Crown Prince if the malady were cancer, replied: 'I am sorry to say, sir, it looks very much like it, but it is impossible to be certain.'[1] That day the distracted Crown Princess wrote to Queen Victoria:

....I am in a desperate hurry to catch the post, and so can only say that in the last few days Dr Hovell has perceived a new swelling in a new place, the appearance of which he did not like, and he wished Sir Morell Mackenzie to see it as soon as possible. Sir Morell arrived this morning, and is not satisfied with the look of the place; it has a malignant character about it and symptoms which do not please him. He will, however, not give a decided opinion about it, nor is he at all certain that it is really bad! I can say no more now, except that this makes me very miserable. The doctors have communicated their fears to Fritz, which has depressed him very much. We have let the Emperor and Empress, our three eldest children, and Prince Bismarck know of this out of pure prudence and conscientiousness. Two other doctors (Professor von Schrötter of Vienna and Dr Krause of Berlin) will come to consult with Mackenzie, but not those who made such a mistake this spring. There is no need for alarm, still one cannot but be uncomfortable. All was going on so well! His voice had nearly quite returned. Of course it is gone again now. Fritz has a good deal of pain at times, but all over the throat, not in that special place! This sudden and rapid change in his state has taken us very much aback.

His general health is as good as possible, but these last two days he looks worn and anxious, poor dear! It is really a hard trial.

The consultations and investigations that now took place between Sir Morell Mackenzie, Professor von Schrötter, Dr Krause and Dr Moritz Schmidt, who was sent by the Emperor, destroyed the last vestige of hope. Cancer had the royal victim in its grip. As a result of the consultation the Crown Prince was given the choice of total removal of the larynx or the palliative operation of tracheotomy.[2] He decided in favour of the latter. Two days later the Crown Princess wrote to her mother:

I should have written before, but I was really so worried and tormented that it would have been a confused letter. Many thanks for your two dear telegrams! Any little line from you - by letter or telegraph - is a comfort to me now....

The doctors have arrived and consulted. They read to me their Protocol - cruel indeed it sounded. I hardly expected much else, still when the crude facts of one's doom are read to one, it gives one an awful blow! I would not break down before them of course. It will be sent to you and to the Emperor. My darling has got a fate before him which I hardly dare think of! How I shall ever have strength to bear it I do not know!! (In confidence I must tell you that Dr Prof Schrötter impressed me most unpleasantly. I thought him rough, uncouth and arrogant; perhaps he did not show to advantage before me.) I cannot enough repeat how wise, and kind, how delicate and considerate and judicious Sir M Mackenzie is - such a real comfort and support - and always calm and collected - also Dr Hovell; I should not have known what to do without them.

I will write more tomorrow - for to-day let me end! William has just arrived, not by our wish, and just at present is rather in the way.

To this letter the Crown Princess added the postscript:

I hope and trust and believe that the dread hour will be put off for many months, if not for years, for more I know I dare not hope.

The following day, November 10, the British Military Attaché in Berlin, Colonel Leopold Swaine, wrote to Queen Victoria's Secretary, Sir Henry Ponsonby, from Berlin:

This news of the Crown Prince is too dreadful, and we are giving up all hopes of his recovery.

In addition also comes the rumour that the Empress is far from well and court officials whisper that Her Majesty is sinking. But I have been unable to obtain reliable information on that head. It appears that the Emperor, though still weak, is recovering, and is by no means as depressed at the news from San Remo as we all are. He views the situation far more hopefully.

I look with sad forebodings into the future if the Crown Prince is taken from us. As you know I have the greatest admiration for Prince William's abilities, but I think His Royal Highness's best friends will admit that he is still too inexperienced and could hardly expect to possess the full confidence, as his father naturally would have, of those older German Princes, like the King of Saxony and the Regent of Bavaria.

The Emperor cannot last much longer, and Prince Bismarck, continually ailing, is also an old man. As long as the latter's life is spared, Prince William would fully adhere to his counsels. But he also gone, would leave the young Prince face to face with the task of selecting a Chancellor for the Empire. Might not such a question at any moment place him in opposition to the more experienced heads of the German Kingdoms and Principalities that make up the Union? It is a very anxious moment.

On the following day, November 11, the Crown Princess wrote to Queen Victoria:

Sir Morell Mackenzie tells me he has written to you, so I will only add a few lines. You do not know what we have been through!! The anxiety about Fritz was so great at Berlin that they again resolved on that awful operation and it is to Sir Morell Mackenzie alone, and to his quiet, clever, wise management, that we owe it to have escaped being dragged to Berlin and having this forced upon us! Please do not let this out, except to some of the family! I hope you will see Sir Morell when you are back at Windsor and let him tell you all that passed! Fritz is quite happy and hopeful and the depression and anxiety has gone off, but oh! what it is to me, I cannot say. Yet I cannot and will not give up hope. Mistakes of the strangest kind are made and the evil may be arrested, or may cease to grow, etc., for a time, or even for good, though I know it is not likely. I must do Prof Schrötter the justice to say that he performed the very difficult and delicate task of imparting to my poor darling the result of the consultation very well indeed! To say the truth I do not think Fritz realised the whole meaning of what he said. He spoke of the operations that could be performed and might be proposed, but neither urged nor advised them! The others all agreed and have left. We have only kept Krause. I was in an agony of terror this morning for fear these gentlemen might put their opinion in too plain language and give Fritz a terrible shock, so I remained in the room, but it all passed off well. I hope now we shall have a little calm and be left in peace and be able to nurse our dear patient as is best for him, undisturbed. I hope the excitement will subside, and we shall be less tormented with letters and telegrams which come pouring in. But the load of dread and anxiety which is upon me will remain it is almost unbearable.

On the following day, November 12, 1887, the German Official Gazette announced in an unsigned bulletin that 'the disease is due to the existence of a malignant new growth'? which was of a 'carcinomatous' character.[3] The next day the Emperor summoned Bergmann, Gerhardt, Tobold, Schrötter, Lenthold, Moritz Schmidt, Krause and Landgraf to Berlin to answer two questions. To the first, as to whether, in spite of the Crown Prince's refusal, the radical operation of the removal of the larynx should be advised, they replied that the patient's will must be decisive in view of the danger of the operation, and that no further attempt should be made to persuade him. To the second, as to why, when the operation had been abandoned in May and June, it was suggested again at so late a date, they replied that ' the responsibility for its non-performance until too late had been incurred by that physician who had overlooked, nay, even denied, the increase of the growth',[4] The consultation resulted in the opinion being unanimously arrived at that the life of the Crown Prince would best be prolonged by no attempt being made whatsoever to remove either the whole or the affected portion of the larynx. After considering this report, the Crown Prince himself decided that the operation should not be performed. The following day the Crown Princess wrote to Queen Victoria (November 13, 1887):

....Tomorrow morning Sir Morell Mackenzie goes, and I shall feel like a ship cut adrift from her anchor! However, happily Dr. Krause, whom I like, and who seems very nice, is going to stay. Sir Morell must come back after a while. We hear there is a perfect storm of excitement and criticism raging at Berlin. It is very unfair and unjust! You will hear a great deal from Sir Morell when he gets back, though his news will have become rather stale by the time you return from Scotland; still, you will hear what we have been through.

Fritz has slept well, and eats well, and feels comfortable. We must pray that he may remain so as long as possible. The sickening dread of what his sufferings may be drives me quite wild at times; and then I hope and trust there may be no suffering.

The weather is splendid, and I hope he will be allowed out again soon, as he enjoys walking and driving so much.

All the world was now interested in the unusual event of an Emperor and his heir-apparent both on the threshold of death. The Emperor, William I, was already declining slowly - his son in the grip of a mortal disease: the agonising race with death had begun. The German press was beside itself. The conclusion was speedily reached that the life of the Crown Prince would be sacrificed because of the mistake of a doctor - an English doctor - who had, they asserted, been called in by the Crown Princess. German doctors, who had been correct in their diagnosis, had been deliberately set aside in favour of an incompetent foreigner! Prince William was not slow to reflect Berlin opinion, and arrived at San Remo with Dr Schmidt to make his own inquiries. On November 15 the Crown Princess wrote to Queen Victoria:

My darling Fritz is going on very nicely as regards the temporary swelling and inflammation of the throat (Oedema). This has nearly disappeared - he is no longer obliged to suck ice all day, and to have ice bandages (ice bags) tied round his neck day and night, and to sleep in his dressing room. But he is not allowed downstairs - not out of doors yet. I have meals alone with him, and sit in his room all day when I am not out walking. He is very cheerful and quite comfortable, busies himself with reading and writing a great deal and sleeps very well. He has promised he will not read about himself in the newspaper and he has kept his promise.

The violent and shameful attacks upon poor Sir Morell Mackenzie in the German press and Berlin public make us very indignant; they are as unjust as they are hasty. We feel so very grateful to him that it pains us doubly.

You ask how Willy was when he was here ! He was as rude, as disagreeable and as impertinent to me as possible when he arrived, but I pitched into him with, I am afraid, considerable violence, and he became quite nice and gentle and amiable (for him) - at least quite natural, and we got on very well! He began with saying he would not go out walking with me 'because he was too busy - he had to speak to the doctors'. I said the doctors had to report to me and not to him, upon which he said he had the 'Emperor's orders' to insist upon the right thing, to see that the doctors were not interfered with, and to report to the Emperor about his Papa! I said it was not necessary, as we always reported to the Emperor ourselves. He spoke before others and half turning his back to me, so I said I would go and tell his father how he behaved and ask that he should be forbidden the house - and walked away. Upon which he sent Ct Radolinsky flying after me, to say he had not meant to be rude and begged me to say nothing to Fritz, 'but that it was his duty to see that the Emperor's commands were carried out'. I instantly said I had no malice, but I would suffer no interference. So it all went on quite smoothly and we had many a pleasant little walk and chat together. He was also quite nice to Sir Morell, etc....William came with the intention of insisting on this terrible operation being performed and therefore brought Dr Schmidt without our knowledge, as it was feared the other doctors would not urge it, and Schmidt was brought to press it on them, and to carry us off to Berlin for that purpose! It would simply have assassinated Fritz. William is of course much too young and inexperienced to understand all this! He was merely put up to it at Berlin! He thought he was to save his Papa from my mismanagement!! When he has not his head stuffed with rubbish at Berlin he is quite nice and *traitable*, and then we are very pleased to have him; but I will not have him dictate to me - the head on my shoulders is every bit as good as his. If it were not I should be the first to give in to him....

Now good-bye, dearest beloved Mama - if you do write to Fritz, I hope you will do so as cheerfully as you can! Letters in a melancholy tone such as he does receive a good many - depress him. He hates being thought very ill, or appearing so!

The tension between mother and son did not tend to lessen as time went on; nor was the Crown Princess overpleased with the sending of Dr Bramann (Professor Bergmann's assistant) to San Remo to perform the operation of tracheotomy if this should suddenly become necessary. On November 16 she wrote to Queen Victoria:

Though I wrote this morning, yet I must send a few more lines tonight to thank you for your dear letter of the 12th which I have just received. All your dear kind words touch and cheer me so much, and your love is a true comfort and support! I cannot say how grateful I am for it. Fritz sends you his best love and thanks for all your sympathy....

William's telegram is too foolish! He told me he had sent it and I said 'How could you!!' It is too impudent! Just like him! He never reflects. He had heard that very morning that Münster had advised us not to send everything *en clair*, as it was all read, so William thought he would give them a piece of his mind and was rather proud of this telegram of his, as a bright idea! I failed to see it in that light!!

We have had fresh annoyance from Berlin today: Count Stollberg telegraphs that the Emperor has sent a surgeon here, Bergmann's assistant, with orders to stay near us! We had twice protested and declined, and said that if a surgeon were necessary we should let Bergmann know! In spite of all this, they force this person on us! They do tease and torment us, and the press goes on quarrelling and fighting about Fritz! Political questions and national feelings and prejudices get mixed up with all this, so that one gets driven nearly wild! But the sincere sympathy we meet with from so many many sides is most touching, and we are deeply grateful for it.

To this letter Queen Victoria replied on November 18:

You have every reason to feel angry and annoyed at the excitement and shameful publicity and disgraceful arguments respecting our beloved Fritz's illness. But on the other hand some allowance must be made for the fearful anxiety of the nation about their beloved, noble and heroic Prince.

I will certainly see Sir M Mackenzie on my return at once and will hear everything. I hope, however, that dear Fritz knows the alternatives and that it is he who has decided not to have the operation? for else the responsibility of others in positively deciding against it would be fearful. The German Surgeons and many, I believe, in England, do not consider that operation so dangerous and there are many instances of its success, for in that way the disease can be really eradicated. Some people also think that Sir M Mackenzie's judgment is not quite equal to his great skill in the internal operation. I only feel it my duty out of love for you both to say openly what strikes me, for the importance and value of beloved Fritz's precious life is such that one must overlook nothing. Of course I am still greatly in the dark as to the exact state of everything and therefore only write this to you as I know you would wish me to be quite open.

This letter crossed one from the Crown Princess written that same day, in which she had poured out all her fears and hopes to her mother:

I received your dear letter of the 14th yesterday evening! So many most affectionate thanks for it! But I should reproach myself if you tired yourself, or gave up too much of your precious time by writing to me, so please do not write oftener on my account than usual. I know how your time is taken up, and though you know what a comfort and pleasure your dear letters are, still I should fidget very much if you wrote more than is convenient to you in any way! Our dear patient continues to do very well! The interference, the attacks, the advice continue to pour down upon us from Berlin, *i.e*, upon me, because we trouble Fritz as little as we can! The newspapers are filled with absolute lies and yet one does not know whether it be wise or advisable to contradict them! They are for the most part very spiteful innuendoes. You know there is a party who have their representatives at this moment even at our court, who no doubt from good motives, but with a deplorable lack of common sense and knowledge of medical affairs, insist that I am at the bottom of all the mischief - prevented the operation in May, forced Sir M. Mackenzie on Fritz, and have kept everyone else away! They also say that this horrible operation would kill or cure Fritz and that I have prevented both the chances! They dread a war or European complications. They think William would be better than an Emperor suffering from an incurable malady, they also perhaps think they can get rid of me, which they would be glad of, as they find tie Emperor and William far better tools. This is so grossly ignorant and false and ridiculous that it is hardly worth fighting. The trouble is that as long as there is breath in me, I shall see that the right thing is done for Fritz for the prolongation of his life, for his comfort and happiness. They are (many of them) angry with me for appearing cheerful and unconcerned before Fritz and for trying to make the time pass pleasantly and keep his mind free from care and from dwelling on painful things! They say I try to hide the gravity of the situation from him, that he ought to feel more what danger he is in. This is not at all true, as he is in no danger of any immediate kind now, thank God! They say that I buoy him up with false hopes, which is also not true, as I carefully avoid speaking of the future in order not to be obliged to say what I do not think! When first Sir Morell told him in the gentlest, kindest way that he was afraid the growth might be a malignant one, it depressed Fritz so frightfully that he shed the bitterest tears and had a heartbreaking outburst of grief! 'To think that I should have such a horrid, disgusting illness! that I shall be an object of disgust to everyone, and a burden to you all! I had so hoped to be of use to my country. Why is Heaven so cruel to me! What have I done to be thus stricken down and condemned! What will become of you? I have nothing to leave you! Who will fight Moretta's battles?' But I did all I could to console and pacify him, and tell him all I could think of which was comforting and reassuring, though consistent with the truth! I said we must leave the future in God's hands and not trouble about it, but fight this illness as well as we can, by remaining cheerful and hopeful, taking care of health, etc.

 He was quite relieved and comforted and what the other doctors afterwards said to him made no impression! He listened quite calmly to them, but he did not realise exactly what they meant! This, of course, is only known to very few people, Sir Morell, Dr Hovell and Moretta! Nor must it be known, or the others would lose no opportunity of saying 'Oh, you are much worse than you know. Your wife is concealing it from you. There is no hope for you anywhere, you had better resign all hopes of succeeding your father. You should have gone back to Berlin and submitted to the operation.' Even good and well-meaning people have not *le tact du coeur* and would not try to save a person one moment's agony or distress of mind. You know how sensitive and apprehensive, how suspicious and despondent Fritz is by nature! All the more wrong and positively dangerous (let alone the cruelty of it) to wish him to think the worst! We should not keep him going at all, if this were the case. Some of his friends think there is something grand in making the worst of everything, the biggest fuss they can, and among the letters and telegrams he gets (in spite of my trying to keep them away from him) are most injudicious, regular funeral orations. This keeps me in a continual fear, as it is really too bad to have him tormented and upset, instead of encouraged and supported, and it makes my task very difficult, as you can imagine! The publicity with which all our affairs have been treated at Berlin, is very painful, and the indiscretion and want of delicacy are very offensive to our feelings. This I am sure you will understand and feel with me!....

How long it may please God to leave our darling with us we know not, but this thought, though it embitters every minute of my existence, shall not cast more gloom over him than I can help! Even in uncertainty there is an element of hope. Small as it is, it is enough to be held out to him in a vague way, which cheers and comforts him and makes him willing to do what the doctors wish, which he would not do, if he were convinced that it was all no use! I have written you these details, as I thought you would wish to know.

I am so thankful we are not in Berlin, where they would half kill us with interference, where they quite lose their heads with excitement.

I do not know, but I think Prince Bismarck would be on our side. The Emperor is marvellously well again, the Empress I hear very conflicting accounts about, so that I really do not quite know....

The continued absence of the Crown Prince from Berlin was now being resented by certain elements in the German court, and the fears of the Princess seemed to be justified when on November 17 the Emperor delegated his authority to Prince William in the event of his illness. Four days later the Empress's second son, Prince Henry, had arrived at San Remo, and the distress occasioned by his visit may be gauged from the following letter from the Crown Princess written on November 21:

At Berlin they had done what is exceedingly wrong. The Emperor has appointed William to sign all the state papers in his stead, whenever the Emperor feels unable! To do this without asking Fritz, or consulting him, is an irregular proceeding and exceedingly *rücksichtslos*. Two days ago a notification of this fact arrived, signed by Bismarck, not even in his hand! As Fritz was on that day much excited and annoyed by an assistant of Bergmann's being sent here by the Emperor's orders - without Fritz's wishes and against my written and telegraphic protest, the doctor wished him not to be worried, so I put by this paper and did not give it him! Henry arrives, pulls a paper, or rather a letter, from Willy out of his pocket, in which letter it says that he has been appointed as *Stellvertreter des Kaisers*, and gives it to Fritz, who was much upset, very angry, and much excited, talked a great deal (which is very bad for him) and said he would go instantly to Berlin, etc....and took a long while to calm and pacify.

Now I must tell you that the court, military and government people are so mad and foolish at Berlin that they imagine Fritz's illness to be in far more advanced a stage than it really is! I may also say their wish is father to the thought! They think that as the Crown Prince is given up, the quicker another takes his place the better for the state (and for them). They think that I, Sir Morell and Dr Hovell, and Dr Krause take care of our patient, and think only of him, his welfare, and of prolonging and if possible saving his precious life; which of course they (the Party) think utterly impossible and ridiculous. They know that Sir Morell, Dr Hovell and Dr Krause are perfectly independent, are not state employés of the German Government, and will take no orders from Berlin, but are simply guided by their duty towards their patient! The Party consequently wish to get rid of them, and are only too glad to avail themselves of the shameful and disgusting polemic in the press, which they even favour and encourage! The Party think that if they could only get rid of me, they would then send Fritz's doctors away and put people of their own choosing, whom they could direct, about Fritz, whose duty, they calmly say, it would be to make Fritz see that his case is hopeless, and that it is his duty to resign his claim to the Throne, the sooner the better. This plot is being worked - and Fritz guesses it - and is very suspicious. All worry is so very bad! The sympathy in Germany is so very great and the affection for him so strong, but the consternation is also very great. People have heard that Fritz knows the worst - that he has accepted it with stoicism, and therefore they think he must be going to die immediately and are astonished that he does not return. Others again think if the Emperor were to be either taken, or so ill that he could not do any business, the Crown Prince must be past doing business, so Prince William must take his place! This latter opinion was expressed by Henry this afternoon to me in, I am sorry to say, a most unbecoming manner. I am not angry with the boy, because he is ignorant, green and misled, and does not understand, but he preached to me as if I were a little girl! He is devoted to his Papa - and thinks everyone in office at Berlin must be right! All these torments are rather hard for me to bear, with all the anxiety gnawing at my heart night and day! I think they will calm down at Berlin and come to their senses....

Thank God dear Fritz feels well and comfortable today, worry and annoyance excepted. He sends you his tenderest love.

Of the future [she added in a postscript] I have not dared to think today. I leave it in God's hands, and do not desire to know what is coming....

Other letters from the Crown Princess to her mother during the remaining six weeks of the year 1887 are mostly in this strain. In the main they give news of the fluctuations of the Crown Prince's illness - one day she would be buoyed up by hope, and the next utterly depressed. She resisted strenuously efforts to replace Mackenzie, Hovell and Krause by other doctors. The continued criticism in the German press worried her considerably, as did the thoughtless and often provocative actions of her sons, Prince William and Prince Henry. 'Henry', she wrote on November 29, 'maintains that his Papa is lost through the English doctors and me....He becomes so rude and impertinent that I really cannot stand it.'[5] On December 2 she again wrote:

It is hard enough to hear myself abused, everything found wrong that is done for Fritz - the doctors, who are acting so wisely and conscientiously, torn to pieces by ignorant excited people - but it is harder far to see one's own children side violently with these people and refuse to hear or believe a word one says. Henry is quite dreadful in this respect!! He is so prejudiced, and fancies he knows far better than his Mama and all the doctors here, and that we do not speak the truth. It makes me feel so bitter at times. However, I think that when we have been here longer, he will perhaps be brought to see things in their true light. He is as obstinate as a mule.

You cannot think how much perfidy has been used in misrepresenting things to the German public, to excite them against Sir Morell Mackenzie, against me, against Dr Krause and Dr Hovell....On this ground the political intrigues have grown. General von Winterfeld, who had been the greatest support and comfort at Baveno, instantly gave everything up, lost his head, and took upon himself to stir up the whole court and military party at Berlin. He persisted in telegraphing the most alarming things, and created the scare at Berlin, which was kept up and increased by the violence of General v. Albedyll and his friends, who were of course terrified, and thought Fritz would be taken from us in a few months and kept bombarding us with orders to do things we could not do. Winterfeld and all the Party at Berlin wanted to pack us up instantly and go back, - put Fritz into the hands of Gerhardt, Bergmann and Tobold and force the operation on us! I need hardly say that the journey would have prevented the acute inflammation from going down and that in all probability the operation would have cost Fritz his life.

Against this it was my duty to fight! Now the same Party will not see and refuse to admit that Fritz is doing relatively well. They had based all their calculations on his not succeeding his father, or on his being obliged to institute a Regency immediately, which would put all the power in William's hands. They are making their arrangements accordingly and I have as yet no knowledge of what Bismarck's attitude is - whether he believes the Party and goes with them, or not! This is the truth of the position we are placed in. They mean it patriotically and for what they consider the good of the country, but it is really foolish and wrong, wicked and cruel, and certainly not in accordance with what the German nation feel, who daily give fresh proofs of affection and confidence, sympathy and loyal devotion.

I must bear with all this injustice, ingratitude and folly for a time. The future will show who was right.

It was during her visit to the Crown Princess that Lady Ponsonby, one of her most valued friends, wrote to her husband, Sir Henry Ponsonby, on December 3, 1887, a letter that sheds an interesting light upon the social conditions which obtained at the Villa Zirio:

Just returned from dining at the Villa Zirio with the Crown Prince and Princess and seventeen at dinner. We were - let me see - Bruhl, Perpignan and four princesses, self and Maggie and Mlle. de B, the governess, made nine women; Crown Prince, Prince Henry, his equerry Seckendorff, Von Rabe (a mysterious man in spectacles), our Seckendorff, and a small dark English doctor were the party. I sat next the Crown Prince, who looked beautiful, with a fresh colour and a good appetite, and whom I had the greatest difficulty to prevent talking....

I have just had a long visit from Baron Roggenbach, an old friend of the Prince and Stockmar, and one of the few people the Crown Princess really trusts. He says he was almost the first to be alarmed about the Crown Prince and told me the history of the case from the beginning. Whatever his opinion is of Mackenzie *at home*, and it does not seem to be favourable, he thinks he has behaved honourably and straightforwardly here. He quite agrees with him that the operation at any time was out of the question whether the evil were cancer or no, so that he (M. M.) was justified in saying, so far as evidence went at first, there was nothing to prove it to be malignant. He never disguised from the Crown Prince it might become so. R. told me a great deal more, but post is going. Crown Princess here for a little and took Maggie with her and Princess Victoria. We dine there tonight.

Must just add that I think Roggenbach quite the most shrewd German I have seen with them. At this moment he says it is a case of surprise, general health and colour *excellent* and each day better. At all events, the mischief is not progressing, tell Jenner.[6]

Bismarck's attitude during this period was one of sympathetic interest, and the Princess wrote with pleasure on December 8 of 'a civil and pleasant letter' she had received from him:[7]

Henry [she continued] is quite nice and amiable now, but I have never returned to the subject of his papa's illness, or the doctors, or the way which people went on at Berlin, as I cannot be spoken to in such a way again! In all other respects he has now calmed down considerably, and makes himself agreeable. He is always nice when he has been with us some time, but not when he has been set up by others, and his head stuffed full of rubbish at Berlin....

Six days later Lady Ponsonby wrote to Queen Victoria:

... The Princess told me yesterday that the fact of a fresh small growth having appeared on the vocal cord has been made known to Your Majesty, also that it has been decided to call Sir M. Mackenzie again in consultation.[8] This has been a source of trouble and anxious thought, not so much that this appearance makes the doctors fear the existence of cancer more than they have lately done. It is to be regretted, of course, as the expectation of another consultation so soon depresses the Prince, and many similar operations will have necessarily a lowering effect, but the great question of all, what exact form of throat disease is the Crown Prince suffering from, remains unanswered as yet, and this growth (precisely the same in character as that which Sir M. Mackenzie operated upon before) does not in any way prove one thing or the other. But this return of the milder form of illness makes a complication in the Princess's position which it is difficult to decide how to meet. With the existing jealousy on the part of the German doctors it may not be wise to call in the English doctor alone. If, on the other hand, the consultation takes in two or three and four doctors, a panic will arise and all the peace which has lately prevailed will be at an end. Besides Princess Charlotte and her husband are expected here shortly. It is difficult to decide whether this prospect of another consultation should be told them or not. In talking over it with the Princess I submitted that in my humble judgment it would be better to hide nothing. The doctors cannot come here without comment from the press and public. If the Prince and Princess arrive expecting to find the Crown Prince as well as the accounts of the last fortnight have made him out (most truly) to be, but instead of that find him shut up in his room, as he must be for the moment, it will strengthen the impression (which I believe the son-in-law shares with Prince William) that the real truth is kept from the relations and from the public, and it would only add to the mass of deplorable misrepresentation under which the dear Crown Princess suffers. I think the Crown Princess has decided that at this very moment only Your Majesty shall be told, but I told Count Seckendorff of my fears, and he said the Princess thought as I did and would make this relapse (it is almost too strong a word) known a little later and before the Prince and Princess arrive.

We dined last night at Villa Zirio and I begged not to sit next the Crown Prince. He is so very very kind and cordial and it is almost impossible to prevent his speaking. If one tries to avoid this by talking oneself, then he will answer. If one is silent, then he will begin the conversation, so I sorrowfully relinquished my place, and Baron Roggenbach being gone (with whom he had long conversations) I think the Prince was persuaded to be more silent and played at billiards instead of talking.

The Crown Princess has had a headache and slight cold and naturally her spirits vary according to the state of affairs. It is perfectly insufferable that she cannot do the simplest thing without its being known at once in Berlin. I daresay

H.I. Highness told Your Majesty of the telegram *en clair* she sent to the Duchess of Montpensier, upon which the Crown Princess receives a message from Berlin before the answer arrives, to say it is wished H.I. Highness should not meet the Orleans family! It must have happened that the information came from someone at Villa Zirio. This is the saddest part of the dear Crown Princess's position. There is not *une âme qui vive* to whom she can speak openly (I am speaking of the ladies). If she does it is always taken with a twist, with suspicion, misrepresented, exaggerated and turned against her. Mdlle. de Perpignan is far and away the kindest and most just person, and the Crown Princess seems to have quite forgiven their little differences. H.I. Highness told me Count R. had shown which way the wind blew when he said things are so altered that now it does not signify there should be anyone (Ct Seckendorff) independent of the Government with influence in the Crown Prince's Household. In the meantime they sat next each other at dinner last night, which amused me, and they speak (which I think does both credit) though they never can be friends. Whatever faults (and I perfectly see them) Count S. may have, there can be no manner of doubt that the advice he gives the Crown Princess is always sensible, honest, open and fearless. Situated as she is, I cannot but think these are great merits. Princess Victoria is a great comfort to her mother and has, I think, a great deal of character. The Crown Princess is, however, very very lonely and it makes me wretched sometimes to think of it....

Lady Ponsonby's reference to the Crown Princess's relations with the Duchess of Montpensier bore allusion to another cause of tension between the Crown Princess and those in power at Berlin. The Crown Princess had always been on friendly terms with the Orleans family, and hearing that the Duke and Duchess of Montpensier were at Cannes (where the Crown Princess's brother Leopold had died in 1884), decided either to pay them a short visit there or to invite them to San Remo. The moment the news of this project reached Berlin, Bismarck promptly forbade such an exchange of civilities, and on January 22 the Crown Princess wrote to Queen Victoria:

Fancy that I am forbidden to go and see the Duke and Duchess of Montpensier and Marguerite and Chignite, or to ask them here. They all so very kindly asked to come here to see us!! It makes me furious to have to find excuses and appear so rude when I am so anxious to see them all! Therefore I cannot go to Cannes, and yet am so anxious to see the house in which our dear Leopold breathed his last, and the Church erected to his memory! It is really too bad and so ridiculous; besides I wish they all knew that it is no fault of ours. It is Bismarck's newest fad. I am quite at a loss to see what possible harm it could do anyone, or anything, if I saw our relations and friends who are always so kind and civil and agreeable. It seems to me so *kleinlich*. I suppose that the idea is the French Government are not to imagine that Germany has the faintest sympathy for the Orleans family or their cause - on the contrary hopes they will not return to the Throne! Prince Bismarck is convinced that they are a great danger to peace and to Germany, which I do not and cannot believe! He thinks if they returned to power, Russia would instantly make an alliance with them and begin war upon Germany, whereas the Czar's dislike to a Republic restrains him from allying himself with France at this moment. I fail to see that this Republic is a safeguard at all.

It was while Lady Ponsonby was still at San Remo that she wrote to her husband, Sir Henry Ponsonby, in December 1887:

... I declare I think the unfairness about the Crown Princess is unbearable. The German press all adopt the tone that the real truth is kept back, and if she quotes Dr Krause (the German doctor here who works with Hovell) they say that he has been won over. Bismarck (*the old one*) and the Emperor and Empress are kind, which helps her. The Crown Prince trusts implicitly in her, so that is a great compensation, but the *hochements de tête* of the children, Henry and the little ones, and the *visage d'événement* of Bruhl irritate me. I don't think M Mackenzie has entered into all the details with Reid. Hovell gave me a long detailed account which with Roggenbach's and the Crown Princess's I have written out while I remember it all.

The Queen's letter is very interesting. I think she has been *envenimée* against M. Mackenzie by Uncle,[9] who is in charge of his nephew William, and thinks and says the English doctor is only trying to feather his nest. Yesterday was the first day she, the Crown Princess, broke down before me. She is generally in apparent excellent spirits, though preoccupied at times; but yesterday it was too much to find him reading a recapitulation of the doctors' former opinion with a paragraph pointing out the difference between this and the present bulletins and leaving their readers to make their own inference. The poor Crown Prince turned to her and said, 'Why will they take every ray of hope away? What good is done them by this?' and pointed to the paragraph. She was quite cheerful to him and then came into the next room where I was and cried. She is so wonderful generally that it fills one with pity. The Crown Prince was full of chaff last night, taking off Maggie, delighted with the thought of the children's enjoyment of the Christmas tree....[10]

The Christmas of 1887 passed with the usual interchange of cordial wishes between the Crown Princess and her mother, and her last letter to Queen Victoria in 1887 bore testimony to the ever-widening gulf between the Princess and her son William. On December 28 she wrote:

So many affectionate thanks for your dear letter written on Christmas Eve. This will be my last letter in the Old Year, your Jubilee Year, never to be forgotten, which has brought much happiness, also much anxiety. It is not without the usual uncertainty that the New Year begins - but still I am full of hope, as Sir Morell Mackenzie is even more satisfied this time than he was before, and more reassured about the appearance of Fritz's throat than a week ago. You will hear from him all he thinks, so much better than I can put it, that I leave the details to him. His visit has been most useful and a great comfort.

Dear Mary Ponsonby has left today - how much I shall miss her, and how thankful I was to have her here for a little. She, too, can tell you much more than I could write....

I am rather amused at the *Times* correspondent at Berlin saying that the 'Mission' at Berlin is for the development of Evangelistic Church life and Christian charity. It is by no means a harmless thing; the people that belong to it are the most violent enemies to all my charitable undertakings (I have always avoided the violent Sectarians, Anti-Jews, and Anti-Catholics, thinking them intolerant and uncharitable). William, and more especially Dona, have always favoured the opposite 'Clique' - who are all violent Bismarckists, Conservatives, etc. Therefore when this meeting was held, at which Dona and William were present and the latter made a very foolish speech, I was in no ways astonished; it created great indignation, however, in the Liberal and *Bourgeois* world at Berlin, and has made William still more unpopular than he already was, with the mass of the population. We said nothing to him about it, not thinking it worth while. He must buy his own experience, as he does not listen to us. The people who for almost 30 years have been nasty to Fritz and especially to me, are the very same who run after William, who have him quite in their pocket and Dona also, the same people or clique as used to persecute my parents-in-law, as long as they were Prince and Princess of Prussia, and who only became such devoted admirers of the Emperor since he dropped all his old principles and all his old friends, and took Bismarck in 1863, and the retrograde era began. Their hope, their wish is that William shall continue the style of Government they are so sadly afraid will be modified if Fritz ever is Emperor. William knows all this! The Court-Clergy at Berlin are most pernicious elements, false, ambitious, narrow-minded and servile, much disliked by the educated and independent middle class. It is sad that the children should not take their parents' side! Fritz and I stuck loyally and faithfully to all the Emperor's old friends, Schleinitz, Usedom, Hatzfeldt, Pourtales, Arnim, Camphausen, Bonin, Prince Hohenlohe - all such excellent, high principled men, tolerant, courteous, cosmopolitan!! Bismarck swept them all away and then the rule of 'blood and iron' - the principle of 'opportunism' was inaugurated and we withdrew into silence and reserve. We could not approve of all that was done, but people who tried to do the Emperor and Empress harm, or who criticised them with disrespect, we should never have taken up!! Much will change if we ever have a chance of putting straight and conciliating. The Emperor's great age accounts in a great measure for all this Party strife! But I must not bore you with these things, which can only be of secondary interest to you.

The new year brought little joy to the Crown Princess. It had barely begun before the discovery was made that the right side of the larynx was attacked by the growth. On January 5 the Princess wrote to her mother:

Fritz is a little hoarser these last few days, and the right side (which was not attacked till now) shows signs of congestion and a little swelling. It is very tiresome, not but what we must expect the like in a state of chronic affection as his is. Still I had hoped we should have escaped it! I have told Dr Hovell to write to Dr Reid about it!

Fritz's illness has made everyone feel what a blessed thing it would be if this regime of Bismarck's omnipotence were not to last for ever, if other motives and sentiments and another spirit were to pervade the German Government. B. is very great, a man of genius and power, does his best and has done great things for his country. One must be just and grateful, but as you cannot gather grapes of thorns or figs from thistles, so can you not expect from him that which modem Germany lacks and which it thirsts for, and that is peace among its classes, races, religions and parties, good and friendly relations with its neighbours, liberty and the respect of right instead of force, and the protection of the weak against the oppression of the strong....

Three weeks later the Crown Princess wrote to Lady Ponsonby (January 28):

The Crown Prince has been feeling very seedy this last fortnight, but it is only the consequence of the last attack, when he had such a violent cough, and such fever and sleepless nights, - all that has passed off, but has left him feeling out of sorts and with headache and a little neuralgia. I hope it will soon pass off; there are no new unfavourable symptoms in the throat! Tomorrow Sir M. Mackenzie returns, and we are very anxious to hear what he will have to say.

We have been much teased from Berlin and dear Count Radolinsky wrote me two most violent letters, that I can only call insane. I showed them to no one and burnt them and shall not answer or take any notice! They were a heap of surmises - (on the old subject) each one as false and fantastic as it could be! winding up with a series of dark threats!!! It is really terrible that he who means to be so loyal to us, should be so credulous, so excitable, violent, imprudent and injudicious - one really does not know how to deal with these wild mad words! He was like a lamb here, but when he gets back to his people he is more like a bull in a china shop - and for no reason. We have also been having great trouble with the press, etc. I am often quite exhausted with trying to keep things straight, *les bras me tombent*, and I wish for you back so much! -

Now to another subject. You know I have a great opinion of Sir H. Layard's talents and knowledge and experience! I know quite well all that is said against him, but also that his capacities could be turned to good account! A man who at his age can write two good books in one year has a deal of energy left. I know the Queen has great prejudices against him; poor Odo used to tell me to do what

I could to smother these! Both parties, Tories and Liberals, had grievances against him - still there was an idea once of getting him into the House of Lords and giving him a peerage. He could get into the House of Commons if he liked - but the work is too hard for him at his age! Are no more peerages to be given on account of the Jubilee? Do ask your King Solomon - I mean Sir Henry, - I do not like to write to the Queen - can you not tell me whether something can be done? What I am saying is *utterly* unbeknown to old Sir Henry Layard though we have just seen him! I enclose a letter from Sir Wm Gregory on the same subject to a third person, who also takes great interest in the idea.

I had a long and interesting talk with Lord Hartington yesterday. He seems full of vigour and lucidity - which is a very good thing. I was so much interested with Lord Chas Beresford's, Lord Brassey's and the Duke of Cambridge's speeches at that meeting (in the *Times* I received today). Oh how I wish every penny were rightly spent on our army and navy, and loth were as efficient as POSSIBLE. We *cannot* do without!

Dearest Mary I must end here! My girls, especially Vicky, send you and Maggie their best love! They say their Mama is getting more and more absent, and they wonder whether *Maggie's* Mama is in a brown study out walking, or loses her gloves and pocket handkerchiefs, and puts her cap on crooked at dinner!! and commits the like enormities! Can you tell me?

January and February passed with the patient still at San Remo, and his wife ever by his side. Almost every week the illness fluctuated to such an extent as to cause alternations of hope and despair in the Princess. She was, however, pleased to note on January 8 that 'the Emperor spoke kindly about Morell Mackenzie, which I am also glad of'. Early in February, the disease now having been diagnosed as perichondritis, it was decided to insert a canula into the patient's throat, so as to render breathing somewhat easier. On February 8 the Princess wrote to Queen Victoria:

I am quite miserable that Fritz suffers so much from this difficulty in breathing, and this horrid tracheotomy is pending: Of course, I am very thankful that Virchow's report is as good as it is. But I must say I feel a little as if we were 'out of the frying pan into the fire' as one cannot tell how long, nor how bad this perichondritis will be, nor how Fritz's constitution will stand it. His patience gets sorely tried and his spirits much depressed - it is difficult to keep up his courage. He feels how necessary he is, and is so anxious to be cured and to recover. The nights and days and weeks wear one, and we cannot see our way out of the wood yet. All this uncertainty is very hard to bear and one has to put as good a face on it as one can.

To Lady Ponsonby she wrote on the same day:

....I am again very anxious and much tormented because tracheotomy is pending, and you can imagine how I hate the thought of this detestable operation, but if the difficulty of breathing continues and even increases, what else can be done? It makes me miserable, however, that my poor darling should have all this to go through without one's being able to take it away from him, which I gladly would.

As for the subterranean war in the household, I have heard nothing lately. Count Radolinsky is a kind-hearted, amiable and intelligent man, most devoted to us, but *not* judicious - violent, credulous (like a baby), excitable, talks too much and is in consequence often led and not by the best people. This makes it a danger, because he is most imprudent, though he means very well. His intentions now at Berlin are the best, and he only wishes to keep the Emperor and the Chancellor in a good humour about us and satisfied with the treatment the Crown Prince is undergoing. How much mischief may be made by the letters written to him (Count Radolinsky) from here, I cannot tell, nor could I prevent it. I simply ignore all these and listen to nothing. I wish we were over this next month or two...[11]

Five days previously, on February 3, 1888, Bismarck, for reasons of his own, published the text of a defensive treaty against Russia which Germany and Austria had concluded on October 7, 1879, and which had till then been kept secret. On receipt of this piece of news the Crown Princess wrote to Queen Victoria (February 9):

I shall be anxious to hear what Lord Salisbury says to the publication of this treaty of alliance between Germany and Austria. It is all done in the interests of peace, I think.

That day, February 9, the long-deferred operation of tracheotomy was performed successfully by Dr Bramann, and the Crown Princess again wrote to Queen Victoria:

This has been a very terrible day of anxiety and distress. Thank God the operation was carried out well and all went straight - dear Fritz is dozing and I am at his bedside. Of course, he cannot speak! He breathes quite well now, but the sound of the air through that canula is of course very horrid! He was only told this morning that it was going to be done and gave his consent. Bergmann was not waited for! Dr Bramann did it very well - Sir Morell, Dr Hovell, Krause and Schrader were there - next door Moretta, Louis and I. I own I was in terror and agonies, as you can imagine! I was infinitely relieved when it was over. Poor dear, he was so good and patient and made no fuss; I did my best to make none either. The arrangements had to be made in a great hurry. His bed is in his sitting room. He felt no pain, I think, as he was under chloroform. Henry and Charlotte were very nice to me today and Louis most kind. I am feeling much shaken with all the anxiety and I trust all will do well now.

The news of the operation at once excited Berlin, and the rumour quickly spread that the Crown Prince was at the point of death, if not already dead! The Crown Princess, however, still could not believe that the malady was cancer, as will be seen from her letter to Queen Victoria of February 12:

Fritz has spent a good night. Yesterday evening Professor Bergmann arrived and with him Ct Radolinsky. The latter immediately said that he had not expected to find Fritz alive, that all Berlin was in the state of the wildest excitement and alarm. That everyone knew it was cancer and only cancer and that Fritz was irrevocably lost, and that at Berlin no one thought of reckoning with him, he was already considered as belonging to the past! This rubbish only shows you what is thought in the circles in which Radolinsky moves. We have asked Sir Morell to put down his views in a short statement, also to publish Virchow's last statement, as everyone at Berlin and my three eldest children are still firmly convinced that Virchow has pronounced it to be cancer as the result of his investigation. Ctss Bruhl almost cuts me, Fritz's two gentlemen make the longest and stiffest faces. All this means that they disbelieve all that is favourable and insist on believing the most unfavourable! Bergmann (who can know absolutely nothing about Fritz's throat except by hearsay) says it is cancer. As he is the first Berlin Surgeon, of course, many of the Germans believe him, as they cannot know or understand that he has nothing but his conjectures to go by!

I had rather a stormy evening last night with all these dear people, who really seem to lose their senses whenever there is extra reason to be calm and collected, firm and judicious. They mean very well, but are uncommonly troublesome to deal with.

The following weeks showed no great change, neither in the condition of the patient nor in the hopes of his wife that all would be well and that he would recover, nor, indeed, in the temper of the Berlin party. On February 20 the Princess thought that 'Fritz is really a little better today....so I am comforted a little, and think he is turning the corner and beginning to mend'. Referring to the excitement in Berlin she added, 'When Fritz is really better, and the excitement and alarm subsides, then all will be much easier. All the gossip at Berlin and here is quite ridiculous. The main thing is Fritz's health, and please God all these pessimistic views are very unnecessary at present.' To the 'spiteful and unkind opposition' she determined to turn the blind eye 'like Lord Nelson...it is best not to see things which are foolish and only intended to irritate one'.

A week later there was another consultation over the patient. Mackenzie, Bergmann, Schröder and Prof Kussmaul of Strassburg were present, and a squabble between their varying views was unfortunately unavoidable. On February 26 the Crown Princess wrote:

Today has been a very painful day for me! As I foresaw, they only sent for poor old Professor Küssmaul from Strassburg to endorse their opinion! He is not a specialist, and cannot see with the laryngoscope one bit, but notwithstanding this, he tried to make an examination of Fritz's throat, which was a very comical proceeding I assure you! He saw nothing, but imagined he saw a great deal and describes quite fantastically what he did see! The principal result was this! He declares Fritz has nothing whatever the matter with the lungs! I told Bergmann that when Sir M. Mackenzie was once allowed to adjust the tubes and treat the throat, the bleeding would leave off and that when Fritz slept better he would eat again, etc., and be a different person. Bergmann said '*Ach wenn das nur möglich wäre*,[12] - he will never recover from the state he now is in! He can only get rapidly worse!!' I asked the Herr Professor to wait a little time and see Fritz again in a fortnight He agreed to this with a pitying incredulous smile! Küssmaul said that the evidence of cancer was so without doubt and so abundant that he needed no other proofs! To all this Sir Morell can only say: 'The first pathologist in the world has found nothing of the kind! What I see of the larynx points in the opposite direction - both these things together make it impossible for me to affirm that it is cancer. Cancer may be there, but I have no convincing evidence! I know more about the throat than these gentlemen, who are, the one a celebrated surgeon, and the other a general physician, who chiefly treats complaints of the stomach, and Virchow's microscopical examination seems to me more reliable than that of Bergmann, Bramann, Krause and Schröder!'

Pray excuse my mentioning such horrid disagreeable details!

You can fancy how painful it is to me to hear these opinions pronounced with such obstinacy - so positively. They fail to convince me, but of course they do easily convince the family, the court and the public of Germany and Berlin! They can do Fritz no harm, as they cannot give him a disease he has not got; and my life is made quite intolerable, as people think me a maniac for not bluntly accepting what a German Professor says. I may not even have the benefit of doubt. It is very tiresome that Fritz has lost his appetite so completely, and very sad that tracheotomy has certainly not answered well. These last three weeks have been a great strain and a great pull on Fritz's strength, and I do not wonder his being shaken and looking pale and ill, poor dear! Küssmaul and Bergmann mean to go away soon and I hope Fritz will gradually resume his usual habits, but the haemorrhage and expectoration are very troublesome and worrying still and make him very dependant, as a doctor has always to be in the room day and night to attend to the canula.

I hope and trust that the rest of Bergmann's and Bramann's diagnosis and prognosis may be as true as that Fritz is bleeding from the lungs.

Of course, I am tongue tied. I dare say nothing against the infallible wisdom of the German medical authorities, or I should be torn to pieces. Whenever I say that things may go all right, I am met with incredulous faces of distrust and implying rebuke and censure. It is really very unpleasant! However I do not care a rap, so long as we can get Fritz on, and of that I do not despair.

Ten days later she wrote to Queen Victoria:

I ought already to have thanked you for your dear letter of the 1st and now I have a new one of the 3rd to thank you for too! I was so much out of spirits these last two or three days that I could not have written a cheerful letter. You will have heard that this Prof Waldeger of Berlin, whom I have not seen and do not know, says he has found undoubted evidence of cancer, *i.e.* such an immense quantity of 'Nest-cells'. This quite convinces Bergmann, Bramann, Schröder and Krause, as it confirms what Küssmaul said! I own it fails quite to convince me, although it increases the evidence on their side, yet there is the fact that Virchow is the great pathologist and microscopist, and as you have read yourself, he found no such evidence, as he does not consider mere nest-cells as an undoubted proof. Furthermore all the other signs from November till now do not bear out the theory of cancer, therefore whilst admitting that it may be, yet I do not feel without some doubts. Virchow gave a negative opinion and these give a positive one. The trouble with the bleeding and the canula is going on, but much less since Sir Morell has changed the tubes! This last night was the best Fritz has had, less cough and much less bleeding! He ate rather better yesterday and really does not feel ill and shaken now at all. Bergmann told Willy that his Papa had six months to live! With this idea William has gone away; of course this is nonsense, a mere guess and a conjecture. It all went straight between Willy and us and was quite harmonious. He left yesterday morning! Not one word of sympathy or affection did he utter, and I was distressed to see how very haughty he has become, and what tremendous airs he gives himself! It is no doubt the effect of being told so often that he may be Emperor in less than a year. His visit did not do any harm, and he did not meddle this time.

I am feeling very troubled and anxious and unhappy with all this; and it is hard to feel that people are provoked with me for refusing to give up all hope, and not rushing back to Germany now, when I know how dangerous it would be for my beloved Fritz! No one thinks of that. All they want is to be able to say that he is in Germany. I say we must wait till the middle of April; then we can go slowly home!

The Emperor has not been well these last few days, but is up and does his business as usual.

The next day, March 7, the Crown Princess wrote to Lady Ponsonby:

I have been longing to write to you for such a time and have never had a minute. Of course, you know all the news I send from here through the Queen. Again as before, the German medical authorities have given the very worst verdict; again it seems to us to lack convincing power, as so many signs of which they affirm are wanting. They base all on their newest microscopic examinations

- to which we are to trust, seeing that what Virchow so explicitly said so short a time ago in no way corresponds with what Waldeger now says. I am more troubled and distressed than I can say - quite miserable sometimes, and yet I cannot bring myself to see things irrevocably in the very worst light, there are so many 'ifs' and 'buts'.

I think my dear husband's general condition much improved these last few days; though that odious bleeding goes on, and the nights are much broken. His appetite is really improving and he looks much better.

We are rather alarmed about the Emperor this afternoon as he is said to be weaker than usual. Heaven grant that we need not be whisked off to Germany where it is terribly cold now. The Crown Prince has not sufficiently recovered to be able to bear the strain of all the business and responsibility which would suddenly fall upon him, and my anxiety would increase tenfold, as you can imagine.

This is not a very cheerful letter, but I am really oppressed with all these cares and anxieties and long for a ray of hope and light in all this darkness.[13]

The concluding sentence about the Emperor foreshadowed a long-expected event. The following day the news indicated that the end of the nonagenarian monarch was near. The Crown Princess viewed this event with no elation, no rapture. Any possible pride or joy there might have been in the thought that his death would elevate her to the dignity of Empress was entirely swamped by the dread certainty that 'Fritz' would have to leave the sunshine and warmth of San Remo for the wintry weather and bustle of Berlin, and to her mother she wrote on March 8:

As you know, the news of the Emperor is such as to oblige us to prepare for all eventualities! I am in terror when I think of the journey to Berlin and yet it cannot be helped, or avoided, if really the change takes place! Fritz must be there to assume the responsibilities of his position, but it is grievous to think of the risks he runs and of the painfulness of the whole situation! He feels it most bitterly - when most he wants his physical powers, all his strength and energy, he finds himself an invalid struggling to recover from the effects of an operation, and in a delicate and sensitive state! Still he will do his duty as best he can and I will help him as well as I can. He feels very much the idea of his father being perhaps taken from this world without his being able to say a last farewell and ask his blessing, or without his being there to be a comfort to his mother! All this is very sad, but I am thankful to think that Fritz in his present state of health will be saved from witnessing the sad and painful scenes and all the mournful details which would upset him too much. We shall leave on Saturday morning and go straight through without stopping, but not to our house. I could not venture to let him stay there in the midst of the public, a perfect prisoner; we shall go to Charlottenburg to Bernhard's and Charlotte's rooms, whilst they will go to our home in town! There will at least be a semblance of privacy and quiet, and we shall not be so overrun.

We are now packing everything so as to be ready to go together *en bloc*!! It does seem too grievous to leave the sweet place, the sun, the sea and flowers. Six weeks more would have set Fritz up and he would soon have begun his walks and drives again, and it would have done him so much good. Now I do not know how we shall get on if sleep and appetite fail. It is all like a horrid dream! I shall miss seeing you, which breaks my heart! We have so much to do and to think of, to arrange, write and telegraph, that I must end here, dearest beloved Mama! I feel sure your heart and your thoughts are with us in this time of sore trouble and anxiety.

In view of the facts given in these letters of the Crown Princess with reference to the development of the Crown Prince's illness, it is not perhaps out of place to quote somewhat extensively from Herr Ludwig's recent book. *Kaiser Wilhelm II.* In his second chapter he states:

Ever since William's unhappy birth, Victoria (*i.e.* the Crown Princess) had stubbornly clung to the nonsensical idea that the German physicians were to blame for her son's disability. This *idée fixe* induced her - so all her surviving friends agree - to underline her distrust of German therapeutics by calling in an Englishman for her husband....At the same time (in 1888) Bismarck wrote in his unmistakable style an article in the *Norddeutsche Allgemeine Zeitung*, the purport of which was that Mackenzie now declared that he too had quite clearly recognised the disease from the first, but that the Crown Prince had confided to him that he did not wish to be pronounced incurable, but on high moral and practical grounds desired to reign for a short time....It is now established beyond question that an unimportant English physician of radical political opinions took upon himself to play the Privy Councillor, and interfere directly in the history of the German nation.

By this semi-official declaration Bismarck, before all the world, displayed his old enemy Victoria as nothing less than the indirect cause of the premature death of her husband; he plainly hinted that she preferred to be the widowed Empress rather than the wife of an abjuring Prince, the victim of cancer....But we must do Victoria the justice to say that she was certainly no tigress, but much the reverse - an emotional affectionate woman; and therefore not to be blamed for hoping against hope that her husband's life might be saved.

She stands indicted, nevertheless, for serious indiscretion. She summoned from her native land an undistinguished physician, simply because she attributed a shortcoming of nature to the physicians of the land she had adopted. Or did she wish, in love and sympathy, to conceal his doom from her husband?

The course of events, moreover, sustains Bismarck's indictment. Through all that year Victoria maintained the fiction that the Crown Prince was only slightly ailing, that he was better, that he would soon be well - not only by numerous despatches and protests to the public at large, whom on political grounds there was perhaps good reason to delude; but with her personal friends and with her children she acted this part for thirteen months, during which her husband was visibly failing at her side. Immediately after the fateful decision in June came her mother's Jubilee. Was she to be absent from that? And was her eldest son to bask in that reflected glory? No - and against the advice of her most trusted friends Victoria forced her suffering, already wellnigh voiceless husband to ride high upon his horse in the London procession, in the hope of silencing by that parade the whisperings of rumour....

Then the English party prevented the Crown Prince's return to Berlin, and they wandered, without German physicians, from one spa to another; yet when one considers the unremitting care shown by Victoria during all this time, one is again persuaded that she really thought it impossible her husband could be suffering from cancer.

At the beginning of November, a sudden change for the worse. A sojourn at San Remo, decisive position taken up by the doctors, *communiqué* in the *Reichsanzeiger* that the heir to the throne was attacked by cancer; nevertheless an operation was not to take place, for the patient did not desire it, and moreover it was probably too late. 'Prince William is entrusted with the Regency.'

From this day forward the Prince's every nerve was strained. He was now in point of fact Crown Prince, and had only to await the speedy departure of a nonagenarian, and a fatally stricken, forerunner. And now the hatred of the parents for their son reached a commensurable intensity. Thirty years of waiting - and then Nothingness! And this crude boy was to step into the vainly-longed-for sovereignty like an idle stroller not one hour of patience or of struggle! Frederick's Regent? Then already he was looked upon as dead? 'I am not yet an idiot, or incapable!' exclaimed the sufferer, when he heard of his relegation.[14]

The difficulties that beset the would-be historian are well illustrated by this account which comes from the pen of Dr Emil Ludwig. With every wish to write a true version of these events, this eminent historian had to rely for his particulars on the accounts of the German doctors and on the articles published at that time in the German press. The only book that attempts to present the other side of the controversy was written by Sir Morell Mackenzie, and was not only an *ex parte* statement of fact, but was also universally condemned by the medical profession both in Germany and England.

Divorced from national prejudice, medical rivalry and political bias, the story of the Crown Prince's illness seems to run as follows. When the Crown Prince first showed symptoms of an affection of the throat, the principal doctors and surgeons were by degrees summoned. Among them were some of the most eminent men in the profession: probably no more able men were to be found in Europe, but not one of them was a specialist in throat diseases. These German doctors unanimously came to the conclusion that the probabilities were that the malady was cancer, but they could prove nothing.

This was at the time, in view of the medical ignorance on this vast subject, a fairly safe opinion to give, and in most cases would be right. Mackenzie, however, was then sent for, and the weight of evidence proves that he was sent for not by a Princess of English birth who was reputed to have a bias against German doctors, but in consequence of the intervention of Prince Bismarck and on the advice of one of the German doctors to which the others assented. Mackenzie, on his arrival, knew that a swelling of the nature from which the Crown Prince was suffering did not necessarily indicate cancer. On three different occasions he removed tiny portions of the affected part of the larynx, which he submitted to Professor Virchow, a pathologist of European reputation. Virchow, after a most thorough investigation of each of the four fragments, states that no trace of cancer was to be found.

Mackenzie thereupon refused to admit the presence of cancer until some proof was forthcoming, and it must be admitted that he played on the uncertainty of the diagnosis for all it was worth. The fact remains that although the German doctors eventually proved to be right they were only relying on surmise, while Mackenzie based his opinion on scientific analysis which proved to be misleading.

The Crown Princess, delighted at Virchow's reports, then praised Mackenzie and made tactless remarks which not unnaturally the German doctors resented.

The controversy then ceased to be a medical one, and became a question of whether the English doctors (for Dr Hovell was now also in attendance upon the Crown Prince) or the German doctors were right. The Crown Princess supported the British specialist, and the whole German nation supported the German doctors, while the Emperor and Bismarck did nothing. It was not until the Crown Prince arrived at San Remo that proof was forthcoming that the malady was cancer, and it was one of the English doctors, Dr Mark Hovell, who raised the alarm. All Germany then rushed to the conclusion that Mackenzie was a quack and that the Crown Princess had deliberately sacrificed her husband's life to gain her own ends, while both Mackenzie and Queen Victoria were accused of having interfered unduly in what was essentially a German question.

It is unfortunate that Dr Emil Ludwig has had at his disposal the evidence relating to one side only of this tragic story. Such misrepresentations of history are hard to correct: judge then the feelings of the Crown Princess at the time, when these inaccurate and biased statements were being made in the German press, while she was unable, on account of her position, to enter the polemical arena and give her account of the facts of the case as she knew them.

## NOTES

1 Morell Mackenzie, *Frederick the Noble*, p. 65.
2 The Autobiography of Sir Felix Semon, p. 156.
3 Sir Rennell Rodd's *Social and Diplomatic Memories*, vol. i., p. 123.
4 *The Autobiography of Sir Felix Semon*, pp. 157-8. Also the *Standard*, November 14, 1887.
5 Prince Henry was then twenty-five years old.
6 *Mary Ponsonby*, pp. 259-61.
7 Busch, p. 232, records that among the Chancellor's letters there was a long one dated November 22, 1887, from the Crown Princess, 'giving the Chancellor particulars of her consort's illness and of the doctors; and also Bodelschwingh's communication, on the top of which the chief had written in pencil "Old hypocrite"'.
8 Apparently the Crown Princess ignored the reports published in the German Official Gazette that the new growth was of a carcinomatous character.
9 Duke of Saxe-Coburg and Gotha
10 *Mary Ponsonby*, pp. 264-5.
11 *Ibid.* pp. 265-6.
12 If that were only possible.
13 *Mary Ponsonby*, pp. 267-8
14 Emil Ludwig, *Kaiser Wilhelm II*. pp. 33-7.

# XI. The Reign of the Emperor Frederick

ON March 9, 1888, the nonagenarian, William I, died, and there began that short ninety-eight days' reign of the Emperor and Empress Frederick. The new Emperor, now in his fifty-seventh year, showed visible signs of his terrible malady, but was still a dominating figure and still mentally alert. He was at the Villa Zirio, San Remo, when the news was brought of his father's death, and immediately the household of the new monarch gathered in the drawing-room of the Villa. A little later the new Emperor and Empress entered, and the Emperor, moving to a small table, wrote out the announcement of his own accession as Frederick III. His next act was to invest his consort with the ribbon of the Black Eagle, the highest order within his gift. He then greeted Dr Morell Mackenzie and wrote for him the words: 'I thank you for having made me live long enough to recompense the valiant courage of my wife.' How often must they have talked over what they would do when they ascended the throne, always imagining the splendour of Berlin as the scene! But here they were in the drawing-room of a villa in Italy, merely a small party with their own suite. It was all rather pathetic, but the indomitable pluck of the Emperor and the devotion of his wife made it impressive as a ceremony.

It was essential that the new Emperor and Empress should at once proceed to Berlin. The decision to go was made by the Emperor, and within twenty-four hours they were en route. Much criticism was levelled at the new Empress for bringing back the Emperor to Berlin, but the decision was his. Always he had put duty before comfort, and he was not the man to abdicate or fall short even on the brink of the grave. Before they left San Remo the Empress wrote to Queen Victoria (March 9):

> The sad news has just come that the dear Emperor has passed away! Fritz is deeply affected, feels intensely being absent from his post and is determined to go there, come what may, and to run the risk. I cannot tell you how anxious I feel and how nervous, and yet I am sure he is right! Your thoughts are with us I know! I dread the journey even less than all we shall find when we get there. Sir Morell has taken the greatest trouble to ensure all possible precaution being taken, and we must leave the rest in God's hands.
> 
> Thank God that the end was gentle and peaceful and without pain! What a long and strange career that has been! To think of my poor Fritz succeeding his father as a sick and stricken man is so hard!! How much good he might have done! Will time be given him? I pray that it may and he may be spared to be a

blessing to his people and to Europe. Excuse my ending here - we are overwhelmed with business and packing, etc.

The journey was swift, and on the evening of March 11 the Imperial party arrived at Berlin. The Emperor at once took up the reins, although the change from the warm, sunny, equable climate of San Remo to the sleet and slush of Berlin must have been a terrible hardship. More than that, the change from the quiet, health-giving leisureliness of San Remo to the business and bustle of the German court, where everything was at sixes and sevens, was one that might have tried the constitution of even the fittest.

Two days of such hectic energy were sufficient to send the Emperor back to bed, and it was a distressed wife who wrote to Queen Victoria on March 13:

How can I thank you enough for your dear letter of the 10th, so kind and loving and so precious to me! I wish I could kiss your dear hand for it directly I know you will forgive me if I cannot write today as I should like! It is all like a dream and I am so overwhelmed with business of all sorts and kinds, things important and unimportant that have to be seen to. I am not in our own home and cannot find my things yet! One's heart is torn and tortured with fears and anxiety and yet I am glad to think that my beloved Fritz has the satisfaction of feeling that he is at home, though this is also full of pain as you can understand.

The journey was a great risk and a great fatigue and has done him harm, but I hope and trust in a few days the effect may be got over. The night was not good. Of course, the change is immense, from the life of an invalid to one of business and excitement, far beyond what he is at present fit for. I do what I can to help him, but the difficulties are immense. I will write and tell you all as soon as I can! I am feeling dreadfully knocked up and cannot sleep! Darling Fritz has had to remain in bed today, as the doctors were not at all satisfied this morning! I hope this night will be better!

The poor Emperor looked so peaceful sleeping in his coffin and yet the sight of death to me just now, when so many fears fill my heart, was agony! I cannot say more. The Empress I think wonderfully calm and composed, and looking better and stronger and a little stouter than when I saw her last! Louise and Fritz of Baden are marvellously calm and collected!

All else I would say, I must put off till another time - questions, letters, telegrams, visits come pouring in, and I like to devote all my time to staying with Fritz.

In some quarters the accession of the Emperor Frederick was expected to see the end of the power of Bismarck. The opposition of the Emperor and Empress to parts of Bismarck's policy was widely known, and it was expected that one of the first acts of the new reign would be the replacement of the Chancellor by someone more in accordance with the liberal ideas of the

Emperor 1888 and Empress. But between Bismarck and the Imperial pair there was, in spite of surface differences, a fundamental and mutual appreciation. The Empress, as Bismarck himself said, 'shared with him (the Emperor) the conviction that in the interests of the dynasty it was necessary that I should be maintained in office at the change of reign'[1] and one of the new Emperor's first acts was to write to Bismarck a letter inviting him to continue as Chancellor. The message, dated March 12, ran:

MY DEAR PRINCE - On assuming power I feel the necessity of addressing you, the long- tried first servant of my father, who now rests in God. You have been the faithful and brave adviser who gave shape to the aims of his policy, and secured their successful realisation. I and my House are and remain most grateful to you. You, therefore, have, above all, a right to know the principles which will direct me in my rule.

The constitutional and legal regulations of the Empire and of Prussia must, above all, be consolidated in the respect and customs of the nation. It is, therefore, necessary to avoid, as far as possible, the shock caused by repeated changes of the institutions and laws of the State. The furtherance of the task of the Imperial Government must leave untouched the bases on which the Prussian State has hitherto safely rested. In the Empire the constitutional rights of all the Federal Governments must be as conscientiously respected as those of the Reichstag; but the same respect for the rights of the Emperor must be demanded from both. At the same time, it is necessary to keep in view that these mutual rights are only intended for the promotion of the public welfare, which remains the supreme law, and that new and unquestionable national needs must always be fully satisfied. As the necessary and certain guarantee of the undisturbed furtherance of this task, I look to the maintenance unweakened of the defensive forces of the country, of my tried Army and growing Navy, which has serious duties before it in the protection of our possessions beyond the seas. They must both be maintained at their present perfection of organisation, to which they owe their glory, and which insures their future capacity to accomplish their duty.

I am resolved to conduct the Government both of the Empire and of Prussia with a conscientious observation of the stipulations of the respective Constitutions of the Empire and of die State. They were founded by my ancestors on the Throne in wise recognition of the necessities and difficulties incident to the social and political life of the nation, and they must be respected by everyone in order to give proof of their power and beneficial influence. I will that the principle of religious tolerance, for centuries past held sacred by my House, shall also for the future be maintained as a protection to all my subjects, to whatever religious community or creed they may belong. Everyone of them is equally near to my heart, for they have all given equal proofs of like devotion in days of danger. In perfect accord with the views of my Imperial father, I shall -warmly support all efforts destined to further the economic progress of every class of society, to conciliate their divergent interests, and to mitigate, as far as possible, unavoidable social inequalities without, however, exciting the expectation that this can be done by State interference. Closely connected with the social question I consider that of the cultivation of youth, and the efforts to this end must be on a higher scale and be made more widely accessible. 'We must, therefore, avoid raising fresh dangers by partial education, and awakening demands beyond the economic capacity of the nation to meet. We must also take care that through one-sided efforts for increased knowledge, the task of education shall not remain neglected. Only a generation trained up upon the sound basis of the fear of God and simplicity of morals can possess sufficient power of resistance to surmount the perils which in a time of rapid economic development arise for the entire community through the examples of the highly luxurious life of individuals.

It is my will that in the public service no opportunity should be lost of offering every opposition to the temptation to inordinate expenditure. My unbiased consideration of every proposal of financial reform is assured in advance, unless the long-proved economy of Prussia does not permit. The imposition of fresh burdens is to be avoided, and an alleviation of the demands hitherto made on the country to be effected. The self-government granted to the larger and smaller communities in the State I regard as 1888 beneficial. On the other hand, I would suggest for examination the question whether the right of taxation conferred upon these communities, which may be exercised by them without making allowance for the burden concurrently imposed by the Empire and the State, does not weigh unfairly upon individuals. Similarly, it will have to be considered whether simplification in the arrangements does not appear admissible by which a reduction in the number of officials would permit of an increase in their salaries. Should we succeed in maintaining the vigour of the principles of political and social life, I shall have special gratification in watching the full development of the rich progress of German science and art.

For the realisation of these my intentions I rely on your oft-proved devotion, and on the support of your tried experience. May I be destined thus to lead Germany and Prussia in a course of peaceful development to new honours, with the unanimous co-operation of the Imperial organs, of the devoted activity of the representatives of the people and of all the authorities, and with the confiding assistance of all classes of society. Not caring for the splendour of great deeds, nor striving for glory, I shall be satisfied if it be one day said of my rule that it was beneficial to my people, useful to my country and a blessing to the Empire.

Yours very affectionately,<br>FREDERICK III.

The new Empress still could not realise that at most her husband could live but a few months: on the other hand many members of the German medical profession, and many of the chief officials of state, were certain that the Emperor was already *in articulo mortis*. The result was a clash between the Emperor's party and those who looked forward eagerly to the displacement of a speechless sovereign by a young and reputedly able prince.

The Empress had only been in Berlin three days when these intrigues came to her notice, and on March 15 she wrote to her mother from Charlottenburg:

I think Fritz's proclamation and also his letter to Prince Bismarck produced the right impression; I think Bismarck was surprised at receiving these papers all ready for publication and written out in Fritz's own hand!

It is very evident that all sorts of intrigues were going on before he came back and that some were very glad at our return, others taken aback; most people supposed Fritz would return merely to resign! Underlying everything is the belief that the present reign will only last a very few months, and this has all sorts of consequences! Most of those who have seen Fritz think him far better and looking more unchanged than they expected....

The Empress's relations with the Iron Chancellor were certainly more cordial after the accession than ever they had been before. The Empress found him 'civil and nice', and the Chancellor for his part realised that it was essential to conciliate the Empress.

On March 16, 1888, at Berlin, the solemn national funeral of the late Emperor took place. The new Emperor, unable to attend, watched the funeral cortege from his palace window. The Prince of Wales had arrived to represent Queen Victoria at the obsequies, and his presence did much to smooth the path of the Empress Frederick. That day she wrote from Charlottenburg to Queen Victoria:

This trying day is over at last, and I feel so thankful that Fritz has stood all the painful emotion and excitement so well. It was all so hard for him! My thoughts wandered during the ceremony in the Dom to you and our beloved grandmama, who was taken from us this day 27 years ago. All went off well, there was no hitch in spite of the bitter cold weather sharp frost and deep snow! The public was respectful and silent, there were no great crowds. The service I thought rather conventional, stiff and cold; the singing was very good! One can hardly talk of service in the German Church, as it is only an address and an extempore prayer, both of which I did not think very happy on this occasion! The hearse was very simple indeed! On account of the bitter weather Fritz could not leave his room, and I was unable to be with him at the sad moment. When the hearse passed close under his window he quite broke down and was overwhelmed by his feelings, as you may well imagine! Directly afterwards we went to him and he was calm again and is now resting a little in bed. He had rather a better night and does not feel uncomfortable. Yesterday he saw far too many people and was too much fatigued today he has kept comparatively quite quiet.

To have dear Bertie here was a great comfort, though alas, I have not seen a very great deal of him! There is an immense deal to do as you can imagine and all is most difficult and complicated. I think people in general consider us a mere passing shadow, soon to be replaced by reality in the shape of William. I may be wrong, but it seems to me as if the party that opposed and ill-treated us so long, hardly think it worth while to change their attitude, except very slightly - as they count on a different future!

It is an inestimable blessing to be relieved from a thraldom and tyranny which was exercised over us in the poor Emperor's name, as now the right thing can be done for Fritz's health! But oh - if it is not too late! too late! This agonising thought haunts me! Yes, we are our own masters now, but shall we not have to leave all the work undone which we have so long and so carefully been preparing? Will there be any chance of doing the right thing, any time to carry out useful measures, needful reforms? Every German who means well, asks himself this question with bitter pain! It is hard, it is cruel! I hope on and live - *du jour an lendemain.*' Enough for the day is the evil thereof, let the morrow take care of itself.' All the more we shall strive to do what is wisest and safest and best! Prudence and caution are necessary now where fresh and vigorous regeneration of many an obsolete and used up thing would have been desirable! You know and feel all this, I am sure! Prince Bismarck has been civil and nice and I think feels quite at his ease.

A month later, in mid-April 1888, Queen Victoria, accompanied by Prince and Princess Henry of Battenberg and attended by the Dowager Lady Churchill, the Hon Harriet Phipps, Sir Henry Ponsonby and Major Bigge (afterwards Lord Stamfordham), paid a visit to her daughter and dying son-in-law at Charlottenburg. Just before her arrival, all Berlin was agog with rumours of the resignation of Bismarck. The wishes of the Emperor and the Chancellor were at that moment in grave conflict, and the subject of their disagreement was once more the future of the twenty-two-year-old Princess Victoria, the second daughter of the Emperor and Empress Frederick. The parents still favoured what they believed to be a love match, and rumour was rife that the Princess was shortly to be engaged, if not already engaged, to Prince Alexander of Battenberg.

It will be remembered that while Prince Alexander was still on the Bulgarian throne the projected alliance had only been prevented by the determined interposition of Bismarck. Possibly Bismarck foresaw that Prince Alexander would have but a brief tenure of power at Sofia, and was then actuated by a kindly desire to save a Hohenzollern Princess from associating her fortune with a Prince whose destiny was so uncertain. Whatever his motives then, his reasons during the crisis of 1888 seem to have been dictated solely by considerations of political expediency. There was still a party in Sofia that would have welcomed the return of Prince Alexander, and Bismarck saw that the Prince's marriage would strengthen the hopes of this party, and possibly embroil Germany with Russia in the confusion that would follow.

The rumoured resignation did not appear to affect in any way Queen Victoria's plans or make Her Majesty hesitate to visit Berlin on her way home from Florence, but she was relieved to receive the following message from the Empress on April 5:

Please be in no anxiety. Crisis of Chancellor is an invention: we have never been on better terms and the understanding is perfect. Your visit must on no account be given up.

This message was, however, somewhat neutralised by a letter which Queen Victoria received from Lord Salisbury a day or two later, dated April 6. In the course of his letter Lord Salisbury said:

....Sir E. Malet telegraphed to Lord Salisbury last night privately that the Chancellor had spoken very earnestly to him about the proposed marriage between the Princess Victoria and the Prince Alexander, stating that he should retire if it took place. Sir E. Malet asked as to the course he should take as to this communication. Lord Salisbury advised him that so grave a communication should not be withheld from Your Majesty: but he thought it should be sent direct, as it was too closely connected with Your Majesty's family to be admitted into official communications with this office. Count Hatzfeldt renewed the subject this afternoon. Lord Salisbury repeated the same opinion to him. Count Hatzfeldt however said nothing about Prince Bismarck's resignation, but only that such an event would force Germany into taking a much more Russian line of policy than otherwise she would be inclined to do.

Three days later, April 9, Queen Victoria sent the following message to Lord Salisbury:

Queen has heard from Empress Victoria that she had long interview with Bismarck on 6th, which was very satisfactory on all points, and she begs Queen not to notice absurd statements in newspapers.

This again seemed to be somewhat at variance with other accounts of Bismarck's attitude, for on April 8 Lord Salisbury cyphered to Queen Victoria:

I have received several private telegrams from Sir E. Malet showing that Prince Bismarck is in one of his raging moods about the proposed marriage.
He shows temper against Your Majesty and as at such times he is quite unscrupulous he will probably try to give currency to statements which are

designed to make Your Majesty personally responsible for any evil results of his own violent passion. He has a vast corrupt influence over the press and can give enormous circulation to rumours. I would humbly advise Your Majesty to avoid any action which could operate with the controversy which is going on. The newspapers say that Your Majesty is going to Potsdam or Berlin. I would humbly submit that this visit at this time would expose You to great misconstruction and possibly to some disrespectful demonstration. German Chancellor is reported by his son to be in a state of intense exasperation....

The Queen was, however, very angry at the way her daughter was being treated and sent the following instruction to Sir Henry Ponsonby on April 9:

Perhaps Sir Henry would write to Lord Salisbury about the outrageous conduct of Pce. Wm, and of the terrible *cercle vicieux* which surrounds the unfortunate Emperor and Empress and which makes Bismarck's conduct really disloyal, wicked and really unwise in the extreme! The Queen sends the Empress's letter to enable Sir Henry to quote parts of it. Russia really *cannot* care a *straw* about Prince Alexander's marriage *unless* they admit the probability, if not likelihood, of his returning to Bulgaria!!

*How* Bismarck and still more William *can* play such a double game it is impossible for us honest, straightforward English to understand. Thank God! we *are* English! The Queen will also write to Lord Salisbury by messenger leaving tomorrow. It troubles and distresses the Queen very much. But the threat thrown out by Russia is one which the Queen thinks impudent and impertinent beyond measure.

The Queen got a letter by messenger from Lord Salisbury explaining the whole thing, but she only saw it after Sir Henry left yesterday, but which she will send Sir Henry later.

Meanwhile, the belief that with the approval of the Empress, Prince Alexander had engaged himself to the Princess Victoria, caused a domestic and political crisis in Berlin. Bismarck professed to regard the betrothal as a nefarious plot on the part of the Empress to embroil Germany with Prince Alexander's enemy, the Tsar, and he found Prince William vigorously supporting his attitude.[2]

Queen Victoria now found the situation very puzzling, and on April 7 her Private Secretary, Sir Henry Ponsonby, wrote to Sir Edward Malet, who had been appointed British Ambassador to Berlin on Lord Ampthill's death in 1884:

Reuter says Princess Victoria betrothed. I ascertained that the Queen is opposed to it and so are Prince and Princess Henry (of Battenberg). I was allowed to tell you this, but it is not desirable to repeat it to the Empress.

Two days later Sir E. Malet replied to Sir Henry:

I am most grateful to you for giving me the information contained in your letter of the 7th, and I have made use of it in the particular quarter where it appeared absolutely necessary. There has been a terrible storm here on the subject, a regular blizzard, and I was most glad of the ray of sunshine coming from you. It will go far to dissipate the cloud.

Four days later, April 13, Queen Victoria, still at Florence, noted for Sir Henry Ponsonby:

The Queen got this cypher (a private one which is similar to one used between Dr Reid and the doctors) in answer to her letter in which she told him of Lord Salisbury's cypher. She cannot understand how this agrees with Sir E. Malet's letters! That it is all got up for a purpose the Queen does not doubt and also that Herbert Bismarck and Wm are at the bottom of it.

The Empress's reception on her rapid journey has shown to that wicked clique at Berlin *how* popular she and her dear Emperor are in the country!

'(Repeat it.)'

That day Sir Henry Ponsonby wrote to Sir E. Malet:

I am commanded by the Queen to thank you for your letter of the 7th instant which Her Majesty received last night by messenger, in which you communicate to her an account of Prince Bismarck's reasons for intending to resign, which you consider were of such a private nature that you could not give them in an official despatch but which were communicated to the newspapers immediately after or possibly before His Serene Highness had spoken to you.

The Queen is quite unable to understand how the visit of a private individual, such as Prince Alexander of Battenberg is now, could have aroused distrust in Russia to such an extent as to have made such an event a cause of danger to the peace between the two countries, and she must confess that she is surprised that Germany should be dictated to by the Czar, who has, you say, a craze against Prince Alexander which as far as the Queen can learn is not shared by the Russian nation.

Nor is it easy to see how the marriage of Prince Alexander and Princess Victoria could in any way cement the union of Russia and France against Germany or cause estrangement between England and Germany. Surely the prognostications of such great European changes arising out of a marriage of this sort are absurd. Prince Bismarck appeals to the Queen, who, he supposes, favours the marriage. He is as much mistaken in this supposition as he is in his other conclusions, if he imagines that the Queen has urged this marriage. No doubt she would be glad if the Prince and Princess wished to marry and if the Imperial family of Germany welcomed such a proposal, that it should take place, but all the details could have been easily and privately discussed without making a state affair out of a family matter.

As far as the Queen can learn, the Chancellor allowed his intended resignation to be announced to the world before consulting the Empress upon this question, and it would appear that after he had seen Her Imperial Majesty matters were arranged.

This storm might therefore have been avoided if Prince Bismarck had only taken the trouble to inform himself more fully of the facts of the case.

That same day, April 13, 1888, Colonel Leopold Swaine, the British Military Attaché in Berlin, wrote to the Prince of Wales, and sent a copy of his letter to Sir H. Ponsonby:

....As regards the 'Marriage Question', I have the following statement to make which I believe to be perfectly authentic. Already within the first week of their Majesties' arrival in Charlottenburg the Empress determined to bring this matter on without delay and Prince Alexander was invited to Berlin. Whether he was only to arrive on Princess Victoria's birthday or already earlier is not quite clear. At any rate nothing as to this proposed visit was made known to the Chancellor. There is no doubt that he heard it by accident and many odd stories are told giving the supposed authoritative version how it became known to him.

Most persons are agreed that the moment was inopportune for starting this project which had been so warmly condemned by the late Emperor; and also, that it should have been done without in any way acquainting the Chancellor, who had so strongly supported the late Emperor against it for state reasons, is equally blamed.

I understand it was the latter more than the former which irritated the Chancellor, but whether he absolutely threatened to resign or not I cannot say. I am inclined to doubt it; although it is probable that he stated it would be impossible for him to remain in office if the marriage took place.

It was a fortnight ago yesterday, or will be tomorrow, since the Chancellor heard of it, and the *pourparlers* had been going on for nearly a week before we learnt anything about it....

I have heard from several sources that Prince Alexander is by no means anxious himself for the marriage. He had a good political reason for it when Prince of Bulgaria and, while trying to shake off Russian influence, he was anxious through this marriage to ensure German support. But all that is past and he is now reported to have *ein zärtliches Verhältniss* with a member of the histrionic art.

We are living in sad times here in Berlin. Not sad alone because we have an Emperor at death's door, nor sad only because there are family disagreements, but sad, doubly sad, because almost all officials - perhaps with exceptions, but I know them not are behaving in a way as if the last spark of honour and faithful duty had gone - they are all trimming their sails.

It seems as if a curse had come over this country, leaving but one bright spot and that is where stands a solitary woman doing her duty faithfully and tenderly by her sick husband against all odds. It is one of the most, if not the most, tragic episodes in a country and a life ever recorded in history.

The Emperor was far from well yesterday, indeed I believe that there was a moment of grave anxiety. A new 'canula' had to be inserted. But the night was a good one and His Majesty was in town this morning.

This is a letter full of painful facts and I can assure you, Sir, that we all feel it most grievously - no one is telling the truth, and all are intriguing for self.

To this letter Colonel Swaine added the 'Very private 'postscript: 'We have been told that not only the Queen, but also Prince and Princess Henry of Battenberg are strongly opposed to the marriage.'

It was about this time that Queen Victoria sent the following message to the Empress: 'Don't contemplate marriage without full consent of William. It would never do to contract a marriage he would not agree to. Sandro's marriage might ruin his whole prospect in life.'

On April 13 Queen Victoria sent the following message in cypher to Lord Salisbury, the British Foreign Secretary:

I cannot understand Bismarck's excitement. Three weeks ago I advised the Empress to take no steps at present in the matter. Prince Alexander's family do not favour his marriage, particularly under existing circumstances, and unless accepted by one person it would be impossible. But Bismarck's tyranny is unbearable, and I cannot abandon my intention of seeing the dear suffering Emperor whom I could never see at San Remo.

Queen Victoria had now taken up a very decided attitude, and on April 21, while still at Florence, wrote to Lord Salisbury:

The Queen thanks Lord Salisbury for his letter and wishes just to say in continuation of what she sent by cypher yesterday that she is sorry to see how Sir Ed. Malet seems to see things through Prince - and still more Herbert - Bismarck's eyes. She cannot conceive what the object of their conduct has been in repeating things as they did and above all in Prince Bismarck's conversation with Sir Ed. Malet and in his sending what almost amounted to a message! to the Queen. It was too outrageous. In the last letter the Queen received from her daughter, dated 13th, she says: 'I do not wonder that you should have been startled and alarmed as many people were, by the *senseless*, ridiculous and violent storm in the press, about Vicky and Sandro! If you knew why all this row was made, you would see more clearly, that the reason was a futile one! *Our* relations with the Chancellor never have been more cordial or agreeable; and you well know that Fritz is too calm and prudent and experienced to jeopardize peace or the interests of Germany in any way. Fritz wished to have Sandro here on Easter

Monday, to give him the order *Pour le mérite* and a *Brigade* (not even a Division). 'Whether or not a *Verlobung* was to have followed was a question which had not been raised. Prince B. did not wish Fritz to carry out the intention (which he has had ever since Sandro's return from Bulgaria) of employing him in the army (for he is their fittest General) and said that he considered that step one which would *affront* the Czar (what an humiliating position for Germany to be in), while quite admitting that it was most regrettable the Czar *should* look upon it as an offence.'

Intrigues of William, etc., followed, and someone must have put it in the papers! It is disgraceful double dealing, and altogether a dreadful business and state of affairs. That poor quiet Baroness E. Stockmar should be distrusted and her letters watched and possibly tampered with is too bad. The poor Empress is not to have a single true friend. What makes the Queen so angry is that Sir E. Malet believes everything which the Bismarcks tell him. He should be warned to enquire from Sir H. Ponsonby before believing such things about people.

With the Queen's arrival at Charlottenburg on April 24, Bismarck seized the opportunity to put before her what he considered to be the facts about the projected matrimonial contract, and through the British Ambassador made tactful inquiry as to when the Queen could see him. On April 24 Sir E. Malet wrote to Sir Henry Ponsonby:

I have communicated with Prince Bismarck and he will wait upon the Queen at 12 tomorrow.
If Her Majesty could also see Count Bismarck for a moment at some time or another I think it would be useful. He is very English in his likings and would be greatly pleased at such attention from the Queen.

The following day, April 25, the interview between the Queen and the Chancellor took place. Both were in agreement that the Battenberg alliance would be a mistake, and when the Empress found her mother ranged with the opposition, she yielded. Bismarck had won, and the price, so the Empress thought bitterly, was her daughter's happiness. Bismarck's own account of the interview runs as follows:

....Grandmamma behaved quite sensibly at Charlottenburg. She declared the attitude of the Chief in the Battenberg marriage scheme to be quite correct, and urged her daughter to change her ways. Of course it was very nice of her not to forget her own country and to wish to benefit it where it was possible for her to do so, but she needed the attachment of the Germans, and should endeavour to secure it; and finally she brought about a reconciliation between Prince William and his mother.[3]

In a later conversation, Busch records that he mentioned to the Chancellor 'what Bucher had told me about the sensible attitude adopted by the Queen of England at Charlottenburg, which he (Bismarck) confirmed, adding that at the interview which he had with her he had in part prompted the admonitions which she addressed to her daughter'.[4]

But a more correct version of the visit is contained in two letters written by Sir E. Malet to Lord Salisbury on April 28. In the first he says:

> There is no doubt that the Queen's visit to Berlin has been a political success.
>
> The circumstances under which Her Majesty's journey was undertaken, had induced a vague apprehension that it might be more prudent for Her Majesty not to come. Acting on a complete misapprehension with regard to the attitude of Her Majesty in connection with an anticipated betrothal of Princess Victoria of Prussia to Prince Alexander of Battenberg, the portion of the press which is supposed to write in accordance with inspiration from the Government had denounced foreign influence in the internal affairs of Germany, and although the fundamental error of the argument had been almost officially exposed, the flood of insolent writing which had been let loose did not quickly subside, and it was feared that the greeting which might await Her Majesty on arrival would not be cordial, and that on this account the feeling between England and Germany, already somewhat estranged through misrepresentations of the press, might be further embittered. It is therefore with no common degree of satisfaction that I am able to record that the exact reverse has taken place. The breach, such as it was, has been closed, not widened. The hearty cheers with which Her Majesty was greeted by dense crowds during her drive through Berlin, proved how little effect the venom of the press had upon the people, and the general feeling with regard to the result of the visit is that it has done great and, it is to be hoped, lasting good.
>
> I may say that this view is shared by many with whom I have spoken, of whom it cannot be said that their opinion is the result of the wish being father to the thought.
>
> It is believed that the interchange of personal communication of the Queen with the Empress Augusta, the Crown Prince, and Prince Bismarck, has been of the highest value in freely brushing away industriously woven cobwebs, and the spiders, of which unfortunately there are too many, have had to retire to their holes.
>
> Prince Bismarck has openly expressed the great satisfaction which he derived from his conversation with the Queen, and has said that if the action of England should correspond with the sound sense and practical character of the views held by Her Majesty, the danger of a European war would be minimised.
>
> The grateful tribute to the Queen, which appeared in last night's *North German Gazette*, of which I have the honour to enclose a copy and translation, is a fitting epilogue to the Royal visit, which has ended so happily and shown that good will and cordial relations between England and Germany are once more the order of the day with the inspired press.

The second letter ran:

You will, ere this reaches you, have heard all about the Queen's visit both from Her Majesty and the Duke of Rutland. There is no doubt that it has done much good and that the evil spirits of contention and slander have had to slink away for the time being.

Prince William (the present Crown Prince) spoke about it to me in warm terms and seemed to be delighted at having had an opportunity of conversing with Her Majesty. He told me also that the Chancellor was greatly pleased with his conversation with the Queen and that he had said to Her Majesty that her visit to Italy, Austria, and Germany, was like an officer going the round of the outposts and seeing that the pickets were all doing their duty, and that it would have an excellent effect in strengthening and encouraging the league of the Central Powers. Altogether I may say that on this side there is an evident desire, not to say anxiety, to come round to the point at which we were when the 'Chancellor Crisis' arose and caused our confidence to waver.

At the dinner at the Palace at which the Chancellor sat opposite to the Queen and the Empress he ardently did his best to be amiable and agreeable, and I could not help being amused when at dessert he selected a large bonbon adorned with a photograph of the Empress and, after calling Her Majesty's attention to it in some graceful words, unbuttoned his coat and placed it next his heart. In short to the outward eye there has been a general healing of mental irritation.

The Queen looked extremely well and was, I believe and hope, much pleased with the whole visit.

Late that evening, April 25, Queen Victoria left Berlin for England, via Leipzig and Dresden, and the British Minister in Dresden, Sir G. Strachey, wrote to Sir Henry Ponsonby (April 25):

I was very sorry that the Queen passed through Leipzig in the night.

That town, which is hyper-Bismarckian (especially National-Liberal) and Dresden, which is ultra-Conservative, have shown a maximum of hatred of the Empress and the Queen. The Leipzig Nat-Lib. *Grenzboten*, an equivalent (in a weak fashion) to our Fortnightly, which has been often utilised by Bismarck, published the other day a long tirade against the two royal ladies, in which the insolence and venom of the Prussian 'reptiles' were almost surpassed. The folly and vulgarity of the similar lucubrations here pass belief. The *freisinnige* party in Saxony is weak, so that their voice cries in the desert; but they have defended the Emperor, the Empress and the Queen, with great courage, and pertinacity, and their Dresden organ exhausts the superlatives of eulogy every day in praise of all three. As in Berlin, the Radicals (who, after all, are only on the political level of our Tories) are admirably loyal, while the Bismarckites are behaving like Anarchists.

For the moment, it would seem as if the 'reptile' press had received a hint to prepare for a change of front. One of the Berlin gang has the audacity to dilate on 'the Reichskanzler's touching, devoted love for his all-highest master', which may indicate that Bismarck thinks that the Emperor's recovery is possible.

At the great official dinner on the King's birthday, I found that all the political summits agreed that Bismarck was the moral, perhaps the material, author of the whole *Hetze*, and although the majority present were 'gravediggers' no one much dissented from the very undiplomatic language in which I relieved my feelings at his expense.

Queen Victoria arrived in England on April 27, and two days later she received the following letter from the Empress:

It all seems like a dream! Your dear visit so ardently wished and hoped for has come and gone like lightning! But not without having left much comfort and gratitude behind it, especially in my heart!

I am indeed thankful that you were able to come and that the pleasure and emotion did dearest Fritz no harm! Alas, there was too much to make your visit terribly sad, but still it is sweet to share not only the bright, but also the dark hours of life with those one loves!! Why those dark hours are sent we shall never know, nor understand! Our ideas of justice, of mercy, etc., are too small and too human, to help us to fathom the reasons that govern the Universe immutably, by the same great Will that called all into existence; therefore we must accept and believe that what is our individual misery and destruction is good and right and necessary for the whole of which we are so infinitesimal a part; but our own soul writhes and sends up a bitter cry - so long as we live and hope and work and aspire and think and look forward! The greatest of helps is the sympathy and love of those near and dear to us - it is the balm that Heaven has placed within the reach of the suffering - at least, which is not denied to many! and I am truly thankful for this most precious treasure! Your motherly kindness and affection has done me good and has refreshed my aching heart!

I have been back into your empty rooms with a heavy heart! I fancied you in the cold, wintry night, on your way to Flushing, and yesterday on the dear yacht, which I am sure tossed a good deal, and this morning at dear Windsor in your own comfortable and splendid home!

Your visit gave much satisfaction here and I did not hear or read one remark to the contrary. Fritz has really had less fever and has taken his food quite nicely (comparatively speaking) and has dozed a good bit by day! The cough has not been very frequent! I hope that the impressions you took away were not altogether only painful ones!

Lord Salisbury perhaps aptly summed up the effect of the visit and Bismarck's attitude when he wrote to Queen Victoria on April 30:

Lord Salisbury with his humble duty respectfully returns Your Majesty's memorandum, which he has read with the profoundest interest. It shows, what also appears from Prince Bismarck's subsequent conversation with the Duke of Rutland, that Bismarck was deeply gratified at Your Majesty's visit to Berlin, and reception of himself; and it gives good hope that he will behave loyally to the Empress, if dark days should come. But it leaves in as much mystery as ever Prince Bismarck's extraordinary language with respect to Your Majesty's supposed action, and the supposed intentions of the Emperor and Empress about the marriage. However it is evident that the Prince as Your Majesty saw him was in his habitual frame of mind; and that the two memorable conversations with Sir E. Malet must have been held under circumstances of mental excitement and depression which passed rapidly away. This anxious incident has ended as well as it possibly could have ended.

In the meantime, the health of the Emperor Frederick had undergone no improvement; indeed, his malady had been somewhat aggravated by the maladroitness of Professor Bergmann, which proved to be one of the turning-points of the case. The facts would appear to be that in the early morning of April 12 the Emperor was seized with a severe attack of coughing, which slight adjustments of the canula relieved. At 8 A.M. Sir Morell Mackenzie arrived, and after consultation with Drs Krause and Wegner it was decided to try the effect of a shorter tube. This, however, did not prove satisfactory, and Mackenzie then decided to try a canula of a new pattern, and invited Professor von Bergmann to come to witness the change. Bergmann arrived at five o'clock in the afternoon, and he, Mackenzie and Hovell went into the Emperor's room, where they found him writing. Bergmann now took out the shorter canula and inserted the new one, but with such an unhappy effect that the tube had to be withdrawn and a violent fit of coughing and haemorrhage followed. Again Bergmann tried, and again the tube had to be withdrawn, and its withdrawal was followed by renewed coughing and streams of blood. Bergmann now asked that his assistant, Dr Bramann, who was waiting in his carriage outside, should be sent for, and on his arrival at once yielded the case to his assistant, who, taking a moderate-sized canula, passed it with the greatest ease into the trachea. But it was hours before the coughing and the haemorrhage subsided.[5]

Bergmann's roughness was never forgotten by the Emperor, and a pathetic proof of the agony the Emperor endured owing to his maladroitness is contained in one of the last scripts which the Emperor wrote. On June 12, in reply to a remark about his medicine, or a question as to his condition, the Emperor scribbled in pencil upon a half-sheet of notepaper: 'There is such a funny taste in the larynx.' In response to another question the Emperor wrote: 'The same Hovell just tried before Bergmann ill-treated me.'[6]

Four months later, on August 24, 1888, the Empress referred to this unfortunate incident in her letter to her mother.

....The end [she wrote] was hastened and the strength to resist the disease was impaired by Bergmann's mismanagement of the after-treatment of tracheotomy, and by the injury he inflicted on my poor darling Fritz by so awkwardly forcing the tube back into its place when no force was required, only skill and patience, and when Sir Morell was going to do it properly himself, Bergmann snatched the canula out of Sir Morell's hands and proceeded to do it in the most awkward and bungling way....

The result of this unfortunate episode was that Professor von Bergmann retired from the case on April 30. His formal retirement occasioned further vitriolic outbursts in the German press against Sir Morell Mackenzie and the Empress, who, on May 9, wrote to Queen Victoria:

I regret very much all this wrangling in the newspapers. Certainly such things have never happened before!! We have been singularly unfortunate in this respect! Party spirit in Germany runs very high and under Prince Bismarck's high-handed rule has become very bitter. This accounts for the so-called 'National' element being mixed up with all this!
Poor Sir Morell Mackenzie is really *sur les dents* with the constant anxiety about and attendance on Fritz. I think his health and nerves are seriously tried, and this makes him perhaps look less calmly on all the attacks of the press! Prof Bergmann has behaved badly towards us and towards him, besides having been most unsuccessful as a surgeon - on this case. But I am not going to complain of him, or accuse him in any way. He goes every day to William! Bergmann has also been made a tool of! The newspapers began about Fritz's case long before Sir Morell was called in. There was already a hot controversy so that Sir M. was brought in against his will. However, I hope and trust there will be no more of it now and that it will drop!....It is very bad for the country and very hard for us.

It was about this period that Sir Morell Mackenzie and Dr Hovell, smarting under the bitter and unfair attacks upon them in the German press, suggested that a true account of the illness and treatment should be published. An article was then prepared for publication, which was submitted to the Crown Princess, whose pencil comment ran:

This is all right and puts it all straight, only one must take care that it does not look as though you used the press to defend yourself, or it might degenerate into a duel between Bergmann and yourself in the press about your patient. When *untruths* are *purposely* circulated I think that we ought to have a *communiqué* (worded by you or as you like) sent to a newspaper through Count Radolinsky, as it is not thought etiquette *here* that the medical men should communicate themselves to the public any news which they had to give, without being authorised on each special occasion. Bergmann, Gerhardt and Schmidt have broken through this etiquette, but would not own up to it, and I do not like the official world here to reproach you with doing what others are not allowed to do.

Whatever you think not right ought to be contradicted and in the way you wish, but I think it ought to go through the official channel! - or it will be difficult to come down on the others in the way they deserve. I am so unhappy that our dear Dr Hovell is so annoyed at this shameful attack. I can sympathise with him, as I suffer in the same way. I shall take every measure for his defence.

Then I am afraid that the details about where Wegner lives, and that he was 'allowed' to come twice a day and when specially called, might hurt his feelings, as he is *Leib-Arzt*. Then it is not necessary to let the public into the fact of where your rooms are, etc. I am afraid they will say that the *Germans* are absent and are kept out of the way. Pray excuse my saying this, perhaps my fears are groundless, only I wish to smooth the plumage of popular opinion, which has been artificially ruffled.[7]

In the result the Empress's wishes were respected, and for the moment no step was taken that might have further exacerbated German opinion.

Matters now seemed to be approaching another crisis between the Empress and her eldest son, 'William', she wrote to her mother on May 12, 'fancies himself completely the Emperor - and an absolute and autocratic one! Personally, we got on quite well, because I avoided all subjects of importance!' Six days later she again wrote:

Fritz is going on nicely, thank God, only the terrible cough is very frequent and troublesome - so disturbing and fatiguing for him by day, but more so by night.

William asks Bergmann to dinner as demonstratively as possible, which considering his strange behaviour, is, to say the least, not very good taste.

For all those who are not staunch or true to us, in the house, Bergmann was a most convenient tool, and we are thankful to have someone else. We have no difficulties amongst the doctors now, nor should we ever have had with Langenbeck or Wilms, whom we know so well and liked so much! Of course, Bergmann did his best and meant well, but he was not the right person, no more were Schröder and Bramann, though I do not blame them.

We were most unfortunate with Prof Gerhardt and most of all with that disagreeable Landgraf who misled Wegner and so many others! Now all these difficulties are overcome. If those with the adverse Party were, we should indeed have an easier position and easier life!

Prince William, indeed, seemed to be doing all that he could to annoy his parents, though the Empress, eager to palliate his offences in the eyes of his grandmother, did not think that he was always conscious of the offence he gave. As the Empress wrote to her mother on May 19:

What I said about William is in no way exaggerated. I do not tell you one third of what passes, so that you, who are at a distance, should not fancy that I complain. He is in a 'ring', a *côterie*, whose main endeavour is as it were to paralyse Fritz in every way. William is not conscious of this! This state of things must be borne until Fritz perhaps gets strong enough to put a stop to it himself. You have no idea of the vexations and anxieties, the troubles and difficulties I have to endure. I shall not torment you with an enumeration, perhaps not knowing the persons concerned, the intricacies, etc., it might even be very difficult for you to understand.

Five days later, on May 24, the marriage of the Empress's second son, Prince Henry, to Princess Irene of Hesse, was celebrated at Charlottenburg. It was a happy, joyous day in the midst of illness and despair. A week later the Emperor, visibly dying, was conveyed by boat from Charlottenburg to the Neue Palais. It was in the Neue Palais that he had been born, here that he had spent the happiest days with the Empress and, as if to emphasise this, he now changed its name to 'Friedrichskron'.

Ill as he was, the Emperor roused himself to deal with one event that annoyed him. The Minister of the Interior, Puttkamer, a typical Bismarckian, was one of that clique who held that an Emperor who could not speak should not rule, and it was he who had been responsible for the official announcement of the old Emperor's death which contained no allusion to the new Emperor. The Emperor Frederick had borne this slight in silence, but when early in June he was called upon to sign a Bill prolonging the life of the Reichstag to five years, he made it a condition of his signature that the Minister, who had encouraged corruption in the German elections, should retire. On June 7 it was certain that Puttkamer would go.

It was in the midst of the 'Puttkamer incident' that Dr Hovell was recalled to England by the death of his father, and the Empress, full of sympathy for the untiring doctor, wrote to Queen Victoria on June 8:

It is most awkward our invaluable little Dr Hovell being absent just now! One feels such absolute security when he sits up all night! He has lost his father as I told you and is in England. I am so afraid poor Sir Morell will knock up - he has to be on his feet all day long and is sometimes rung for three times in ten minutes!

We have felt anxious and tormented about Fritz in more than one way! The weather has been cold and wet and he has not got on as we should wish in more than one respect - Sir M. will write details - still he has done a good deal of business! We have had great trouble and annoyance - the Ministers do many things of which Fritz disapproves, but there is instantly a ministerial crisis about everything as soon as he remonstrates and one has to be very cautious. It is most difficult! If we could clear the place of all spies and traitors, and surround Fritz with trustworthy men and true supporters, it would counterbalance the power of the Ministry. To get the right things done, the wrong ones prevented, and yet not to fall out with Bismarck is a terribly difficult game to play, and yet it has to be done. Fritz has after much difficulty and some diplomacy got rid of Puttkamer, which I consider a great step! He will be able to carry all sorts of other things if he can break through the wall of opposition already so cleverly organised at San Remo, and in which William is so deeply involved. He would be different to us, I am sure, when these people and influences have gone, that use him for their purposes against us! He would be much more amenable and reasonable then I am sure. You cannot think how hard and difficult my life is! If I could think we had a year before us! How much could be done, but that is so uncertain!! and then?? I cannot think of it all, my heart is too near to breaking.

Here at this place the contrast is so great with the life we used to lead - with Fritz about everywhere, and yet it does not do to think of that, one must be thankful that one has him at all! What will it be next year?!!

The clique are of course enraged with me, as their one idea is to isolate me completely, and prevent my having anything to say about Fritz; to set the children against me and to make it impossible for me to get on with Prince Bismarck, or William, and make me unpopular in the country by inventing constant lies and calumnies; this they began last year already because they thought it opportune as the Emperor was old and Fritz was ill. I do not care one rap, and they have not intimidated me as they thought they could! I receive constant proofs of affection, sympathy, loyalty and confidence from other circles, so that they are rather baffled in their attempts to injure me! and what if they do succeed? If Fritz goes, I do not the least care what becomes of me. I do not want these people's love and I scorn their hatred. Fritz and I shall be more than avenged some day by the course events will take when these people come into power....

Now the people are patient because they know their Emperor is on their side and would fight for their just wishes and aspirations if his will were not kept in check by the Government and the Clique Cartell Partei, who take advantage of his illness to wield the same power as they did over the Emperor William, who was quite on their side and had no will of his own, except to retard all progress.

It is a curious state of things! I am sad and depressed, but not abashed, and shall fight and struggle to the last. Not with force or by open opposition can one gain anything; it is by the greatest caution and wariness.

The Puttkamer incident, however, only served to accentuate the growing differences between Bismarck and the Empress. Puttkamer's resignation was gazetted on the 11th - an event which Bismarck signalised by giving a dinner at which Puttkamer was the guest of honour!

All knew that the Emperor's days were numbered. The Empress - isolated, friendless, heartbroken - could only write to her mother on June 12:

> I have not the heart to write - I do not feel able! and yet I do not like to leave you without a line! Things are not going well! I have not much hope left, but how long our precious one will be left to us I do not know; it may be for some time yet, it cannot be for very long! Pray do not spread any alarm, it makes our position ten times more painful and difficult, and to be able to do the best for him, make him as happy and comfortable as we can without impertinent interference, and without all the brutal heartlessness I had to submit to when Fritz was so ill - after the 12th April - is all I can crave for! I am' too miserable, too wretched to write more! You who went through December 1862 will understand all!

The next day she wrote:

> My days and nights pass I know not how! I hardly leave Fritz's room, or the one next door, only going upstairs to sleep....Sir Morell has with wonderful skill and dexterity succeeded in feeding him with a gutta percha tube, so that enough nourishment can now be taken quite well! But what it is to me to see my poor darling so changed! He is a perfect skeleton now and his fine thick hair is quite thin. His poor throat is such a painful and shocking sight, that I can often hardly bear to look at it, when it is done up, etc. I have to rush away to hide my tears often! It is very difficult to keep the air pure in the room, so it is a great comfort that the weather permits his being on the terrace! Oh, the bitterness of looking round our pretty home and knowing that my three darling girls will have to leave it for ever, with all its sweet and sad recollections! It was the long slow work of years to put it straight - not for us to end our lives in; but these are minor considerations.
> How much I have to suffer in a thousand ways you do not know....
> You ask what you can do for me!! It is too kind and dear of you; now I know of nothing, but later there will be a great deal, and I shall often ask your advice. I feel so like a wreck, a sinking ship, so wounded and struck down, so sore of heart, as if I were bleeding from a thousand wounds. Writing makes my tears flow, thinking also, speaking with friends - too! It is only dry hard business I am fit for, and there even my memory seems to fail me, and at times I can remember nothing but the pain!!

Two days later, on June 15, 1888, the Emperor Frederick died at eleven o'clock. That evening the distracted Empress wrote to her mother:

> On the 14th December 1862 you found time and strength to write me a line in your overwhelming grief, and I, through agony, half-distracted, yet must send you a few words! I cannot tell you what hours those were, and what images

torture my mind, what impressions rend my heart. Oh! they will haunt me for ever! The wrench is too terrible - when two lives that are one are thus torn asunder, and I have to remain and remember how he went from me! Oh, the look of his dear eyes, the mournful expression when he closed them for ever, the coldness and the silence that follow when the soul has fled. Oh! my husband, my darling, my Fritz!! So good, so kind, so tender, brave, patient and noble, so cruelly tried, taken from the nation, the wife and daughters that did so need him. His mild just rule was not to be. Forgive me if I write incoherent nonsense, but it is almost too much to bear!

Thank God his kind heart does not suffer what mine does now!!! I have taken my last leave, my last look. I am his widow, no more his wife! How am I to bear it! You did, and I will too. You had your nation, your great duties to live for! I have my three sweet girls - he loved so much - that are my consolation. When they want me no more, my time is at your disposal whenever you care to have me with you! I tried to help him with might and main, to be useful to him, to save him all trouble, annoyance and pain. I think I succeeded to a certain degree! I always said I was his watch-dog!! Now all struggles are over! I must stumble on my way alone! I shall disappear as much from the world as possible and certainly not push myself forward anywhere! Those who really loved him will be kind to me for his sake!

I must end here, I feel ill and sick, sore and broken, but not tired, alas! no - I feel as if I should never sleep again.

## NOTES

1 Busch's *Bismarck*.
2 Sir Sidney Lee, *Life of Edward VII*, i. p. 501.
3 Busch's *Bismarck*, vol. iii. p. 187.
4 *Ibid*. p. 198.
5 This account follows substantially that of Sir Morell Mackenzie in his *Frederick the Noble*, pp. 143-53. Professor von Bergmann's own account differs in only one particular that when he came in to see the Emperor he found him 'on the point of suffocation'.
6 Part of this script was published in facsimile in the *British Medical Journal* of October 13, 1888, where the Bergmann and Mackenzie accounts are considered side by side.
7 Extract from the Hovell papers, communicated by Mrs Mark Hovell.

## XII. The Emperor William II

WITH the death of the Emperor Frederick, the Empress lost for the time being all hope, all desire. Life with her husband gone, was empty and bitter. All that she desired was solitude and peace, but scarcely had the Emperor's eyes closed in that last long sleep than there broke out a virulent campaign of vituperation against the Empress such as few have had to endure.

The Empress was much pained to find that her son could scarcely bring himself to express sorrow for his father's death, and that he gave the impression that he held his memory in small esteem. The Bismarcks, father and son, followed the Imperial lead, and shocked the ex-Empress by heaping disparagements on the dead man's name. Count Herbert excelled his father in offensiveness and spoke of the Emperor Frederick as an 'incubus' and an 'ineffectual visionary'.[1] In a conversation with the Prince of Wales he bluntly suggested that 'an Emperor who could not talk was unfit to reign'. The Prince of Wales subsequently admitted to Prince von Hohenlohe (afterwards German Chancellor) that he found the greatest difficulty in restraining his temper at the time.[2]

Bismarck now became all-powerful again, and no humiliation or pain was spared die ex-Empress, either by the Chancellor or his new master. As soon as it was known that the Emperor Frederick was dying, a cordon of soldiers was secretly drawn round Friedrichskron, so that no documents might be removed without the knowledge of the new Emperor. The Master of the Household hastened to promulgate the order that 'No one in the Palace, including the doctors, is to carry on any correspondence with outside....If any of the doctors attempt to leave the Palace, they will be arrested.'[3] The Empress and her suite were practically under arrest.

Immediately after the death of the Emperor Frederick the scene was transformed. 'It was', as Ludwig recounts,[4] 'as though a monarch had been murdered, and his hostile successor, long prepared, had seized upon the newly acquired authority. "Divisions of training-battalions approached the Palace at the double; round all the terraces was a regular system of guards with loaded guns. Major von Natzmer, one of the intruders of the night before, sat ready mounted, and the moment death was announced he galloped round the Palace, giving orders, inspecting guards. Suddenly the Hussars appeared at a trot; divisions established themselves at all the gates of the Park; the Palace was, in the military sense, hermetically sealed." Anyone who wished to leave had to have a permit from the new master's aide-de-camp; telegrams had to bear his visa.'

Vainly did the Empress Frederick appeal to the young Empress; equally vainly did she request Bismarck, the day after the Emperor's death, to grant her an interview. Curt and uncompromising the reply came that Bismarck had no time as he was so fully occupied with his new master.

The following day the Empress, with her three daughters, fled from Friedrichskron to her farm at Bornstedt, and on June 18 she wrote to Queen Victoria:

I have fled here to our little farm with my three darling girls - their Governesses, Frau v. Stockmar and three other ladies (friends of mine).

They are going to bury him now! - to carry him out of the dear house in which he was born, in which he died, where we have spent nearly thirty happy summers, and which we considered as our home. How pleased and proud he was to call it his own - for the first time - how many plans he had for beautifying and completing it! He only passed a short fortnight of sickness and weariness in it, but surrounded by love and affection, tended and watched with loving, tender and devoted care, and now he has left it for ever!! Oh God, why was I not allowed to go with him - why, oh why this separation? You bore it, and I must bear it! It would not be right nor grateful to mourn against God's decree. But more cruel suffering was never laid on human soul than on mine at this moment!

On this sad day,[5] once a glorious day of victory, when Germans and English fought side by side, my sweet precious little Sigismund was torn from us! We were not together, and I passed through those bitter hours alone, and I remember well that I was glad his kind and tender heart was spared all those agonising scenes. Now again the same bells are tolling. Are they really for him, the good, the noble, the brave, patient, enduring, pure and kind!! Oh, such men should not die! They have no right, I think. They are wanted in this sad world, but they also have much to suffer!!

I have received your dear letter and have it with me here and read it with grateful heart! Your love and sympathy does my bleeding, aching, broken heart good! and consoles me! Yes, you say right! Your angel husband left your side, left you alone, but you were permitted to continue his work, you could live with his dear memory and spirit inspiring and guiding you - for the same task and duties as he lived for!

I see others take his place, knowing they cannot fill it as he did! Their aims and aspirations, their principles are other ones, and all the nation feels this with me, with the exception of those who loved us not and who opposed and crossed us - for thirty years. Theirs is now the power!

I disappear with him. My task was with him, for him, for his dear people. It is buried in the grave where he will be buried today! My voice will be silent for ever! I feared not to lift it up - for the good cause for him!

I would have fought and struggled on! We had a mission, we felt and we knew it - we were Papa's and your children! We were faithful to what we believed and knew to be right. We loved Germany - we wished to see her strong and great, not only with the sword, but in all that was righteous, in culture, in progress and in liberty. We wished to see the people happy and free, growing and developing in all that is good. We tried hard to learn and study and prepare for the time in which we should be called to work for the nation. We had treasured up much experience! Bitterly, hardly bought!!! - that is now all wasted. It does seem cruel that he who had no other thought but to be just, to help others, to make peace, heal many a wound and dry many a tear, to do good, should be taken away, the hand stayed that worked so willingly, the eye closed that looked so kindly on all that approached him!

Where shall I go, what will be my home, I know not, neither do I care. I am his widow and that is enough for me! My three darling girls that feel all as I do, that loved him as tenderly as I did almost, will not leave me until they have homes of their own! He blessed Vicky, he sent his blessing to Sandro, he told me to write to Prince Alexander - he wrote to Willy and spoke to our friends, and we shall wait in silence and in patience until we know whether William will do his father's bidding, respect his wishes and carry out his intentions! With a disposition like his it is no use to drive him, or hurry him! Now you will have no reason to be against us, or not to help us, when the right time comes! We are no longer people of political importance! How my Fritz loved you! He kissed your photo the other day, his whole dear face brightened and was lit with a smile when I read bits of your letters to him! *Die gute Mama! wie liebt man sie!* - he always said, and was so pleased when you sent him messages! He did so love and admire England, was so proud of being popular there, and of being your son-in-law. He would have been a true and faithful friend and ally! He was so anxious to bring the two countries as near to each other as possible. The British nation, so true and free and generous, will not forget him, I feel sure!!

I must end here - my grief overwhelms me and I cannot write properly. Goodbye, goodbye.

This letter brings out the fact that although the Empress must have been cut to the quick by her son's behaviour, not one word of reproach or complaint escaped her lips. Her humiliation she bore in silence.

One of the dying wishes of the Emperor Frederick was that his son should place no obstacle in the way of the marriage of Princess Victoria with Prince Alexander of Battenberg. In his will, dated April 12, the father had written: 'In case I am....summoned hence, I wish to have set in evidence as my unbiased personal opinion that I entirely acquiesce in the betrothal of your second sister with....Prince Alexander of Battenberg. I charge you as a filial duty with the accomplishment of this my desire, which your sister Victoria for so many years has cherished in her heart....I count upon your fulfilling your duty as a son by a precise attention to my wishes, and as a brother by not withdrawing your co-operation from your sister.'[6] The son showed his respect for his father's dying wishes not only by breaking off the engagement, in which proceeding he had Bismarck's veto to appeal to, but in his letter of explanation to Prince Alexander he claimed that the rupture was because of 'the profound conviction previously held by my late deceased grandfather and father'.[7]

The ex-Empress returned to Friedrichskron a few days later. Here another humiliation was in store, for her son, the new Emperor, let it be known that he objected to his father's name being perpetuated in the name of the palace, and that its former title of Neue Palais would be restored. In such a way were all the wishes of the dead Emperor disregarded.

On June 25 the Emperor William opened the first Imperial Parliament of his reign with great pomp and pageantry, and in his opening speech promised to 'follow the same path by which my deceased grandfather won the confidence of his allies, the love of the German people, and the goodwill of foreign countries'. Many there were who interpreted this statement to mean that he did not intend to carry out any of the wishes of or liberal ideals of his father. In his own *Memoirs* he himself gives ground for this opinion when he states: 'The tragic element for me in the matter of Bismarck lay in the fact that I became the successor of my grandfather - in other words that, to a certain extent, I skipped a generation.'[8]

On June 29 the ex-Empress wrote from the Neue Palais to her mother:

I pass hours of utter listlessness and a feeling of despair comes over me, then again I reproach myself with not having done enough for him, for having left for 'Ost-Preussen' when his days were numbered. Then I feel burning with indignation and disgust at the disgraceful language and behaviour of certain people, and then I feel how small that is, compared with the tide of tears and mourning, of true love, sympathy and admiration, which wells up day after day from the heart of the nation. So I am tossed to and fro. Many a stab and smart makes me writhe, but I try to forget it as soon as possible. I close my eyes and ears to the official world and find it the only way not to feel the profoundest irritation with 'W. I am only too ready to make all allowances for him when I think of the deplorable friends he has had, and of all the nonsense with which his head has been so systematically stuffed....

I saw Sir Edward Malet yesterday. There is nothing settled yet about my plans. I cannot make any until the 'Will' has been carried out and I know what *pied à terre* I can have here, and also what place I can have as my own private property. Two have been offered which would do exceedingly well, but more enquiries about terms, etc., have to be made.

I busy myself every day in Fritz's rooms, by degrees replacing them in the state they were in before his illness, as I shall have to give up this dear house. I do not like others to turn everything topsy-turvy. It is quite deserted and silent, but the quiet, sad as it is, does one good.

The whole pageant and pomp about the Reichstags Eröffnung I thought very silly and absurd and out of place....The significance was that Prince Bismarck wished to show how delighted he was at the commencement of a new era, so much more to his taste than the three months of Fritz's reign. Of course a whole chorus echo this sentiment. Fritz of Baden, who has the vanity of taking the lead in all those things and is fond of protégé-ing the Empire, never sees how he plays into Prince Bismarck's hands on all occasions; so do most of the German sovereigns. Of all this, on which one could speak volumes, I will be silent now....

Queen Victoria welcomed these frank expressions of opinion from her daughter, and soon made it evident to the new Emperor that she disapproved, if not of his actions, at least of the actions of those of his staff who were encouraging him in his truculent attitude. Particularly did she dislike General von Winterfeldt, who as the emissary of the Emperor William now came to Windsor to announce the accession of the German sovereign. The choice of such a man as the special envoy - for Winterfeldt had been one of those who seemed to glory in the early death of the Emperor Frederick - filled Queen Victoria with dismay, and her reception of the General could scarcely be described as cordial. A few days later (July 4) Colonel Leopold Swaine, the British Military Attaché in Berlin, wrote to Queen Victoria's Private Secretary, Sir Henry Ponsonby:

....The young Emperor spoke to me this morning of the cold reception his special Envoy, General von Winterfeldt, had received at Windsor. After what had passed between us in the picture gallery and what you wrote to me in your first letter I was in hopes it was going to be otherwise. But, alas, it has not been so. The Emperor is much hurt. I gather from my interview with him after the parade today that he feels he is treated as a grandson and not as German Emperor. I don't think he will resent it this time, but I am very anxious even on that head, for there are many advisers here who, feeling as he does, are ready to recommend it. No man is striving harder than Malet to bring about and foster a good understanding between the two countries, and it is literally cutting away the ground from under his feet if all he does is undermined by our court.

I know you are doing all you know to throw oil on the troubled waters, and you will see by what I now tell you how necessary it is to continue to do so at every opportunity. I am quite upset by this unfortunate turn matters have taken and am longing to get away from here.

The letter was passed on to Queen Victoria, who appended the laconic comment:

The Queen intended it should be cold. She last saw him as her son-in-law's A.D.C. He came to her and never uttered one word of sorrow for his death, and rejoiced in the accession of his new master.

Sir Henry Ponsonby utilised this note as the basis of his reply to Colonel Swaine, and the young Emperor quickly learnt that although he could do what he liked in Germany it was necessary to be careful where Queen Victoria was concerned.

Queen Victoria's replies to the letters of her daughter brought no little measure of consolation, but the Empress Frederick's cup of bitterness was not yet full. It was not sufficient that she had withdrawn from all active participation in affairs of state: not sufficient that she desired to be left alone; all the machinery of vindictive interference was now brought into play. Her every action during the Emperor Frederick's illness was now to be put under the magnifying glass of an inquiry. As she wrote to her mother on July 5:

A thousand loving thanks for your dear letter of the 3rd (the day of the Battle of Königgrätz). It is so kind of you to write so often! I am so grateful for it! My days pass wearily and the pain gets no better and many are the stabs I feel! The whole of the new Court, their doings, etc., grate on my feelings of course!1 It would be wrong to wish others to be as miserable as I am! But to see them all full of life and hope and in the place he ought to fill and yet so unlike him, so unable to understand him or me, is intensely painful.

Yesterday all the Ministers came to take leave of me, then all the Aides-de-Camp, then a deputation, the wives of the Berlin Artists, who mean most kindly! As I have my veil down during these audiences, they can luckily not see my face.

The language of the official press, *Norddeutsche Kreuz-Zeitung* and *Post* continues to be shameful and disgraceful!!! but the generality of German papers are most nice!

Bergmann, who did so much harm to my beloved darling, is continually received by William, and has now been charged by William to write a pamphlet about Fritz's illness. I begged William to let this controversy cease, as it gave me so much pain and was so useless, but he has taken no notice of what I said!

Prince Bismarck has not asked to see me, to take leave, or to condole!

A splendid place on the Rhine has been offered me, which I should like of all things, but I fear I should not have the money to buy it, though the Crown would give me something towards it, as it was Fritz's intention to give me a sum to buy myself a place! I do not think it ought to be out of Germany, for different reasons which I can explain to you!....

Oh! there is so much would wring your heart if you knew all I went through. Yes, indeed Fritz will be terribly missed, there is no one to appeal to. The King of Saxony, Louis and Fritz of Baden are too anxious to be well with the present Government to be just or impartial.

The reigning party here are anxious to wipe out all trace of Fritz's reign, as of an interlude without importance, and the spirit of which they think unjustifiable. William II succeeds William I - in a perfect continuity of system, aims and tradition! Frederick III would have had to be submitted to, but he has been happily removed by Providence before he had time to set his mark and his stamp on the German Empire; the sooner he is forgotten the better, therefore the sooner his widow disappears the better also. How little in harmony with the German nation this is, they well know, or they would not take so much trouble to attain their object! Of course, as these people are friends of William and Dona, their object is not easily perceived, and W. and D. would be shocked if they could view it all as it is. On the other hand their opinions in general are completely that of the party who have fought and worried us for so many years, and the Empress Augusta and Louise of Baden refuse to see all this as it is, that they are really blinded to these facts. I am glad to see and hear of it all as little as possible, and am very nearly indifferent to all this, so deep and intense is my disgust and contempt for these people and their doings, and so great my gratitude for all the touching sympathy and love shown for those for whom Fritz was so anxious to work and to live.

On July 10 the *National Zeitung* published a long extract from the advance sheets of the German doctors' reports upon the Emperor Frederick's last illness. It is noteworthy that this publication contained nothing from the pen either of Professor Virchow or Sir Morell Mackenzie, nor even from Dr Krause or Dr Hovell. Gerhardt and Bergmann were the main authorities quoted, and in its entirety it constituted an indictment of the diagnosis and treatment by Sir Morell Mackenzie, and sought to prove that Professor von Bergmann was right from the first in his diagnosis of cancer. The distress this report occasioned the Empress may be gathered from her letter to her mother, dated July 12:

The publication about my darling Fritz's illness, permitted and authorised by William, makes me quite ill! It is an outrage to all my feelings, I think cruel and disgraceful! He has no heart, he cannot understand how insulting it is to have all the details which concern so harrowing and painful a thing as the illness of one's own dear husband, father of one's children, officially dragged before the public, in order to satisfy the spite and vanity of four people, Bergmann, Gerhardt, Bramann and Landgraf! They are to be considered first, and I afterwards! It is quite unusual to publish secret state documents deposited in the Archives of the Haus Ministerium.

Now I hear that a fresh coup is meditated against me, which is already beginning to appear in hints in the *Cologne Gazette* - to make the public believe that I have tried to get Ernest of Cumberland replaced in Hanover. It seems so ridiculous that no sensible person could believe such rubbish, but it is already half believed because it emanates from the Wilhelmstrasse. I fancy they will find it rather difficult to prove such a thing! but it does not prevent them from trying it. *Calomniez toujours - il en reste toujours quelque chose* - this is the principle they go on!....

An indication of how the Empress bore her misfortunes may be gathered from a letter written on August 4, 1888, by her sister, Princess Christian, to Lady Ponsonby. The letter ran:

I thought it best merely to write you a business letter and then to write another letter all about my beloved sister. Thank God I can *really* give you a good account of her *on the whole*. Her health is good when one considers the tremendous strain on it, but her nervous system is so shaken that she oftentimes feels wretched and ill when *not really* so. She does not like being told that she looks pretty well or better than one expected, so I never make any remarks. This horrid damp weather and perpetual deluges of rain have given her bad rheumatism, from which she has been very suffering, but I am thankful to say that is better today. I think her much aged, and at times her face is pinched and drawn, otherwise she is unchanged.

It is most touching to be with her, and my admiration is beyond words. I never saw such a courageous woman - for crushed and broken-hearted under a load of sorrow and care such as few have ever had to bear, she always pulls herself together, determined to face whatever comes, and thinking all the time of how she can help others and what she can do for the good of her country.

She has terrible bursts of grief and despair at times, but generally she is very calm and quiet - at times almost cheerful - full of interest in everything and all that is going on.

At times it is all I can do to keep my tears back when I look at her dear face with that expression of mental pain and suffering on it.

Her future plans are all uncertain, and she has no idea at present where she will make her home. She has the Palace at Berlin, but that is all, and she may have the use of the Castle at Homburg or at Wiesbaden! I think she would like to find something that could be quite her own, not a Crown property. She has heard of several places - but has not decided on anything as yet. I shall be truly glad when she has, for this uncertainty is most tormenting.

The young Emperor has returned and so far he has been very nice and pleasant with his mother, but of course he *does* do a thousand and one things which hurt and pain her, and which one would give worlds he did *not* do. But I really think he does them out of thoughtlessness and certainly *not* from premeditation. I have said and done my very utmost to try and smooth down matters and have implored her to take him as much into her confidence as she can by consulting him about trifles. This would flatter and please him - and she would unconsciously gain a far greater influence than she at present has any idea of. I hear from all sides that he *does* wish to be nice and kind to his mother and does think very much about her. Of course there are that set who are determined to try and prevent him getting on well with his mother and whose one object in life it is to keep them apart, yet I am *not* without hope that things will by degrees become far more comfortable between mother and sons. But Vicky has endured so much - has suffered so cruelly - has been so tormented and persecuted - that she has much to forgive.

I am so thankful I have been with her, and she makes me so happy by saying that I am a comfort and help - would that I *could* do *anything* to lighten her burden! Ah! dear Mary, my heart is so sad and heavy - and even *here* one can sometimes scarcely realise the terrible truth. One misses him at every turn - dear beloved Fritz!!

I leave for Homburg on Monday night, but my sister has asked me to return to her again towards the end of September, which I shall only too gladly do....

Nine days later (August 13) the Empress wrote to Queen Victoria:

Of course it pains me much to see how little there is of mourning at the Marmor Palais and many other things I do not approve of - of course I do not say a word and never shall again. I do not see much wisdom or prudence, and can only sigh over the things which would have been so differently treated and handled, had beloved Fritz remained only a little in the place he was so well prepared and called to fill. With years William might have gained experience and insight, and under his father have been trained to carry on his work with judicious care. Such was not to be Germany's fate! The ruling party try to accentuate in every way how William is his grandfather's and not his father's successor; this party broke Fritz's heart by taking our sons away from us - and trying to force them into another mould, another direction, which they never would have had if they had remained under our influence! Nobody worked harder at this than the Empress Augusta, or triumphs more at this moment, sad to say. But my beloved one's name is fast becoming a watchword with the people, and the whole moderate Liberal and progressive Party will rally round it! Kaiser Friedrich's proclamation embodies what they hoped and wished, and what they will work for! They will never get it from Prince Bismarck, nor from William. All that is so sad!!....

The Empress's withdrawal from affairs of state was quickly seized upon by her enemies to mean that henceforth she was to be treated as a *quantité négligeable*, and there resulted a lack of courtesy, of consideration, that finally led the Empress to protest. As she wrote on August 22:

It is most strange to watch things here now. In my deep mourning and overwhelming sorrow, they do not even annoy or irritate me, but I cannot help smiling sometimes. For instance: the Empress Augusta sees everybody, audiences and dinners every day regularly. She especially receives all people who are William's protégés or appointed by him! There is a continual intercourse between the Marmor Palais and Babelsberg. Messages carried to and fro - they ask the Empress Augusta about everything. This house does not exist! William never comes, and I am taken no notice of! It seems to be more and more adopted that I am the third here at Court! You know how very indifferent rank and etiquette, honours, etc., are to me, but yet I am often shocked at the want of courtesy and considerate behaviour I meet with. I am quite ready to give way to the Empress Augusta on account of her age and her being my mother-in-law, but to have to knock under to my own daughter-in-law besides, makes it rather trying and almost ludicrous sometimes....

It is no secret and a fact that as far back as March 1887 people at Berlin, of that certain Conservative set, talked loudly of Fritz not succeeding his father, that he ought to give up to William, who was the only proper successor to the old Emperor, and that Fritz and I ought to live retired in some Schloss as private individuals!! This was their wish! Hence their rage at Fritz having reigned at all, because it spoilt their programme, hence their fury that Sir M. Mackenzie would not pronounce it a cancer and incurable, in May, and would not recommend the operation. Hence their ceaseless endeavours to obscure Fritz's memory, - and to calumniate me and run me down in every imaginable way! Forgive my writing all this, but it is a page in the history of the Bismarck era, and is true! All that is foreign, especially all that is English, is hated, because it is thought to have a Liberal tendency! They did not understand Fritz, he was too good, too noble and too tolerant and enlightened. They would have had to obey him, and had he been well and strong and spared to reign, he would have scattered this impertinent, daring, and good-for-nothing set to the winds! They know it so well and they are therefore so thankful to have escaped. In silence and solitude I carry my cross and find it very hard, very cruel and bitter, but I know that the wise and the peace-loving, the moderate and the right-minded of all nations mourn with me one who never can be replaced, and feel how great is the loss to every good cause! Amongst the Liberals I have many good and true friends. Also amongst men of science, letters and art, but these people are not noisy or powerful.

Three other friends the Empress had who never deserted her, and never allied themselves to the party that were endeavouring in every way to belittle and calumniate the dead Emperor - these were her three youngest daughters - Princess Victoria, who had suffered from her brother William's and Bismarck's action in forbidding her engagement to Prince Alexander; Princess Sophie, the Duchess of Sparta; and Princess Margaret (Princess Frederick Charles of Hesse).

Bismarck now definitely let it be known that it was his opinion that had the German doctors been entrusted with the care of the late Emperor, events might have had a happier sequence. Sir Morell Mackenzie was abused far and wide, and the main indictment in the abuse was that he had been selected by 'that Englishwoman', the Empress Frederick. On August 24 the Empress wrote to Queen Victoria:

I ought to have added that when this terrible operation was recommended last year, I was not clearly told of all the dangers and of the chances of success! When I complained of this later, I was told 'If the Crown Prince and Crown

Princess are told all, they will not be got to consent and submit to it'. Surely that was not right! I should have protested violently before Sir Morell Mackenzie was called in had I been aware of all the facts connected with the operation. I fancy Wegner very reluctantly agreed to the idea of the operation, but he let himself be guided by Bergmann and Gerhardt, who had taken the responsibility, and I went entirely by what they said! How could I do otherwise!! Bergmann said to Wegner, '*Es ist nicht gefährlich*'[9]- and to another acquaintance of ours, a Herr Hesse, '*Es ist eine Operation auf Leben and Tod*',[10] so that this poor gentleman was terribly frightened. Now of course Bismarck makes capital for himself out of these conflicting opinions - it is decreed that it is in the interest of Germany to make it appear as if German science had been set at naught by me, a foreigner, and in consequence Fritz's precious life has been lost - that I preferred a foreign 'quack' to a German Professor and high dignitary of science, and thus by my obstinacy sacrificed Fritz's existence, whereas German science was in this case represented by a Russian (Bergmann) and by one Prof Gerhardt, who surely might make a mistake with the best intentions without compromising German science. Gerhardt was only too glad, then, that Sir Morell Mackenzie should undertake Fritz's treatment, as he, G., had nothing else to recommend than this operation. If Fritz had submitted to it, he would only have done so from ignorance of the danger, and if they had lost him, he would have been sacrificed indeed to their recklessness! The disease took its course! When it really began, we do not know, and of this there is no proof! He was so well managed, so carefully nursed and tended by Sir Morell and Dr Hovell, and afterwards Leyden, that he suffered less than others would have done. The end was hastened and the strength to resist the disease was impaired by Bergmann's mismanagement of the after-treatment of tracheotomy, and by the injury he inflicted on my poor darling Fritz by so awkwardly forcing the tube back into its place when no force was required, only skill and patience, and when Sir Morell was going to do it properly himself, Bergmann snatched the canula out of Sir Morell's hands and proceeded to do it in the most awkward and bungling way![11] He used force with another patient of his, and the man died in consequence, but I do not dream of putting down his awkwardness to German science! That is a cry got up to show how Bismarck and William protect all that is German and how patriotic they are, and that a foreigner always must be wrong and an evildoer; - this I beg leave to say is not, and never was, the standpoint of German science, which is strong enough in itself, and which no one ever attacks! Prince Bismarck's dodge is always to make the Germans think they are going to be attacked, wronged, insulted, and their interests betrayed if he were not there to protect them. There are many who are silly and ignorant and shortsighted enough to believe all this trash, and who would sacrifice their rights and liberties and their prosperity if only Prince Bismarck would stay and protect them!!! From what? Against what? I really do not think they know!! Herbert [Bismarck] would wish it to be thought that Fritz would have been tempted to sacrifice Germany's interests, for instance, as regards Alsace-Lorraine, or Hanover - or anything in 'short', and that I am the serpent who always proposed such things!! Also that William was too staunch a German to be capable of such a thing!!! Is it not a shame to act such a comedy? Fritz often defended German interests in 1866-1870, when Prince B had lost his courage and his nerve, but no one knows that, now that Fritz's lips are closed!! Fritz's and Prince B's ideas of German interests did not always agree!! They often did, but not always (as I said before).

Excuse my pen running on, but I wish you to know the truth; people in Germany are being purposely blinded and misled! A foreigner and a Liberal must necessarily be an enemy of Germany - and a traitor!

On the following day the Empress again wrote to Queen Victoria, who in her letter had written asking if the Empress had had any indication of the seriousness of the illness when she visited England with the Emperor Frederick (then Crown Prince) in the preceding year for the Jubilee celebrations. The Empress's reply ran:

You asked me in your letter whether I was alarmed this time last year when I said goodbye to you? Indeed I was not! I was often very anxious, but full of hope! I knew that a malignant disease was not proved and that what Gerhardt and Landgraf pretended to see, or thought they could see, was not to be seen! They made a guess as to the cause of the hoarseness, etc., which afterwards came true, but they could not be sure! The voice improved so much in Scotland and at Baveno before the 18th October that I had no reason to despond, though I had always a dread and fear of the eventuality.

I have now heard of two cases which are very similar indeed. As for the operation, it was out of the question! Many German doctors know and say this; and the special wickedness of Bergmann is now to say to William, Henry, Charlotte and the public, that the operation would have been a mere nothing (as he does) and would have saved Fritz, whereas he told others it was a matter of life and death! But if he had been honest he would have told us then, that there was not one case he could show of a person who was operated for malignant disease either by laryngotomy or laryngal fissure who had ever lived longer than three or four months, and that they had all died from the effects of the operation! The people who are now living who have had this operation performed (I have seen two) never had malignant disease, their larynxes were injured by another cause, one from being driven over! Our most celebrated surgeon for this operation here is Hahn (the one who operated on Mr Montague Williams). Hahn is very timid in expressing an opinion and would not for the world offend Bergmann, who is as vindictive as he is vain and powerful, but Hahn was horrified last year at this operation being performed! He knows the danger, the terrible state the patient is reduced to, and the improbability of its curing this disease, as it reappears elsewhere or comes again in the same place. Moreover Hahn thought Bergmann far too inexperienced and Fritz not a fit subject for such an operation! The terrorism which is exercised here by the

Government makes even celebrated men like Hahn afraid to open their mouths. I could send you a list of the cases we know about!!....

Bergmann is known to be exceedingly untruthful; he does not care what he says, he is a thorough Russian intriguant. We should never have had this trouble and row if we had had old Langenbeck or Wilms!! (You know Langenbeck refused ever to perform this operation at all, as he considered it was too great a risk for the patient.) With Hahn or with Langenbeck we should not have had any difficulty. Gerhardt and Bergmann were together at Wurzburg and one supports the other!! How badly Prince Bismarck and Herbert Bismarck specially have behaved in this affair, I cannot describe! It is quite indifferent to them and yet they thought right to *chauffer* German susceptibility and vanity and chauvinism, to please William, to harm Fritz and me, and to excite dislike against everything English!

They were pleased enough that our darling lived no longer, therefore it was not out of love and devotion! The operation would have effectually put a stop to all chance of his succeeding his father, and we should most likely have lost him directly! I must do this justice to Prince Bismarck, that at the time he was quite against the operation and had the perspicacity and good sense to see how imprudent and rash a proposal it was, and wished all else tried before; but when he saw that Fritz's days were numbered he turned round and thought he would get more advantage both with Willy and the public from taking the other side and crying down Sir Morell Mackenzie. And oh, it was so treacherous, mean, false and shameful - just like those wretched people! and William is in their hands!!....

There was now some indication that those who believed in the Empress Frederick were anxious and willing to take up the cudgels on her behalf against the ever-increasing number of insinuations and innuendoes. Prudence and the fear of displeasing the all-powerful Bismarck or the young and arrogant monarch, however, led many to keep silence, but the first indication of this defensive attitude on the part of some of her friends gave the Empress no little satisfaction.

It was about this time, too, that the rumour went round that the Prince of Wales, in conversation with Count Herbert Bismarck, had stated his opinion that Germany ought to return Hanover to the Cumberland family and treat the inhabitants of Alsace-Lorraine with greater kindliness. The new Emperor, in a speech at Frankfort-on-the-Oder, when he unveiled the monument to his cousin, Prince Frederick Charles, a prominent Prussian commander in the war of 1870, showed his irritation at what the Prince of Wales was reputed to have said, by concluding his speech with these words:

There are people who have the audacity to maintain that my father was willing to part with what he, in conjunction with the late Prince, gained on the battlefield. We, who knew him so well, cannot quietly tolerate, even for a single moment, such an insult to his memory. He assuredly cherished the same idea as we do, namely, that nothing should be surrendered of what had been gained in those great days... On this point there can only be one opinion, namely, that we would rather sacrifice our eighteen army corps and our forty-two millions of inhabitants on the field of battle than surrender a single stone of what my father and Prince Frederick Charles gained.[12]

After this 'silly speech', as the Empress described it in her letter to Queen Victoria of August 25, 'he turned to General Blumenthal and said, "I hope my uncle, the Prince of Wales, will understand that"'.[13] 'Herbert Bismarck', the Empress continued, 'had told William that Bertie and Alix wanted Hanover back for Ernest of Cumberland and had criticised German administration in Alsace-Lorraine; I thought it very nasty of Herbert Bismarck.'

This rumour much disturbed the Empress, and on August 26 she wrote to her mother:

Many thanks for your dear telegram from Balmoral. I am sure you feel reminded of last year. I send you a little article which takes my part against the new attacks against me in the official press. Why do the Bismarcks wish to make me responsible for what Bertie and Alix said about Ernest of Cumberland? I told you yesterday they wish it to appear that I instigated Bertie and Alix, which is most absurd, as I really hardly know what they did say. I am sure they meant most kindly, but as it happened it has been rather unfortunate that anything was said, as the Bismarcks use it as a weapon against me. Not only have they represented it so to William and caused him to make that foolish speech at Frankfort, but they also spread it through the *Norddeutsche* and *Kolnische Zeitung* to injure me, and it is then largely believed. I am utterly innocent of all this, and the Liberal press of course is not taken in, but everybody else is. It is rather silly, to talk of my intriguing for Danish aspirations, as Fritz and I always did what we could for Schleswig-Holstein aspirations and not Danish ones, and were attacked and persecuted for it in those days. One is really ashamed of such rubbish, but it all profits the Bismarcks and William in the eyes of a widespread class in Germany. Their superior patriotism is aired again on this occasion, and distrust sown against me, and doubt cast on Fritz's intentions.

It is an abominable game and apparently always succeeds with a certain set.

The truth of this rumour, as usual, was slow to see the light of day. What had happened was this. The Prince of Wales, who had always admired the noble aims and integrity of the Emperor Frederick, believed, rightly or wrongly, that he contemplated the restoration of Alsace-Lorraine to France and of Schleswig to Denmark; and further understood it to be his intention to restore to the Duke of Cumberland, who had married the Princess of Wales's youngest sister, the private property of the royal family of Hanover, which had been sequestrated by Prussia after the war of 1866. It was during the Prince of Wales's visit to Germany for the Emperor Frederick's funeral that he asked Count Herbert Bismarck if there was any truth in the Emperor Frederick's designs of reparation. Count Herbert at once reported the question to his father - the question now being transformed into a suggestion. Not unnaturally Count Herbert's version exasperated the new Emperor who, in his turn, understood that the Prince of Wales had suggested that Germany should give up all that she had won by right of conquest during the preceding quarter of a century.

The moment this embroidered version came to the ears of the Prince of Wales he stigmatised it as 'a positive lie'. He had asked Count Herbert 'whether Fritz would have wished to give back the provinces of Alsace and Lorraine if possible', and Count Herbert had replied 'there was no foundation for such a rumour', and, added the Prince, 'there the matter ended'. Of Schleswig and the royal family of Hanover he had spoken quite vaguely, as he wrote to Prince Christian on April 3, 1889.[14] Bismarck, however, was not disposed to let such an opportunity slip, and the virulent campaign against the Empress Frederick was now intensified. It was hinted that she had incited the Prince of Wales to offend German pride in this manner, and that when all was said and done she was nothing but 'an Englishwoman' and cared nothing for the national aspirations and military glory of the German Empire.[15]

## NOTES

1 *Die Grosse Politik*, vol. vi. p 326.
2 *Memoirs of Prince von Hohenlohe*, vol. ii. p. 391
3 Ludwig, *Kaiser William II*. p. 54.
4 *Ibid*. pp. 54-55.
5 The anniversary of Waterloo.
6 Hartenau Archives, quoted by Corti, p. 336.
7 Ludwig, p. 56.
8 Ex-Emperor William's *My Memoirs*, 1838-1918, p. 3.
9 'It is not dangerous.'
10 'It is an operation that means life or death.'
11 See supra, p. 242.
12 The German Emperor's Speeches, translated by Louis Elkind, p. 17.
13 Sir Sidney Lee, *Life of King Edward VII*. vol. i. pp. 647-648.
14 Sir S. Lee, *Life of King Edward VII*. vol. i. pp. 647-648.
15 *Die Grosse Politik*, vi. pp. 326-333

# XIII. The War Diary of the Emperor Frederick

THE Empress Frederick was now anxious that neither she nor her late husband should be for ever under the stigma of the abuse and criticism which continued to be directed at her from Berlin. Already she had made some tentative steps towards this end. A year earlier the Emperor Frederick, on his visit to England for Queen Victoria's Jubilee, had taken with him three boxes of papers which he deposited for safe custody at Windsor Castle.

Four or five months later the Emperor (then Crown Prince) determined to send over to England the manuscript Diary which he had compiled during the Franco-German War of 1870-71. The Crown Prince and Princess were then at San Remo, surrounded by servants and officials in the pay of Prince Bismarck, and it was realised that to attempt to send away documents by ordinary methods would simply result in their falling into the hands of the Chancellor. The Crown Princess, not knowing what to do for the best, then took Dr Hovell into her confidence, and this shrewd and ingenious gentleman devised a means by which the spies of Bismarck and Prince William were eluded. For several days the three volumes of the Diary were placed ostensibly on the table of the principal drawing-room of the Villa Zirio, for all the world to see, read and handle if need be. Suddenly one night Dr Hovell received an urgent call. Hurriedly he packed his things, disturbing only his valet. At the last moment, passing through the drawing-room, he took the three volumes of the Diary and started off post-haste to visit his mythical patient. Early next morning the hue and cry was raised. It was known that at the best Dr Hovell could not get to England for two or three days, and agents were warned to cover every route to England which he might possibly take; their instructions were that by hook or crook Dr Hovell's luggage was to be lost - it being understood, of course, that it would eventually be found again minus the Diary. Every port and every important railway junction en route for England was covered, but Dr Hovell was not traced.

On the third day Dr Hovell returned to San Remo, and his arrival was duly reported to Berlin, but the disquieting news was added that the Diary was still missing. In point of fact it was now in England! The astute doctor, realising that all routes to England would be carefully watched the moment his departure from San Remo was reported, headed straight for Berlin - the very last place that the emissaries of Bismarck would expect him visit, and a route on which it was unlikely that any watch would be kept. He arrived there in the early hours of the morning and at once went to the British Embassy, where, of course, no one was about. On being told that he must wait an hour or two before anyone in authority could see him, he replied that he must see the Ambassador immediately, as his business admitted of no delay. He was so insistent that eventually Sir Edward Malet himself was woken up and came down in a dressing-gown to see him. Quickly grasping the situation, the British Ambassador saw the necessity of instant action, and despatched a special messenger to London with the Diary, while Dr Hovell returned to San Remo.

Such a procedure may seem strange, that the private papers of the ruling house of one country should be sent to the royal archives of another, but as the Crown Princess wrote in her own Diary: 'He (the Crown Prince) unfortunately could not consider them in safe custody in Berlin, and....he regarded his papers as being in a better place of concealment 'under Mama's care' than in our house in Berlin.'[1] There was a fear, a fear well-grounded, that any papers or records of the Emperor Frederick's might be suddenly seized and perhaps destroyed - a proceeding which had precedent to warrant it, and the Empress was now anxious to add to these existing records at Windsor.

The work [she wrote on September 14, 1888] of making extracts from my letters to you will be immense, perhaps you could find someone else to help also?? as Sir Th Martin will not do. Fritz kept a journal, I do not. His is very precious to me now. Some day the world shall have a true picture of him and all he suffered, but now it is much too soon. Poor darling I can hardly believe that he was snatched from his home, carried away by this horrid disease, in spite of his fine strong frame and wiry constitution, in the midst of all he had to do, day after day. I live through this last year and think how often our hopes were raised in the midst of our doubts because he seemed to be so well and strong in spite of his throat, and how grateful we were for each little sign that made one think his health was not being undermined, until February came, and he was so mismanaged after the tracheotomy, which made an inroad on the store of strength and power of resistance, which would not have been so tried if only Sir Morell Mackenzie and Dr Hovell had had him in their own hands. Their patient was completely snatched out of their hands, and I never saw such bungling treatment or such obstinacy as Bergmann's, Bramann's, and Schrader's - it was enough to send one mad.

Sir Morell showed an amount of patience and good temper which was quite extraordinary under these most trying circumstances, but only for Fritz's and my sake; as he would have gone away directly from another patient seeing the case taken out of his hands and utterly mismanaged. I implored him to stay. I had no confidence at all in these other gentlemen, but I tried not to show it so as not to upset Fritz and make him lose faith in the doctors about him, but it was difficult enough, as he had very little confidence in them and only liked Sir

Morell to touch him - with his light, gentle, dexterous fingers. It annoyed Fritz to have so many around him, but he bore it out of civility and courtesy and with angelic patience. I felt miserable because I could not help seeing that we were losing ground and time, by their not understanding the canula and not stopping the bleeding; which weakened Fritz so terribly and distressed him so much. Sir Morell succeeded in stopping the bleeding when the others were gone and had left off interfering. What an agony of anxiety I was in, I cannot forget, and how these spiteful creatures used to misrepresent everything purposely to William, Henry and Charlotte and intrigue with the Aides-de-Camp, and write and telegraph to Bismarck and Stallberg behind our back. It was too bad, and I who had to smother everything down, so that Fritz should not be angry or irritated, and yet not keep him in ignorance completely of the game they were playing, so that he might be able to defend himself - and not fall completely into their hands! May I never meet any of these creatures again, I do not think I could look at them. Of course poor little Schrader did it all for the best and in the innocence of his heart; he is devotedly attached to us, and I have remained on the best terms with the lit de man, also with poor old Wegner. Forgive my alluding to all this again. It haunts one night and day. That Fritz's mind was kept easy and his spirits tolerably good was due to Sir Morell's untiring efforts alone, and enabled me to get along and do what I could, or really I should have been utterly crushed and trampled under foot by the daring audacious intrigues and attacks of those who opposed us! Thank God darling Fritz never knew what I went through! He used to ask with the greatest surprise, *'Warum sind deine Augen so rot?'*[2] It is all over now, but one cannot forget it! It was so unnecessary! There was sorrow enough without it all! But people were not only and always purposely bad! They were very stupid and ignorant, did not and could not understand, were misguided and misled, which made them lose their heads, and behave so strangely.

It was about this time that in accordance with a decree of the new Kaiser William II, concerning the unsealing and inspection of the Emperor Frederick's literary remains, the widowed Empress asked Queen Victoria to return to her from Windsor the three boxes which had been deposited there in the preceding year. A thorough inspection of these was made by German ministers of the crown appointed for the purpose, and a selection of the papers was deposited in the domestic archives at Berlin, including the four successive manuscript editions of the Emperor Frederick's War Diary during the Franco-German War of 1870-71.[3]

Years before this, in 1873, one of the most trusted advisers of the Emperor Frederick - Professor Heinrich Geffcken, a German diplomatist and jurist - had had access to the Diary. Now, in August 1888, Geffcken prepared for the press a series of extracts from the Diary - in all, less than twenty pages, and in the October number of the *Deutsche Rundschau* (published late in September) these were given to the world. The publication created a furore on account of the frankness of the diarist and the way in which he showed how Bismarck had wrongly arrogated to himself some of the credit for the creation of the German Empire which should have gone to the Crown Prince.

A few days after the publication the Empress Frederick wrote to Queen Victoria:

The Marmor Palais and Berlin are in a state of fury and excitement about the publication of Fritz's *Tagebuch*. It does not suit the 'powers that be' at all of course. William was in a rage and called it 'high treason' and theft of State papers! Of course this is nonsense! I was much surprised and also annoyed at the publication which is extremely injudicious and indiscreet! Of course it is all true, and all these portions of the public who are unbiased and devoted to Fritz are delighted, especially the Liberal press of which I send you a little sample. The part that Fritz played at Versailles in Jan. 1871 is of course not known by the public!! The German Empire is supposed to have been called into existence by the Emperor William and Bismarck - whereas it was Fritz who got it done! Therefore this comes in the light of a revelation! I cannot imagine how it got into the *Rundschau*. Fritz had several copies lithographed and gave them to his more intimate friends (I think he gave you one also?). One of these copies must have been seen by the person who wrote the article in the *Rundschau*. Everyone now thinks I have done this and to play Prince Bismarck a trick to revenge myself, etc. Of course, this is all a mischievous lie! in order to excite his party, William, etc., against me.

The article was evidently put in by somebody with the best intentions, but it reminded me of the story of 'Meyer' at Windsor in 1848 - publishing a poem, signed 'A' - so that everyone thought dear Papa had written it! Do you remember? I was advised to put a denial into the newspapers, that I had anything to do with the publication - this I refused to do! I was also advised to write in the same sense to Prince Bismarck, which I also refused. But I have sent him word that I could not understand who could have published this, and that it appeared to me a want of tact and judgment to print what partook of a private and intimate character while the people named in the book were alive.

Here is another pamphlet about Fritz's illness, which is good and fair.

Our weather is very fine, I am sadder than ever, worn, worried and badgered. The sum that Fritz wanted me to have to buy myself a place, and which they had as good as promised me in June, I am not going to have. The Haus Ministerium say the Crown cannot afford it William did not even say he regretted it and seemed to think it quite natural! I am glad in one way, as the less I am under obligations to the present system the better pleased I am; independence is a grand thing.

Two days later, on September 26, 1888, she wrote:

Alas, the evil passions are all abroad (of the Govt. and Bismarck party) and their violence is untold! This publication utterly infuriates them. Where it was got from, what it is, I do not know! I possess nothing of the kind in my papers, and yet every word is true, and the facts are correct, - the writing seems to be Fritz's own, they are his words and opinions, but I never saw them put together in this form!

An outburst of delight from the public has been followed by an outburst of fury from William, who bitterly criticised his Papa to me, and said how could he write such imprudent things down, etc. I only thought to myself how deeply is William to be pitied for so little understanding his Father. The vile *Post*, a Government paper, draws a simile between Fritz and the Emperor Joseph of Austria, saying that the latter had been a failure, and implying what a blessing it was for Germany that Fritz had not reigned longer as his principles must have led to a failure!! These are the sentiments and this is the language which has been held during 30 years, but especially during the two last, in government, court, society, and Berlin military circles, with which our three eldest children have been imbued. By nature they do not understand politics, nor do they care about them; they only join the general cry of the circles in which they move, and support William with all the roughness and violence of his disposition. They were so completely in the hands of the 'clique' that Fritz found it impossible to let them into his complete confidence, as they did not keep things to themselves, and it was easy for others de *leur tirer les vers du nez*. We looked forward to a time when 'authority' - to which William and Henry were always ready to bow - would be represented by him alone, and they then be more disposed to enter into their father's views, and it would no longer have been dangerous to enlighten them! This time, alas! has never come, and the golden opportunity for influencing these young people has been snatched out of our hands. May they never have to learn by stern experience the truth of what their father and their mother would so gladly have told them.

This publication is not apocryphal - but how it has come out is impossible to say. G von Normann is dead and Krug, who often acted as clerk and copied for Fritz, is dead too! It has been put in by some friend - anxious to do honour to Fritz's memory, which it does! but not considering that many things in this publication are calculated to embitter my enemies and expose me to still more unkindness than I have come in for already.

I send you a horrid article from the Post and two nice ones from a Liberal paper and I also send you the original publication in the Rundschau in case you have it not already!....

I am indeed blessed [she added] in having so kind and dear a Mother to whom I can pour out my bitter sorrows and speak of my many trials, and am truly grateful for this mercy.

Bismarck, after much cogitation, decided that the best way of countering the revelations in the Diary was by treating it as a forgery. 'As you will have seen from what you have read', he told Busch about this period, 'we must first treat it as a forgery, a point of view from which a great deal may be said. Then, when it is proved genuine by the production of the original, it can be dealt with further in another way.' Busch then asked the Chancellor if he had spoken to the Emperor on the subject, 'and he replied in the affirmative, saying "He was quite in a rage and wishes to have strong measures taken against the publication"'.[4] From this admission it is evident that both the Chancellor and the new Emperor knew that the Diary was genuine, but the world had not yet learnt that to these two, and to Bismarck especially, all weapons were of equal value when it came to diminishing the prestige or fame of the dead Emperor or his surviving spouse. On September 27, the Empress, who was about to leave her beloved Friedrichskron for ever, wrote to Queen Victoria:

The Diary is perfectly and completely genuine, word for word, and I now know where the original is. It is in the archives of the Haus Ministerium, and was among the papers I gave up! Of course it was not my intention to give it up; I thought it was purely military, and had not read it. On the one hand I am now terrified that if William hears where it is he will have it burnt because Prince Bismarck has officially said it is "apocryphal"'. On the other hand, there is no better proof for my enemies that I had nothing to do with the publication. But who has done it? and to whom could Fritz ever have lent it? This I do not know....The Conservative party here think it is the grandest thing Prince Bismarck ever did to deny the authenticity of this diary. It is very possible he did it *bona fide*....

Leaving this (Friedrichskron) is an agony to me. I seem to hear my darling's voice everywhere - see him, etc., and feel as if he were so near - here, or coming soon. In another place it can never be the same, and yet I cannot continue to live here as I did. I am more miserable than I can say.

The new Emperor was now fast acquiring a reputation for pageantry and military demonstrations, and his rapid sequence of journeys early in his reign to the courts of St. Petersburg, Vienna and Rome led the wits of Berlin to contrast the three German Emperors as 'Der Greise Kaiser, der Weise Kaiser, und der Reise Kaiser'.[5] On September 28 the Empress wrote to Queen Victoria:

....You can imagine how it pains me to think of William's renewed journeys to so many courts, and of all the receptions in Italy, a country to which we were so much attached and for which he does not care. Since our terrible loss not two days have been devoted to mourning, or to quiet, or a little care to his mother!

It has been one whirl of visits, receptions, dinners, journeys, parades, manoeuvres, shooting and entertaining. Of course it jars on my feelings, and I have to get accustomed to be a person who is not considered or remembered by the present regime, and I find it rather hard.

Leaving Friedrichskron is too terrible!....No more to be able to go into Fritz's sitting room, or dressing room, all just as they used to be, and never again to go into the room where he closed his eyes for ever seems so very hard. Yet many a widow has gone through the same. I always have a feeling that he would have wished me to stay in the house which was so dear to him, and guard the sacred spot where he died, but I know it cannot be....It is perhaps unreasonable and absurd to complain like this, but I can hardly tear myself away from what has been our Home for thirty years without a bitter pang....

I hope to hear that the place near Cronberg is secured in a few days, and then I shall set the architect and gardener to work, and shall hope to show it to you some day. It will be two years before I can get into it, alas!

Meanwhile, Bismarck, after the most thorough investigation, had learnt that Professor Geffcken had been responsible for the publication of the extracts from the Emperor Frederick's War Diary. He now decided to admit that the Diary was genuine, but further decided to prosecute the unfortunate Professor for 'high treason'! On September 29 (the anniversary of her betrothal) the Empress wrote to Queen Victoria:

This is our dear *Verlobungstag* thirty-two years ago. Oh how it wrings my heart! How I pine and long for him, and for his kind words and looks, and for a kiss I! It is all gone and over. Day by day I feel more lonely and unprotected. No one to lean on and the difficulties I have to face alone are really too terrible. Yesterday I felt very near putting an end to myself! So many loving thanks for your dear letter by messenger, and for Sir Theodore Martin's letter! You can imagine how indignant I feel at the tone in which the Government and Bismarck papers dare to speak of Fritz and of his Diary. It is not *überarbeitet*, there is not a word that is not his very own and in his own dear writing. Of course it ought not to have been published without my permission and not now. It was done with a good intention, and the public are delighted! The facts, long known to me and which now leak out, are of course odious to the government and Bismarck party, and the opinions which Fritz so modestly and simply puts forth are of course 'gall and wormwood' to them, as they are the very principles they have been treading and trampling down, and holding up to opprobrium for twenty years, calumniating and persecuting each individual who dared to uphold them. Now this party try to cast doubt, contempt and ridicule on Fritz's word and on his character, which makes me feel quite savage! They may attack and run me down as much as they like. I have nothing to lose, they have done all they could, but that they should venture to attack him when he is no longer there to defend himself, is mean, cowardly, ungrateful and abominable.

I want the *Tagebuch* back. I am so afraid William and Bismarck will order it to be burnt, and it is such a valuable and precious record of the real truth of things, that if they do that, I do not see how I can ever be on a footing of peace with them again!

It is really too much to bear all at once. I do not mind the truth being known in England.

I have not published this Diary, nor had anything to do with it! I fear it was Dr Geffcken who did it, - it was imprudent and indiscreet, but I will stand up for every word that is said. Mischke, Blumenthal, Stosch and many others can testify to the absolute historical truth of all it contains, but I certainly should not ask them to come forward, as they and all our friends are suspects to the government and might be treated *à l'Arnim*. Oh dear, it is all so sad and so complicated! My fate is to be trodden down and ill used now they have nothing to fear from me, and I shall never find redress anywhere....

These are the last lines I shall ever write to you from this dear house of such sacred memories to me, where his cradle and coffin stood, where he opened his dear eyes on this world, and where he closed them, with a soul as pure as a child. This page of my life closes here, and with bitter tears the new one begins.

The news has arrived that the purchase of the Villa Reiss is concluded, and now it is mine! Somehow or other I feel keen about it no more. Perhaps I shall begin to care again, but just now I am too wretched and miserable, and feel as if I could not rise any more from under the load of sorrow which oppresses me....

Three days later (October 2) she again wrote:

No doubt it was a foolish thing to do to publish that Diary, and that certainly it was not an opportune moment! How poor old Geffcken got hold of it I do not know, but you know he is a good soul and meant no harm, and was devoted to Fritz! The way Bismarck has behaved and how the matter has been treated is simply disgraceful, much, much worse than the indiscretion and the want of tact in publishing the diary! They have now arrested Geffcken! It will create an immense sensation, and will make the Government profoundly unpopular, though not so much, I fear, as it deserves! These arbitrary acts of high-handed despotism seem to go down with the people of Berlin in the most extraordinary way! The 'Party' are of course exultant and triumphant. 'Brutality' in every shape and form is what they admire, practise and preach.

The feeling of love for Fritz is very strong in the nation, and it is with indignation that all right-thinking people read what B. has written in his report and feel that I too have again been insulted.

The resounding scandal and embittered controversy caused by the publication of the extracts from the Diary now seemed to be approaching their zenith. Once again the Empress had the agony of seeing many whom she had counted as her friends ranged against her. Even some of her own family were in the opposite camp, but it must be admitted that she at times hardly made allowances for the difficult position in which they were placed. They were not in a position to know the inner details of the dispute, and yet, if they took her side, they ran the risk of affronting not only the omnipotent Bismarck, but also the Emperor William II. As the Empress wrote to Queen Victoria on October 11:

There is not a doubt that Bismarck only puffs up Geffcken's misdeed of publishing this Diary as much as he can, in order to be able to strike a blow and terrorise all people who might be inclined to speak a word of truth and to raise their voices for Fritz and for me! Bismarck's fear is that anything about the Regency which the 'Party' worked so hard to obtain might leak out, and it is to strike terror into the press that he makes this row for fear of any revelations which might be disagreeable to himself! All must be done to raise William on a pinnacle, because he is Bismarck's pedestal, which Fritz would never have stooped to be! So Fritz must be diminished in the eyes of the nation, and I must be calumniated, accused, vilified, because being Fritz's widow, the love the people had for him is still too warm for me! I must not be left a leg to stand on. I must be made to leave the place or to remain an object of distrust and dislike. This is not very agreeable to bear! Independent people are silent, cowed into holding their tongues. The whole machinery of the press is in Bismarck's hands - in Berlin alone the Government employé's are 33,000 people; all of these have no other opinion than what he orders them to have! Caprice, tyranny and despotism are rampant. It is very sad indeed. When will reaction against this intolerable state of things come, and of what nature will it be?

William allows his Father and me to be insulted and attacked, and sanctions it! I try to be patient and resigned and remember that silence is most dignified. Fritz of Baden, Louise and the Empress Augusta are on Bismarck's side. Fritz of Baden especially has completely changed in politics, and sails with William. It is his interest to do so. Louise is the only one who at least feels and understands my position. Charlotte has shewn neither tact nor feeling the whole time! She now fawns on William and has gone to Rome to see his arrival, etc., which, considering our mourning, has hurt my feelings very much! The first thing William did at Vienna was to receive Prof Schrotter, who did not behave well to Fritz, as you know.

I hear that already all the official papers have their articles against Sir M. Mackenzie ready written, by order from the Wilhelmstrasse.

You do not know all I have to endure. Good little Dr. Delbrück said yesterday if our darling Waldie were alive and 21 now he would call anyone out, the Chancellor himself, if disrespect were shown to his parents. I am sure he would, he was so staunch and so affectionate. Seeing my sons side with our enemies makes me guess what Caesar felt when Brutus stabbed him.

The following day she wrote:

You may be quite certain that I shall patiently endure all persecution, and not stir! I must say - I felt strongly inclined to prosecute Prince Bismarck for libel and go to law. But it is not proper in such deep mourning so to come before the public and possibly the *Staatsanwalt* (Procurator-General) would have refused to prosecute! Then that would have been a second insult to me!

What am I to think and feel when I see my own son approve of and encourage the insults to his father's memory and his mother's reputation! He is either too lazy and careless, or he does not understand, or he intends to break the 5th Commandment, or he is so blunt of perception and so blind - in his prejudices - that he does not understand how disgraceful is the part he has played, is playing, or is made to play!! He has had a long and careful training and preparation in the Bismarck atmosphere, so that his sense of right and wrong, of gratitude, chivalry, respect, affection for his parents and pity for those who are so stricken has been thoroughly destroyed! It well-nigh broke Fritz's heart, when he saw how his sons were having their minds warped and their judgment and opinions prverted. They were young, easily caught - and their Grandparents contributed largely to this result!....

The Villa Liegnitz at Potsdam they have asked me to give up, as they want it for William's gentlemen ! I have nothing at Potsdam now, except my little Bornstedt, *i.e.* a few little rooms there. I can sleep at the Stadt Schloss at Potsdam if I like, but must ask for permission each time, which, of course, I shall avoid! Consideration for me and my feelings has been so completely set aside, that the less I come across the present court the better; especially as I am afraid I could not promise yet always to keep my temper under so much provocation, and I do not want to give them the satisfaction of seeing how much they annoy me.

Whilst the quarrel over the Diary was still raging, another publication led to a further embitterment between the Empress and those who sought every possible opportunity of vilifying her and her dead husband.

On October 15 there was published by Sir Morell Mackenzie a small volume entitled *The Fatal Illness of Frederick the Noble*, which gave his account of the Emperor's illness and death. Had he kept to the medical issues involved, the resulting controversy might not have been so bitter, but he went out of his way to prove that the German doctors were incompetent and that their maltreatment of the patient had hastened his death. A few days earlier the Empress had written:

I send some interesting newspaper cuttings. You will see a letter from me to Sir Morell Mackenzie in the newspapers. He has not published it, nor has he anything to do with it! I am glad it found its way into print, as it will clear up the one point on which he is so much attacked here, - that he purposely ignored or out of stupidity failed to recognise the nature of the illness.

And now, on October 20, she wrote:

I have felt almost distracted these last few days! As time goes on it is so difficult to bear the constant longing which gnaws at one's heart with patience, and yet one cannot make it cease! Every sort of annoyance about Geffcken and about Sir Morell's book continues to worry me! Some of my best friends think it is a plan of the Bismarck and Government party, and perhaps of himself, to try and exasperate me so that I may leave the country altogether in disgust and return no more! They are every day on the look out for some reproach to make, or to try and put me *dans mon tort*. You saw the vile tone and calumnies in Bismarck's *immediat Bericht*. Some say I ought not to let it pass, but ought to remonstrate with him and William! This would be of no earthly use. Bismarck would laugh and answer civilly or with a fresh pack of lies, and the official press would be hounded on again. William does not read letters, - if they are unpleasant to him he tosses them on one side! He does not see or feel what is an insult or injury to his parents, and does not think it worth while to trouble about it; - to get on easily and undisturbed with the Chancellor, to do exactly what he pleases with as little bother as possible is all he cares about. His Mama is a consideration he never dreams of remembering! As Prince Bismarck and Herbert know this very well, they become more and more daring, as they know and feel that against my darling Fritz, against me and mine, they may say, write, print, do what they like with complete impunity! I have no one here to defend or advise me!! The two men on whom I ought to be able to rely are Min. Friedberg and the Haus Minister, but they are servants of the state, of William and Bismarck, and have neither the interest nor the courage to defend me where I am wronged.

I have only my sense of right, my good conscience, and the affection of many sections of the public and the Liberals to rely on nothing else! For all that, I shall not allow myself to be driven away from Germany, nor shall I abandon those who are true to beloved Fritz's memory and principles.

My Household are, with the sole exception of Ct Seckendorff, all in the other Camp, though they are very nice to me and Ctss. Brühl does all she can to show her sympathy for me now! Still all these important subjects I can never mention before them. They think everything right that is done at court and by the Government, and Bismarck is the first consideration!

The Empress Frederick was fortunate enough to have among her suite a certain number of very clear-headed and high-minded people. Although they were devoted to her and sympathised with her in all her difficulties, their devotion did not blind them to the fact that the persecutions which she had undergone often made her suspect a slight when no slight was intended. Like true friends they never hesitated to tell her frankly what they thought, although it must often have been difficult to do so without giving the impression that they were not wholly on her side.

There was Countess von Brühl, who had been many years with her; Count von Seckendorff, her secretary, who was a great art connoisseur and who had been with her ever since the Franco-German War; Countess

Perponcher Sedlnitsky who, although appointed since the Emperor Frederick's death, was her constant companion and friend; and Baron von Reischach, a man of great ability and reputed to be the best judge of a horse in Europe. At one time it was thought that he would be appointed German ambassador in London, but he remained with the Empress till her death and was later appointed Master of the Horse to the Emperor William II, when he succeeded in bringing the royal stables in Berlin to a height of perfection hitherto unknown in Germany.

The sale of Morell Mackenzie's book was now temporarily prohibited in Germany, and Mackenzie, by way of a riposte, secured the stoppage of the sale in England of the German surgeons' report of the case.

The Emperor William II during this period had taken up the attitude that both the publication of the extracts from the Crown Prince's Diary and Sir Morell Mackenzie's book had been instigated by the ex-Empress, and he appeared to be willing to accept any version of these affairs rather than his mother's. There was indeed good reason for the Empress to write to Queen Victoria on October 30:

Here things are most unsatisfactory; something new, painful and disagreeable and serious turns up every day! W. made a most ill-judged and *mal placé* speech to the Ober Burgermeister and Town Council when they came to congratulate him on his return. He was very rude to them, which made a painful impression. He has not come near me yet, so I have at last sent him word that I wish to see him, and I will try and speak to him on all these different matters. They say he is full of rage and distrust against me, as he still insists on believing that I had allowed the publication of his father's diary and that people had access to it in England ! One can make him believe anything, except the truth!! The more fantastic it is, the more unlikely, the more ready he is to believe it. Instead of suspecting the bad people that surround him and take a pleasure in maligning me and exciting him against me, he distrusts his own Mama! It is really too hard upon me! It has been growing steadily for two or three years, but his Papa was there, and he did not dare carry it to the extreme he now does. G. v. K(essel), with a wickedness and audacity I could hardly have credited even in him, now swears on his *Diensteid* that the cypher (which he found in his table drawer the other day) was not there when he last looked, and insinuates that it has been put there by someone in this house!! Is it not too bad? He was careless, forgetful and untidy, and the whole time I thought it must be amongst his things and said so, and said it was sure to come to light; but William preferred the cock-and-bull story I wrote to you before and which K. spread about everywhere. Now he does not like to own it was his own fault, so he invents this in order to cast blame and suspicion on others!

Some letters of our dear Roggenbach were found amongst Geffcken's papers; as they were old friends they corresponded together! Roggenbach is now at Bonn. Since he has been there the Police have broken into his home - at

'Schopfheim' in the Grand Duchy of Baden - with orders from here, - broken open the drawers of his writing tables and ransacked all his papers!! These things are allowed and sanctioned by William against his Father's most trusted and oldest friends!!!

The Police have by Bismarck's order a list of all people who were Fritz's friends or mine, or our habitués, or in any way connected with us, both ladies and gentlemen, even innocent Frau v. Stockmar, and we hear that the houses of all our friends are going to be searched! What for and with what intentions no one can tell, for besides its being disgraceful and shameful, it is exceedingly silly. Prince Bismarck wishes to strike terror and show that if anyone dares to have been friends with the Emperor Frederick or with me, they must be held up to the public as dangerous, as intriguants, as enemies to Germany and the Empire!! and liable to be put in prison!

Meanwhile Geffcken had been put on his trial for high treason, but the prosecution was soon abandoned. Bismarck, however, now took the opportunity to make a report to the young Emperor in which he questioned 1888 or denied the accuracy of a number of the statements in the Diary and made a venomous attack on the author, endeavouring in every way to belittle the prestige of the Emperor Frederick, and to expose and disparage his political liberalism.

A great call now was made for the publication of the entire Diary, but the late Emperor had left strict injunctions that it should not be published until 1922.[6] On November 2, 1888, the Empress Frederick wrote to Queen Victoria:

Prince Bismarck has instigated the publication of a pamphlet, in order to contradict, as it were, all that Fritz says in his diary. He wishes it to appear to the German nation, that you and our family were always the most dangerous enemy of Germany, and that Fritz, under my pernicious and dangerous influence, had made himself the tool of this policy.

Prince Bismarck, his clique, the government and society here (with few exceptions) are bent on tearing down beloved Fritz's memory, which is idolised by the people, and on proving that he would have been a danger for Germany, that he would not have protected her interests and that his Liberal ideas, his sympathisers and his friends, would have been the ruin of the State! I, being Fritz's widow and your daughter, must be held up to suspicion in the eyes of the public. All I do, even now in my solitary and retired existence, is criticised, misrepresented, etc. How far this nonsense is carried may be illustrated by the fact that Bernhard[7] goes about saying he hopes they will not let me go to England, as I only want to intrigue against the German Government ! It is not surprising of him as he was always a mad *chauviniste*, but it is not kind as a son-in-law on whom I lavish much affection and kindness and who was much more devoted to beloved Fritz than his own sons were! It only shows you how the talk and the unhindered efforts and workings of that clique blind people's judgment even against their own better feelings! There is nothing to be done now, but to bear it; I share the fate of all our friends, all the best, most experienced and enlightened patriots who would have been our support and help. War to the knife is waged against them all, with the most unheard-of and unjustifiable means!

It is now a struggle for Prince Bismarck's power to shake off all obligations and fetters which might be a *gêne* - to those belong Fritz's memory and my person! I must be run down and annihilated, as I am a relic of that fabric of hopes and plans he wishes to destroy once and for all! He fears that William might some day fall under my influence and therefore this must be prevented in time by making me out a danger to the state and an enemy to the Government.

It is very sad, not for me alone, but for poor Germany, Fritz's beloved country.

If this mad dance is carried too far, and I see nothing to stop them, there will be internal troubles of no small magnitude and no short duration. The phrase one hears again and again among the people is '*Wir meinen es sehr gut, aber wir lassen uns nicht knechten*'.[8]

The town of Berlin is very independent and after they have given such touching proofs of their loyalty and made such sacrifices to prove it, *i.e.* spent such sums on decorating the town for the Emperor W's funeral, given me such a fine gift (*N.B.* At which William is quite furious, and says his permission ought to have been asked) and now offered William a beautiful and very expensive fountain he admired, to be put up before his windows, they will not brook such rudeness and such treatment as they experienced at William's hands the other day.

Bismarck could not have a better tool than William. He has carefully had him prepared by his own son Herbert for two years. All other voices and views are excluded. W. reads only the papers prepared for him, does not understand or care for all the difficult and intricate questions of internal Government and is utterly ignorant of social, industrial, agricultural, commercial and financial questions, etc., only occupied with military things, with a little smattering of foreign affairs, and constantly being fêted, travelling about, having dinners, receptions, etc. Bismarck wishes his head to be thoroughly turned, his vanity and pride to be still greater than they are already, and then he will of course dash into anything they may propose. It is sad indeed for me as a mother, but it is not surprising. The clique supported by the Emperor William and the Empress Augusta (who both meant no harm and thought they were right) have brought this about and we could not prevent it. Fritz saw it all and it broke his heart, and I am sure the mental worry and distress predisposed him to this disease, which was then developed by Gerhardt and Bergmann's rough treatment! Oh, what a tragedy it all is!

Of course it must be our endeavour that the relations of England and Germany should not suffer in spite of Prince Bismarck's wickedness and

William's folly. You and dear Bertie and I and your Ministers will do all that is possible to keep everything on the best footing, but still I hope that this state of things is not ignored in England, and that all the sorrows and sufferings of your daughter are known, as well as their sources and reasons.

England under Lord Salisbury has shown a patience and caution and courtesy towards the German Government which are truly admirable. The English press has been fair and moderate in its estimation of the present state of things; its affection and praise of our beloved Darling would only be looked upon with anger and suspicion, by the Government. You and yours have always showered attentions, civilities, generosities, etc., on the German Court, and you know that the German unbiased public love and admire you and dear Papa, and you saw how well they received you in Spring.

The B. party hold the following language, 'We mean to show England that we do not want her - we must break up the connection between the English Royal Family and Germany'.

You know that I have no blind hatred or prejudice against Prince Bismarck, that I have tried hard to get on with him, and be as civil as I could. I have always given him his due and also taken his part where I thought he was misunderstood or his notions mistrusted when they were good and honest ones.

Fritz and I were intensely anxious not only that the Government and Ministers should get on smoothly and well, but that the two nations should understand each other, and sympathise in common aims and interests and that they should work hand in hand, assisting each other in the cause of true culture, civilisation and progress! We hoped that the bonds of affection and confidence between the reigning families so closely allied by such sacred ties would grow stronger and stronger. Fritz considered himself the representative not only of his family tradition, but of beloved Papa's ideas - how he loved you and how he loved Bertie more and more every year!

Fritz did not need Bismarck and his diplomatic band to keep up good relations with other Powers! He possessed the friendship and confidence of the rulers, and the sympathies of their people! This always was gall and wormwood to Bismarck, who feared a rival in prestige, and would have had to do Fritz's bidding if Fritz had been well and could have enforced his will Bismarck was quite nice and tractable when you were here, because he thought Fritz's life might be prolonged for another year, but the moment he saw on the 11th and 13th June that this would not be, he turned against us and thought to free himself from everything that could possibly give him the least trouble! His pupil and present Sovereign has neither scruples nor conscience to stick at anything, so they go on hitting out right and left, offending everyone all round (except Russia) and trying to crush and annihilate all that is in any way Liberal, or independent or cosmopolitan. Alas, I do not exaggerate, I merely relate what is history and what is no use cloaking! With the younger generation there is no use talking, reasoning or expostulating. We older ones of steadier heads and longer experience must maintain a prudent and dignified silence, until such time comes as we can speak with effect. I am not actuated by a feeling of revenge or bitterness. I can afford to forgive 'them that trespass against us', but in my deep unspeakable sorrow, I grieve to see so much that is so low and so bad! So much falseness and cruel ingratitude and such utter reckless folly and ignorance. I can but stand aloof and pray God to take pity on me and my three girls, on this country and on *les honnêtes gens* in general.

So many thanks for your very dear letter of the 30th, which was such a comfort to me! I have had a very dear letter from dear Bertie! Of course I had no idea of what happened at Vienna.[9] I am so ashamed and so indignant. Any want of respect or gratitude or courtesy to Bertie from a son of mine I resent most deeply, as he has been the very kindest of Uncles to all my children. Here Bertie was blamed for having left Vienna, in order not to see William, and to be purposely uncivil to him! Of course I know this was not and could not be, but was far from guessing that it was the other way round! I am quite disgusted and feel it more than any rudeness to me, as, alas, I am used to that.

Pray excuse this unusually long letter. If it seems opportune and desirable I wish you would let dear Bertie see it.....

William considers any public mention of his father's name or mine an offence to him! So have they succeeded in working him up and stuffing his head full of rubbish - mingling flattery with accusations against his parents - *il gobe tout* because he is so green and so suspicious and prejudiced!!

This letter from the Empress Frederick shocked and distressed her mother, Queen Victoria, who was now nearing her seventieth birthday, and the aged Queen endeavoured to find some means of reconciling not only her son, the Prince of Wales, with the new Emperor, but also her daughter. Her letter of the 6th brought the following reply four days later:

I thought you would be shocked and distressed at all that has been going on here! It is indeed terrible for me! William does not mean to distress and wound me as he does, I daresay, but it makes it none the less hard to bear. He has so little feeling himself that he does not know other people have, and that a want of respect, courtesy, consideration and fairness, coming from him is an offence and keenly felt! More disagreeable things than I have written have taken place, but I hope the Haus Minister, who is very calm and quiet and most anxious for peace and harmony, and to whom I spoke for two hours yesterday, will be able to smooth matters down a little.

It was very kind of you and of Bertie to keep from me all that had happened at Vienna, and I hope Sir Edward Malet knows the rights of it and also Bertie's feelings and will be able to give them expression if possible. I feel so ashamed when I think how little William knows how to behave, and so angry with the people who admire this *Rücksichtslosigkeit* and autocratic behaviour, this utter want of consideration for others! Alas, he is exceedingly dependent on those around him in his judgment and opinions, and I know them too well to hope that he can improve at present. He is considered the right and real *représentant* of his Grandfather's view and Prince Bismarck's policy, and is much elated at this. Much flattery is poured upon him, so he never doubts that all he does and thinks is perfect, and there is no counterbalance or moderating influence in his wife that I can see! She quite approves the present system, gives it her full support and is very happy. He never for one moment remembers that whatever popularity he may have in other circles, except the official ones, is due to his being his own dear father's son, and that it is hoped that through being my son and your and Papa's grandson, the antediluvian and autocratic ideas of most of the Hohenzollerns will be modified by a wider, more humane, liberal, tolerant and moderate spirit. There are many who imagine that this will and must be the easel I, alas, do not; as he is too obstinate and also as the people who might influence him in the right direction are either totally unknown to him or have no means of approaching him, and his whole mode of thought is so completely different that he would never read or understand or study anything which could open his eyes. He has never travelled and he has not one eminent man as a friend - as we, I am happy to say, had so many. My influence has been purposely and ingeniously destroyed and counteracted! Fritz's entreaties were systematically put on one side.

The words with which the [old] Emperor William told Herbert Bismarck that our son was to be employed at the Foreign Office were '*Damit seine junge Seele vor Irrthümer bewährt würde*'.[10] I have it from Herbert's own lips. The 'errors' were - his father's and mother's wishes and opinions, - their house and their friends! Certainly the [old] Emperor William succeeded - alas for Germany - and no one helped more to destroy whatever she once thought right than the Empress Augusta! We wanted nothing else than what she gave herself endless trouble to effect with her own son. She wished him to have less prejudices, *einen freieren, weiteren Blick*,[11] than the rest of his family and did him an immense service thereby, but she completely turned round of late years, and did all she could to deprive us of any influence over William! In this she was seconded by her daughter and all the Emperor William's Household. I often complained to you of it! They succeeded - and all we are now suffering are the fruits of this, which used to worry and torment Fritz so much!

*P.S.* - A most curious fact [she added] is that Count Münster, who left Friedrichsruh yesterday, found Prince Bismarck *sehr milde gestimmt*,[12] determined not to have a war with France. He said about William, '*Der Kaiser ist wie ein Ballon, wenn man ihn nicht fest hielte am Strick, ginge er, man weiss nicht wohin*'.[13] Princess Bismarck said, '*Die Kaiserin Friedrich thut mir in der Seele weh. Sie wird doch zu schlecht und zu hart behandelt*'.[14] Either she does not know that all the spite comes from her own people, or they keep it purposely from her! William said to me, 'All my excellent Kessel says, I believe implicitly'. This shows enough how bad the influence is - Lyncker has a bad influence also - not because he is false, but because he is *borné*, violent, rough, always for strong measures and exceedingly *schroff*, whereas Kessel is false, dangerous and a direct mischief-maker. William has yet to learn that one cannot ride rough-shod over other people's feelings and rights and views, without causing them to rise up and protest and resist such treatment! He is really like a child that pulls off a fly's legs or wings and does not think the fly minds it, or that it matters. I do not think he the least understands how I have been insulted and injured and what I have gone through. The people around him incessantly are pouring gossip and calumnies into his ears and poisoning his mind against me and all his father's friends, and he is so credulous that he believes everything without even asking whether it be true or not! It is very painful to me to have to speak out and make him understand that I will not submit to the things they have tried to make me swallow, and that I am deeply wounded by the utter disregard shown to all my feelings.

Nine days later the Empress Frederick and her youngest daughters left Germany to visit England - or 'home' as they all regarded it. Even thirty years of residence in Germany had not quenched in the Empress that ardent love of her native land which was one of her most dominant characteristics.

She was accompanied to the railway station at Berlin by her son, the Emperor William, who now seemed desirous of making amends for his previous behaviour. A few days after the Empress had left for England the British Military Attaché in Berlin, Colonel Leopold Swaine, wrote to Sir Henry Ponsonby, Queen Victoria's Private Secretary:

Although a Sunday, I had to see General von Waldersee on business, and at its conclusion the General volunteered the remark that he was very glad that the Empress Frederick had left for England, as he hoped that not alone the period of Her Majesty's absence from Berlin must help to make much that had passed here lately of an unpleasant nature between her and the Emperor lose in acuteness, but also that the Queen's influence during the Empress's stay in England would have a beneficial result. On the latter he laid the greater weight, for it was noticed after the two days of the Queen's stay in Charlottenburg her influence had been of so much value.

The General said that at an interview he had had last week with the Emperor, His Majesty had expressed himself as most regretful at the strained relations existing between his mother and himself. He had stated that he was most anxious and desirous that this should cease, but that there were some points on which it was impossible for him to give in, and he hoped Her Majesty's stay in England would put an end to these for ever and make them disappear for 1888 good and all.

He said that the Emperor was young and that it consequently pained him more than it would an older man whenever it was forgotten that he was Emperor and consequently head of the family, and that in matters concerning the country he was frequently treated as a son without its being remembered that he was also Emperor. He instanced the Empress Augusta, who, he said, never left Berlin to go to Coblentz or change her domicile anywhere without previously informing the young Emperor, thereby showing him that she considered him as the head of the house.

The whole thing, if I may so express myself, appears silly vanity. But if these little attentions are likely to have good results and would tend to bring about a more affectionate *rapprochement* they are worthy of a trial.

I know the Empress Frederick does not like Count Waldersee and looks upon him as one of those who are priming the Emperor with bad advice, but I can positively state that this morning he spoke with great feeling and great regret, and I do not think that he is acting otherwise than for the best to diminish the difficulties existing between mother and son. He complained bitterly of the tittle-tattle that was going on, and on which he lays the whole blame of the situation.

The Emperor saw the Empress Frederick off this morning and as far as outward signs went nothing could have been more affectionate.

## NOTES

1 *The War Diary of the Emperor Frederick*, Foreword, p. v.
2 Why are your eyes so red?
3 *The War Diary of the Emperor Frederick*, Foreword, p. vi.
4 Busch's Bismarck, pp. 194-5.
5 The 'white-haired Emperor', 'the wise Emperor', and 'the travelling Emperor'.
6 For full text see *The Diary of the Emperor Frederick*, translated by A. R. Allinson, MA
7 Her son-in-law, Prince Bernard of Saxe-Meiningen.
8 We mean very well, but we won't become slaves.
9 Both the Prince of Wales and the Emperor William II. were due to visit Vienna early in October 1888, and on August 15 the Prince wrote to his nephew that he would be glad to meet him under the Austrian Emperor's roof. William II, making no reply direct, promptly stipulated to the Emperor Francis Joseph that no other royal guest should dim the glory of his own stay in Vienna. The Prince of Wales tactfully avoided any contretemps by visiting the King and Queen of Roumania at Sinaia during the German Emperor's visit to Vienna.
10 So that his young soul may be guarded against errors.
11 A freer, wider outlook.
12 In a gentle mood.
13 The Emperor is like a balloon, if one did not hold him fast on a string, he would go no one knows whither.
14 The Empress Frederick makes my heart ache. She is indeed being treated too unkindly and too roughly.

## XIV. The Emperor William's Visit to England, 1889

THE Empress Frederick and her daughters returned to Germany from England at the end of February 1889, and her return was marked for the moment by a much better relationship between her and her eldest son, who now sought from Queen Victoria an invitation to visit England in state during the course of the summer. Queen Victoria, whilst anxious not to do anything that would give the impression that she took sides with the Emperor against his mother, was desirous that there should be no cause for Anglo-German differences, and therefore accorded her grandson the invitation he sought.

During this period there had been much perturbation over the publication by Ernest II, Duke of Saxe-Coburg and Gotha, the brother of the Prince Consort, of his frank memoirs under the title of *Aus meinem Leben und aus meiner Zeit*. The first volume appeared in 1887, and the second and third followed in die succeeding two years. Beyond the fact that these volumes are one long eulogy of Bismarck, it seems difficult to account for the hostility with which the Empress Frederick regarded them, and certainly there seems to be nothing to justify her complaint that they contained attacks on Queen Victoria. Most of the references to the Crown Prince show him in a favourable light, and the general impression given is one of affection and admiration for both him and his wife. Certain passages, however, probably did appear to the Empress as derogatory to her late husband, and to anyone accustomed, as the Empress was, to fulsome praise of him, even a slight criticism might have seemed like abuse.

It was to these topics of the Emperor William's visit to England and the Duke of Saxe-Coburg's memoirs that the Empress alluded in her letter to Queen Victoria of March 15, 1889:

> I quite understand about William's visit [she wrote] and your position with regard to it. I know you could not do otherwise, but I am sure you will also understand what my feelings must be. No amends have ever been made to me for all I have been made to suffer, no explanations offered, nor excuses, and I cannot forget what has passed.
>
> What is your advice about Uncle Ernest? I begged Lenchen to write to you about it. This is the second infamous pamphlet written against me, with covert attacks against you, from his pen. This, added to the misrepresentations in his newly issued Memoirs, is doing a great deal of harm and especially creates in the minds of my three elder children a totally false and very mischievous impression.

It is too wicked of him. It is generally known that I was very fond of him, so people think that he must know what is going on.

You remember William's speech at Vienna the other day to poor Rudolf,[1] who in confidence told Bertie of it, which fully bears out what I say. Some person or other ought to be found to set this straight.

I thought you might like to know what the treasonable letters are which Roggenbach and Geffcken wrote to each other. A friend of mine with great difficulty got hold of one of the printed copies which were circulated - in this Bundesrath, but not elsewhere allowed and copied them hastily. These are the papers which were taken out of these gentlemen's boxes and tables in their absence - a piece of unheard-of audacity and law-breaking. Please keep them among my papers.

How William and Bismarck can think without blushing of what they did, I do not know, but you see what one is exposed to now in Germany; *die reiche Bourgeoisie bei uns ist feige, wer aber für sein Brot arbeiten muss und nicht als Beamter abhängig ist, knirscht mit den Zähnen über das Junkerregiment.*[2]

Some think when Bismarck is no more that all this party will be scattered to the winds; for as he has no principles he cannot build up. The party have a leader, but no programme. They will follow him everywhere and are in constant admiration, but with no firm institutions and principles a party cannot hold together when the leader is gone. Still the mischief will not be over when he disappears, as he has thoroughly corrupted all moral sense in the young men who will come after him. Where is the hand and the mind to take up Bismarck's position and work on the lines of honesty and moderate rational progress for the development of true freedom? I see none. That is why my beloved darling said, '*Ich darf ja nicht sterben; was würde aus Deutschland?*'[3]

I am afraid I shall bore you, but you know I have no one to speak to here in the house. No one cares, knows or understands, and in my half-sleepless nights I lie and ponder on these sad things, hoping and praying that it may be well with Germany, but feeling that this is not the road to safety, prosperity or liberty - to a wholesome state of things. How many good and excellent men who are persecuted and calumniated are suffering and sighing in silence and despair as I am.

A week later. March 22, the Empress again wrote to Queen Victoria:

I have just received your dear letter by messenger, for which many affectionate thanks. This is the old Emperor William's Birthday. I wrote a long letter to the Empress Augusta, and as this is the warmest answer I have received since June, I send it for you to guess what the others must have been like!

About Uncle Ernest, I will try and furnish you more decided proofs, so that something may be done! He ought at least to be made to feel that such behaviour is unworthy of our dear father's brother and of a gentleman! How cruelly ungrateful it is to you, to Fritz and to me! He boasts of leading and advising

William, and of having 'opened his eyes' about me and my family!!

The cold and indifferent attitude of her son had now produced in the Empress a feeling that was a mixture of resignation and injured pride. She agreed with Queen Victoria (March 28):

> that William is not quite aware of the insults and injuries I have suffered at his hands, though I certainly did my best to enlighten him! As he does not feel for his mother he cannot be surprised if she who gave him so much love and care, now can only remember with pain that he is her son. Perhaps years may change this, but at present I am too sore and have suffered too much! He has it in his power, if he likes, to change this. I can do nothing, nor will I ever give way and humour him, and bear all in patience and silence, as I did from last June to last November (for his sister's sake) again. He simply accepts that and thinks he can continue to ride rough-shod over me; there he makes a mistake. I think he simply is so wrapped up in himself, his power, his vanity, his plans, his position, that he does not remember my existence.
>
> I so thoroughly and utterly disapprove of all that has been done since that dread day, with very few exceptions, and have so little hope of its mending, that I strive to hear as little and think about it as little as I can. But one cannot cease to care for the country and its interests, and it is difficult to become indifferent to things which for thirty years and up to last June seemed of vital importance to Fritz and to me, and which we watched with such anxiety.

For the next month there is little of historical interest in the letters of the Empress to Queen Victoria. Family and social news predominate, but there are occasional references to Germany, which she feared (March 29) was becoming 'a sort of military Paraguay', and to 'William and Dona', who, as she wrote on April 6, 'were quite nice and civil, and meant to be amiable, *mais voila tout!*' On April 9 she records:

> I lunched with William and Dona yesterday! No one knows what it cost me to go there and see our own servants and Fritz's *Jäger* serving behind their chairs, etc. Their new rooms are very gorgeous, but it is all rather heavy and overloaded and wanting in real refinement, I think.
>
> Yesterday Prince Bismarck came. It was a bitter pill to me to have to receive him after all that has taken place and with all that is going on. He talked a great deal about Rudolf, and said that a scene with the Emperor (of Austria) had taken place, according to Reuss's account. Perhaps Reuss was wrong. I should think very likely.

Prince Reuss's account, however, was very near the truth of this mysterious episode. It would appear that the Emperor of Austria took strong exception to a certain liaison which his heir-apparent had formed, and the

Archduke Rudolf resolved to break off the entangling shackles to which the Emperor objected. His final interview with the lady resulted in the tragedy of Mayerling, when both he and his mistress were found dead together. On April 20 the Empress wrote to Queen Victoria:

....I have heard different things about poor Rudolf which may perhaps interest you. Prince Bismarck told me that the violent scenes and altercations between the Emperor and Rudolf had been the cause of Rudolf's suicide. I replied that I had heard this much doubted, upon which he said Reuss had written it and it was so! He would send me the despatch to read if I liked, but I have declined. I did not say what I thought, which is that for thirty years I have had the experience of how many lies Prince Bismarck's diplomatic agents (with some exceptions) have written him, and therefore I usually disbelieve what they write completely, unless I know them to be honest and trustworthy men. Szechenyi, the Ambassador at Berlin, whom we know very well, tells me that there had been no scenes with the Emperor, who said to Szechenyi: *'Dies ist der erste Kummer, den mein Sohn mir macht.'*[4] I give you the news for what it is worth. General Loe heard from Austrian sources that the catastrophe was not premeditated for that day! but that the young lady had destroyed herself and, seeing that, Rudolf thought there was nothing else left to him, and that he had killed himself with a Förster Gewehr which he stood on the ground and then trod on the trigger. Loe considers, as I do, poor Rudolf's death a terrible misfortune. The Chancellor, I think, does not deplore it, and did not like him!....

Preparations were now well under way for the state visit of William II. to England in the August of 1889, to which both Germany and Britain looked forward as an expression of Anglo-German amity. Germany's young colonial empire was now proving something more of a national interest than Bismarck had imagined, and it was to these subjects that the Empress alluded in the same letter of April 20, which contained the references to the Archduke Rudolf's death.

When I was at Berlin I saw William three times: once he and Dona called, when we arrived, to return my visit; once we lunched with them, and on Vicky's birthday they had supper with us. No subject of any interest or importance was touched upon! He came to the railway station when I left, as he was just leaving himself for Wilhelmshafen! The whole time he was gay and merry, but quite indifferent, never asking me one question about myself, and not one sympathising or kind word was uttered!
Their going to Friedrichskron is a pang to me I cannot describe! If one could think they went there with the right feelings it would be so different - if only it had been left one year uninhabited after all that happened! To think of the room our beloved one closed his eyes in now simply used as a passage, - strangers going to and fro and laughing, etc. All the rooms we inhabited and where I

suffered such untold agonies, after one short year occupied by others, and the home ringing with noise, laughter and merriment before a year is out, pains me so bitterly! I know it is foolish, but I cannot get over it!....

If you wish for my impression on politics, I will give it you, I think it totally different from the one that for instance Christian has! He has mixed in society and with officers and people of the court and Conservatives and Bismarckites! These say William is very popular and things are going on beautifully. This is not my impression. I think 'William is totally blind and that the Government make one mistake after another. Herbert Bismarck's influence is supreme, - his old father toadies William as he never did his grandfather or his father! The evil party have everything in their hands and all the power, and do absolutely what they like. William is quite one of them. All serious, important and well-informed people think the state of things sad and dangerous and feel that they cannot last, that the serious questions which will arise cannot be dealt with after the fashion of Prince Bismarck and his party, but that one cannot tell when, or whether, the veil will be rent which so completely obscures William's eyes, and when they will be opened to the real facts.

Many - amongst others Friedberg and Prince Radolin - implore me not to leave Berlin, and say that my very existence there is a silent protest against many things and a little check on those who now drive William in the direction they like! I am not of this opinion. Wherever I can be of any use to William or to the country in ever so small a way, I am always ready - but after the way in which I have been treated, to live on there and accept smilingly all they choose to heap on me, and be the butt for their calumnies and intrigues, would soon kill me, *je me consumerais*! My life would be more or less an imprisonment. I had best keep quite quiet, lie still, and keep out of the way of the Berlin Court and Government, until they are forced to see the error of their ways! I shall always go to Berlin from time to time, but it would be far too soon to spend the coming winter there, quarrels and disagreeables would be unavoidable.

I am sure William will make himself amiable and agreeable in England - as he was cross during the Jubilee because his father and mother were there, and he could not play the first part! Now he thinks he will have all to himself and can afford to be gracious. Prince Bismarck is anxious now for England's friendship, as well he may, as it suits him for the moment not only with his Zanzibar and Samoa businesses, which have been so shamefully mismanaged, but in view of European complications which he is anxious to avoid, but which I fancy are beyond his control. He has made a fatal mistake with Austria! He has so weakened her that she becomes almost useless as an Ally! His policy of allowing the Balkan States to become powerless is a great blow to Austria! Bulgaria under Ferdinand is a reed to lean on, Servia - without King Milan - will hardly withstand Russian influence, and Panslavism is working hard to upset Charles of Roumania and seize upon his country! If Russia is the Master in the East and the Russians have finished getting ready their regiments in Poland (which are not quite ready) she will attack Austria to a certainty, in spite of the Czar's dislike to such an undertaking.

Prince Bismarck has weakened Austria by incessantly preaching to her to give way to Russia in everything! Poor Rudolf knew this and saw it so well.

The French wish for peace because of their Exhibition and because their new infantry rifles are not all ready; they will be so in April next year, and ours in Germany will not. If the Russians attack Austria and we are forced to help the Austrians, the French will not be able to resist the opportunity of falling upon us! We should then have to drop Austria and face both French and the Russians!! How awful that would be!! Of what use the Bulgarians, Servians and Roumanians might have been in assisting Austria!! Perhaps all this need not come to pass, but we seem to be drifting in this direction. The clouds seem to gather, but they may disperse again!

With regard to the Colonial policy, Prince Bismarck is caught in his own trap! He never seriously thought of having Colonies or fighting for them, but he encouraged the misguided and artificial enthusiasm about Zanzibar and Samoa, because he thought he could use it for electioneering purposes, and that flourishing the patriotic flag, and blowing the national trumpet, would make him popular, and enable him to get what he wanted from the Reichstag. Meanwhile not only the Chauvinistic party but William have taken it quite *au sérieux* and wish it followed up. The Chancellor does not dare to say that it would be wiser to drop all such undertakings for the present and while the state of European peace is so uncertain, but I have no doubt he thinks it.

Many of the letters which the Empress Frederick had written to Queen Victoria were now shown by the Queen to Lady Ponsonby, the Empress's trusted friend. The following letter of thanks from Lady Ponsonby, which Queen Victoria kept among the Empress's letters, gives some idea of the way in which people unthinkingly widened the breach between the Empress and her son by repeating every unkind word that the one said of the other. That the Empress should have had in her service persons who reported to the Emperor all her references to him is perhaps hardly to be wondered at, but it is interesting to find that among the Emperor's suite also there were those who never lost an opportunity of telling the Empress all he said of her. They can have had little to gain by doing so, since the Empress was practically friendless and powerless, and the obvious inference to be drawn is that they wished to keep the breach open and to prevent any possible reconciliation between mother and son.

It seems sometimes [Lady Ponsonby wrote to Queen Victoria on May 4, 1889] as if it were impossible to unravel all the troubles and complexities of the Empress's position and to disentangle what is important in the difficulties to be overcome - to separate the grave matters too hard almost for Her Majesty to overlook, which in spite of the deep sorrow and tragic suffering of the past year have been forced upon her, from the smaller troubles which might possibly be smoothed over and explained away in time. The Empress has, in her gracious kindness, often spoken to me of the puzzled and nearly hopeless confusion in which the problem of her future position and existence seems to be involved, but when Her Majesty is calm and free from the *rapportage* so fatal to her peace of mind, which is so deeply to be regretted, I think the Empress judges the whole situation in as wise and patient a manner as can be expected, and it is this frame of mind which it is devoutly to be wished her friends should encourage.

The Empress is far too clever to mix up the bitter feeling of revolt, which the evils of a cruel destiny must inevitably at times raise in the mind of one so gifted and capable of ruling, at being as it were set aside, with the just indignation aroused by unworthy treatment, and I have often heard Her Majesty recognise the fact that dignity and strength will be best shown in acquiescing in the inevitable silently. A Frenchman has said, '*Les médiocres ne s'aperçoivent pas combien il y a de mépris dans un certain silence, mais les gens d'esprit ne s'y trompent guère*'.

The inevitable: the young Emperor must be *first*. He must be *very* German. He is not a boy, and however right Her Majesty may be about the mistaken policy of the German Government, to oppose it, or to speak against it even to the most confidential friend would, in my humble opinion, as I have often expressed it to Her Majesty, cause her own difficulties to increase without effecting the smallest iota of change in the policy pursued. The regrettable and reprehensible manner in which the Emperor lightly treats his father's memory and his mother's feelings and wishes, must harm His Majesty more than it can do the Empress, and if it were *possible* (how *difficult* it will ever be, everyone who loves and sympathises with the dear Empress must feel from the depths of their heart) for Her Majesty resolutely to abstain from listening to the reports and repeated words which, perhaps well-meaning, but certainly officious friends hasten to furnish, this would be a great gain. I ventured once to suggest that if people existed who never lost an opportunity of recording every unpleasant impatient word or speech to widen the breach between mother and son, how likely it was that others could be found who acted in the opposite direction on precisely the same principle, and that every syllable of criticism pronounced by Her Majesty found its way back to the Emperor. It is true that as the Empress remarked there is no adverse influence in Her Majesty's entourage to correspond with the baneful and calumnious effect of the Emperor's immediate advisers, and it is at this point the exceptional difficulties start up. It seems almost more than human nature can bear to know that misrepresentation and lies are freely circulated and yet to take no notice. Even here, silence would, I venture to think, in the long run carry a more crushing refutation than retaliation. The Empress Frederick is a very powerful personality in Europe, and as such, quietly, silently, but very surely, as I believe, this strong individuality will gather round one centre all that is first-rate in society and in the artistic and literary world; later, it is probable also in the political world, but for this it is obvious that anything like *interference*, active or passive, in politics, would be fatal to Her Majesty's peace.

There is one subject touched upon by the Empress on which I am presumptuous enough to disagree with Her Majesty. At the time the difficulty arose between the Emperor and the Prince of Wales, the matter got into the newspapers, and the outside world expressed pretty freely its opinion to the disadvantage of the German Emperor. At the same time more than one *German* remarked to me: now is the moment for the Empress Frederick to play the *beau rôle* of smoothing matters for her son. Her Majesty says nothing could be easier than for the Emperor to write a short letter which would set everything straight; if Her Majesty *could* be induced to *suggest* it, her son could not fail to recognise what a noble forgetfulness of her wrongs this desire to conciliate English opinion showed.,..

During the early months of 1889 signs had not been lacking that all was not *couleur de rose* between the new Emperor and Prince Bismarck. William II, according to his own *Memoirs*, was a devoted admirer and pupil of the Iron Chancellor, but it was an uncongenial fact to him that while he was the nominal ruler of Germany, Prince Bismarck was the actual ruler. Their first outward and visible sign of difference occurred over the Chancellor's treatment of certain elements in the industrial situation in Germany. Early in May 1889 the Krupp works at Essen were compelled to close down owing to a strike of the Westphalian coal-miners for increased pay and shorter hours of labour. Bismarck at once saw to it that troops were available to maintain order. The result was a conflict between the troops and the miners on May 7 in which three miners were killed. Within a week 100,000 strikers were out, and on May 14 the Emperor received three delegates from the miners, to whom he made a characteristic speech. In the following days the dislocation spread to Silesia and another 20,000 men ceased work.

A law dealing with the working classes was now about to be passed through the German Parliament - a law promulgated by Prince Bismarck to compel the workers, with government assistance, to provide for old age and infirmity.

On May 18 the Dowager Empress wrote to Queen Victoria:

The Strike of the Coal-miners is a very serious thing! I was more than horrified at William's speech. 'Wm. told the men that if they had anything to do with the 'Social Democrats' *ich werde Euch alle über den Haufen schiessen lassen*.[5]

It is just like him! He uses *les gros mots* wherever he can and thinks himself very grand! I think such words in the mouth of a Sovereign, and so young and inexperienced a man, most brutal and unbecoming. But this is his style and that of the present regime. Never would my beloved Fritz have uttered such a threat, or thought of bettering matters by holding out the prospect of such violent measures. It sounds so childish besides! The Liberal members of the Reichstag have taken the greatest trouble to put the matters straight between the employers and men on strike, and I think have succeeded to a certain degree!

The new Law, Alters und Invaliden Versorgung, which has been so hastily pushed through, is not a good one, and while purposing to be a great boon to the workmen, is in reality not an advantage to them, and all men who have thoroughly studied the question think this Law ill considered. Of course it takes in the public, who do not thoroughly know the question, and sounds like an immense benefit to the working classes.

The Westphalian coal strike ended on May 31 by a compromise between masters and men - but the ensuing year was to see a further recrudescence of trouble in this area.

June 15, 1889, was the first anniversary of the death of the Emperor Frederick, and all the poignant memories of that period found expression in the letter of the Empress Frederick to her mother of June 14:

What an agony it is [she wrote] to remember each little detail of last year!

I cannot even now realize that such a sorrow as this has indeed come to darken every day and hour of my life; and when such an Anniversary as the 15th June comes round - no words can convey what one's feelings are! The cruel haunting memories - the agonising thoughts, which being brought back so vividly, increase one's misery and desolation and quite overwhelm one with almost unbearable heartache! I remember how he kissed Sophie and gave her the flowers, etc., and seemed cheerful and ready to think of all the little things - for the day.

To me it hardly seems as if a year could have passed since those fatal days - and yet how long and weary those twelve months have been - what days and weeks of misery they have contained! and yet life has to be faced, and lived and struggled with, and duties remain. The battle seems almost superhuman sometimes! But how your love and care and sympathy and kindness have cheered and helped me on and given me courage; and the faithful affection of my few real friends - the sunshine of my three dear girls' presence! What a blessing those three dear young lives are to me, and how grateful I am to have them - his dear children! I am not ungrateful for this - nor for the fact that our beloved Fritz lives on in the heart of the German nation at large in spite of detraction and calumny, and that his bright image and noble example will not be forgotten. This is very soothing to me - and this even our enemies cannot destroy! '*Das Andenken des Gerechten bleibt ein Segen.*'[6]

When I think of the first year of the new reign!! mistake after mistake - blunder after blunder! How many people persecuted, wronged, offended, injured and calumniated!! hardly one generous or noble action done! Alas! also inseparable from the memories of those days in June at Friedrichshof are those of the cordon of Hussars round the house - the orders to the doctors against my beloved one's wishes - the brutal treatment of Sir M. Mackenzie and those who assisted me in nursing and tending our angel! - the sanctioned pamphlet of

Bergmann and Gerhardt; the treachery of Kessel and Winterfeldt, the false heartlessness of Prince Bismarck, the daring impertinence of his son; the accusations and calumnies against me and all Fritz's friends - above all the disregard of Fritz's last wishes, of his last letter, the ruin of two dear young people's hopes! the spirit in which all arrangements were made and all those by Fritz upset and undone!!

These are things which I cannot forgive or forget! I can bear them in silence, I can refrain from trying to find redress, or from retaliating. Time may soften these impressions and also undo some of the harm which has purposely been done me in the eyes of Germany - it may some day open the eyes of my three elder children to the fact that their mother is not a conspirator against Germany and a traitor to the country, as she has been made out to them to be, and as they have allowed themselves to be led to believe; but it can never wipe out from my remembrance what has passed during the first twelve months of W's reign! It will be my duty some day to endeavour to let the truth go down to history and not the lies that suit Prince Bismarck and the Government and all those who court its favour!

Queen Victoria's sympathetic reply brought the Empress to a more equable state of mind, and the following letter, written on June 21, gives some indication of the influence which the aged Queen exerted over her eldest daughter and of the wise counsel she gave her. Judging by the replies from the Empress, her mother invariably urged moderation and did everything in her power to bring the Empress and her son into much more amicable relations.

You are right [the Empress wrote] in saying I ought not to say 'I will never forgive' - indeed the example of Him who forgave his enemies and taught us to pray 'Forgive us our trespasses' is ever before me. It is wrong to say I cannot forgive and I do not think I possess a revengeful or vindictive disposition, nor that I find it difficult to forget and forgive when I have been injured, or offended; but I do find it hard to forgive the wrong done to those I love, to my husband and my child, to our friends, and quietly accept what those in power may think fit to dare to do! When one is not *un chiffon* one feels very intensely the gross insults to which one has had to submit, and thinks that some sort of amends ought to be made and that it is not necessary for everyone to try and smooth the path for the oppressor who rides rough-shod over one! The good of both countries and political considerations go first, but the triumph of those who have behaved so shamefully to me is very hard to bear. They get everything they want, are flattered and honoured and made much of, and revel in the thought of the injuries and humiliations they have inflicted on me. However, I will try and steel myself against all these stabs.

I was so anxious you should know the rights about this new Law passed at Berlin, as your Embassy and the *Times* would only give you the official view, that

I put down in German my views, which are those of our friends, and asked Miss Green to translate it, which she has done, and I now send it, begging you would kindly return it when you have read it! It might also interest Sir H. Ponsonby. The present regime strikes violent blows against all that is Liberal, progressive and independent, - a gradual, steady, moderate development of Liberty it will not tolerate and seeks to destroy, and favours Socialism to flatter the masses and have their support for despotism and Caesarism. It is very much the system of the Emperor Napoleon and still more the creed of Prince Napoleon, but it is bad and dangerous! William has never studied these questions - does not care for them, or understand them, - has no opinion of his own, but takes up that of the Bismarcks with violence and obstinacy. Anyone who dares to point out the danger of such a course is put down as a traitor and malefactor, so those who care for their own ease, peace and comfort are silent! I am silent because I should not be understood, and it would be of no use. Still I wish that you should know the drift of what has lately been done in our poor Germany. To me much of it seems blind folly and ignorance - to the followers and admirers of B. it appears sublime wisdom.

In the following month the Empress made many endeavours to arrive at a more satisfactory intercourse with her son William. But the memory of her humiliations still rankled. On July 19 she wrote to Queen Victoria:

I wish so much to say a little more about William so that you may be quite *au fait*. I have struggled with myself very hard, and I think I am now in quite a calm and forgiving frame of mind, not anxious to rake up all grievances, etc., but I wish those who are so good and kind to me to know that I am particularly careful to do my duty *vis-à-vis* of William, and not to give any handle to those who wish to turn all against me! I only wish to be left in peace and quiet, not persecuted and not constantly calumniated. I have, as you know, no ambition to possess any influence, or to meddle and interfere with anything the present regime does! I cannot approve of what it does, nor of the persons who are in power, so I am only anxious to see and hear as little as possible about them and keep out of their way altogether. I can make many an allowance for William, as he has had his mind systematically poisoned against me and has been told for years that it was die greatest misfortune that his Papa listened to me and had confidence in me, and that I was an enemy of Germany and held dangerous opinions, etc....

Of late it has been the endeavour of all those around him to increase his distrust of me, to which Charlotte has, alas, greatly contributed.

Therefore no effort of mine to be on good terms with him is of any use. There is no confidence, and he does not in the least understand me, or indeed know anything about me!

I believe he considers himself a good son, and does not perceive how during this whole year he has not only cruelly neglected me, but also allowed injuries and insults to be heaped upon me. I cannot enumerate again all that has been done since June 15th, 1888 - you know the things which have wounded my heart, and offended my dignity. It would be of no use if you were to tell him this, or to say I had many subjects of complaint that I could not forget, but it might be of use to tell him that there was a great deal of sympathy for his parents in England, and that you thought it would be his duty to defend and protect his mother and to try and make up to her for the cruelly hard fate she had to suffer! This might make an impression! He is so selfish and has already been so *rücksichtslos* to us, that it has become a perfect habit, and he would be very much astonished if he were told how badly he has behaved to us, and how shamefully his Government and entourage have treated me! The treachery and want of respect to his Father - the insolence, enmity to me! He does not see or understand that he had no better friends than his parents; he never understood his Papa, and he thinks all women dolts or idiots. His wife has shown no tact and no nice or kind feeling towards me and above all no gratitude. This is all very sad, but it is so, and I shall suffer from it as long as I live, but I have made up my mind to this and must content myself with a footing of outward civility, which I shall do all to maintain! One thing must not be forgotten, that all the accusations heaped upon me have never been refuted, and that until William is convinced by circumstances, or by someone or other, that they are lies, and is anxious to atone in some way for the insults offered to me, I cannot feel otherwise than deeply hurt and offended I This I am sure you will not think strange and would do the same in my place.

Treitschke received a public reward after his abuse of us, Puttkamer the 'Black Eagle' after Fritz had dismissed him in displeasure, Bergmann and Gerhardt decorations and favours after Fritz was so dissatisfied with their services, and so I could name a long string of deeds, one and all directed against Fritz and me - whether they were meant so by William or not. Of his words and his speeches I say nothing, for he can always follow the example of Bismarck and his son, and flatly deny, when it suits him, what he has said before! This belongs to their system; when they have vilified and injured a person to their hearts' content - because it seems politic at the moment - they afterwards pretend to forget it, and are much surprised that their victim still remembers it. I saw Prince Radolin two days ago and he said Herbert Bismarck complained that you had said you did not wish Kessel to go to England, and how strange it was that you should know anything about the Emperor's Aides-de-Camp, or have a preference for one or the other, and again referred to General Winterfeldt having been so badly treated at Windsor. Prince Radolin, of course, gave him a very good answer! Please keep this to yourself.

Whilst the moderating influence of Queen Victoria was thus making itself felt in the relations between the Empress and her son, there was steadily growing in the German court another influence that was destined to have the most deplorable effect upon the Emperor William II. For some years there had been in his immediate entourage a Prussian officer of chauvinist views - Count von Waldersee, who, in the various campaigns since 1866, had proved his undoubted military ability. In 1881 he became Moltke's Chief of Staff, and when Moltke retired, Waldersee stepped into his shoes as Chief of the General Staff. There were now signs of a growing rivalry between Waldersee and the Bismarcks, and to her letter of July 19 the Empress added the postscript:

You may have heard about the rivalry between the Bismarcks and Count Waldersee - the latter has a pernicious influence on William, and I am told by many - also by Hintzpeter - that it is he who has set William so against me for years! Waldersee is a great friend of Bernhard and Charlotte. Neither the late Emperor William, nor Fritz, could bear him, and distrusted him very much - he is not nearly as clever as Moltke, and a very shifty and changeable individual. She (Countess von Waldersee) is a very good woman, but violently Low Church, a partisan of Stöcker's and a very great friend of Dona's. The Stöcker party are hated in Germany, and Prince Bismarck is sharp enough to know that to patronise it openly (though it consists of his own followers - Conservatives, etc.) would not do, therefore he was secretly anxious to get rid of Puttkamer, who was their great supporter. Now, of course, he disclaims having anything to do with Puttkamer's fall, and all to please William; and it is said that I took advantage of Fritz's weakness to get rid of Puttkamer.

On August 1 the Emperor William II, with a German fleet, arrived at Spithead on his state visit. Honours were lavished upon him. He was created a British admiral, a grand naval review was arranged for his pleasure on August 5, and two days later he was present at manoeuvres at Aldershot. The Emperor's reply to his being made a British admiral was to make his grandmother, Queen Victoria, a colonel of a German Dragoon regiment. On August 8 he left England, much pleased with his reception.

During the stay Queen Victoria had endeavoured, without, however, much success, to induce her grandson to treat his mother in a better manner. He listened attentively to what she said, but hardly was he back in Germany than the old attitude of indifference and hostility reasserted itself. In her letter to Queen Victoria of August 24 the Empress reviewed the events of the past five years. Mortifications are often harder to bear, and cause more distress, than real calamities, and try as she would, the Empress could not forget the many humiliations that had been heaped upon her by her son William. What she felt most of all was the fact that it was impossible to tell him anything. Surrounded as he was by men who did not dare tell him the truth or who knew little or nothing of what was transpiring behind the scenes, he remained in a fool's paradise. The one person who could have enlightened him was Bismarck, but Bismarck kept silence.

The Empress's letter, dated August 24, ran as follows:

I am also very grateful that you spoke to William and I hope it may have a good effect, though I am not sanguine about it. As you say, he hears such nonsense about and against me. But his mind has been thoroughly poisoned against his parents for the last four or five years by the circles in which he moved, the people with whom he associated for political purposes, and the influence of his Grandparents (without their meaning to do harm) was exercised in this same direction. I do not see how, with a credulous and suspicious disposition as his is - without much judgment or discernment, or experience - this is to change, as he is surrounded by people whose interest it is and who incessantly try to malign me. None have done more harm than Uncle Ernest, Herbert Bismarck, Charlotte and G. v. Kessel.

You say I am not to listen to things told me against him. I have no one about me to speak against him. My entourage are his creatures and the system of *rapportage* and espionage is so great at Berlin that they would not venture to open their lips. Besides there is not one who is of my way of thinking politically, as you know. From Fritz's friends and mine I am completely cut off; and everyone I see always tries to make me think William in the right. Needless to say they do not convince me, and often even irritate me, as I feel the injustice of being told to swallow still more, and to forget the things that are too insulting to forget. I judge William's feelings to me, not by the things he says alone, which are no secret, as everyone knows them, but by his deeds. His conduct during the whole year 1887 and 1888 - surely I need not repeat it all. From June 15th to the day when the name of Friedrichskron was abolished, it was a string of insults. My wishes and his dear father's set at nought - about his precious remains before the funeral. My feelings outraged. The soldiers round the house, our telegrams stopped. The treatment of Sir M. Mackenzie, the publication of Gerhardt's and Bergmann's vile book; the confiscation of the answer, the treatment of Sandro, the brutal way in which W. broke off his sister's marriage and treated us, disregarding his father's orders and Friedberg's advice. The press campaign against me paid by his Government. The affair about the Foreign Office cypher, which I am still supposed to have appropriated, whereas Kessel had it. The Fêtes given and the official journeys taken during the first three months of deepest mourning. The affair of Fritz's Journal. The insulting *Immediat Bericht* of Bismarck, calling Fritz and me foreign spies, before the whole of Europe. Then the accusation that I had made away with state papers, which has never been contradicted. The ostentatious way in which the Emperor William is constantly alluded to and Fritz never, or only in a few short words. All the orders which Fritz had given for new organisation of the Court *cassirt*, his arrangements upset. Puttkamer decorated with the Black Eagle; Bergmann and Gerhardt received to dinner and decorated. Treitschke, who called Fritz's reign *eine traurige Episode*, received W's official thanks printed in the newspapers. General Mischke and G. v. Roder simply dismissed. These and many other similar things are what I have had to submit to, and which I resent. They are not *Klatsck* but facts which will be recorded in history. The Geffcken affair, the treatment of Roggenbach, General v. Loe and Stosch. The table drawers broken open, the private correspondence of these gentlemen stolen and published. The Morier affair. These are a little too much to forgive, unless I am righted again in the eyes of the public, and unless William begs my pardon some day. These offences are not a year old - since April he has not come near me and has written twice.

For all that, I wish peace to reign and do nothing in the world to provoke him, or give rise to any difficulties for the present, and keep out of the way of a regime for which I have the profoundest contempt and the greatest disgust for the public good and that of our two countries. I rejoice when matters go smoothly between England and Germany, and think it a blessing, but all the while I know that the 'Entente' could and would have been a very different one under beloved Fritz, and more to be depended on than the momentary caprices of Prince Bismarck and William.

On the whole I trust the visit to England has done good in many ways. It will take years before I can feel less sore, and though I may feel no resentment later against him personally yet I can never excuse, or approve of what he has done, of the principles he governs with, or the people that surround him.

Excuse this lengthy explanation. I promise you I will be very good and not feel *unversöhnlich* towards him; but some day I must be righted in the eyes of Germany, and the calumnies must be refuted which are still believed, and which W chooses to believe to a great extent.

## NOTES

1 The Austrian heir-apparent, who had committed suicide on January 30.
2 Our rich middle class is cowardly, but he who must work for his bread and is not dependent on Government employment gnashes his teeth over the 'Junker' Government.
3 I must not die; what would become of Germany?
4 This is the first vexation my son has caused me.
5 I will have you all shot down.
6 The memory of the just is blessed.

# XV. The Fall of Prince Bismarck

THE differences that had arisen between the Emperor William and Prince Bismarck in the May of 1889 became considerably accentuated during the course of the following months, and as the year came to its close it became evident that another 'Chancellor-crisis' was sooner or later inevitable. In the fierce struggle for power and mastery that ensued, the Empress Frederick took no part, though its result was bound to affect her own fortunes and happiness. In none of her letters does she give any indication of taking sides with either of the contestants, and it was mainly of other matters that she wrote to her mother during this period.

Of particular interest to her, however, was a somewhat peculiar matrimonial tangle. In the year 1888 Prince Bismarck had appointed as German Ambassador to London Count Paul von Hatzfeldt-Wildenburg, who had married years earlier Helen, the daughter of Mr. Charles Moulton of New York and Paris. They had been divorced in 1886. In the following years, however, Count and Countess Hatzfeldt's daughter Helene became friendly with Prince Max of Hohenlohe-Oehringen, whose desire to marry was checked by the fact that he wished to avoid the social stigma which then attached to the daughter of divorced parents. As a result of this, Count and Countess Hatzfeldt desired to remarry, but there were legal and other difficulties in the way, not the least of which was Prince Bismarck's opposition. The Empress Frederick, who had sought the aid of Queen Victoria in this matter, now wrote to her mother on September 13, 1889:

> I saw Paul Hatzfeldt the day before yesterday and he was so grateful to you. He speaks with the tears in his eyes. It will all be right in a week or two, and he will at least have a home and his children can talk of their home and parents without blushing.
>
> Prince Bismarck and his son have played a most odious part in all this, and now make William believe that they never made difficulties, whereas the very reverse Is the truth. A promise, a given word, is nothing to them and never meant to be kept. I know that and have learnt it to my cost in twenty-five years. Lies are considered quite legitimate. At any rate these two gentlemen seem to grow fat on them, whilst those who were gentlemen enough to believe them have fallen victims. Fritz Holstein and Arnim are in their graves, Sandro has been driven to desperation, Keudell nearly died, Roggenbach can hardly get over it, and Geffcken is annihilated. Hatzfeldt would have added one to the list, but the fates have willed it otherwise at the last moment. If William had people like Ct

Hatzfeldt and Keudell and Prince Radolin about him, he would not live in a world of fiction about so many things as he does. But the net is so inextricably knit which surrounds him that it is useless to attempt to put the truth before him now. One must have patience - later perhaps it may be done. Hatzfeldt is never allowed to be alone with him. None of my friends have access to him, while our declared enemies and those who have behaved worst to us are about him. Under such circumstances my life and position are very odious and painful. But I know it cannot be otherwise for the present and am determined to bear it with as much calmness, patience and philosophy as I can. Every remonstrance, every appeal to truth and justice, or better feeling, would only make them enjoy the game of bullying me still more. I am powerless while they wield the weapon of authority and abuse their power to any extent....

A fortnight later the Empress wrote again to her mother (September 27, 1889):

When I saw Hatzfeldt at Homburg, he told me that his 'Civil' marriage would take place as soon as he had the formal written consent from the Foreign Office, or from the Chancellor (I do not know which of the two he meant), and that he hoped to receive this document in ten days, or a fortnight, which time must now have elapsed. Some one mentioned yesterday that Ct Hatzfeldt's *Civil Trauung* had taken place on the 22nd, but whether that is so, I do not know; I am inclined to doubt it.

What Sir Edward [Malet, British Ambassador at Berlin] alludes to I do not know, but I am certain that if there is any doubtful point still in the situation, it would be for the best if Sir Edward talked it privately over with Ct Hatzfeldt. That a *piège* is always to be apprehended I have long known and, I believe, always said, but Hatzfeldt is so cautious and prudent *et si fin*, so calm and quiet, that I imagine he will not fall into the traps they have always dug for him. You can have no idea of the duplicity, the utter want of faith and principle of Prince Bismarck, his son and their band of employees at this Foreign Office.

To carry out their wishes and plans, their intentions - the web of lies and intrigues, the number of persons used to weave them are quite untold. William was drawn into this three years ago, without having the experience or insight necessary in these things. You remember how in his enthusiasm for Prince Bismarck's system, etc., he allowed himself to be used against his own parents. He trusts those people, with all of whom Kessel is hand in glove, and they know how to manage William; so that no one, neither Hatzfeldt nor anyone else, would have William's support and help against any villainy which might be planned. I am in exactly the same position! Prince Bismarck attacked me violently in his paid press - before all Europe, calumniated our beloved Fritz's memory, and all his party followed the lead. William never attempted to stop it, never defended us, never caused the truth to be said, and their lies succeeded!! Roggenbach, Geffcken, Loe, Morier, Stosch, Sir M. Mackenzie are all proofs of the same fact that we are all without any protection; anything that this party choose to do, or to say, they have the power of doing! They have now made the most they could out of William's reception in England - it does not surprise me and I knew it beforehand! They say that no Sovereign was ever so feted, and that it was not true that anything which had been done in Germany since March 1888 had ever been disapproved of by public opinion in England, or by you; this was all an intrigue and merely a spiteful invention of mine, of which their Emperor had plenty of opportunity of convincing himself!

I cannot say it makes any very deep impression on me, as I was so prepared for it by what Prince B. and his son said to me, - the triumphant and defiant tone they adopted!

I am completely isolated and my life can only resolve itself into one thing for the present: learning to endure with fortitude. There is no one to defend, support, or help me, no one to ask redress for the wrongs I have suffered and always suffer, because all I do is systematically blamed and criticised.

Kind Hatzfeldt, with whom I also talked, said so truly that there is nothing to be done, explanations, attempts at justification would be of no use - as the net cast about William is too strong, he would not be able, or even be allowed to hear the truth, or see through all the cleverly wrought machinations to bring about a certain conviction in his mind! Circumstances may change, people may die, or go away, or others may by a happy accident gain his ear, and then a time will come when perhaps justice may be done to me! Perhaps I shall have ceased to care, or ceased to live. Hatzfeldt always hopes and prays and thinks that in time you may gain an influence on William, and perhaps Bertie might too, I think. But, alas, the feeling that Bertie has had to give way, and has completely got over the story of last year, makes them still more daring and less afraid of offending - they think that they can do what they like and explain it away after, and that everybody is bound to accept their explanations! Believe me, the powers that be only behave well to those of whom they stand in a certain awe! They are insolent to all whom they are not afraid of! They treat Russia with the utmost consideration and *ménagement*.

As long as the two Bismarcks, Waldersee and Kessel have paramount influence, it is easy to see that I can only have a terrible time of it! Even Stockmar and Lyncker,[1] who are honest men in their way, and whose part I have always taken, do not like me, and you know how Charlotte and Bernhard have gone against me, encouraged by the King of Saxony, Fritz of Baden, and even the Empress Augusta, though personally she is quite nice to me!

This is the situation, it cannot be helped. In private families such a situation could hardly exist! Wronged and persecuted as I have been, I could have appealed to you and all my brothers and sisters to seek redress for me and to fight my battles with me! But this I could not do in my position. England must appear to ignore what are affairs of the German Court and see that the relations between the two great countries be not disturbed or affected by family affairs! Both out of courtesy and political reasons my brothers - English Princes - cannot be as outspoken with the Emperor of Germany as if he were someone else....

This, my defenceless position, is, of course, greatly to Prince Bismarck's convenience and he and his party take as much advantage of it as they can. Our friends have never been blind partisans of his Government, and the blows he deals at them, he deals at me. I am not complaining and hope I do not bore you too much with all this. I thought you might care to hear from me, now I am here, what I feel the situation to be!

Another time I will write and tell you what I think of the political situation here; I never remember the outlook having been as dark as it is now, because it is so utterly without hope! The Bismarck system and policy will not disappear when he does, as William has identified himself with it; but I trust that when Prince Bismarck dies the bad measures will be more successfully fought and opposed, as his prestige will no longer be there to bear everything down before it. For foreign policy his death would be no gain, as his name still keeps Germany's foes in check, and at his age he is so determined to prevent war, he is cautious and his cunning is very useful in avoiding things which give offence. Waldersee is imprudent and thoughtless and William utterly so, and so we should have rushed or blundered into no end of dangerous enterprises (viz. Visit with the King of Italy to Alsace-Lorraine, Colonial enterprises in Africa, etc.) so that perhaps Prince Bismarck's still being where he is, is in some ways a good thing though it increases tenfold the dangers in home affairs! The despotism and chauvinism, the retrograde movement in all things cannot fail to exasperate those who are not simply actuated by self-interest.

The enormous sacrifice the nation is called upon to make for the Army creates a deep-seated discontent in the masses of the people, of which William is totally unaware, and for which Bismarck cares nothing.

Her letter continued with a reference to her recent visit to Denmark, where she found:

The Queen of Denmark most kind and amiable - she adores the Russians. The King was charming as always. Frederick's oldest son is a bright boy and very nice....Dear Alix [later Queen Alexandra] was the flower of the flock with her two sweet girls. Dear Tino [Constantme of Greece] and Georgy [later High Commissioner of Crete] are certainly the finest of the young men, and also the most intelligent. Alix of Greece was sweet and dear, but like wax, so terribly anaemic. She and Paul seem very happy. The noise they all made, and the wild romps they had were simply indescribable....Once or twice I was obliged to laugh right out when they were all carrying each other. It was certainly a very novel and original sight, very absurd sometimes, and they seemed happier and to enjoy themselves more thoroughly than children of five or six. Tino and Georgy are as strong as two young Hercules! I only wonder no arms or legs were broken. The Queen of Denmark's furniture must be unusually strong - one sofa, I believe, had to have the springs renewed at different times....

Finally, the Empress concluded her long epistle with a shrewd comment upon Bismarck's attitude towards England at this period:

Hatzfeldt [she wrote] is eyed with much jealousy and they would be glad to play him some trick if they could, but he is always on the alert.

To make quite plain what I said before, Prince Bismarck of course encourages all that now is a demonstration of civility to the English Government. He wishes his Germans clearly to understand that he was only inimical to an England which sympathised with the Emperor Frederick and with which any other *rapports* existed except those arranged, suggested and sanctioned by him! The England which sympathised with the present regime and his Government alone, is the one that he wishes to be friends with and will certainly be friendly to!! This was the meaning of the storm he raised in April 1888, and in June and July of the same sad year, and of the campaign against Morier. I think he has great confidence in Lord Salisbury and also in Lord Rosebery; the latter he takes for a pure Bismarckite, and is perhaps not altogether mistaken! I do not envy Lord Salisbury, but certainly his way of 'getting on' with Bismarck is admirable, and he shows a patience, tact and sagacity which are very great.

Fritz always looked to Hatzfeldt as the future Minister for Foreign Affairs; and certainly he is the only one I know who could succeed the Chancellor for that branch of affairs; but, of course, I see no chance of his being selected. If ever Bismarck retires, his dreadful son is certain to succeed him; it will be such a pity.

A few weeks later Count and Countess Hatzfeldt were remarried, and in the early months of 1890 they had the satisfaction of seeing their daughter become Princess Max of Hohenlohe.

On October 27, 1889, another wedding took place, that of the Princess Sophie to Prince Constantine, Duke of Sparta. The Empress Frederick, the sovereigns of Greece, Denmark and Germany, the Prince and Princess of Wales, and the Tsarevitch of Russia were all present at the ceremony in Athens, whence the Empress that day wrote to Queen Victoria:

In the midst of all this bustle and hurry I must write you a few words to say that the wedding is over and that all has gone off very well. Tino and his little wife are in their new house, a tiny place, smaller than Osborne Cottage (a good deal), but light and cheerful and comfortable - arranged like a little French villa, reminding me much of our 'Villa Zirio' at San Remo. My darling Sophie looked so sweet and grave and calm, my little lamb, and I felt - oh, so miserable during the Service, thinking of my beloved Fritz and how he would have liked to see his child and how we should have comforted one another at having to part with her. Her dress and wreath became her so well. Her neck and throat looked so white and pretty, and the wreath fitted so nicely and close round her head. The gown was of white satin with a *tablier* of cloth of silver trimmed with lilies on lace and garlands of orange blossom and myrtle. The train was of white satin embroidered all over with silver thread in a Genoese design of the 16th century. The only *contretemps* was the veil having disappeared. It most likely was forgotten at Berlin. She had to wear a plain tulle one. She had a necklace of pearls round her neck and a few diamond pins in her hair to keep on the veil. The ceremony in the Greek Church was very long, but I thought it solemn and impressive, and the church though modern is fine. All the Bishops with their round mitres and long beards looked very well. All the arrangements were very well made. The King himself had settled everything. The weather was splendid, like on your Jubilee Day, but not too hot; there was pleasant air. We drove in our low gowns in open carriages. I drove with dear Bertie, which was a great comfort to me. How much I thought of you and dear Papa and my wedding when I saw the dear young people standing at the Altar. They held a lighted taper each and had to walk three times round the Altar (as you know). The Protestant Service was very short, but nice in the little Chapel here. The King's Chaplain and Kogel officiated, the former married the young couple and the latter gave the blessing and said a prayer; two short chorales were sung and then we went upstairs to a family luncheon. I felt dreadfully upset, but tried to be brave. The Queen of Denmark and dear Olga were most kind and good to me. After the lunch Sophie appeared in a very pretty and becoming white and gold dress and bonnet, and drove away through the town. Poor Moretta and Mossy could keep up no longer and sobbed bitterly. Olga, the King and I hastened on foot to Sophie and Tino's house to receive them there, Olga blessed them and gave them a picture of our Saviour to kiss (which is the custom), and then we left them in their new abode where they are now resting until the Gala Dinner when they will appear again. Sophie's train was carried by Dita Perponcher, Mdlle de Perpignan & Mdlle Soutso, her new Lady-in-Waiting.

Victoria of Wales has been unwell and could not appear, but she was up and came to see Sophie and sat in the Protestant Chapel. Olga is in great beauty just now; she has the face of a Madonna. The Queen of Denmark is wonderful to be able to stand all this fatigue. My dear *Kleeblatt*, my trio as you used to call them, is broken up now and I feel it bitterly. I suppose one will go after the other, but it will be hard indeed when the day comes. When I look at my poor Moretta and think what might have been and ought to have been, it gives me a great pang, especially when I see Sophie with her Tino. Tino was delighted with your lovely fruit baskets and will thank you himself as soon as he possibly can....

The Empress now continued her holiday in Italy, but even whilst holidaymaking the Empress's mind would turn again and again to those tragic events of the preceding year. Even had she wished to forget them it would have been difficult to do so in view of the constant stream of articles and pamphlets dealing with the illness and death of the Emperor Frederick. One of these in particular caused her much perturbation. Towards the close of the year the celebrated German novelist Gustav Freytag published a volume of reminiscences under the title of *Der Kronprinz und die deutsche Kaiserkrone*. The Empress had made Freytag's acquaintance in the early years of her married life and he had early been the confidant and friend of her husband. Her uncle, Duke Ernest of Saxe-Coburg-Gotha, was also a great friend and patron of the talented novelist. Now, in his reminiscences, Freytag drew such a picture of the dead Emperor that it could not fail to distress the ex-Empress. Freytag averred that the Emperor Frederick as Crown Prince was subjected to foreign influence and entirely under the sway of his pro-British wife, and it was insinuated that through the Crown Princess, Princess Alice and other members of the British royal family, important German military secrets had reached the French commanders during the course of the Franco-German War.[2] The letters of the Crown Princess published in this present volume, and the publication of the Emperor Frederick's War Diary of 1870-71 in are sufficient to disprove these baseless innuendoes, but at that time they were accepted by the majority of Germans as indications of the truth, and neither Bismarck nor the Emperor William made any step to contradict the delicately veiled charges. Freytag, in fact, was warmly complimented in high quarters on his libellous work. On December 14, 1889, the Empress wrote to her mother from Naples:

....It is significant indeed that poor Geffcken, whose publication was a piece of indiscretion and imprudence, was imprisoned and all our friends made the subject of persecution because it was done with a view to show the people what dear Fritz was. Of course, Geffcken had no business to do so, but the intention was a good one. Now what Freytag writes is in a spirit of *dénigrement* to show the world that Fritz was overrated and I a danger to Germany. For this Freytag has been complimented and remains, of course, quite unmolested because this acceptation suits the government - my own son's government. Uncle Ernest congratulated Freytag and asked him to dinner at his Minister's. Uncle Ernest is quite delighted with the book.

There was a Director of the Gotha Museum, a Doctor Aldenhoven, of whom we always had a high opinion. He was well known to Fritz Holstein and poor Fanny Reventlow. He is a sincere Liberal and one of the very few honest and respectable men in Uncle's service. Old Seebach liked him also. Now Aldenhoven has resigned because Uncle sent him word that it would compromise him (Uncle) in William's eyes if a Liberal *deutsch Freisinniger* remained in his service. Is it not disgusting to see how Uncle pays his court to Bismarck, William, etc. He ought to be too proud and independent, but alas, I fear Uncle is capable of anything and everything that is undignified now.

I hear now this Freytag is going to bring out a Biography of Normann - this annoys me very much, as Normann was in our house for upwards of 20 years. It is sure to touch upon things connected with us, and in a spirit which will not be what I should wish, and I dread new disagreeables....

A few days later the Empress received a great and unpleasant shock. Among the papers of the Emperor Frederick which had been taken from Friedrichskron the day after his death there was a sealed letter addressed to the Empress containing his wishes regarding his funeral and other matters. For eighteen months this letter was held back from her owing to an 'oversight', and it was not until December 17, 1889, that the Empress received this pathetically intimate letter. Three days later she wrote to Queen Victoria from Naples:

> I think you will feel for me, dear Mama, when I tell you what a shock I had three days ago, which upset me most terribly. I received a letter from William's Hofmarschall, H. von Lynker, who was formerly with us, and opened the cover quite unconsciously - it contained a sealed letter directed to me - in my darling Fritz's handwriting. This letter to me contained his wishes, directions and orders about his funeral and all that was to be done - and not done, and what he specially forbids; begging me to see that this be carried out.
>
> This letter Lynker had had all the time in a box which he had forgotten to open and look through and now examined by accident. It made me quite ill and reminded me of those terrible days and how they refused to listen to my prayers and entreaties to leave those dear, sacred, precious remains of my darling undisturbed. How brutally and cruelly those whom I will not name behaved to me. Perhaps they would not have dared had I been able to show this letter; though William ignored other letters expressing his father's wishes, and though they seemed to dare everything that was shameful and bad.
>
> I felt sure Fritz must have left some directions, but as you know, none were ever found, and now a year and a half after, they are found in William's Hofmarschall'ss box!
>
> I have not been able to sleep properly since, I am still so upset. Lynker is much distressed. I am certain he did not mean it at all and it was an oversight, pure carelessness and accident, but it gives me great pain. I told him that I bore him no grudge. But my wrongs and woes rise up again in my memory with a vividness which is an agony.

The effect of the publication of Freytag's reminiscences was to cause a recrudescence of the bitter controversies over the Emperor Frederick's actions and Ideals, and a Doctor Harmening entered the lists on behalf of the dead Emperor. Unfortunately, he gave Duke Ernest of Saxe-Coburg-Gotha the opportunity to charge him with libellous statements, and in the result the Doctor was sentenced to six months' imprisonment. Harmening's pamphlet had been written as a counterblast to another pamphlet in which the belittling of the late Emperor was carried to a further pitch, and the Empress, rightly or wrongly, thought that this scandalous publication was due to her pro-Bismarckian uncle, Duke Ernest. On December 24, 1889, the Empress wrote to Queen Victoria from Naples:

Another thing which has sadly annoyed me is that the man (a Doctor Harmening, not personally known to me) has lost the lawsuit in which Uncle Ernest had him accused of libel. It is a great pity. Uncle was very sly and supported by clever lawyers. The result is, that Uncle, who *is* the author of that villainous pamphlet, escapes free, whereas the man who boldly defended Fritz, me and you, and spoke up in a manly tone, is sent to prison for six months and has to pay the costs. Uncle considers this a new triumph. It is deeply regretted by all our friends in Germany. I send you a newspaper extract containing the trial. Uncle, who has avowed, to people I know, having written the monstrous pamphlet against us, now finds himself sheltered from public indignation, by avoiding letting the proofs be found. This result is most unfortunate and unjust, but it is pretty well known now everywhere that he is the author and that Dr. Harmening, as ill luck would have it, was not able to prove it and bring it home to him. I could if I liked, but of course would not and could not do such a thing against Papa's own brother, and also for Alfred's sake - besides the disgust at creating such a scandal. Uncle, knowing all this, allows the man to be condemned for libel who has only spoken the truth.

A fortnight later the Empress returned to Berlin for the funeral of the Empress Augusta, her mother-in-law, who had died suddenly on January 7. On January 11 the Empress wrote to Queen Victoria:

I ought to have written yesterday, but I was so knocked up with the journey that I felt both shaken and excited and my eyes sore, so I hope you will excuse me. We rushed away from Rome on the most lovely day, warm and fine, a deep blue cloudless sky, the place looking so splendid in its stately beauty. The King and Queen and many friends whom I was so sorry to leave were at the station. The journey reminded me cruelly of the one from San Remo....

William was at the station and I made him take me to my house - the empty desert silence in all the rooms made my heart ache. I just changed my clothes and went to the Schloss and into the Chapel where the poor Empress lay in her coffin, which looked like a bed as it was so covered with flowers. You would have thought she was just going to a fête, or a soirée, her face was so calm and peaceful and had grown younger. There seemed not a wrinkle, and the eyes that used to stare so and look one through and through were closed, which gave her a gentler expression than I ever saw in life. Her false hair in ringlets on her brow, the line of the eyebrows and eyelashes carefully painted as in life - a golden myrtle wreath on her head and an ample tulle veil, very well arranged, flowing and curling about her head and neck and shoulders, hiding her chin, her hands folded, her bracelets on and her wedding ring. The cloth of gold train lined and trimmed with ermine which she wore for her golden wedding was very well folded and composed about her person and over her feet, and flowed far down the steps in front. She looked wonderfully well and really almost like a young person. I felt that if she could have seen herself she would have been pleased. She was 'the Empress' even in death and surrounded with all the stiff pomp and ceremony she loved so much.

Still I think there is something indescribably touching about that last sleep and the expression it sometimes gives to countenances. Only one I could not bear to think of, and it half kills me to remember, and that was my angel - her son.

Yesterday evening at 9 o'clock I was there again (but without the children) to take leave, and attend a short service before the closing of the coffin. The Schloss Chapel was suffocatingly hot and all filled with lights. There was a number of the family there, and I felt so lonely, so helpless among them all, and among all those Court officials. No one took me up or down stairs and one feels so set on one side, so forgotten, that to all my pain it gives me a feeling of bitterness difficult to describe. Dona means quite kindly, I suppose, but her grand condescending airs aggravate one so much...How all this would have affected Fritz. He would have felt his poor mother's death terribly. His kind and tender heart gave more affection than he received.

The Empress Frederick now hoped that at last she might be of some little use again, and she was especially desirous of taking up the Red Cross and hospital work, which had been continued since 1871 under the direction of the Empress Augusta. But here again she was to be disappointed, for the Emperor calmly ignored her, and made his wife, the Kaiserin, head of the various societies in which the Empress Augusta had taken so much interest. On January 13 the Empress Frederick wrote:

I am indeed distressed not to be able to send a line with General Gardener, but yesterday I had to receive people all day long; I could not find a moment for writing. I was going to tell you what has hurt my feelings so much. The Empress Augusta was at the head of the Red Cross Society and the *Vaterländischer Frauenverein*. These are very large societies and might be made exceedingly useful if well and efficiently worked and directed. Ever since 1870 it had been Fritz's great wish and his intention that I should succeed the Empress Augusta in this capacity whenever she felt too tired, etc., to go on with it, or in case of her death. I have for years taken trouble to prepare everything for this, as General v. Bronsart, Prof. Esmark, the Duke of Ratibor, Wegner and others can tell you; and when my affliction came, everyone who was not my direct enemy rejoiced at the thought that this branch of activity and usefulness would be left me, as everything else, *Louisenorden, Stiftfallen*, etc., has passed to Dona, who has all the social duties, representations, etc. I wrote to Louise of Baden about it last year. I also asked Count Seckendorff to speak to Kneseback. It was I who helped the Empress Augusta with the sick and wounded in 1864, 1866 and 1870-1871, and since then I have continued to study the subject. On arriving the other morning I spoke to William and said that I was ready now to take over these two Societies - of course, I did not mention the Augusta Hospital nor the Augusta Stift, as I thought Dona would have the patronage. He answered, 'You need not trouble yourself about it, my wife arranged with the Empress Augusta a year ago that she would take her place and also take Knesebeck into her service'.

Therefore my daughter-in-law and my mother-in-law both thought fit to ignore me and cut me out, and to prevent my having a work which would, of course, become very important in time and give me a certain amount of influence. My gentlemen and ladies are so annoyed and shocked that they can hardly believe it. You see how I am treated, dearest Mama, and how much the assurances of William are worth when he says he wishes to do everything to please me. It will take me a long while to get over this. Please say nothing about it; the thing is done. The Stöcker party, into whose hands all these things will fall, more or less triumph and rejoice at this new affront to me. The thing is done and in the most offensive way to my feelings, so there is no use saying a word more about it, it only makes it impossible for me in 'Charities', etc., to work with Dona - this I should refuse to do. I have a little experience, not so much as I should like, but certainly more and I believe, without vanity, a little more education and knowledge than Dona, so that it will be to the detriment of the interests of the public and also prevent these Societies from developing into what they might be. In the case of war, which Heaven prevent, I should simply have nothing to say, and be under Dona's orders, a thing I should most certainly not submit to. Pray excuse my troubling you with these affairs of mine - they are, of course, very insignificant compared with larger and more general interests; but I think you too will be sorry that I should have the grievous disappointment and this treatment at the hands of my mother-in-law and my children. Poor Empress, she is gone and I do not harbour any feeling against her that is not kind or right; on the contrary I feel that she was Fritz's mother and that he would have mourned her loss most sincerely, but after having been her daughter-in-law for over thirty years, I think that a proof of her confidence or affection would have been *versöhnend* after all I have gone through, and that it would also - in Dona and William's eyes - have done me good.

It now became evident that there were elements in Germany which were becoming more and more disatisfied with the dictatorial and autocratic regime of the Emperor and Prince Bismarck, especially with regard to their treatment of the press. Finally, utterance was given to these sentiments in the Reichstag by Prince Henry Carolath, who, in the January of 1890, voiced the growing dissatisfaction. On January 26 and January 31 the Empress Frederick wrote to her mother:

....I send you an extract from a newspaper containing a speech made in the Reichstag by Prince Carolath, to whom Fritz was always very kind, and who has the courage, as you will read, to censure a state of things which, while muzzling the press in every way, allows attacks on Fritz and me and you - such as contained in Uncle Ernest's vile pamphlet - to go unnoticed and people who protest against the lies in these pamphlets to be sent to prison for having libelled Uncle Ernest. It is very honourable of Prince Carolath to have spoken up; it will draw down the wrath of the Government and die Court upon him, but all honest and unprejudiced people will applaud him.

I send you [she wrote again on January 31] this article about Prince Carolath's excellent speech and Uncle Ernest's shameful pamphlets. The matter is not at rest and Uncle has caused Tempeltey to deny that he (Uncle) has ever written them. He boasted before of having done so, and I told you in 1887 of the mischievous effect of this pamphlet (the first one) and of how my three eldest children believed every word of what William then said. It sowed the seeds of distrust in William's mind against his father and me - this was fostered by the Bismarck party and false ambitious people, and so perverted William's ideas that it caused him to do all he did in 1887-1888. It will take years to clear the nonsense and lies out of his head and show people and things to him in their true light, as there is no one about him who could have a good and wise influence and also the authority to convince him of all the misapprehensions he was a victim of and still labours under. As long as Prince B. lives, as long as Herbert and H. v. Kessel remain about him and he believes them, of course, it would be hopeless to attempt to clear things up. They have weapons with which a simple outsider cannot compete; and besides it is of the utmost importance to them not to be shown up.

One must have patience and keep quite quiet and say nothing. The day will come perhaps when the truth will come to light, and to attempt to hurry on that day would be to spoil all....

Uncle Ernest has much to answer for. His behaviour to you, to Fritz and to me is simply disgraceful; it is too grievous, as we have all been so kind to him and really fond of him and I never thought he had a bad heart, though I always knew he was most unscrupulous and unprincipled and had an imagination which played him the most extraordinary tricks....

Meanwhile, Bismarck, ever the avowed opponent of Socialism, was seeking an amendment of the repressive Socialist Law of 1873, which definitely combated Socialism, in such a manner as to continue its provisions indefinitely. This brought about a sharp difference of opinion between him and the Emperor William, who pointedly remarked that so far from wishing to handicap the working classes, he wished to be like Frederick the Great *un roi des gueux*.[3] In spite of the Emperor's opposition, however, a bill for amending the law was introduced in October 1889, but was rejected on January 25, 1890, and parliament was now closed by the Emperor. A few days later, on February 4, the Emperor issued two rescripts in which he urgently recommended action for the improvement of the condition of the working classes, and towards this end suggested the co-operation of England, France, Belgium and Switzerland. It was on February 15 that the Empress wrote to Queen Victoria from Berlin:

I know absolutely nothing of what is going on - except what I read in the newspapers, or can only pick up from one of my friends. When I visit William, which is very seldom, we talk of the weather so that I am very much more out of everything than I was when I arrived here a girl of 17!! Of course, this is unavoidable since all that happened two years ago.

This playing at State Socialism appears very dangerous to me and always has! My beloved Fritz was so much against the passing of the Socialist Law! He foresaw what the Liberal party always foresaw and which has now happened, *i.e.* it would only encourage the growth of Socialism and teach the Socialists to organize themselves into a body secretly. This is now done. They have grown with extraordinary rapidity even since last year, and all the miners who sent a deputation to William last year have since joined the Socialists. For years Bismarck and his party have prevented William from seeing with other eyes than theirs. He (William) is absolutely ignorant! He has never studied politics or these questions, which are so serious! He hardly knows a single political man. Of the Liberals in Germany he does not know one!!! He always was taught to avoid all our friends, and now there is no one to tell him the truth. He never asks what his father thought and would have done, but takes the advice of the oddest and most incompetent people whom he meets by accident and who are mere amateurs.

How true is the proverb, 'Fools rush in where angels fear to tread ' This new *Staatsrath* is made up of the strangest and most incongruous elements and not one member of the Liberal party!! Men who have spent their lives amongst the working classes, who have watched the whole of the development of the so-called 'social question' (such a stupid word) for the last thirty years, who represent no class interests, and want absolutely nothing for themselves, and are anxious to save William from danger, for his father's sake, are ignored! They have no means of approaching him or of making their views heard, of giving a timely word of warning. Prince Bismarck, whose fault the present situation is, of course sees the rashness of what is done and does not approve it! He often talks of retiring - right and left! I think he counts upon William getting into a dreadful mess and a scrape, and his then being appealed to to put everything what he thinks straight again. He is so shrewd that he understands marvellously how to make the best for himself out of other people's mistakes - also out of his Sovereign. William is so green that he makes blunders which take one's breath away. He is perfectly delighted with himself, and the flattery which is continually lavished upon him makes him think himself a genius!! It makes me very unhappy to see my own child surrounded with dangers and rushing headlong into things of which he does not understand the drift! He listens to Hintzpeter on the subject of Christian

Socialism. His ideas are very good to listen to, but, alas, too doctrinaire and theoretical to be the only ones to go by. After all Hintzpeter is not a political man by profession. He is extremely kind and charitable to the poor, but he has a one-sided view of the question. William also listens to a Count Douglas (a great donkey) and Geheimrath v. Heyden, an amiable man, a painter, who was a miner thirty years ago. How all this will end I do not know! I think the proclamation most unconstitutional, and it is not counter-signed. No one knows what to make of it! Those who have, as I have, watched the unwholesome development of German politics for the last twenty years, cannot be surprised at the muddle and mess and confusion they are in now, and a young, totally inexperienced, totally ignorant man at the head of affairs, who is a very great despot and wields a great power and has no wise heads about him. Coquetting with the 'mob' and making independent men hold their tongues always has been part of Prince Bismarck's programme as it was the Emperor Napoleon III's.

However, if this curious Staatsrath only does a little good, one may be glad. But I fear there are troublous and stormy days ahead for Germany!...

The parliamentary elections early in 1890 resulted in an increased Socialist representation in the German parliament. Meanwhile, England, France, Belgium and Switzerland had considered the Emperor William's proposals for an international agreement on questions affecting the working classes, and a Labour Conference was mooted. On February 19 the Empress wrote:

Is it not rather embarrassing to know what to do about this international Labour Conference? I think it is very imprudent and ill-advised to come forward with an international scheme before having privately enquired whether the different Governments find it convenient or possible to accept proposals! It is true the Labour question exists in every country alike, but still under very different conditions. A Conference of this kind, or a Congress, is very different from a 'postal telegraph' or 'monetary' Conference - or from a scientific Congress! One must be a very great authority on these subjects, or possess a vast experience to venture on such a step as a proposal to settle this question. To stir it up without arriving at some very striking, important and satisfactory result, is the worst thing that could be done. It raises expectations doomed to be disappointed and excites the masses instead of calming them, which is the very thing to be avoided and will lead to a struggle here - to coercion - and perhaps violence - and then reaction. Prince Bismarck sees this most likely - does he wish it or not? Will it profit him and his party in the end or not? I cannot tell you! I think Cardinal Manning makes a great mistake in extolling William's step to such a degree. How differently beloved Fritz would have gone to work and handled these delicate dangerous questions! There is such a difference between courage and foolhardiness. How much study and knowledge, experience and wisdom and good counsel are necessary for great reforms! Why not assemble the best heads in Europe to discuss these questions unofficially and privately - such as Sir L. Mallet, M. de Lavalaye, M. Anatole Leroy-Beaulieu, and many others? The question would ripen gradually, and by consulting the German Liberals, who are the most learned of all, one might arrive at a conclusion which William's Government might submit to the Reichstag. Now I fear there will be much confusion and very little result. There is too intimate a connection between economic questions and the Labour question to be able to solve one quite without the other! I think such men as Lord Brassey and Lord Armstrong would admit that Prince Bismarck's protectionist policy, which William admires so much without understanding it, is at the bottom of many of the evils we are suffering under - the high prices of food, etc., which are dreadful for the working classes, of course make low wages much worse, and consequently the amount of hours of work too great. But it is too vast a subject to approach in a few words. Fritz and I never ceased to study it, therefore it is nothing new to me! 'Look before you leap' I should like to write in big letters over William's table - though it would be of very little use, I fear.

*Feb. 20*

Prince Bismarck and his wife came to see me yesterday. He spoke a long while on the subject of William's newest coup! He also spoke of retiring soon, as he could not keep pace with innovations so suddenly resolved on and carried out in such a hurry and on the advice of people he thought in no way competent to give it. I daresay he quite means what he says in this instance, but I do not suppose his resignation would be accepted. It seems to me that he was quite *de bonne foi* with William and that he tried his best to dissuade him from an experiment which he thinks not only a great risk, but for which he sees no likelihood of success. Seeing that William was bent on it, especially at the instigation of Hintzpeter, who told William he would find it 'a mine of popularity for himself and it would make him a great man, etc.', and a Count Douglas (such a stupid man), a M. de Berlepsch (whom therefore Prince Bismarck instantly proposed as Minister), and the painter, G. v. Heyden, Prince Bismarck, as he said, concentrated his endeavours on trying to make the step as harmless as he could; he re-wrote the Erlass and he begged that everything diplomatic might be left out of the proposed international Congress or Conference. So far, I think Prince Bismarck was very wise, and acted very loyally towards William, and I could only agree with him! Of course, he did not discuss principles of policy; with those you know I could not agree. But I certainly think the advice he gave William in this case was prudent and sensible and practical and I am very sorry it was not taken.

I thought Prince Bismarck looked remarkably strong and well and inclined to take things very philosophically. He is exceedingly fond of William and he never was of Fritz (this is quite natural), but I fancy he is uneasy at the very great self-confidence and the *naïveté* with which he exercises his will and takes responsibilities, and also at the curious people who have access to him and are listened to.

Please look upon all this as confidential. I watch all these things as a perfect outsider and impartial observer.

*Feb. 21*

Since I wrote the above I see that poor Sir Louis Mallet is dead. How very very sorry I am, he was such a distinguished man !....

I have just received your dear letter by messenger, for which so many thanks. Of course, everything done for the working classes for their real good and their real interest is a step in the right direction and one everybody would hail with pleasure. But William has never troubled his head in the least about the poor, or the working classes, and knows absolutely nothing about them, or he would have consulted more people, tried to obtain more information and have carefully prepared the step he has taken. He has never mentioned affairs or politics before me since 1888. I should most certainly never make a remark before him - or offer an opinion if it is not asked - after the way in which I have been treated - the slights and insults and impertinences which I have had to swallow! I should neither be understood nor listened to, therefore I could do no good! Perhaps the time may come, but certainly it has not arrived.

He seeks no advice nor cares to know what his own parents thought on these subjects - he fancies he is gifted with supreme wisdom, therefore one must let him alone. Perhaps he will all the sooner be inclined later to see things as they are, then I shall certainly not refuse to make myself of use to him, but to take the initiative would be a great mistake on my part and a want of proper pride - and that is the last thing one clings to when all else is taken from one. The adulation and flattery which is heaped upon him you would hardly believe. His mother is the only one who will not stoop to this - and is naturally considered a bore in consequence. There are so many who are anxious to get rid of me as the last remnant of Fritz's reign and of his ideas, that it is only by remaining perfectly quiet and passive that I can be safe from their accusations, their attacks and intrigues, and their constant *Heizerei* and *rapportage* at the Schloss.

I think, however, on the whole it is better and not worse, and that they are less bent on persecuting me than they were, but the terrain here is perfectly intolerable, - personal ambition, spite and jealousy and intrigue are rife, and displayed with still more impudence than they used to be. I think everyone feels this! But as they see that I want nothing and do not care to have so-called influence, and have no curiosity to know their doings and their secrets, and that they cannot frighten or drive me away with their shameful calumnies, they rather leave off throwing stones at me - and think me harmless and *sans conséquence*, which of course makes William and Dona less suspicious and on the defensive, or on the look out for offences, which really was quite unbearable.

When we meet we are quite friendly and comfortable, and no one sees the wounds and the daggers in my heart - nor how profoundly I feel all the wrongs Fritz and I have suffered.

A fortnight later, March 7, she wrote:

> What a pity it is the *Times* makes such superficial and prejudiced remarks about our elections! The *Freisinnige* are not republicans or democrats at all - they are as like English Whigs as they can be - they want constitutional government - as little state interference as possible - and free trade, no Socialism, no repressive laws, no persecution of Jews or Catholics. Of course they do grumble about the army budget sometimes and they oppose the taxes on wheat, bread, tea and coffee. They are specially detested by Prince Bismarck and consequently calumniated in every possible way. I do not see why the *Times* should stick up for such unfairness. The *Cologne Gazette* had an article on the 4th of this month which I really think was the most abominable one I ever read. I sadly fear it was inspired by Prince Bismarck's entourage.
>
> I fear poor William thinks all will be very easy and that he has only to dictate his wishes, etc. - a rather childlike idea. He is most despotic and arbitrary in all his instincts and one cannot well govern that way nowadays.

The path of an autocrat is strewn with difficulties, but even if he succeeds in trampling them down he can never work with or under another autocrat. The Emperor had learnt from Bismarck the secrets of autocratic government and was beginning to assert himself, with the inevitable result that they were gradually coming to loggerheads over the Socialist question. On March 15 the Empress wrote:

> Today these delegates arrive on their curious mission. How one does bless a Constitution like the British one, when one sees a young man, totally without knowledge and experience, playing the despot, without anything to prevent him from running into danger or mischief. It would be a curious Nemesis if, for all his past sins, Prince Bismarck were to fall, just the very time he happened to be in the right - not one older man or older relation is there to give a little timely advice, to warn and give a gentle hint, both in political and important matters, or in family and court matters. If we could have had William to ourselves the last four years, or if I had him even now, a great deal could be prevented, and he would not be as blind and ignorant as he is. I am sorry to say poor Dona is not a help but an obstacle. Her pride is so great and she thinks she knows better than everyone, because she is the Empress, and she is always on the defensive and ridiculously *exigeante*. The flattery that is lavished on both of them is enough to turn any lady's head and it is no wonder that hers is turned. They never ask or consult me on any one subject, great or small; but only invite me to their family dinner, just as they would an aunt or a cousin. They have not a single wise or steady head about them; some very respectable and well-meaning people, others who are dangerous and intriguing, but not a single superior man or woman.

I am quite away and out of everything and know very little of what goes on at the Schloss. I only meet William or Dona at family dinners, amongst all the others, which, of course, are painful occasions to me, and I try to make the hour pass pleasantly and hide all my sad and bitter thoughts and feelings.

Dona enjoys her position intensely and her whole face expresses the most intense satisfaction. She is convinced that all William and she do and think and say is perfect, and this is certainly a state of beatitude. She meddles in everything the family does, every little trifle is reported to her, and she orders and directs in a way very galling for the others from so young a person.

Three days later, on March 18, 1890, Prince Bismarck suddenly resigned, and the Emperor appointed General Georg von Caprivi in his place as Chancellor. Meanwhile, Queen Victoria had received the Empress Frederick's letter of the 15th, and in her reply had asked why it was that she had been 'so keen' on Dona's marriage to her son William. On March 22 the Empress replied:

....You say: why did I wish so much for William's marriage and fight so hard to obtain it? Because amongst those young Princesses I knew (as it was not thought advisable he should marry a cousin) Dona seemed to me the most likely to make an excellent wife and mother. We had a great esteem and affection for her father, who had great confidence in us and with whom we were so intimate. I then hoped and thought she might be grateful and affectionate to me and show me confidence - in that my hopes have been completely disappointed! She has quite forgotten, or does not like to remember, or really does not understand what she owes me. She has a great sense of duty, but she does not seem to see what her duty towards me is! She is an excellent wife and though not a judicious yet a devoted mother! I am glad to see her so happy - and that she and William and the children are all so prosperous, etc., and of course I am thankful for that, but for myself, my comfort in my loneliness and sorrow, as a support, they, alas, do not exist! This may change in time, though I much doubt it. This is not the moment to try and open their eyes on the subject of all I have had to endure, which they simply ignore. If other people surrounded them and could explain it all to them and show them how infamous the conduct of so many towards us was in 1887-1888, against me in 1889, and how untrue were all those accusations, I daresay they would feel sorry and also feel differently and behave differently towards me, and I might then forgive it all, though I could not forget it.

I cannot approve of the way in which Prince Bismarck's resignation came about and think it in some ways a dangerous experiment, as I do raising this so-called 'Social question' at this moment! I am afraid nothing good will come of it! The love of playing the despot and of showing off is very great. General Caprivi is a General of whom Fritz thought a great deal, and whom he had always hoped to have some day later as Minister of War! He is an honest, straightforward, respectable man, of great energy - a very stubborn and determined will, not given to any compromises and rather violent. I should not think he understood politics in the least, but he is incapable of saying what he does not mean, or of an intrigue of any kind!

The system Bismarck [created] was intensely corrupt and bad, - this, however, is not the reason that William wanted the change, and this he does not even see through. The genius and prestige of Prince Bismarck might still have been useful and valuable for Germany and for the cause of peace, especially with so inexperienced and imprudent a Sovereign, and I fear that he will be missed in that respect, as I also fear that the combination which is to replace him will not be strong enough! William fancies he can do everything himself - you know he cannot - a little modesty and *Selbsterkenntniss* would show him that he is not the genius or the Frederick the Great he imagines, and I fear he will get into trouble. If Prince B. were to retire - a Ministry could have replaced him with Prince Chlodwig Hohenlohe as Chancellor, Hatzfeldt as Foreign Minister, Caprivi as Minister of War and a Liberal as Minister for Home Affairs - we should have had nothing to fear, and could not look upon Prince Bismarck's retirement as a misfortune! Wise and experienced and conciliatory men would have had the confidence of Germany and of Europe, and in time, I am sure, would have had the best influence on William, and the barrier which exists between him and me would also soon have melted away, and all the eminent men in Germany who were kept away by the machinations of the Bismarck system would gradually have come forward, their opinions would have been heard and discussed, and an era of peace and stability would have commenced such as Fritz's reign would have been! Now I see nothing but confusion - sudden resolutions not sufficiently considered - suddenly carried out, with a truly Bismarckian contempt for people's feelings, but without the *coup d'oeil de maître* which Bismarck often had! What was wrong in him and what would be right to do now, William does not see and there is no one to tell him, as all those are kept away, or have been purposely discredited in William's eyes, who could have advised him! You can imagine that I am not very happy or comfortable about the state of things....

Three days later (March 25, 1890) the Empress wrote:

Prince and Princess Bismarck came and took farewell, and General Caprivi paid me a long visit, and I thought him extremely sensible and only hope he may succeed; but he is a very conscientious man, and thoroughly in earnest, and if William means (as he says sometimes) merely to have people who 'obey him' and 'carry out his orders', I fear he will find it very difficult, almost impossible, to fulfil all the duties of his office, which in the eyes of the nation has an immense responsibility! I am afraid William is a most thorough despot and has some very queer ideas on this subject in his head. Prince Bismarck told me much that was very interesting to hear! He did not exactly complain, but I think he feels very deeply that he has not been treated with the consideration due to his age and position. We parted amicably and in peace, which I am glad of, as I should have been sorry - having suffered so much all these long years under the system that it should appear as if I had any spirit of revenge, which I really have not. Many feel the son's coming departure as a deliverance. I think General Verdy Duvernoy was the principal instrument in getting rid of Prince Bismarck....

The fall of Bismarck, however, did not bring about any of those political or social changes for which the Empress Frederick had hoped. As she wrote to Queen Victoria on March 29:

....The confusion to me seems extreme, and the state of things most anxious and unsatisfactory. Changes in those things which were most to be regretted in Prince Bismarck's administration are not contemplated, as I hear William wishes to have the son [Herbert Bismarck] back again soon. It would be a very great mistake. The only good I see in all that is being done, is having so honest a man as General Caprivi at the head of affairs, but I doubt very much whether he can or will remain.

The Conference, I believe, has worked quite well, but what the result will be, and how much of that result will be carried out and put into practice, is another question, to which I think but few can give a sanguine answer....

Whether or not the Empress was right in believing that her son desired to retain the services of the younger Bismarck as Secretary for Foreign Affairs, Count Herbert resigned on April 1, and was succeeded in that office by Baron Marschall von Bieberstein. A week later, on April 8, the Empress Frederick wrote to Queen Victoria:

I cannot tell you much about what is going on here in the way of politics, but I look with alarm to the future! Everything must be done in a hurry and be startling! and emanate or seem to emanate from one source! I think a Ministry composed of Jules Verne with Lord Randolph Churchill and Lord C. Beresford as steadiest elements, and with General Boulanger and a few African travellers (poor Mr. Gordon Gumming, if he were alive) and certainly Richard Wagner, if he were alive, would be the sort that would best suit the taste in high quarters, and we might no doubt pass through phases most refreshing and sensational in their novelty and originality, and adventures of all sorts would not be wanting. Sometimes one does not know whether to laugh or to cry! I wonder how long Caprivi will last and what he will be able to do! He is a very steady man, honest and determined, very conservative and very military!

The new Minister of Foreign Affairs has never so much as written his name down in my book, nor has Herbert Bismarck announced his *Demission* or been to take leave, which is very rude, as he was Fritz's Minister, but I am heartily glad that I shall be spared having to see him, or speak to him!....

It seems to me [she added in a postscript] that the German Emperor is to be converted into a sort of Tsar, and Germany to be governed by ukases.

Bismarck had fallen, William II was now supreme, but the event, instead of bringing the Empress Frederick back into any position where she might usefully give service to the country of her adoption, resulted in her being, except for one brief and transient mission, relegated to the furthest possible point in the German political and social background.

## NOTES

1 Herr von Lynker, Court-Marshal to Emperor William II.
2 *The Empress Frederick: A Memoir*, p. 328.
3 The ex-Kaiser William II's *My Memoirs*, p. 37.

# XVI. Caprivi's Chancellorship

THE fall of Bismarck, wide though its influence was upon the destiny of Germany, made for the moment little change in the life of the Empress Frederick. It was true that she had now no longer an inveterate enemy at the head of the German Government, for the new Chancellor, General von Caprivi, wisely abstained from interfering in matters outside the scope of his office. But her son, the Emperor William, although freed from the influence of Bismarck, showed little sign of any slightly kindlier attitude towards her; and in all other respects her position was unchanged. For her part, the Empress maintained her attitude of non-interference in state affairs, and occupied herself not only with the many works of charity in which she had always taken a keen interest, but also with those artistic activities which gave her so much pleasure. One form that this activity took was the building of a house after her own heart, and it was at Cronberg that she acquired an estate of a villa and a few acres from Dr Steibel, the son-in-law of Mr Reiss, a Manchester manufacturer, who had given it the name of the Villa Reiss. Adjoining properties were also bought, so that the estate was enlarged to about 250 acres. The Villa Reiss was practically demolished, and in its place there gradually arose a model *domus regalis* which bore upon its front porch the inscription 'Frederici Memoriae'. The house was designed by a celebrated German architect, Herr Ihne, but was regarded by people in Germany as being rather an English country-house than a German castle, and there was some truth in this assumption, for the architect had been advised to go to England by the Empress to study the more modern houses. 'Friedrichshof', as the Empress's new residence was called, was completed in the year 1893, but from 1889 to that date its planning, decoration and development were a constant source of interest to the Empress. It was here that she now housed the large number of art treasures that she had acquired, and there was ample reason for the comparison of the galleries and saloons of the ground floor with the finest of the German museums.

Here, at Cronberg, the Empress soon made hosts of real friends among the inhabitants, and in an extremely short space of time began to be regarded by them very much in the same way as Queen Victoria was regarded at Balmoral.

The Empress's retirement to Cronberg seemed to emphasise her determination to give her enemies no excuse for accusing her of meddling with political affairs, yet she still continued to take a vivid interest in all that concerned the welfare of Germany and her native land. Particularly did the activities of her son, the Emperor William, engage her attention, and when, on May 6, 1890, he opened the new Parliament with a speech in which, while professing an ardent desire for peace, he asked for 18,000,000 marks for the increase of the German army, the Empress wrote to Queen Victoria four days later:

....The speech at the opening of the Reichstag has created much disappointment in this part of Germany. Not only were people astonished at the change of ministers not being mentioned, but many another thing that was expected and hoped for was not spoken of, such as the determination not to renew the Socialist Law, the restitution of the *Guelph fond*, the abolition of the terrible and useless passport vexations in Alsace on the French frontier; things that are just and necessary, that Fritz always intended to carry out, and which would strengthen the present government and make it popular, though no great reforms in themselves....

It seemed, indeed, as if it was still the intention of the Emperor William to ignore all that the Emperor Frederick had planned or projected. It was therefore a pleasant and touching experience for the Empress Frederick to learn that her husband's memory was revered in Berlin and that the town wished to erect a monument to his memory. The Emperor William, however, refused to permit any such thing, and it was with feelings of exasperation and sorrow that the Empress wrote to Queen Victoria on June 3, 1890:

The town of Berlin wished, as you know, to erect a monument to our beloved Fritz; it is the first time they have done so for one of their sovereigns! They have the money already! They informed me of this and I told them how much it touched me, and how this token of loyal affection would have touched him much more than a monument ordered, executed and paid for by the government. They sent in their plans and have been waiting over four months for an answer, and now William has refused to grant them the permission and says that the state will do it! This pains me very much indeed, as such a spontaneous demonstration of respect to Fritz's memory is a very different thing from a state order, which is just as one would order a bridge, or new barracks, and it ought to have been gratefully and graciously accepted. He might also have asked me, or let me know, or have consulted me! The town of Berlin said the monument should be made according to my wishes. Now, of course, all is spoilt! William ignores my existence in everything.

Queen Victoria's answer was to invite her daughter to England, and to point out that as Berlin was already erecting a hospital in memory of the

Emperor Frederick a second monument was perhaps superfluous. To this the Empress Frederick replied on June 13, 1890:

So many thanks for your dear letter by messenger, which I will answer today, as we leave tonight and I fear I shall have no time to write tomorrow. What day may we arrive in England? The 28th? You return from Balmoral on the 26th, I believe?....
I think you misunderstood me about the monument for my beloved Fritz. The town of Berlin gave a sum of money on October 18th, 1888, to found an institution which was to bear his name. I gave it to die children's hospital which is now being built. This was a different thing! This was to be a large equestrian statue! The State has ordered one of the Emperor William, and the town of Berlin voted the money already last year to erect one to Fritz. They had to ask leave and they did not wait a few months, as I said last time, but a whole year for the answer, which has now been given in the shape of a refusal, after I had told them how pleased and grateful I was at the idea. That I should feel hurt and aggrieved, you cannot wonder, as it again appears as if W. did not wish historical evidence of Fritz's popularity to go down to posterity. As history books for all the schools in Prussia are arranged by the Ministerium, his life, his character, his views and short reign can be made as little of as is thought advisable, and all can be coloured as the present Government please! as they did about his illness and his Diary, whereas I should like the truth known and justice done to him and his friends, which implies its being done indirectly to me also. If the Government wish to erect a monument themselves they might have done so and yet have allowed the town to carry out its intentions. I call it most autocratic and calculated only to annoy. *La raison du plus fort est toujours la meilleure* and it is quite curious to see how all W. does meets with approval in England; a glance at the *Times* shows this, and it is not surprising that he should therefore think himself infallible and his conduct towards his father and mother without fault; he does not see how he abuses the power so prematurely put into his hands.

The Empress's dissatisfaction with the way in which she had been relegated to the background is further evidenced in her letter to Queen Victoria of December 13, 1890:

Many thanks too for the paper about Greece, which I return, having read it with much interest. You say that for the first time I have written to you on a political matter since 1888. It does indeed seem strange to me that now I am 50 I am completely cast off from the official world - not a single official person ever comes near me and what used to be *mein tägliches Brod* has quite ceased. How I used to work for Fritz and how he used to tell me everything! Now I might be buried alive, for, of course, no one comes near me. As matters are, it is far better so, as one would not like to be responsible for even the smallest unfortunate result. All the more, I can look about and study and pick up information on different subjects, and my former friends not in official positions are far more outspoken now than they used to be. I do not run after the official world - on the contrary I avoid them; I am too proud to ask any questions if I am not told things or asked my opinion.

Influence on the course of events I have not the smallest, or faintest, but as a member of the thinking public I do not stand alone and have many who care to exchange opinions with me. At home I used to follow with such interest all in which dear Papa and you were concerned. There was a time when the Emperor William and the Empress Augusta used to talk over everything with us. Now that my experience is perhaps worth something, there is a dead silence and one's existence is forgotten.

I have not the faintest ambition to play *un rôle* in the present regime, indeed I should scorn to do so after all that has happened, but it is impossible to lose one's interest in the affairs of this country, and in the course of peace and progress in the rest of the world. When I go to Italy or to Greece, it is a pleasure to talk with King Umberto and with Willy of Greece. I do not speak of home, as of course what goes on there I watch with the same affectionate interest as since I was a child.

For the first time in two years the Empress now expressed her point of view on a question of foreign policy. Apart from Germany, England and Russia, the two countries in which she had been most interested during the preceding lustrum had been Bulgaria and Greece. In Bulgaria after the abdication of her protégé, Prince Alexander, Ferdinand of Saxe-Coburg-Gotha had ascended the throne, and in spite of plots and intrigues was gradually consolidating his position.

In Greece the Empress Frederick's interest had been quickened by the marriage of her daughter Sophie to the Duke of Sparta. The province of Macedonia, still under Turkish rule, was seething with unrest, and both Bulgaria and Greece cast covetous eyes on the land of Macedon.

To her letter of December 13, 1890, the Empress added the comments:

With regard to Greece, I should like to add one word. The most dangerous and ticklish question for peace is in the East and the one that is always turning up again is the Macedonian question. Both Bulgaria and Greece will never resign a claim to a portion of this country, and never be friends until this is once settled and arranged. Once Sandro had made a most excellent plan of how both could be contented in the event of this province being lost to Turkey. I often wonder whether England, Austria, Germany and Italy could not try to arrange the Macedonian difficulty peaceably for these smaller powers and thus do away with a dangerous apple of discord which may set the East at odds at any moment, and give the Russians the much-desired opportunity for interfering.

I saw a friend of mine the other day who is on the Committee for the Anatolian Railways at Constantinople, and he told me he thought the

Bulgarians the most promising of all the Balkan nationalities and thought the State was capable of greatly developing and having a very good future before it - it had made great strides and it owed everything to Sandro.

The attitude of her son still caused the Empress bitter heartburnings, especially when his arrogant conduct was extended to his sister Sophie, the Duchess of Sparta, who had been on a visit to Berlin to discuss her conversion to the Greek Church a project that the Emperor strongly opposed, going so far as to say she would never be allowed to visit Germany again. On December 27, 1890, the Empress wrote:

Yesterday evening a messenger arrived, who leaves again today at two, and brought me your dear letter, for which many affectionate thanks. I thought it was impossible that we should not think alike on this subject. I hope too that it will blow over when W. has been made to see that he cannot carry out threats of the kind if they are ever so solemnly made (as these were) without consequences which must destroy the peace of the family for ever and show him in the light of a tyrant and bully, which I think, in spite of his love of showing his power and authority, he would not like. That such heartlessness and *Rücksichtslosigkeit* have left a deep impression on me you cannot wonder, as it has again revealed to me the spirit in which I have been treated these three years, when I was striving to dwell as little as possible on his conduct, hoping that it would improve. Peace is the only thing I hope for. Gratitude, affection, confidence, sympathy, I shall never get from that quarter. They do not understand me - they did not understand their dear father. They do not want me they are full of suspicion against me, though they might know that I interfere in nothing and am far too proud to do so. These sentiments burst out on the smallest provocation, and as it is impossible for me to know and guess who it is who perpetually is trying to repeat gossip to W. and tell him things to irritate him against me, though I know it is the interest of many, I shall always be exposed to this sort of thing. But I feel his rudeness and undutiful conduct to me far less than I do his rudeness to his sister, who has gone away most deeply disgusted and hurt. He has no heart and Dona has no tact, and they are both so convinced of their own perfection that they will ran with their heads against a wall some day in all *naïveté*.

The best course now and the one I shall certainly adopt is to drop the matter altogether. What the King of Greece will do or write, of course, I do not know.

In the preceding month a fourth son had been born to William II., which led the Empress Frederick to comment:

I also think a daughter would have been an advantage and I asked W whether he would not have liked a daughter. He answered 'Girls were useless creatures, he did not want one and far preferred to be without'. For him I daresay boys (Recruits) to be ordered about are far more to his taste but some day to provide them all with means and with homes will be no easy task....

The year 1891 opened for the Empress Frederick without any indication that life was likely to be smoother for her. She had now passed her fiftieth year, and, as many observers noted, was growing more and more like her mother, the septuagenarian Queen Victoria. On February 22, 1891, the Empress wrote to her mother:

> I get told here very often *Comme vous ressemblez à la Reine d'Angleterre and I always answer Cela n'est pas flatteur pour ma mè, je voudrais lui ressembler, - ce qui la rappelle c'est mon deuil, qui est hélas le même − qu'elle porte depuis 29 ans.*
>
> You say that I have not inherited from you the love of looking about at things, but I have a special reason. First of all you always live amongst beautiful things, therefore you do not feel the want so much *de vous meubler la tête* as I do, who do not live in so interesting a milieu. Then you never had the time or opportunity to make art a special study, and lastly you can get everything arranged for you, whereas I must direct the arrangements of my house and myself, and choose and collect every single thing, and cannot leave it to other people. There are but few at Berlin who quite share and understand my taste, while in London and at Paris there are hundreds, and a great many in Italy. In Germany there are very few real amateurs and collectors, and this taste is nearly confined to the Artists and Professors. But the interest has greatly developed in Germany during the last twenty years, and the Exhibitions do a great deal of good.

The Empress's life of quiet routine at Cronberg was, however, now interrupted by one last active participation in an affair of diplomatic importance. It was at the request of her son, the German Emperor, that in the early part of 1891 the Empress paid a semi-official visit to Paris. The Emperor was at this time desirous of testing the real feeling of the Parisian populace towards Germany, and thought that the best means would be a visit by a near relative. The Empress Frederick had paid several visits incognito to Paris since the conclusion of the Franco-German War, and on each occasion had been well received; there was therefore some reason for the assumption that she would be the most likely member of the German imperial family to sow the seed of a *rapprochement* between the Empire and the neighbouring Republic.

Accordingly, on February 19, 1891, the Empress, accompanied by her daughter Princess Margaret and a considerable suite, arrived in Paris. That day an official communique was issued to point out that the Empress was visiting Paris to thank those artists who had promised to exhibit pictures at the forthcoming art exhibition in Berlin, of which she was patron. The first three or four days in Paris passed off well. The Empress visited a large number of studios and picture galleries as well as one or two of the curiosity shops for which Paris is famous.

The German press, however, now began to hint that the visit was a move towards a reconciliation between the two countries - a hint that aroused the Boulangist party and caused somewhat inflammatory speeches to be delivered in Paris. This spark was fanned into flame when a day or two later it became known that the Empress had visited the Palace at Saint Cloud (which had been destroyed by the Germans in 1870) as well as Versailles (where her husband had been stationed) and the neighbouring battlefields. Memories of *L'Année Terrible* now surged back, and when it became known that a laurel wreath placed at the foot of the monument to Henri Regnault, the celebrated French painter, who had been killed in the last desperate sortie from Paris, had been removed on the occasion of the visit of the Empress to the Ministry of Fine Arts, all attempts at politeness and courtesy were abandoned. Passions now blazed up to fever point The French press thundered against these '*Insultes aux Français*', and the Empress, avoiding the tempest, left hurriedly for London.

But the storm did not abate with her departure. The French artists now withdrew their promises to exhibit at Berlin, and the Berlin press retaliated with uncontrolled abuse of their Gallic neighbours.

This was the last intervention of the Empress Frederick in public affairs, and for months the consequences of it caused her the deepest distress and mortification. On March 29, while still at Sandringham staying with her brother, the Prince of Wales, she wrote to her mother:

I shall continue to be much tormented about all the reports circulated at Berlin purporting to come from Paris and to be written by people of the Diplomatic Corps and notables from Paris - such lies. It seems at first they feared in Berlin that Count Münster (the German Ambassador in Paris) had not quite understood the situation, but they are now satisfied on this score and all the blame is laid on my entourage. Really it is too bad.

I had insisted on going to see the French artists in spite of the warning and entreaties of 'the people whose business it was to keep up the *bonne entente* between France and Germany'. This is a wilful distortion of facts. Count Münster told me to go to Bouguerau and to Detaille, which I did. Emile Wauters, Madrazo and Munkaczy are not Frenchmen, but a Belgian, who wears the German *Pour le Mérite*, a Spaniard and an Austrian. Messrs Lefèbvre and Galland are Frenchmen - the latter I have known for years and have often visited, though Münster has never heard his name....

Other crimes are that I went into shops and bought nothing. This is not true; I went into two jewellers' shops - people who had worked for me and whose bills had just been paid. I am supposed to have gone to all sorts of Jewish collectors. I went to see the great Spitzer collection, and he certainly was a Jew when he was alive....It has annoyed me horribly....I think at 50 and after having seen so much of the world I might be credited with enough tact not to make a fool of myself as they represent me to have done....

A few days later, on April 3, she wrote from Buckingham Palace:

....Hatzfeldt is also much annoyed about the nonsense they believe at Berlin about my visit (to Paris) and that my entourage are blamed for the impression my visit is supposed to have made, which in reality it did not, but only was described by the bad press as having done so. I hope we shall hear no more about it. But I did not cut the Russian Ambassador, nor would I have dreamt of doing such a thing....

Gradually the storm died down, and the Empress resumed her interest in matters of artistic interest. Two such examples of her devotion to art may be mentioned. In her letter to Queen Victoria of April 2, 1891, after a visit to the National Gallery in London, she wrote to her mother:

....I went today to see the National Gallery and admired all its glories again. It is the best chosen, the best lit and arranged collection of fine pictures in the world, and that is saying a great deal. Of course the gallery is not a large one, but I think one enjoys it all the more, whereas the Louvre is quite overwhelming.

This afternoon I went to Mr Alma Tadema's studio. His whole house is a work of art imagined, planned, and arranged by him and the scene from which his lovely pictures are taken....

Four months later the Empress, who had now returned to Germany, wrote to her mother a letter in which is given her opinion of the 'Marseillaise'.

I am very sorry [she wrote on August 26, 1891, with reference to the visit of the French fleet to Portsmouth, when the officers dined with Queen Victoria at Osborne] that the horrid Marseillaise should now be the French Anthem, associated as it is with the horrors of the Revolution and used by the Socialists as the symbol of violence and all their mad Labour principles. A respectable Government, such as a peace- and order-loving Republic ought to be, does not choose a melody to which any such stain is attached as '*Aux armes citoyens, Formez vos Bataillons, Marchons, Marchons, qu'un sang impur*, etc. (which meant the blood of kings, aristocrats and priests and now means that of capitalists, bourgeois and Jews). *Tremblez, tyrans et vous perfides, L'opprobre de tons les partis; Tremblez, vos projets parricides Vont enfin recevoir leur prix, Tout est soldat pour vous combattre*' etc., etc.

I must say I felt sorry that you should have to get up to such strains as that, though you had no other way of doing the French honour and most people forget the words of that savage song and the occasions on which it was used, and what wretches sang it....

The Empress's relations with Bismarck after the Chancellor's fall now began to assume a mellowness and sympathy which had never been known during his term of office. A slight indication of these changed relations may be gathered from a reported conversation between Busch and Bismarck about this period.

I took the liberty [Busch records] to ask further what sort of woman the Crown Princess was, and whether she had much influence over her husband. 'I think not', the Count said; 'and as to her intelligence, she is a clever woman; clever in a womanly way. She is not able to disguise her feelings, or at least not always. I have cost her many tears, and she could not conceal how angry she was with me after the annexations (that is to say of Schleswig and Hanover). She could hardly bear the sight of me, but that feeling has now somewhat subsided. She once asked me to bring her a glass of water, and as I handed it to her she said to a lady-in-waiting who sat near and whose name I forget, "He has cost me as many tears as there is water in this glass". But that is all over now.'

This incident about the glass of water evidently much impressed Bismarck, for he told it to Busch again some months later, when he said of the Crown Princess, 'She is in general a very clever person, and really agreeable in her way, but she should not interfere in politics'.

The Empress for her part watched with interest Bismarck's activities, and on January 6, 1891, she wrote to Queen Victoria:

....I have just seen some people who have been staying with Prince Bismarck, and they say he never was so well and strong and active, and is very cheerful and in good spirits, but that his relations with his son Herbert are not nearly so confidential, affectionate or intimate as they were, and a certain coldness has set in. Bismarck is working hard at his Memoirs. I have no doubt they will be strange and piquant....

In the remaining nine years of the Empress's life the Empress never interfered in political matters, and her letters for this period are mainly full of domestic or family details. She did not, however, lose her interest in her eldest son's actions and speeches, and it was with a keenly critical eye that she read his orations in the columns of the German press. Whilst refraining from any public comment upon his oratorical efforts, tactful or otherwise, she was, in correspondence with her mother, frank in criticism of her son's many official utterances. One such speech he delivered at Erfurt in September 1891 on the eve of the meeting of the Socialist congress at that town.

The speech at Erfurt [she wrote] was another of those unfortunate imprudences of William these are daily specimens, Caprivi cannot prevent them. William neither understands or values advice, he neither asks nor takes it, and as he is in many ways very green for his age, constant blunders and *bévues* are the result. *Ich dulde keinen neben mir Jeder der gegen mich ist, werde ich zerschmettern.*[1]

He is so vain, and all the flattery has made him so conceited that he delights in making speeches on all occasions, and they are usually very *mal à propos* and have to be corrected and arranged afterwards so that they should not make too startling an impression. One is inclined to smile if it were not so serious and so dangerous. Fritz was so prudent and careful and wrote out his speeches before and changed them over and over again. Emperor William I was *not* very happy in his speeches but they were rare. His letters as you know were funnily blunt and the *tournure de phrase* not very happy, so that they often offended people very much, which he did not at all intend, as he was so very civil and courteous and meant to be kind although a military despot, and he was such a gentleman and *grand seigneur*. His great age and prestige made people take differently what, coming from a young man, who has not done anything particular in the world to boast of, sounds differently. His way of speaking of Napoleon, though he was certainly *un fléau*, I thought most unbecoming, for he was a great historical personage and soldier and a vanquished foe, and after 1870-71 it does not seem necessary to say another word; but as you will perceive by this little newspaper cutting this speechifying is encouraged by a certain silly party who find it quite to their taste, though it offends that of all more cultivated people.

The Emperor William, however, did not confine his remarkable statements to the spoken word, and on the occasion of his visit to Munich in November gave evidence of his Caesarian ambitions when he wrote in the book at the Town Hall the classical tag:

Suprema Lex Regis Voluntas [2]

All parties without exception were offended by the Emperor's phrase, and the opinion of the Empress coincided with the opinion of the majority of Germans when she wrote to her mother on November 15, 1891:

....I was distressed at what W wrote in the book at this Town Hall at Munich:

Suprema Lex
Regis Voluntas.

I think he can hardly understand what a *bévue* he is making when he writes such a thing. A Czar, an infallible Pope - the Bourbons - and our poor Charles I - might have written such a sentence, but a constitutional Monarch in the 19th century!!! So young a man - the son of his father and your grandson - not to speak of a child of mine - should neither have nor express such a maxim....I can say nothing, give no advice. I am usually completely ignored.[3]

Another provocative speech was made by the Emperor William six weeks later, when addressing some new recruits for the German army. At this period a certain section in the German political world was working hard for a *rapprochement* between the Emperor and Prince Bismarck, and it was to this speech and to these endeavours that the Empress alluded in her letter to Queen Victoria of December 5, 1891:

....I don't think the state of things very satisfactory here. W. has, alas, made a terrible new speech to the recruits which is very freely criticised, and the party that wish a reconciliation with Prince Bismarck are working very hard. I was even asked whether I would not try to use influence to bring this about, but as you may imagine I answered that I had no influence whatever, and would never allude to the subject.

There is great poverty, and the working classes have lost a good deal of money and very little business is done. There is just a quiet confidence in Caprivi's honesty and steadiness and moderation, but Miquel has done his best to undermine him. I do not think he will succeed. The principal cause of uneasiness and insecurity as to foreign affairs is the fear that Mr Gladstone will have 'a turn' again before long and that the Russians and French will take the opportunity of making war, as it is assumed that England would not join the Triple Alliance and allow Russia to do what she pleased - both in the East and in Europe - and France what she liked in Egypt.

W is not at all popular. Every question has been taken up and then dropped again, and a deal of irritation caused and nothing of consequence done or reformed. The public utterances are much criticised and the expense of the Army increases tremendously. Still all this would smooth and calm down and settle itself, if only wiser and steadier and more experienced men were listened to....

Further endeavours were now made to effect a reconciliation between the Emperor and Bismarck, and on December 12, 1891, the Empress Frederick wrote to Queen Victoria:

....Politics are in a queer state. Caprivi has done excellently well and has defended his commercial treaties valiantly; but the agitation on the part of the Conservatives and Bismarckites to bring Prince B back is very strong. They want his influence to be all powerful again, even if he does not take office. First they want to obtain a complete reconciliation with W. I have even been spoken to and asked whether I would not try to influence W in that direction. You may imagine how I laughed. The very people who for years laboured and intrigued to destroy my influence and that of Fritz now would wish me to help to patch things up with Prince B. I told them plainly that I had not the faintest influence over the son whom their wickedness had turned against his parents, nor his affairs - they have what they wanted, to all intents and purposes I am dead and gone. I shall never seek to have any influence. My opinion can always be had for the asking - unasked I shall never give it. I should consider it very dangerous for the country and the monarchy to let Prince B have anything more to say. That later on, W should be on a footing of courtesy and civility with him and that he should be received at Berlin I should consider both dignified and proper and good policy, but nothing more.

It may interest you to know that it is Kessel who is the person used to try and influence W towards a reconciliation, and sly as he is, he is hard at work to effectuate this.

You may be sure I shall not open my mouth. May they all reap the harvest of their bad deeds. If I had a shadow of influence I should implore W to make no speeches in public, for they are too terrible, and not to write into books and under photos any more - it makes one's hair stand on end. Here in Berlin people are becoming accustomed to these very strange utterances and think it a peculiar style to which it is well not to attach too great importance - it is put down to ignorance and childish impetuosity, and some of the best newspapers mildly criticise, remonstrate and advise. I send you here a specimen which is very good. I fear, however, it does not make the slightest effect. Oh, how different all might be if that vile party, who brought on 1848 and drove F W IV off his head, terrorised my father-in-law and formed the bodyguard of Bismarckism - broke Fritz's heart and destroyed all the work of our lives - took entire possession of our son, knocked me and all our friends down - did not exist. Bismarck, their stronghold, is gone, but they remain, and until the baneful work they have been at for so many years is stopped, of course, there never can be harmony or understanding between W. and me, nor can he have any knowledge of his father's opinion, or any confidence in his mother - though there may be peace and a more comfortable feeling of outward intercourse. Herbert Bismarck said three months before he left, to a friend of his whom he knew: '*Die Kluft zwischen den Kaiser und seine Mutter muss eine vollständige werden, die nicht wieder zu beseitigen ist.*'[4]

I must wait quietly - perhaps I shall die before justice and truth have their day, but the people who are around him are not my friends, and have no wish that he should return to me. My keeping so completely aloof from everything ought to prove to them how needless it is for them to take such pains to keep me away. For me patience is the best, but it is patience without hope....

The speeches of the Emperor William did not gain in prudence as the months went by. In February 1892, on the occasion of a parliamentary dinner, he gave further proof of his animosity to those whom he considered to be his enemies, and on February 16 the Empress wrote from Berlin to Queen Victoria:

The Government here and W are playing a most dangerous game it seems to me from sheer ignorance of the importance of die question they have dealt with so lightly. I am afraid W makes the most imprudent speeches at these parliamentary dinners (after dinner). Here am I condemned to sit and look on in silence without being able to say one word in warning and knowing that the hideous mistakes made may lead to terrible consequences. After having for more than thirty years been so nearly connected with all that was going on, and collected knowledge and experience of people and things, I now watch as from a grave - more than useless and forgotten - the reckless course pursued by my own son. The other members of the family do not seem to see or to care - no one sensible has any influence - no one about him warns or gives advice. The worst of it is that we shall perhaps all have to pay for his ignorance and imprudence. Of course, far away in England you see and hear nothing of all this.

Dona's people are exceedingly active and make her take part in all sorts of charities and undertakings of many kinds, but only from an orthodox Low Church and Conservative point of view. We never talk on these subjects, indeed between the Schloss and me there is no intercourse whatever. We are on a friendly footing whenever we meet, which is very rare. It needs an unusual amount of philosophy to accept a situation of so much bitterness and disappointment without murmuring. I should never come here any more if it were not my duty, and if there were not things which I cannot and must not and will not abandon and where some good still can be done. It is beloved Fritz's homeland we still have friends I stick to, but with the whole present regime I have absolutely nothing to do.

A week later the Emperor William made another speech, this time at Brandenburg, in which he severely censured the opponents of his political policy, styling them 'grumblers'. The speech made a sensation not only in Germany but also in England, where *The Times* commented unfavourably upon it in a strong leading article. The reproduction of this article in several Berlin newspapers led to their confiscation by the German Government, and it became more and more evident that the Emperor, whilst making the most ill-advised statements himself, was determined to allow no one in Germany to criticise the Imperial utterances.

Meanwhile, the distress in Berlin, Hanover and Dantzig, due to trade depression, brought in its train much rioting and disturbance, and it was to these subjects that the Empress alluded in her letter to Queen Victoria of February 27, 1892:

I send you some really good extracts from Papers of my way of thinking about those horrid riots of the day before yesterday and yesterday. It seems all quiet again now, I am happy to say. These things will happen now and then, but are more dangerous in Germany than anywhere. I also send an extract about my poor W's ill-inspired Speech.

I really feel like an old hen that has hatched a duckling instead of a chicken and sees it swimming away. Only ducks know how to swim and the poor hen's anxiety is needless, whereas here it seems to me that he 'rushes in where Angels fear to tread'. I wish I could put a padlock on his mouth for all occasions where speeches are made in public. It is no use to say anything - the Bismarck education and the school of the Emperor William's entourage have made him what he is, and their teaching brings on these results - his dear father and I are in no way responsible for his extraordinary ideas. We were for constitutional liberty, for quiet steady progress - for an unobtrusive but unobstructed evolution - for individualism and the development of culture, not for Imperialism, Caesarism, State Socialism, etc. We were Whigs of the old school, but the modern most unphilosophical sort of Tory Democrat is an abomination to me - a cajoling of errors and coquetting with mistaken ideas only for the sake of gaining more power, whereas I am for liberty of opinion and individual independence - of which poor Germany has had so little. *Les extrèmes se touchent* where there is absolutism, and where the State is everything there is sure to be Socialism. I wish to see the public at large working for the relief of the poor and the unemployed; charity might be still more liberal in Germany, more general and better organised. But charity is crippled, and self-help and organisation cannot be learnt when the State alone insists on doing everything and others sit and look on.

Two days later, in the course of a letter to her mother expressing her sympathy at the death of Prince Albert Victor, Duke of Clarence, the eldest son of the Prince of Wales, the Empress again made reference to the malevolent influences of the clique into which her son the Emperor William had fallen.

I am sorely tried too; though I have, thank God, not lost my eldest son, he is a source of constant anxiety to me. The pernicious influence of the Bismarcks of certain military circles and Junkers have so filled his head with ideas which I consider most false and dangerous and which he takes up with the conviction and *naïveté* of ignorance and inexperience - there is no one there to advise or counteract the baneful turn given to his opinions. What will it come to? He was snatched out of our hands - all our wise friends were put to silence. Alas, my poor parents-in-law rather lent themselves to this system of playing him off against us. You remember how I used to complain of the poor Empress Augusta flattering him, etc. She did all for the best, I am sure, but she did him a deal of harm. I assure you I tremble for him - with all his rashness and obstinacy, etc., he is a big baby. Henry and Bernhard understand politics no better than he does. Some of his Aides-de-Camp were beside themselves with enthusiasm about this speech, which quite brought the perspiration to my forehead when I read it. The speech was, alas, no ebullition of the moment - he had written it all down before and took it with him and made Oberpräsident von Achenbach prompt him. I should have refused and told him that such a speech was impossible. Afterwards the Ministers tried to weed out all the expressions which were a great deal stronger still, therefore the *Staatsanzeiger*, in which it was printed in its present form, appeared three hours later than usual.

Tonight W presides at a banquet of students of the Borussian Corps at the Hotel Kaiserhof - a thing which in my opinion is not the right thing for a Sovereign to do - still I trust he will be more prudent in his utterances. It is too despairing to see people rushing headlong into mistakes and on quite a wrong track and not to be able to stop them. All those who are blind enough to hate Constitutional liberty admire and applaud him and all the orthodox set. Why is it they do not see that they are playing the game of Socialism as Prince Bismarck was? I so seldom see Sir E. Malet that I do not know what he thinks of all this, and he is so prudent a man that he would not say to me what he thought.

It was, of course, inevitable that some of the public criticisms levelled against the speeches of the Emperor should come to his ears, and the effect of these comments upon him is indicated in the Empress's letter to her mother, dated March 21, 1892:

I think that he was very furious at some of the criticisms on his speech. He will not admit that the speech was a mistake in any way and thinks the criticisms all pure spite and wickedness, but some that were shown him have annoyed him, which everybody is thankful for, as heretofore they have made no impression whatever - and it is hoped this may stagger him a little and make him a little more prudent and careful. I myself do not think so - he is so imbued with false ideas that it would want a constant and daily and powerful influence to open his eyes, explain things in their true light. He does not understand what a Constitution is. He does not know a single member of the Liberal party - he never reads one of the really good sensible newspapers. If he only had the same political instinct that dear Louis had, and that I believe and hope Ernie will have. None of my children care for politics, or understand them, *i.e.*, for the development of a wise and enlightened progress. I think that it was wished that William should be away on the 18th March, which was a very good thing, as it was not certain whether we should not have some rows in the streets again. The Education Bill has been thrown out and Ct Zedlitz has resigned. Everyone is very glad and I think there will be a universal sense of relief. Caprivi has tendered his resignation, but I do not suppose it will be accepted. I should be sorry for many reasons if he went. He is certainly not a statesman, but he is so honest and well-meaning and conscientious and a safe man....

As the year 1892 progressed, it became evident that tremendous efforts were being made to secure a reconciliation between the Emperor William and Prince Bismarck. The Empress regarded any such reconciliation with alarm, and her reasons are clearly given in her letter to Queen Victoria of June 4, 1892:

> I suppose you have heard of all the efforts that are being made to bring about a reconciliation between Bismarck and W. I consider the thing dangerous in many ways. It would take too long to explain it all, but W will soon be quite in the hands of the OstPreussische clique and that of the industrials, such as Stumm.
> The latter was employed in sounding the terrain to see whether Bismarck would go and see W on his way to Kiel to meet the Emperor of Russia, and whether, therefore, W's train should stop at Friedrichsruh. If it were only a mere act of courtesy and civility it would not matter, but the industrials want to have an influence on politics, especially in the sense of protectionism. I fear, if they succeed, that Caprivi would leave directly, which would be a very great pity for many reasons. The Minister of the Interior, Herfurt, is a useful man, the only clever head in the Ministry - thus Eulenburg and the Conservatives are trying hard to get rid of him. There is no stability anywhere....

In the following months it became evident that there was little hope of any reconciliation between Prince Bismarck and the German Emperor, and the attitude of the ex-Chancellor to his former master now began to peep forth in the severe strictures which he passed upon the Emperor's policy at home and abroad. It was very evident that the breach between the two men, instead of narrowing, was becoming wider and wider.

During the summer months of 1892 there occurred in England a change of ministry. The general elections of June and July had resulted in the return of Mr Gladstone to power for the fourth time. The election had been fought primarily upon the issue of Home Rule for Ireland, a legislative and constitutional issue upon which Lord Rosebery, who was now appointed Foreign Secretary in Mr Gladstone's ministry, was not in the fullest agreement with his leader. It was to these events that the Empress Frederick alluded in her letter to Queen Victoria of August 16, 1892:

> ....I was so much relieved to hear that Lord Rosebery had accepted the post of Foreign Secretary, as, though his non-acceptance would have been a blow and a spoke in the wheel to the Gladstonians, yet, even in a short while, without Lord Rosebery at the Foreign Office irreparable harm might have been done and mischief wrought beyond undoing. I felt very unhappy and uneasy for you in the first place and then for our dear country. To think that the greatest and most glorious Empire in the world, whose affairs were being managed (on the whole) as well and successfully and carefully as could be desired, should by a combination of circumstances be plunged into indecision and uncertainty - a troubled sea of fantastic and unreasonable experiments - makes me frantic. I was

most alarmed about Egypt. The folly of abandoning an undertaking on which so much blood and treasure, thought and labour have been spent, seems to me too grievous and, alas, dangerous in every way. You know I am not chauvinistic, and 'prestige' is often a very empty word, but in this case 'prestige' is a power and a reality - to be used for good. Why should we make room for the French, knowing that it would bring a train of calamities after it? If we leave Egypt, we shall never have influence there again - the next Army of occupation will be a French one.

We here in Germany know how the Russians are pushing forward towards the Indian frontier and moving up their forces and their material. Those who wish England well think that 40 or 50,000 men more are needed than we have now in India, and do not consider the number high. It is a small sacrifice compared with that we should have to make, if to reconquer part of the Indian Empire were necessary. It behoves us to be on the watch and not to part with anything which can strengthen our arm - whereas any weakness will only tempt our enemies to attack us. This is my firm conviction.

When I heard that Lord Rosebery was gone to France and was not going to accept, I feared that he might have seen members of the French Government and have heard from them of promises made to France by Mr Gladstone about Egypt. The speech of Sir C. Dilke made me fear this. But on the other hand, if Mr Gladstone is so utterly bent on taking office *coûte que coûte*, perhaps he will give way to Lord Rosebery and also make other concessions? You have been through such difficult times often and everyone admires the way in which you take such things, and of this I always feel so proud.

God forbid that the wretched Home Rule Bill be passed. Some say Mr G will try to abolish the House of Lords if they throw it out, but this is easier said than done. Others maintain he will make a batch of new Peers and so get the support he wants. Then again one hears he wants to abolish the 'Commander-in-Chief' just as the Lord High Admiral was once abolished. But this is more political gossip and surmise than anything else. One thing I am certain of, the GOM, in spite of all his vagaries and vanity and fanaticism and power of thoroughly convincing himself that the course he means to adopt is the right one, is yet sincerely loyal to the Crown. I have often observed that, and it would be unjust not to admit it, or give him credit for the sincerity of those sentiments, while one is obliged to think him dangerous as a politician and cannot possibly agree with the programme he has so often announced and that many of his party will try and force him to keep to, which I cannot help thinking will soon by its utter impracticability end in a breakdown.

Perhaps I ought not to speak so openly, now he is once in office and everyone must try to make the best of it and prevent mischief as much as possible....Meanwhile the Conservatives will be very glad to have a rest....

Interest in Germany was now concentrated upon the army bills that were introduced by the Chancellor, General von Caprivi, in November 1892.

These bills were designed to effect great increases in the strength of the army, and owing to the depressed state of trade in Germany were vigorously opposed in the Reichstag. On January 7, 1893, the Empress wrote to Queen Victoria:

I am afraid the situation here is not at all satisfactory. The Generals and military authorities are perfectly convinced that the army reform is absolutely necessary for our safety. I quite believe what they say and wish with all my heart they could obtain what they want. Alas, the government have gone to work in the most awkward way. Instead of slowly trying to prepare public opinion (especially convincing the Deputies) they came upon the nation with this immense demand for money at a time when all the sad consequences of the Bismarck regime are most felt. The depression of trade and the unsatisfactory state of agriculture, the ever increasing, now almost crushing burden of taxation, alas! W's great unpopularity and the general discontent make this Bill so distasteful to the people that I fear there is no chance of its being passed. A dissolution would make things worse and Caprivi's resignation would be a misfortune. This is all very sad, and I often feel very anxious. In these twenty-one years the Monarchical principle has suffered very much - so many blunders have been made - unfortunate speeches - so many people have been hurt and offended, etc....that there is a very uncomfortable feeling abroad. Every party (the blindest Bismarckites excepted) is anxious to keep Caprivi, whose honesty and conscientiousness are so thoroughly appreciated after the long years of the Bismarck regime, but what is to be done? Neither W nor Caprivi can quite understand or grasp the situation - they have no political knowledge or experience, and the former a great amount of prejudices, etc....the result of the entourage he has lived in. I wish with all my heart one could help him, but his whole education as regards politics *serait à refaire* and a totally different set of people ought to have access and things be explained thoroughly from the right point of view. All my anger and bitterness (for W I have more than just cause) are turned into anxiety and concern and pity, but I am quite powerless to do even the smallest good and can only hope against hope that things may right themselves.

The Empress's attention was now attracted to events in the Balkans. In Roumania the heir-presumptive, Prince Ferdinand, had, in 1888, become engaged to Mlle Vacaresco, a maid-of-honour to Queen Elizabeth (Carmen Sylva). Public disapproval of the match was, however, so pronounced that the engagement was broken off, and Queen Elizabeth left the country. Finally, in the June of 1892, Prince Ferdinand became engaged to Princess Marie of Edinburgh, and in the following February their marriage took place at Sigmaringen.

Scarcely had Roumania settled down to its new Princess than attention was directed to Servia, where the youthful Prince Alexander, on April 14, suddenly proclaimed his majority, dismissed die Regents and their ministry, and appointed in their stead a radical ministry amid every sign of popular approval.

At the same time that these events were attracting attention to the Balkans, the German Emperor was visiting Rome, where he had invited himself to the silver wedding of the King and Queen of Italy.

Poor King of Italy [the Empress wrote to her mother on April 18] - the visit will quite ruin him - he has to pay all out of his own pocket, the Naval and Military Review into the bargain, and it is to cost two million Lire. I live in dread of the Alliance being made so irksome that the poor Italians cannot keep it up. I wish William would see this. They are not at all pleased at Berlin at his going away now, when the '*Militär Vorlage*' has to be fought in the Reichstag. The Quirinal has to be arranged and the enormous Palace at Naples got ready. It is really not considerate to overwhelm the Italian Court with such a suite. I am quite distressed about it.

It is quite true that the Roumanians do not want Elizabeth back, as they are terrified at her having been the tool of the Russians and a danger to Roumanian interests through these Vacarescos, Scheffer, and French people, but if she could once be brought to see and understand what it all was, there would be no danger any more and only advantage to everyone if she returned. Poor Princess Wied knows this all quite well and says she cannot blame the Roumanians.

This *coup d'état* of the Servian boy King seems also to be a Russian Coup and consequently rather to be regretted, though it may be good in other ways. The Queen was always a Russian tool, poor thing, and as King Milan is always in want of money, it is not impossible he may have become one too from this reason. It is not agreeable for Ferdinand of Bulgaria. I shall think of him so much tomorrow on his 'Wedding Day.

In the summer of 1893 the Empress paid a visit to her daughter, the Crown Princess of Greece, at Athens. It was from Athens that she wrote about this time to Baron von Reischach a letter which more than any other appears to embody her opinion of the current political situation in Germany. The general election of June 1893 had resulted in a small majority for the Government, which desired to carry out the policy of strengthening the army in spite of the opposition of the Socialists. The Empress was pleased at the Government victory, and the event gave her the opportunity of summarising the trend of political thought in Germany during the past decade. Naturally, her opinion of Bismarck, now mellowed and in better perspective, owing to the passing of years, comes into the letter, which ran:

I fully agree with you regarding the elections, and do not incline to exaggerated pessimism. But it is a difficult matter to argue on such a theme, and especially in writing. My point of view and political creed differ widely from yours. All my experience, studies and observations have contributed to confirm my opinion. On one point, however, I think we entirely agree - that is, in regard to the ideal we hold of our native country, in the burning wish to see it realised, which does not imply external power only, but internal soundness, intrinsic solidity and power, which means its inner worth. There are many things which still require to be shaped into proper and ordered form. Poor Germany has had an historical development which in some ways has fostered its great qualities, whereas it has tended to cripple others entirely. It is necessary to see below the surface, and to understand how judgment, restfulness, and political aptitude are lacking, and how natural this is, and also to what degree the individual lacks independence in his political thoughts, and for this reason is easily susceptible to doctoring. The wild and poisonous nonsense of Socialism, which is apt to take such a deceptive and seductive form, is composed of nothing but hollow phrases and forced deductions, and would never otherwise have enslaved such strong men. True and sensible freedom worthy of mankind, which makes human beings conservative in a good sense, has never been nursed or taught, nor has it been preached. The great man (Bismarck) who achieved such wonderful things had no grasp of this. But this alone could have stemmed the tide of lunacy called Socialism, for it taught men to think independently, and to recognise where the true interests and duties of the individual lay. That, however, did not suit the political machine, which was priding itself on creating things rapidly which from their nature should have been prepared slowly and from above, the growth of which would have matured of their own accord. Pray do not think that I wish to be unjust towards the Great Man. I do not wish either to underrate his achievements or to revile or criticise him; he had colossal power and represented a potential lever; he gave what he had to give. But the fact of his being what he was brought in its train more than one disadvantage alongside all the brilliant successes of his career, which had attained such dizzy heights. I cannot help thinking that the Emperor Frederick's noble, straight and unselfish nature would gradually, by systematic and cautious opposition and purposeful and well-thought-out counteraction, have corrected these disadvantages, which he, as a tactful and quiet observer, had had ample time to recognise. I feel convinced that he would thus have finished and complemented Bismarck's great work. He alone might have brought this invaluable gift to his dearly beloved people. Now that he is lying in his grave, things will have to go their course and pass through difficult stages. Wisdom and experience may possibly have to be bought dearly. But I suppose that gradually things will evolve out of the chaos and excitement which seem to prevail nowadays. Germany has too many good brains and true hearts at its disposal, not to be able to work out its own salvation dispassionately and wisely. The excitement of victory is past, and its reaction of alarm and exaggerated pessimism will pass as well, and a more sensible frame of mind is bound to be developed out of this ferment, but in my opinion, this phase which we now have to pass through might have been spared the nation. There have always been great men, but not always Sovereigns, who had been trained, prepared and created for their posts like the one whom we shall always mourn. The nation will have to learn to rely on itself and do without such men. I feel convinced that it will be equal to its task, and that it is looking forward to a happy future. Maybe you will not agree with me on all these points. I do not wish to force my opinion on anybody, and do not often express it. And I find that very few people share it. It is the habit of men to consider as vain and impracticable a philosophic theory intended to keep hold of the sequence of historical events. I do not share this opinion. Unless a person has formed a clear idea of cause and effect, and of the consequences of certain principles, he lives from hand to mouth and not for the morrow, and in a continual state of vacillation. Prince Bismarck was a great opportunist, a master in creation of situations; his perception was rapid and the means he employed were clever; his courage was great, but his example was a wrong one to copy, and bad for the training of others. I am speaking without rancour, and bear him no grudge. My husband and myself did not meet with his approval. He considered us inconvenient tools, and the way in which his party treated us and tried to render us innocuous has become a matter of history. I cannot say that it was a pleasant time, and its effect has not yet passed. I suffered greatly, but I have gladly endured it all, and am ready to pay the highest price for it, if it has done any good at all, for I steered the course which I whole-heartedly considered the right one. The fact that my son's soul was alienated from me is the wilful and purposeful work of one party. It thinks it has performed a patriotic deed; it has the power, whereas I had none, and I will most likely go to my grave unknown, alien and misunderstood, for a lonely woman is not able to achieve anything against many turbulent men and their blind prejudices. Fate will not have it otherwise, and I do not impute to the men who trod us under foot any bad motives. I feel convinced that they thought they were serving their country and considered the means they made use of - *de bonne guerre*! Men are perishable, but ideas live. The Emperor Frederick's hopes and what he worked for may some day be realised, but not for a long long time. Maybe they will come after hard times, but I shall not live to see them! Pray forgive my long dissertation: I have had time to think it all out in this beautiful and still night at Tartoi. When my heart is well-nigh bursting with pain and bitterness, when I think of Berlin, then I look up to the golden stars and regain my tranquillity and peace, for sometimes things turn out better than one thinks, and a few decades count in the lives of nations not more than a few minutes to us here. I believe firmly in eternal progress and evolution, whether quick or slow, and whether those men disappear or not who might have sown the seed for this development and prevented an arrest of this process.[5]

Meanwhile, the difficulties occasioned in Roumania by the long absence of Queen Elizabeth (Carmen Sylva) in Germany, now seemed to be approaching a solution. In the October of 1893 a son was born to Prince Ferdinand and his consort, and the event was the prelude to the return of the Queen to Roumania during the following year. Before the return of the

Queen to Bukarest the Empress Frederick had written to Queen Victoria (October 17):

....Poor Elizabeth! I had not the heart to telegraph to her, as I feel the joy cannot be without great bitterness for her....

So many thanks for your dear letter of the 12th. You say in one part that Elizabeth did not like the peculiar position of Herr von Roggenbach in her mother's house. Elizabeth was always devoted to him and owes him an immense debt of gratitude. The moment the intrigues began, Elizabeth took a dislike to him, to her mother, the King and all her old friends. The set that surrounded her heaped the vilest lies and calumnies on the heads of both H. v. R. and the Princess. They are all to be read in that detestable book *Misère Royale*. Now Elizabeth is shocked and horrified and sends for H. v. R. and says she cannot understand how she could misunderstand her best friend. He has behaved, as he always does, with the greatest tact and unselfishness. Those who say he is indiscreet make the most outrageous mistake. He is the very reverse, so retiring, so delicate and so tactful, it is indeed very difficult to get him to come and see one, or write. How often the Empress Augusta used to say that, and what confidence she and Fritz and General v. S. had in him, and those who are alive have still. How Fritz looked up to him!

I think you forget, dear Mama, that it was Bismarck and his whole large party who persecuted him. W sanctioned his house in the country being broken into and the locks of all his boxes forced, his writing table broken open, his private papers seized, copied and shown to the members of the Bundesrath. This villainous act of abuse of power happened just before I came to Osborne in 1888. It is a black spot on the present regime and reign and was in connection with Geffcken's being thrown into prison. This was worthy of Napoleon the First, or of Richelieu, or the Medicis in the Middle Ages. It was no indiscretion of Roggenbach's - it was done in order to make a case against Fritz and against me. I am not so magnanimous as Roggenbach. I cannot forgive and forget all that yet - it was my son who sanctioned and encouraged all this, and that makes the difference; if he had been a stranger, one could have got over it.

The year 1894 opened with the ostensible reconciliation between Prince Bismarck and the Emperor William. The Prince was warmly and honourably received by the Emperor, and a popular ovation marked the passage of the aged ex-Chancellor on his way to meet his sovereign.

The Emperor was now fully determined that Germany should expand wherever possible, and in his colonial policy he was now supported by his former Chancellor, who had changed his opinions on this subject during the past few years. In the June of 1894 Germany took exception to certain clauses in an agreement signed in the previous May between Great Britain and the Congo Free State, by which a strip of territory was leased to Great Britain for the eventual track of a Cape to Cairo railway. This would have interposed a belt of British territory between the Congo and German East Africa, but under German pressure the lease was abandoned. The ex-Empress watched Bismarck's attitude to these questions with interest, and on June 21, 1894, wrote to Queen Victoria:

> I think the German Government are quite wrong about the Congo and that they are making themselves odious for no reason. It is too absurd to suspect England of falseness and treachery - that is not in our line. I always was strongly against German Colonies in Africa. They are of no use to Germany - only an expense and a trouble. They do not understand in Germany how to manage and govern them, and it only makes the Germans quarrelsome and pretentious and always on the qui vive; in short it seems to me very unnecessary to embark on any such adventure. Fritz always thought so. Prince Bismarck used to be strongly opposed to these colonial enterprises and then suddenly took them up. One of his friends, I think it was General v. Schweinitz, expressed his surprise at this change, and Bismarck answered, 'I, too, think Germany would be better off without this colonial policy, but I must have it as a means of stirring up German indignation against England whenever I want it, because the Crown Prince [Fritz] will be too prone to form a friendship with England and I must be able to keep him in check by "German patriotism". I want England's co-operation often, but I will not have the influence of British ideas in Germany - the constitutionalism and liberalism to which the Crown Prince is given. I must also have a means of bringing England to terms when I want her support, and therefore I must stimulate German colonial enthusiasm.' I do not know whether I ever told you this - it is a long while ago, but it comes back to me now. It is so like the cunning old fox - it may be very clever for his own purposes of reigning supreme and appearing to a great many excitable, violent and short-sighted Germans as the greatest patriot of the day, and the one who most wishes to raise Germany's position, uphold her honour and glory and carry her name abroad that it should triumph over the seas. Looked at practically and impartially it is great rubbish. If the Germans wanted a real, useful, good Colony in a place where a great many Germans have settled and colonised, the south of Brazil would be much better, and at one time in Paraguay one might have had a very favourable opportunity after the war when the population was so decimated. There are buildings, roads, navigable rivers, etc., and one might have done useful work, whereas in the Cameroons the climate is impossible and the whole thing is altogether unsatisfactory and a mistake and a failure.
>
> But this is only my private idea. I know you will not betray me. I have Germany's interest every bit as much at heart as Prince Bismarck had, but not to drive Germany to acts of folly by exciting false patriotism. I should like to see her people in the enjoyment of more civilisation, liberty, culture and prosperity, and freed from many a yoke which weighs upon them; I feel convinced that this is quite compatible with being on the best of terms with England and not coming into any collision with British interests, and that true greatness and power He in

the development and progress of the nation. With so huge an Army as Germany is obliged to keep up at present, an unduly and disproportionately large Navy seems to me a mistake, both from an economical and political point of view.

William's one idea is to have a Navy which shall be larger and stronger than the British Navy, but this is really pure madness and folly and he will see how impossible and needless it is. One large enough for German requirements and as good as possible of its kind is all that ought to be aimed at - with prudence and safety. But he has some fantastic idea of Peter the Great, Frederick the Great, etc., who did so much by their own initiative, and forgets how Germany is thirsting for liberty and reform in so many things, and how his true work cut out for him, left him as a legacy by his father, is of a very different kind.

To this letter the Empress added a postscript, which shows that her opinion of Bismarck had not changed greatly since his demission from office in 1890:

What I confided to you in my letter this morning, I should not venture to tell Lord Rosebery. He was and is still, I believe, very intimate with the Bismarcks, and how could I tell whether B might not hear his own words again. I remember that he said them to Schweinitz, who is a very reserved, cautious and discreet man, but B might be furious with him and he would never tell me anything again. Whenever Prince B is no more and nothing disagreeable could occur to Schweinitz, it would not matter who knew it - it would amuse and interest Lord Rosebery then. Prince Bismarck's dodgy, tricky ways - his sharpness in trying to turn everything to advantage - for his own power - were very difficult to cope with. Germany is now saddled with troublesome and unprofitable Colonies - highly flattering to its *amour propre*, and the public in their enthusiasm consider it another leaf in the crown of laurels which surrounds the brows of their great benefactor and patriot, the great Chancellor, but only the wiser few perceive how doubtful a benefit he has conferred on his country. I, of course, am not at liberty to express my opinion and should lay myself out to much misunderstanding and be considered unfaithful to German interests. The German Government once having embarked on this affair, of course, must continue to carry out what it has begun and would consider it most humiliating to abandon the policy into which it threw itself headlong with such rashness. The very sound of the thing is fantastical and charms William, as all startling, unusual, sensational and new things do. I am very glad that a quiet, steady and clever man, such as Hatzfeldt, is in London just now - it would be so easy to make a mess and so difficult to get out of it....

In the October of 1894 General von Caprivi resigned or, as some thought, was removed from the post of Chancellor, and his place was taken by Prince Chlodwig von Hohenlohe. The Empress Frederick had long had a very high opinion of Caprivi, and in her letter to Queen Victoria of

December 18, 1894, expressed it unhesitatingly:

> Caprivi was looked upon by most sensible and reasonable people as a drag on the wheel of the Government and a guarantee that no very sudden adventure would be plunged into. The very quick, easy and unceremonious way in which he was removed (at least to all appearances) made many sections of the public apprehensive as to what might follow. Prince Hohenlohe, who is certainly a wise, calm and prudent man, has evidently been taken by storm and either overridden or has had no time to consider all the consequences of the step that was being taken; and the strong reactionary and ultra-conservative spirit that has for a hundred and more years been the element of all mischief in Germany has gained the upper hand, and the Government has taken a very rash step, which I fear will end in a defeat.
>
> I am only a silent and much-distressed spectator of what goes on. To be able to warn, or to put in a word of advice, one would have to be on the spot and the first to speak. When things have once been misrepresented to W, and he has formed an opinion, which he does in two minutes, and has resolved on a thing and also carried it immediately into effect, it is of course no use to remonstrate. He takes criticism very much amiss, and unfortunately it does not make an impression or have the desired effect of enlightening or convincing him. It only irritates and fills him with suspicion, or offends him....so that whatever shadow of influence one might have on this or that occasion or question would of a certainty be destroyed. There is nothing for it but to shut one's mouth and only seize whatever good opportunity chance may offer one, however rare this may be, to say what one thinks or feels.
>
> Poor Prince Hohenlohe has no easy task.

## NOTES

1 I suffer no one near me. Everyone who is against me I will crush.
2 Literally: The will of the king is the highest law.
3 For an interesting explanation of this incident see Sir Rennell Rodd's *Social and Diplomatic Memories*, pp. 267-268, where he relates that 'there were two registers at Munich in which eminent visitors were invited to inscribe their names. The Emperor had already done so in the album presented to him. It was then discovered that a mistake had been made and that so august an autograph should have been recorded in the Golden Book. The Regent (of Bavaria), however, expressed the opinion that his imperial guest must not be further importuned, and informing him that he had done so, begged that his decision should be respected. Nevertheless, in spite of the Regent's wishes, the book reserved for more important autographs was submitted, and then it was that the Emperor, intending to signify that the Regent's will must be his law, wrote in it instead of his name the much-discussed sentence. The explanation appears

plausible, but it does not enhance the Emperor's reputation for discretion.'
4 The gulf between the Emperor and his mother is bound to become complete, and can never be bridged over.
5 Published in Baron von Reischach's *Under Three Emperors*, p. 140 *seq.*

# XVII. Closing Years

THE Emperor William's choice of a new Chancellor, Prince Hohenlohe, was one which appealed to the Empress Frederick. He had only been Chancellor for three months when she wrote to Queen Victoria (January 4, 1895):

....I saw Prince Hohenlohe lately and he seemed all right and to meet all the great difficulties he has to fight against with the greatest calmness. Not the smallest one is William's impulsiveness. William does not know and understand the rights of things, but speaks and telegraphs with the greatest aplomb and unconcern where it would be better to say nothing, to form one's own opinion very slowly and express it very rarely. It makes me so unhappy to see how great W's unpopularity is in the town here, in the army, in the provinces, amongst the lower orders, etc. Of course, people are often very unjust, but I am afraid it is the great imprudence constantly committed which is the cause. I can say nothing and do nothing. I wish I could hope that there would be improvement in this respect - all the people that surround him are too inferior to be of real use in opening his eyes and a help in forming his judgment. I think Prince Hohenlohe's calm, conciliatory and dignified manner will by degrees have an influence. He is both wise and patient and has great tact and experience....

Hohenlohe, however, was not strong enough to prevent the Emperor from continuing his practice of mating provocative speeches, another of which was made at the opening of the new Parliament House at Berlin on December 5, 1894. Three days later the Empress wrote to her mother:

....There has been a little row directly in the Reichstag. The Socialists refused to get up when three cheers for the Emperor were asked for. The reason they gave was one which I trust William will hear, and which indeed I was almost furious about with them. They could not cheer for a man who exhorted his soldiers in a speech to fire at the rest of the people whenever he ordered it. This is, of course, only an excuse on the part of the Socialists, but it shows the harm these distressing and unfortunate speeches do and how people do not forget them. How unnecessary it is for a Sovereign to be present when recruits take the oath, and then to harangue them! The German press (the Conservative portion) are very Anglophobe just now for no reason - it is too stupid. Their vanity and their jealousy of England have been purposely so stimulated by Prince Bismarck for his own purposes - that now he is gone, that section of the public which he was wont to excite - whenever it suited him - is roused the minute a cry is raised, and their patriotism bursts forth in the most ridiculous and unjust attacks on England's rapacity, duplicity, etc, and the lies they spread, the nonsense they believe, are truly absurd. The only way is to treat it with the contempt it deserves, and the wiser heads and all the Liberals regret it very much and think it very foolish. One must never forget that Prince Bismarck admitted (in private) that he was only animating this colonial fever in order to have a bone of contention with England and a means of setting German public opinion against the English. It was just like him, and it is great folly and very detrimental to real German interests.

Relations between the Emperor William and Bismarck now grew in cordiality, and on the occasion of the ex-Chancellor's eightieth birthday the Emperor presented him with a sword of honour on March 26, 1895, at the ex-Chancellor's residence at Friedrichsruh.

It was rumoured at this time that Mr Gladstone, the veteran English Liberal statesman, was also desirous of paying some honour to the old exponent of Prussianism, and in June 1895, when he was cruising in German waters in one of Sir Donald Currie's ships, the suggestion was mooted that he should pay a visit to Friedrichsruh. The Empress Frederick's comment on this piece of news ran as follows (June 21, 1895):

....What an odd idea of Mr Gladstone and his party to wish to see Prince Bismarck and pay him a visit at Friedrichsruh. Prince Bismarck so cordially hated Mr Gladstone and loathed English Liberals that I think the plan of paying a visit there was naïf in the extreme....

The rumour, however, proved false, and on July 5 the Empress wrote to Queen Victoria:

....I thought it seemed very unlikely that Mr Gladstone had wanted to pay Prince Bismarck a visit. The latter has been again making mischievous and spiteful speeches which in one way I do not regret, as it shows so plainly what his thoughts are and always will be in spite of all the fuss made of him....

It was indeed difficult for the ex-Chancellor to change his outlook on the turn German policy had taken since 1890, and he remained a keen critic of the political situation. On December 21, 1895, the Empress wrote from Berlin:

Here I am sorry to say things are not going well. H. v. Keller has W's ear, and W. is very angry with Prince Hohenlohe for having insisted on K.'s dismissal. If W only knew what a service Prince Hohenlohe has rendered him.

H. v. K. was simply impossible, and to push coercive measures still further against the Socialists and the press and having these constant arrests and prosecuting people for *lèse-majesté* was really not possible and has already created great ill-feeling and discontent and has made W. still more unpopular. Alas, he does not see the danger - he is so ill-informed and does not understand the situation; his attitude is more and more one of an absolute monarch, which here in Germany is an anomaly. If it were not for Prince Hohenlohe, who is so wise and gentle and prudent and tolerant, and has such an excellent way of dealing with people and such a perfect temper, and is so utterly unselfish and disinterested, though he is not a Liberal, many more dreadful mistakes would be made. These terrible Junkers, who brought on the year '48 and later regained the upper hand with my father-in-law, seem all powerful now. The most retrograde nonsense is preached and carried out; pietism is rampant and emanates from Court circles. It is bitter indeed to have to sit still and look on at all the blunders made. I much regretted the visit to Friedrichsruh, though I trust it is not a sign of what is much expected, *i.e.* a Ministry, Ct Waldersee and Herbert Bismarck instead of dear Prince Hohenlohe. It would be the worst thing possible for Germany, but the Court Party are working at it, Keller, etc.

Events in the Balkans now again began to attract attention. In Bulgaria Prince Ferdinand was striving to shake off Turkish suzerainty, and apparently hoped to achieve this goal by courting Russian influence.

....I must say [wrote the Empress on January 4, 1895] I am horrified when I read of what Ferdinand is doing in Bulgaria. It seems that he is dying to be recognised by Russia and the other Powers, and thinks to obtain Russia's favour by all these concessions to the Russophile party, which concessions seem as dangerous to me as they are undignified, and will not buy Russia's' good graces one bit, while they will do Bulgaria harm.

A few months later, in the July of that year, M Stambouloff, the autocratic Bulgarian Prime Minister from 1887 to 1894, was assassinated by Macedonians in Sofia. On July 20 the Empress Frederick wrote to Queen Victoria:

This murder of poor Stambouloff is a very shocking thing and very bad for Ferdinand. The German papers are down upon him in the severest manner - even too harsh, I should think. Still, if he were wise, he would rush back to Sofia, have a strict inquiry made and the murderers brought to justice (even though they may be in the pay of the Russian Panslavists' Committee). Ferdinand seems bent on coquetting with Russia - in the hopes of being recognised, which he never will be. I own the state of the East seems very uncomfortable just now. The horrors that have been committed in Armenia - the lukewarmness and half-heartedness of the Great Powers in obliging the Sultan to stop them. The signs of rising in Macedonia are also very disquieting. How far the Slav population are encouraged and instigated by Russian Panslavists and money to rise, one does not know. If the Slav population, Bulgarians, etc., try to shake off the Turkish yoke now, you may be sure that all the Greek population in Epirus, Thessalonica and Crete will do the same - and no Government can keep them quiet, as for generations it has been their aim and they have dreamed and thought of nothing else. Least of all had the Greek Government the power to keep it down, though it may make every effort to do so....Then we should have the East in a blaze, and the Great Powers of Europe are not of one mind and might be arrayed against each other - indeed probably would, which is terrible to think of and the consequences incalculable.

Do you know that some years ago Prince Lobanoff [who was appointed Russian Foreign Minister in March 1895] elaborated a scheme for putting Bulgaria in order again (in the Russian sense), *i.e.* regaining it for Russia. He submitted it to the late Emperor, but it was laid aside as not opportune, and I am afraid now he (Prince Lobanoff) is in office, he will think the time come to carry the plan out. Does Lord Salisbury know this? It is so unfortunate that the Turkish Government and their management of their home affairs should go from bad to worse - those who must support and maintain Turkey should, if possible, insist on some of the abuses ceasing, but it is very very difficult. The whole of the terrible Eastern question crops up again. How is it going to be dealt with, one asks. So much has changed since the Crimean war, and the situation is no longer the same. I am sure it preoccupies you too.

When one has a grand-daughter in Russia, one in Greece and one in Roumania, one can but feel more than disquieted at the thoughts of a conflagration being so near - the East is a powder barrel and at this moment there are sparks enough flying about....

Some people think the Sultan has more confidence in Russia now than in any other Power - it is most strange.

In the few years that were now left to the Empress Frederick her relations with her son improved in cordial feeling and sympathy. It was, however, very distressing to her that Anglo-German relations, which had been so fair in the previous decade, were now showing an ever- growing tension.

I am naturally anxious to do what I can [the Empress wrote to Baron Reischach from England in 1897] in order to attenuate the points of friction whenever I become aware of them, but it is absolutely impossible for me to make any impression on the press of either country....I fortunately never see the low-class press, but one cannot afford to ignore it. It would be regrettable if the Emperor should make a point of noticing it, for he would get a wrong impression of public opinion. But it is a regrettable fact that, after making allowances for exaggerations, there should still remain a sense of distrust for which the Emperor has only himself to blame. The measure of sympathy which he possessed was very great and rare, and a fine trump card in his hands with which he might have obtained many invaluable advantages for Germany. Time alone can let the grass grow on all that has happened and re-establish the feeling of mutual confidence. But I consider this difficult as long as the whole of the German press continues to act as it has for the last twelve months, when venom and abuse have exhausted everything that could be said against England. Though this is rarely mentioned here and the subject hardly ever discussed before me, the inevitable result will be that England will feel convinced that Germany wishes to be hostile to her on principle, and not only the Emperor, and will eventually be driven more and more into the arms of Russia and France, which would upset all the policy which I have had before me all my life, and which would link together the two Germanic and Protestant States, and this I consider to be the most desirable goal for both.

This fond hope has, I fear, for the present been destroyed; let us hope it may revive again some day. The harm which Germany is doing herself is greater than that which she is inflicting on England. I am afraid that they do not quite realise this in Berlin. I have said before that I cannot notice anything in the way of ill-feeling in daily life. The Queen is constantly praising the Emperor for never missing an opportunity of being courteous and attentive, saying that he had been exceptionally courteous and sympathetic on the death of the old Admiral, Sir Alexander Milne, and you know my mother is very fond of her grandson.[1]

Much of the tension between Germany and England at this period was due to Germany's determination to proceed with the development of her infant fleet and generally to increase her armaments. It was therefore an event of colossal importance when, in the summer of 1898, Count Muravieff, on behalf of the Emperor of Russia, suggested that a conference of all the Great Powers should be held in order to preserve the general peace by some measure of disarmament, and on August 31, 1898, the Empress Frederick wrote to Queen Victoria:

I should like to say one word more about the Russian proposal and all one hears. A great many people are delighted - take it *au sérieux* and say 'What a blessing. At last something has been done in connection with public affairs which is a subject of mutual congratulation amongst reasonable people.' Of course nations have suffered and languished, and none so much as the Germans, under the tremendous strain of our increasing armaments, and no doubt Socialism has grown in consequence, as the country could not grow so rich as it would have done had the money been used for other purposes. Some again think that whatever the immediate result may be (of this proposal) the idea of diminishing armaments which was so advocated by Peace Societies and peace-loving individuals without influence, or by democratic elements, passes into a new phase, as it has been taken up by an Emperor and a Government. Some papers say, 'Why did not such a proposal come from the Queen of England? She was the only person from whom it would have appeared natural.' I cannot help thinking that the suddenness of this proposal, so little in accordance with Russian tradition, with their acknowledged national programme and their later political moves, points to a sudden fear having arisen in their minds. The idea had floated about that the only barrier to their Asiatic plans of conquest would be a war with England, or an alliance between England and Germany, or England and America and Japan. This stroke Muravieff wished to parry, and no doubt this has been done in a clever way. It brings Nicky to the fore - it lends importance and power to Russia and for the moment makes her the centre of European policy. Can she be taken at her word? I think she is only acting in her own interest and is far more astute than any of the Western Powers. Perhaps, too, Russia found the French Alliance rather a hamper now and then, and wishes to free herself of it.

It is certain that for many decades Russia has been preparing for the final conflict with England for the supremacy in Asia. There is hardly a Russian who conceals that from any but Englishmen. Only the other day they ordered ships, naval armaments, etc, for 190 millions of marks. Russia is not ready to fight England at present and is afraid that events in China might run her into the danger of a war with England before she is fully prepared; therefore it is her interest to put off any such danger until her Fleets in the Baltic and the Pacific are increased and modernised, and until the Manchurian and Siberian Railways are finished and she is able to move her troops to the different important points. Russia feels that she has raised suspicion and opposition in England by her advance in China, and fears that England may be prepared to resist her with force. This danger is averted by the manifesto, and the responsibility for hostilities thrown on Russia's adversary - England. It is certainly very clever, but to me it seems a 'Ruse', as they must know that if a Congress assembles the deliberations will come to nothing, but they will have gained time and others will have lost it. That sly fox, Muravieff, has no doubt worked on the imagination of Nicky, who is so noble minded, kind-hearted and well-intentioned, and no doubt sincere in what he proposes to the world. I wonder what you will say to it all.

Do you remember when William summoned the international Congress - for social reform and for considering the labour question and improving the workmen's conditions? I said it would come to nothing and was of no use and would never be taken in earnest, and that I could not share the universal enthusiasm, because to be a reformer, one must feel it and wish it and know the question thoroughly, and be a thoroughly liberal-minded, humane individual. I was right; not long afterwards, the speeches about shooting down democrats were held on all occasions, and the Congress was without results.

Nicky is quite against Constitutions, or liberty for Russia - this I know - and would never grant the concessions which the Emperor Alexander II had lying ready written out in his table drawer, with only his signature wanting, when he fell a victim to the Nihilist bombs. The prisons in Siberia are as terrible as ever, the police as powerful, and the people have no redress the oppression in the Baltic provinces is the same as under Alexander III. Therefore an era of peace seems hardly in accordance with the oppression and suffering of a race still governed by despotism, though the Czar is as good and gentle and kind as a man can be - anxious for the welfare of his subjects, pure in mind and noble of intentions, true and upright, and endears himself to all who know him by his unaffected simple ways and charming manners, so modest and quiet, and his winning expression....

The Empress was right in her surmise that nothing tangible would result from the Russia suggestion. At the Peace Conference which met in London in 1899 the disarmament proposals were left unsigned, although a permanent arbitration court was set up at The Hague.

In the three remaining years of the Empress's life two dominant subjects exercised her mind - the fortunes of the various members of her family, and the wars in which England was engaged in the Soudan and in South Africa, and her letters to Queen Victoria over this period are filled with comments upon the various births, marriages, and deaths among her relatives and friends, and with her opinions on the varying turns and fortunes of the campaigns. Up to 1898 the Empress had enjoyed exceptionally good health, but in that year she had a riding accident, and in the following year she became the victim of that same disease from which her husband had suffered. On September 6, 1898, four days after the battle of Omdurman and the hoisting of the British flag at Khartoum, the Empress wrote to Queen Victoria:

I would have written yesterday to thank you once more for your telegram and tell you once more how sincerely I rejoice at the success of our arms and what is, I hope, the termination of the Egyptian War, and offer you my sincerest congratulations, but was prevented. The fact is I had what might have been a very serious accident, but I escaped with only a slight injury to my right hand. I was out riding with Mossy and Frau v Reischach when my horse took fright at a steam threshing-machine in a field and shied violently. I tried to quiet it, and the groom got off to lead it past the machine, but it reared in one moment and swung round, throwing me off, happily on the right side, and my habit caught in the pommel, which broke the weight of the fall, but it was very dangerous as my head and shoulders were on the ground almost under the horse's hoofs. However, I got up and walked part of the way home and only felt shaken and stiff towards evening. Whether it was a kick or a tread on my right hand, I do not know, but it was extremely painful. I went straight to my doctor, who told me to put my hand in ice, which I did, and the swelling soon went down. I can use it for writing, but not for other things. It was my favourite horse - a thoroughbred - usually so charming to ride, but I perceived on the road that something was wrong with her, as when she first heard the machine she stopped

350

and snorted and I had some difficulty in getting her along she jumped and plunged and finally reared, as I said. But it was a very lucky escape - nothing of any consequence happily - and I am all right today, except for a headache, and much ashamed that it should have happened.

Two months later the Empress visited England for the last time, staying with Queen Victoria at Balmoral and with Lord Rosebery at Dalmeny Park. On her arrival from Balmoral at the latter residence she wrote to her mother (October 31, 1898):

I was so sad to leave Balmoral - sweet place - with a thousand charms, dear and precious recollections. I enjoyed the time there so much and am so grateful to you for having allowed me to come and for all your kindness. The journey went off very well. I admired the drive to Ballater more than ever - the maze of golden birch trees seemed to give quite a glow to the hill-sides. At Aberdeen I caught sight of the Sirdar for a moment before he left for Balmoral - we had a little drive down to the harbour after lunch in the Hotel and before the train started. The line along the coast is very interesting, and passing over the Tay and Forth bridges especially. It was nearly dark and the moon rising when we passed through this fine old Park. Lord Rosebery is looking very well and seemed much pleased at your message. His daughters are very pretty and pleasing, I think.

The following day the Empress wrote:

I wonder how you all are at dear Balmoral, for which I have no small degree of *Heimweh*, This morning was beautiful, but it soon became misty and windy, though fine on the whole. 'We went to Edinburgh in the morning to St. Giles' Cathedral and then to the Castle and to the National Gallery. I found the collection increased and very well hung and lit - some such fine things. Then we walked a little in Princes Street and went into one or two shops, but I saw nothing much that I cared for. Edinburgh looked very fine, I thought, and I was exceedingly sorry that we had no time to go to Holyrood. I hear the Chapel is in the same terrible state as I saw it 14 years ago - when by stooping down I could see through the iron bars of the side Chapel the bones and skulls lying about.

People have an idea that you do not wish anything restored. I said I thought that was a mistake and that you had lately said you thought the tombs should be looked after and put in order. General Chapman was much pleased when he heard that; he too was grieved at the state of utter neglect of this historical spot and place of burial, so near a Royal Palace inhabited now and then by yourself.

This afternoon we went to see Hopetoun - what a stately house and magnificent place altogether! I was much interested in seeing it. The views are beautiful and the trees, etc., so fine.

I think Lord Rosebery's daughters quite charming, so gentle and nice, with such pretty manners, and bright and intelligent. I think them pretty too - with very good figures and lovely complexions....

In the May of the following year Queen Victoria celebrated her eightieth birthday, and the letter which the Empress Frederick wrote to her mother for that occasion exemplifies to a marked degree the affection and appreciation which existed between the two. The letter, dated May 22, 1899, ran:

As, alas, I cannot be with you on your dear birthday, these lines must convey at least a little of all I should like to say.

All the gratitude, the love and veneration, they cannot express, which fill my heart and banish sad thoughts, nor all the heartfelt and tender good wishes and blessings.

Eighty years of grace and honours - of usefulness and goodness of trials and sorrows - with much happiness and many joys such as are given to few, though mingled with troubles and anxieties inseparable from a unique position as a sovereign and mother. Truly a reason for us to praise and thank God for so many mercies, and to pray that bright and peaceful years may crown the rest! The thought of all those who would have loved to have celebrated this anniversary with you, and who are no more amongst us, will, I know, not be absent from your mind, and their dear memory will be recalled, with all the affection they received and bestowed in our dear home, and which can never cease to be missed. I join my sisters in the gift of candelabra for the Indian room and venture to send a tiny locket, which I hope you will put on a bracelet or watch chain.

May the day be very fine and dear Windsor not too tiring for you.

I must not write a longer letter today, as I know the flood of letters which will come in and how many will have to help to send answers!

Good-bye, dearest beloved Mama - once more let me say how deeply grateful I am not only for past love and kindness but for all the tender sympathy which has been such a comfort to me.

Towards the end of that year, 1899, the varying fluctuations of the South African war, which broke out in October, aroused the keen interest of the Empress, who was naturally hopeful of British success. She followed every battle eagerly and read the detailed accounts of every engagement in the *The Times* and the *Daily Telegraph* with a view to understanding the British point of view, for the Germans had from the first taken up a very hostile attitude towards England and had sided with the Boers. The German press rang with tales of British barbarity which found credence with the semi-educated, and published scathing criticisms on British strategy. Powerless to contradict these fabrications publicly, she wrote innumerable letters to her friends putting forward the British version. On October 20, 1899, there occurred the first battle of the war at Glencoe or Dundee, when six Boer guns were captured. General Sir William Symons, the British leader, was, however, mortally wounded in the fight. The victory elated the Empress, who wrote to Queen Victoria on October 24:

Your telegram yesterday caused me great joy. With all my heart I congratulate you on the brilliant success. Alas, it seems to have been dearly bought, and brave valuable lives have been lost. You call the place Dundee, whereas the newspapers call the battle 'Glencoe'. I know the two places are quite near each other and that Glencoe Camp was the place most threatened. How splendidly our troops seem to have behaved - all the boasting and savagery of these horrid Boers and all their fury was of no use to them. Their numbers must have been very overwhelming. I only hope Mr Rhodes is safe, as they have sworn to take his life and intend to attack Kimberley. I am so distressed to hear of poor General Symons being mortally wounded. Is there really no chance of his recovery? Poor man, after his bravery and his excellent management of his troops and masterly arrangements, it does seem so sad. It is pleasant to read the Italian and Austrian papers, in contrast to the French, Russian and German.

I cannot help hoping you will go to Italy in spring and not to France; really the French have been too nasty. I wonder how it will be with William's visit? His foolish telegram to Kruger after all has to answer for a very great deal, and it is a great satisfaction to me that the German Government should in some ways have to eat their words - after that telegram they deserved to have every imaginable difficulty, etc., to show them its folly.

A week later, on November 2, 1899, the Empress wrote from Trento:

The sad news of the reverse at Ladysmith has made me dreadfully unhappy, and I can imagine how it must distress you and what anxiety it must cause you and everyone in England. Our forces were indeed too slender at that place to oppose such an enormous number. I only hope and trust that we shall be able to inflict a signal defeat on those dreadful Boers elsewhere and that our success will not be doubtful in the end. If only part of our Fleet were in Delagoa Bay and reinforcements could reach Ladysmith from another quarter. So much advice is given the Boers from German, French, Russian and Dutch sources that, of course, they know quite well what to do and where our weakest points are. You cannot think how I feel being far away and not knowing what is going on, as the *Times* and the *Daily Telegraph* arrive so late. It does not do to lose heart and see all *en noir* because of this sad misfortune at Ladysmith. The chances of war are always uncertain and 'luck' is a fitful Goddess. I am pining for more and better news. I wish I could fly over to you and help to read out to you and write for you at this anxious time.

My doctor arrived yesterday, and today I am going to begin the electricity and massage cure for this awful lumbago, which till now has yielded to nothing. The constant pain is so wearing and the helplessness very trying. My only comfort in not being with you now is that I should be a trouble and a cumbrance in your house in my present state.

The Empress's ailment, which the German doctors cautiously diagnosed as lumbago, was, however, much more serious, and on November 7, 1899, the Empress Frederick wrote to Queen Victoria:

I suffer very much indeed from my back at night and lying down or sitting in a chair. I can manage a little walking and driving, so that I can be out a good deal, but I am very much hampered in all my movements.

What a mercy that Sir G. White seems to hold out at Ladysmith and that the railway communication with the coast is not yet destroyed, and that the wounded are doing well, and new troops arriving at the Cape. God grant all may go well in spite of all the terrible difficulties in the way.

These letters are typical of the Empress's correspondence with her mother during the succeeding months. British successes would elate her, and reverses distress her. She was most anxious that Germany should preserve a strict neutrality and keep in check the undoubted pro-Boer feeling among certain sections of the empire. By the end of the year 1899 the Empress, who was now in Italy, was compelled to spend the greater part of her day in bed, and her enforced inaction resulted in her letters to her mother becoming more frequent than before. A typical letter of this period is the following, which is dated January 1, 1900:

The first words this morning and my motto for the century: 'God save the Queen'. Never was this prayer breathed more tenderly and devotedly, nor from a more grateful heart.

One hates parting, even from an imaginary bit of a past so precious, and one loves not beginning a new phase and embarking on the unknown, though we do so every day of our lives without thoughts as solemn as those with which we enter upon a new year, and this time a new century.

My thoughts are so much with you all today, and how I should love to talk over the many subjects of deep interest and anxiety which crowd in upon one. I hope the news from South Africa is more reassuring. William wrote me a card saying he hoped peace would soon be made and this useless bloodshed put an end to. These sentiments in this form I cannot echo. Heaven knows each drop of precious British blood seems a drop too much to be shed, but to allow ourselves to be driven into giving up a struggle which was unavoidable and forced upon us at the very moment when it is most unfavourable to us, I should think most deplorable and disastrous - a mistake all round, which would only please and encourage our enemies - anxious for anything that can injure us -

and dishearten and distress our friends.

My opinion is that England will come out of this contest, which she was bound to undertake as part of her mission in the spread and establishment of civilisation, stronger than she went in. She will see who are her friends and who her foes, and she will also see whatever defects there may be in her armaments and will reform whatever is faulty. The Empire will be welded more firmly together than ever by having faced a common danger. England will put forth her strength and, I doubt not, weather the storm.

I am able to be up for a little in an arm-chair and on the sofa. The pain is still very acute. Professor Renvers is coming to see me tomorrow and new endeavours will be made to cure this severe and tedious attack, which causes so much suffering....

In spite of the growing acuteness of her sufferings the Empress was able on one occasion to set foot again on what was technically British 'soil', for the British man-o'-war *Caesar* called at La Spezia. On February 25 the Empress wrote to her mother:

....I feel that you must be very anxious about the struggle between Lord Roberts and General Cronje. One trembles at the thought of all the bloodshed, and yet one knows that nothing decisive can be arrived at without another battle or two. If Cronje is overcome, there remains Ladysmith to be relieved and Joubert's forces to be disposed of, Bloemfontein to be taken and Pretoria reached. It keeps one in a fever of suspense....

I hope I shall be able to manage to see some of the lovely spots round here, wherever the roads are not rough and a long drive not needed. I should love to do some sketches, for there are most beautiful bits of coast, rocks and wooded hills here, much wilder than on the other side of the Riviera. The villages too are almost untouched and most picturesque. A magnificent man-o'-war, the *Caesar*, was in the harbour of La Spezia, and we went on board. I managed it somehow, and was indeed happy to be once more on a British ship. Of course I could not go over the ship, but rested in the splendid cabin of the Admiral....

Two days later she wrote:

Only one line of congratulation and to say how delighted I am to hear this most important and excellent news of Cronje's surrender with 7000 men to Lord Roberts.

I cannot say how thankful I feel for you, for Lord Roberts and Lord Kitchener – for the Army in general and for all England. I am sure it is part of a great load off your mind. Now one only wishes that Ladysmith and Mafeking should be relieved, General Joubert beaten, and Bloemfontein and Pretoria taken, and the war ended. One wishes Sir R Buller to have his share of luck and good fortune, and poor Lord Methuen too. It would be splendid if the decision could be come to before the Paris Exhibition is opened. Our success would be a pill for the French, Russians and Germans to swallow, which they would not like at all and which would do them no harm and only good....

The relief of Ladysmith awakened equal rejoicings, and when, on Queen Victoria's birthday, the news of the relief of Mafeking was confirmed, the Empress wrote from Cronberg (May 24, 1900):

Let me again wish you, with all my heart, every blessing on this day so dear to us – and say how much my thoughts are with you – and with how many a fervent prayer. So many thanks for your dear letter of the 2ist received yesterday and for two telegrams – the one with the news that the report of the relief of Mafeking was officially confirmed, and the other that you safely arrived at dear Balmoral, where I hope you will spend this dear day as peacefully and pleasantly as possible and enjoy a little rest and quiet after so much fatigue. Your visit to the poor wounded must have been very interesting – their pleasure to see you must have been great It is very tiresome that the Boers have gone to Laing's Nek again and are troubling us in Natal and giving Sir R Buller much work no doubt in hopes to affect Lord Roberts' onward march. How wonderfully well Colonel Baden-Powell managed at Mafeking – indeed he deserves all praise possible. I am afraid the war is not likely to end just yet and a good deal remains to be done. Still one feels all confidence that things are going well and will terminate satisfactorily and that there will be no giving way or misplaced generosity and leniency, and that fate will overtake that old hypocrite Kruger in spite of his being as sly as many foxes put together – and the intriguing Leyds, whose lies even now have not abated....

In her letter to her mother of July 4, 1900, there occurs a last reference to her son, the Emperor William, who once again had shocked the Empress Frederick by a tactless public speech.

....Dear William has made [she wrote] a new speech with much fanfaronade. I wish the German Government would give up the policy of constant fireworks, sensational coups, etc., as the vanity and conceit of the public and their chauvinism are stimulated thereby to a perfectly ridiculous degree....I am about again, but in great pain...but nothing can be done, so one has to bear it....

The Empress's last letter to her mother was written on October 5, 1900.

....I have been suffering [she wrote by the hand of her daughter Charlotte] to such an extent, but though in no ways alarming, so I trust you will not worry yourself one moment about me. I shall be prevented for some days from leaving my bed, and the attacks of spasms that seize me in the back, limbs and bones are so frequent that it is difficult to find a pause long enough to write in....

The following months gave the Empress no respite from her terrible malady. It seemed, indeed, as if the last months of the Empress were to be marked by the most agonising suffering and by a successive series of unhappy events. Only three months earlier, on July 30, 1900, her brother Alfred, Duke of Saxe-Coburg, who had succeeded 'Uncle Ernest' in 1893, died at Rosenau. But the sufferings of the Empress were mitigated in no small degree by the tender affection and consideration shown towards her by a few of her friends and many of her relatives. Of these latter, the most considerate was her eldest brother, the Prince of Wales, who on the occasion of Prince Alfred's funeral took the opportunity to spend many weeks at Homburg and to make frequent visits to his sister at Cronberg. The Empress's eldest son also stayed in the same district at the Castle of Wilhelmshöhe for a period. He seemed to share the Prince of Wales's concern at the invalid's condition, and his demeanour towards her and his uncle was unusually considerate.

The last bitter blow that fate had in store for the Empress was the death of the mother she loved so much on January 22, 1901. All through the Empress's life her mother had been a never-failing help, and her tender solicitude and affection had assisted the Empress through all the difficult passages of her life.

The Empress's own end was now not far distant. On July 24, 1901, the Emperor William wrote to his uncle, now King Edward, of a visit he had paid to the Empress on July 15, when he found her very despondent but able to write letters and to interest herself 'in everything that is going on in the world, politics as well as literature and art'. The Emperor thought her no worse than when the King had last seen her, and anticipated no crisis until the winter, but soon it became clear to her two devoted daughters, the Duchess of Sparta and Princess Frederick Charles of Hesse, that she was sinking. A fortnight later, on August 5, the Empress died. By her own direction she was buried by the side of the husband she had loved so well and who had brought her the greatest happiness she had known.

With the death of the Empress Frederick there passed from the European stage one of the most tragic figures in nineteenth-century history. It is difficult in the retrospect to attempt to allocate the blame or praise for those events in her life which caused so much contemporary controversy. Certain it is that in any summing up her complex character cannot be disregarded. As her mother's daughter she quite naturally had from her earliest days a pride in her British birth, but when she married and went to live in Germany no woman could have thrown herself more thoroughly into the life and feelings of the German people than she did. She spoke their language perfectly and had no difficulty in understanding their point of view. Her pride in the German army, her love of the German people, her intense desire that Germany should take the lead in everything, were traits in her character that might have been expected to endear her to all Germans. Although married to one of the great heroes of Germany, an impeccable wife, a warm-hearted friend and a charitable Princess, she was yet unpopular, and the main reason was that she remained *'die Engländerin'* in German eyes, a phrase that, in the Germany of the nineteenth century, bore as much scornful acerbity as the term 'Bolshevist' in England to-day. A truer conception of her outlook is perhaps contained in the description which her son, the Emperor William, gave of her in his book: 'She was always most German in England and most English in Germany'. And that was the main cause of her unpopularity.

Another of the principal stumbling-blocks was that despite her sex she was supposed to interfere in politics, and this was anathema to Bismarck and the Junkers, who had long ago satisfied themselves that *Kinder, Kirche und Küche* were the only legitimate interests for women. Then she was a Liberal. In those days, while the intelligentsia of Germany were in great part Liberal, the reigning families and practically the whole aristocracy gave the cold shoulder to anyone suspected of even the mildest form of Liberalism. Bismarck had succeeded in making the Liberal party thoroughly unpopular, and therefore it required persons of some character to allow themselves to be ticketed as Liberals. Both the Emperor Frederick and the Empress, when they were the Crown Prince and Crown Princess, never hesitated for a moment to proclaim themselves Liberals, but while such ideas were regarded as possible in the case of a great soldier, they were not to be tolerated in the case of a woman, although what was then understood by 'Liberal principles' was vastly different from the interpretation that is placed upon that conception to-day. Liberalism in the middle of the last century was a school of political thought which believed that progress should be made through the means of democratic representation such as England then enjoyed. Germany by contrast was then an autocratic state, in which either the Chancellor or the Emperor wielded supreme power. To have openly found fault with the Crown Princess's Liberal ideas, or to have condemned her because she was a woman interested in politics, might have had dangerous repercussions and led to unforeseen results. Therefore, the safest accusation to bring against her was that she was an Englishwoman intriguing against Germany; this brought together all patriotic Germans, no matter what their politics might be, and created a feeling of distrust for the Empress. Further, in order to give some plausible explanation of the fact that the Crown Prince himself held Liberal views, it was said that he was entirely under the domination of his wife. For these reasons the Crown Princess's unpopularity grew, and, unfortunately, she was not gifted with the necessary tact for so difficult a situation. Able, intellectual and talented, she particularly wished to be of service to the country of her adoption, but she had been brought up to express herself with perfect frankness and she never hesitated to state her point of view, sometimes with tactless honesty.

They have a saying in Spain, 'Clever people say stupid things, stupid people do them', and certainly in the Empress's case this was true, as she never learnt caution. Curiously enough there have been two precisely similar cases in Europe of late years. The Empress of Russia was accused of pro-German proclivities during the war and was said to dominate her husband, when two totally different reasons, her love of mysticism and her infatuation with that sinister figure Rasputin, were the real causes of her unpopularity. The second instance is Queen Sophie of Greece, who would be entitled to have German sympathies, but who was accused of dominating her husband, King Constantine, whereas there is no doubt that all these stories were invented to throw a cloud over the monstrous blunders the British Government made in dealing with the situation in Greece.

The most tragic event in the Empress's life was of course the death of her husband, and the deplorable quarrels that surrounded it. It is difficult even now to see what the outcome might have been if the Empress had placed her whole reliance on the German doctors. Possibly the storm of criticism that assailed her during this period might have been avoided, but it is extremely doubtful whether, since the illness proved eventually to be cancer, any other doctor, or any other treatment, could then have effected the cure of her husband, or even any alleviation of his sufferings.

Since the death of the Empress Frederick the main criticism directed against her has been based on the assumption that she had been harsh in her treatment of her eldest son. But can anyone after reading the letters given in this volume come to any other conclusion but that, in the main, the differences that occurred between them were due to the actions of the Emperor? Until late in his teens there was no shadow between them. In fact, until the Emperor left the parental roof and got into the hands of the Junker party headed by Bismarck and Waldersee, a party that was eventually to lead Germany to world power and downfall, the relations between the two were all that could be desired. Once the future Emperor was caught up in that powerful clique, his sympathy with his mother vanished and henceforth cool indifference was his attitude towards her. When he succeeded to the throne, he had quite made up his mind that he would never allow his mother to interfere in politics in any way. Not only did she hold advanced Liberal opinions which conflicted with his autocratic nature, but he could never dismiss from his mind the sneers of Bismarck at 'Petticoat Government'. Therefore, he resolved that no one should ever accuse him of being influenced in any way by his mother. Whether kinder methods on his part would not have produced the same result it is difficult to say, but he was determined to prevent her taking any active part in political and social life. And the pathetic part of it all was that she was really fond of him. Had her feelings been indifferent, his behaviour to her would never have hurt her as it did, but she loved him and was ever grateful for the occasional signs of affection he showed her.

The Empress Frederick perhaps failed to make allowance for the difficult position in which her friends and even members of her family were placed. Many must have sympathised with her, but to do so openly meant incurring the wrath of the Emperor and Bismarck, and therefore the safest course was to remain silent. Those who did actually espouse her cause, like Geffcken, Roggenbach and others, were so persecuted that their careers were ruined. It is hardly to be wondered at that when she became a person who had ceased to count, no one dared to come forward and defend her.

The Empress Frederick indeed suffered from the disadvantage of being born before her time, and also, paradoxically, of living too long. Up to the year 1871 her life had been one remarkable series of successes. In her birth and childhood she was fortunate. In her marriage she was happy beyond measure: and the wars of 1864, 1866 and 1870-71 had crowned her husband with laurels well deserved. Their union had been blessed by eight children, all, in 1872, surviving with the exception of Sigismund. Here, indeed, was the Princess at the zenith of human happiness, at the pinnacle as it were of her life; after that, blow upon blow assailed her. First came the loss of her beloved child Waldemar in 1879: the next decade saw the promise of a throne, but, with the fulfilment of that promise, the illness and death of her husband. Then followed the gradual alienation of the sympathy of her eldest son, the steadily increasing ring of enemies, until finally we see the deserted widow in retirement with scarcely a faithful friend left. Calumny and vituperation have pursued her even beyond the grave.

She was a Cassandra to whom none would listen: an Andromache for whom none had sympathy. Her Liberal counsels, if followed, might have averted the wrath to come. It is the irony of fate that those who insulted and derided her during her lifetime and after, were also those whose autocratic and militaristic views eventually brought the Germany that she loved to the abyss of disaster. It is in the nature of tragedy to evoke musings upon what might have been. Had the counsels which she gave, and which drew down upon her the disapprobation of the gallery, been suffered to prevail, would Germany have been saved from the disasters that eventually overwhelmed her?

Calumniated, abandoned, distrusted and even hated as she was by Germany in her lifetime and for a quarter of a century after, the time is surely coming when that great country will recognise that in the Empress Frederick it had a sovereign lady who, in spite of her faults, in spite of the defects of her qualities, always devoted her energies to secure for Germany the political and cultural leadership of continental Europe.

## NOTE

1 Hugo, Baron von Reischach, *Under Three Emperors*, p. 179.

# Index

Abdul Hamid, Sultan, 117, 118
Achenbach, Oberprasident von, 331
Acton, Lord, 151
Adelaide, Queen Dowager, 16
Adlerberg, General, 142
Albedyll, General von, 209
Albert, Prince Consort, 16, 17, 18, 21, 26, 28, 30, 31, 32, 34, 37, 87, 88, 115, 127, 277, 282
Albert Victor, Prince, Duke of Clarence, 331
Aldenhoven, Dr, 303
Alexander II, Tsar of Russia, 111, 116, 117, 121, 142, 143, 144, 145, 349
Alexander III, Tsar of Russia, 350
Alexander, Prince, of Battenberg, ruler of Bulgaria ('Sandro'), 156-63, 168, 170, 231-6, 238, 2500-1, 257, 321
Alexander, Prince, of Hesse, 157
Alexander, Prince, of Servia, 335
Alexandra, Queen (Princess of Wales), 48, 49, 51, 76, 79, 104, 109, 129, 261, 301
Alfred, Prince, Duke of Edinburgh, later of Saxe-Coburg, 37, 125, 138, 143, 149, 160, 305, 357
Alice, Princess (Grand Duchess of Hesse-Darmstadt), 16, 67, 68, 69, 78, 98, 136, 157, 303
Alma-Tadema, Sir Lawrence, 325
Alvensleben, Countess, 75
Anhalt, Duke of, 60
Anthony, Prince, of Hohenzollern-Sigmaringen, 63
Antoinette (Antonia), Princess (Leopold), of Hohenzollern-Sigmaringen, 63, 64
Apponyi, Count, 66, 67
Argyll, Duke of, 154
Armstrong, Lord, 311
Arnim, Count von, 214
Arthur, Duke of Connaught, 167, 169, 171, 173, 174
Augusta, Princess (later Queen of Prussia and German Empress), 18, 25, 35, 44, 107, 238, 254, 256, 271, 276, 279, 280, 283, 299, 305, 306, 307, 321, 331, 339
Augusta Victoria, Princess, of Schleswig-Holstein-Sonderburg-Augustenburg, German Empress ('Dona'), 139, 140, 141, 144, 157, 170, 214, 254, 256, 284, 285, 294, 306, 307, 312, 313, 314, 322, 330
Augustus, Duke of Sussex, 16

Bazaine, Marshal, 74, 78, 82
Beatrice, Princess (Princess Henry of Battenberg), daughter of Queen Victoria, 157,

158, 231, 233, 236
Bedford, Duke of, 154
Benedetti, Vincent, Count, 65, 74, 77
Beresford, Lord Charles, 216, 316
Bergmann, Prof. Ernst von, 156, 182, 183, 185, 186, 187, 188, 190, 202, 204, 205, 207, 209, 217, 218, 219, 220, 241, 242, 243, 253, 254, 258, 259, 260, 264, 276, 290, 293, 295
Berlepsch, M de, 311
Bernard, Prince, of Saxe-Meiningen, 133, 134, 135, 171, 221, 275, 294, 299, 331
Bernstorff, Count von, 66, 84
Bernstorff, Countess von, 108
Bieberstein, Baron Marschall von, 316
Bigge, Major (afterwards Lord Stamfordham), 231
Bismarck, Prince (Prince von Bismarck-Schonhausen): views on marriage of Princess Royal of England, 21; vetoes appointment of Sir Robert Morier as Ambassador, 30; summoned to Berlin by King William I, 39; policy of, 39; and Crown Princess Frederick, 39, 40, 47, 53, 90, 103, 104, 116, 117, 118, 122, 128, 150, 151, 169, 170, 195, 215, 222; and Constitution of 1850, 41; ignores Crown Prince's letter, 41, 44; views on breach between Crown Prince and King William I of Prussia, 45 seq.; hostility of Crown Prince, 45, 46; fosters anti-English sentiments in Prussia, 47; views on Germanic Confederation, 47; and war with Denmark, 48, 49; policy of Prussian aggrandisement, 53; attitude to engagement of Princess Helena, 53; growing hostility to Austria, 53, 54, 59, 61; desires war with France, 63; and Ems telegram, 65; on staff of King William I during Franco-Prussian War, 68; on English influence in Crown Prince's circle, 79; for bombardment of Paris, 85, 86, 91; favours creation of a German Empire, 87, 88, 89; signs armistice with France, 99; relations with Russia (1871-78), 106ff; effects the *Dreikaiserbund*, 106; and London Conference (March 1871), 107-8; attitude towards Empress Augusta, 107, 108; suspicion of France, 111; and Roman Catholic priesthood, 111; Queen Victoria's attitude to, 113, 115, 233, 236; difficulties in domestic politics, 119; suggests British occupation of Egypt, 120-3; and Congress of Berlin, 129-30; opinion of Lord Beaconsfield, 130; alliance of Prussia and Austria, 147; autocratic government of, 150; anti-English attitude of, 150; attitude to Bulgarian affairs (1886-88), 156 seq., 231; and engagement of Princess Victoria of Prussia, 157, 158, 231, 232, 234; change in policy (1887), 165; and illness of Crown Prince Frederick, 182, 186, 257, 260; and summons to Sir Morell Mackenzie, 184, 222, 224, 257; twenty-fifth anniversary of appointment, 196; and Orleans family, 212; publishes text of treaty against Russia, 217; and Empress Frederick after her accession, 230, 245, 246; rumoured resignation of, 231-2, 235; Lord Salisbury's account of, 232; and Queen Victoria (1888), 232, 238, 239, 241; attitude on death of Emperor Frederick III, 248, 249 ; and Empress Frederick after death of her husband, 249, 255, 258, 262, 273, 275; espionage system of, 263, 275, 295; and War Diary of Emperor Frederick III, 267, 269, 270, 271, 275; influence on Emperor William II, 276, 277, 309; attitude to Emperor William II, 286; colonial policy of, 287; breach with Emperor William II, 289, 297, 333; old age, etc., insurance scheme of, 289; and Count von Waldersee, 294; fall of, 297-317; opposition to Hatzfeldt

marriage, 297; prospect of retirement or death of, 300, 315; attitude towards England (1889), 301; fails to deny Freytag's slanders, 303; and Socialist Law of 1873, 308; protectionist policy of, 310; resignation of, 314-5; and Empress Frederick after his fall, 315, 316, 318, 326, 336-8, 341; rapprochement between Emperor William II and, 328-9, 332, 340, 345; and colonial policy of Emperor William II, 340, 345; presented with sword of honour, 345; and Mr Gladstone, 345
Bismarck, Count Herbert, 153, 184, 194, 195, 234, 236, 248, 258, 260, 261, 262, 273, 276, 279, 286, 293, 295, 308, 316, 326, 329, 346
Bismarck (-Schonhausen), Countess, later Princess, 86, 89, 120
Bloomfield, Lady, 21, 28
Bloomfield, Lord, 20, 21
Blücher, Countess, 54
Blumenthal, General von, 68, 69, 79, 86, 89, 261, 270
Bonaparte, Louis Napoleon, Prince Imperial, 770
Bose, General, 72
Boulanger, General, 316
Bourbaki, General, 96
Bramann, Dr, 204, 217, 219, 220, 241, 243, 254, 264
Brassey, Lord, 216, 311
Bright, John, 168
Brühl, Countess von, 210, 213, 218
Buchanan, Sir Andrew, 19, 51
Buller, Sir Redvers, 355, 356
Bülow, Prince, 88
Bunsen, Georg von, 38
Busch, J.H.M., 90, 158

Cambridge, George, Duke of ('Uncle George'), 60, 216
Caprivi, General Georg, Count von, 314, 315, 316, 318, 327, 328, 332, 333, 334, 335, 341, 342
Cardwell, Edward (afterwards Viscount), 71
Carnarvon, Lord, 126, 127
Carol I, King of Roumania. *See* Charles, Prince, of Roumania
Carolath, Prince Henry, 307, 308
Carpenter, Boyd, Bishop, 21
Cavour, Count, 108
Chamberlain, Joseph, 153
Chanzy, General, 96
Chapman, General, 351
Charles, of Hesse, Prince (of Hesse), 36
Charles, Prince, of Roumania (King Carol I), 125, 286
Charlotte, Princess (of Wales), daughter of King George IV, 16
Charlotte, Princess, of Saxe-Meiningen, 30, 110, 133, 134, 135, 137, 211, 217, 221, 259, 265, 271, 292, 294, 295, 299, 356
Chlodwig, Prince von Hohenlohe, 214, 248, 315, 341, 342, 344, 345, 346
Christian IX, King of Denmark (Prince Christian of Schleswig-Holstein-

Sonderburg-Glucksburg), 29, 48, 49
Christian, Prince of Schleswig-Holstein-Augustenburg-Sonderburg, 53, 54, 72, 98, 139, 143, 166, 262, 286
Churchill, Dowager Lady, 231; Lord Randolph, 172, 173, 316
Clarence, Albert Victor, Duke of, 331
Clarendon, Earl of, 12, 18, 20, 26, 30, 36, 37, 64
Clementine, Princess, of Bourbon-Orleans ('Aunt Clem'), 98, 169
Cobden, Richard, 19
Constantine, King of Greece (Duke of Sparta, 'Tino'), 300, 301, 302, 321, 359
Crispi, Francesco, 173
Cronje, General, 355
Cumberland, Ernest Augustus, Duke of, 254, 261
Currie, Sir Donald, 345

Dealtry, Thomas, 61
Decazes, Duc, 113
Delbrück, Dr., 271
Derby, Lord, 26, 112, 116, 118, 119, 120, 126, 127, 128, 129, 131
Devonshire, Duke of, 27
Dilke, Sir Charles, 153, 334
Disraeli, Benjamin, Earl of Beaconsfield, 146, 149, 151, 152, 157, 163, 164, 165, 187, 188
Doetz, Dr, 80
Dolgoroukova, Countess (Princess Yourievsky), 142, 144
Dönhoff, Countess Amélie, 89
Douglas, Count, 310, 311
Dresky, Captain von, 80
Dufferin, Lord, 147, 158
Duncker, Professor, 42, 44
Duvernoy, General Verdy, 316

Edward VII, King of Great Britain and Ireland, Emperor of India (Albert Edward, Prince of Wales): birth and education of, 16; visits court of Napoleon III, 17; question of his marriage, 29, 48; Mediterranean tour with Crown Prince and Princess of Prussia, 40; attitude during Danish War (1864), 51, 66; with Queen Victoria at Coburg, 54; alleged sympathy with France against Prussia, 67; reconciliation with Crown Princess, 104, 109; dislike of Bismarck, 104; visits to Berlin and Potsdam, 109, 133, 138, 144; visit to India, 112; and Benjamin Disraeli, 130, 131; and Lord Randolph Churchill, 172, 173; at funeral of Emperor William I., 230; and Count Herbert Bismarck, 248, 260, 261, 262; Vienna visit of (1888), 278; avoids meeting Emperor William II, 278, 289; at wedding of Princess Sophie in Athens, 301; last visits to Empress Frederick, 357; *see also* 38, 157, 172, 173, 235, 289, 324
Elizabeth, Queen of Prussia, wife of King Frederick William IV, 33, 34., 35, 89
Elizabeth, Queen of Roumania ('Carmen Sylva'), 335, 336, 338, 339
Elliott, Sir Henry, 131
Ernest, Duke of Cumberland, King of Hanover, 16

Ernest, Duke of Saxe-Coburg Gotha ('Uncle Ernest'), 16, 48, 53, 68, 69, 135, 282, 283, 304, 305, 308, 357
Ernest Augustus, Duke of Cumberland, 254, 261
Ernst Gunther, Duke of Schleswig-Holstein, 166
Esebeck, General, 72
Eugene, Prince, of Sweden, 161
Eugénie, Empress, 71, 74, 77, 79, 81, 83, 92, 93, 112
Eulenberg, Count, 194, 333

Failly, General, 91
Falk, Dr, 147
Falkenstein, General von, 86
Favre, Jules, 99
Ferdinand, Prince, of Roumania, 335, 338
Ferdinand, Prince, of Saxe-Coburg-Gotha, Prince of Bulgaria, 169, 171, 173, 286, 321, 336, 346
Francis Joseph, Emperor of Austria, 47, 106, 163, 285
Frederick II, the Great, King of Prussia, 79, 308, 315, 341
Frederick III, German Emperor (Frederick William, Crown Prince of Prussia and of Germany): meets Princess Royal of England, 17; seeks marriage with Princess Royal, 18; wedding announced, 19; visit to England (1856), 20; marriage of, 21; birth of heir (Emperor William II), 27, 29; and war in Italy (1859), 30; elected Rector of Königsberg University, 35; character of, 38; Mediterranean tour with Prince of Wales, 39; breach with King William I of Prussia, 40; letters to Bismarck on breach of Constitution, 46, 47; hostility to Bismarck, 37, 48, 57, 128; visit to English court, 40; and Queen Victoria at Coburg (1863), 47; supports Augustenburg claim to Schleswig and Holstein, 48; attitude during Danish War (1864), 49; meeting with Prince of Wales after Danish War, 51; victories during Seven Weeks' War, 58; command during Franco-Prussian War, 68; victory at Wörth, 72. 74; at Weissenburg, 72; on hospital activities of Crown Princess, 76, 80, 82, 91; views on German unity, 79; views on problem of Alsace and Lorraine, 79-80, 258; created Field-Marshal, 82, 83, 104; and bombardment of Paris, 85, 86, 89, 92, 94, 98; favours creation of a German Empire, 87-9, 265; not dominated by Crown Princess, 90; thoughts for future of Prince William, 97; visit to London (1871), 104; friendship with Lord Ampthill (Odo Russell), 106; visit to London (1874), 109, anti-Russian attitude of, 118; on Russo-Turkish War (1877), 123; visit to England (1878), 129; as Regent, 130, 131; and engagement of Princess Victoria of Prussia, 157; illness of, 181-224, 241-3, 253, 254, 258, 302; Bismarck stops operation upon, 182; Sir Morell Mackenzie's attendance on, 186 seq., 272; difference of opinion of doctors concerning illness of, 188-9, 190 seq.; suggested treatment in England, 189; visit for Queen Victoria's Jubilee (1887), 190, 192, 263; journey to Tyrol, 193; in Venice, 195; at Baveno, 197; at San Remo, 199-224, 227; question of operation, 200-3; operation performed, 217; rumours in Berlin concerning, 217; true story of illness of, 224, 242; accession to throne, 226; journey to Berlin, 227; attitude to Prince Bismarck after accession, 227-9; visit of Queen Victoria (1888), 231; death of, 246, 248, 302; affection for Queen Victoria, 250; War Diary of, 263-

80, 275; Sir Morell Mackenzie's book about, 272, 274; Bismarck's attack on memory of, 275; slanders concerning, 302-3; proposed monument in Berlin, 319, see also 249, 252, 256, 257, 250 *et seq.*, 284, 291, 293, 294, 295, 296, 298, 301, 303, 305, 306, 307, 309, 310, 311, 312, 314, 320, 329, 330, 339, 340

Frederick, Empress (Victoria, Princess Royal of England and Crown Princess of Germany): birth of, 16; education of, 17; meets Prince Frederick William of Prussia, 17,; visits court of Napoleon III, 17, 81; hand sought by Prince Frederick William, 18; confirmation of, 18, 20; wedding announced, 20; marriage of, 21, 98; leaves for Berlin, 21; personal appearance of, 22, 40 ; first winter in Berlin, 25; love for England, 26, 38, 125, 195, 280; Berlin residence of, 26; birth of Prince William (Emperor William II), 27-8; residence at Potsdam, 29; holiday at Osborne, 29; birth of Princess Charlotte, 30; influence of Prince Consort on, 31-2, 37; on ministerial responsibility, 32; description of death of King Frederick William IV, 32-4.; visits England on death of Duchess of Kent, 34; and coronation of King William I, 35-6.; twenty-first birthday of, 37; and Bismarck's appointment, 39; Mediterranean tour with Prince of Wales, 40; birth of Prince Henry, 40; on breach between Crown Prince and King, 41, 43, 44, 46; and Prince Bismarck (while Crown Princess), 46, 53, 60, 104, 107, 111-2, 118, 150, 151, 166, 168-9, 171, 196, 214, 215, 232; visit to English court, 47; visits Queen Victoria at Coburg, 47; supports Augustenburg claimant, 48; attitude during Danish War (1864), 51-5; description of Prince Christian, 53-4; foresees war with Austria, 55; birth of Princess Victoria, 55; death of Prince Sigismund, 55-6, 249, 360; hospital work during Seven Weeks' War, 58; on Crown Prince's part in War, 58; praise of Prussians, 59; education of her sons, 61; and physical disability of Prince William (Emperor William II), 61-2, 98; on Hohenzollern candidature, 63-5; birth of Princess Sophie, 64; attitude towards war with France, 66; anxiety during Franco-Prussian War, 68-9; appeal to Queen Victoria for hospital supplies, 69, 71; and christening of Princess Sophie, 69-70; on victory at Wörth, 72; hospital activities during Franco-Prussian War, 73, 76, 78, 80, 82, 91, 94, 99, 103; on government of Napoleon III, 74; on French army, 75; on fall of Napoleon III, 77, 79, 81; views on Alsace-Lorraine problem, 91; on bombardment of Strassburg, 78; on Prussian superiority, 79; on Anglo-German tension during Franco-Prussian War, 83, 92, 100, 102, 103; opposed to bombardment of Paris, 86, 90, 94; slander concerning her influence over the Crown Prince, 90; and Empress Eugénie's screen, 92-3; relations with Empress Augusta, 96; imperial title of, 98; and future of Prince William (William II), 98; on capitulation of Paris, 99; on peace terms, 99; zenith of career, 103; visit to London (1871), 109; reconciliation with Prince of Wales, 104; visit to London (1874), 109; confirmation of Prince William, 109; on the Eastern Question, 114-6, 118, 147-9, 159, 160; anti-Russian attitude of, 118; on European policy towards Russia, 119, 120-1; and British affairs in Egypt, 121-2, 333-4; on Russo-Turkish War (1877-78), 124; advocates British intervention, 124-8; on Lord Derby's policy, 129; visit to England (1878), 129; on Lord Beaconsfield, 131; on marriage of Princess Charlotte, 133-5; on death of Princess Alice, 136-7; death of son, Prince Waldemar, 137, 360; becomes a grandmother, 137; and Prince William (Emperor William II) before his accession, 137 *seq.*, 161, 190, 193, 204-5, 214, 220, 231, 243-4; on Nihilists, 140, 145; on Prince William's engagement and marriage, 139-41, 144, 314, 315; on Czar's morganatic marriage, 142; on assassination of Czar Alexander II, 144; opinion of Gladstone, 152, 153-4, 168; on Lord Rosebery's appointment, 153-4; on Irish affairs, 153-5, 334; estrangement between Prince William and, 156-8, 166, 223; and engagement of Princess Victoria of Prussia, 157, 158; views about Prince Alexander of Battenberg, 159, 162; on decline of British influence in Europe, 163; conversation with Crown Prince Rudolf of Austria, 163-5; on Bulgarian affairs (1887-88), 165-73; and Lord Randolph Churchill's visit to Russia (1888), 172; on British interests in India, 172; and summons to Dr Morell Mackenzie, 183-5, 222; and operation on Crown Prince, 185-7, 257-60; slanders concerning Crown Prince's illness, 188, 222-4; presence at Queen Victoria's Jubilee (1887), 192; journey to Tyrol, 193; in Venice, 195; at Baveno, 197; at San Remo, 199-224; and death of Emperor William I, 221, 226; becomes German Empress, 226; returns to Berlin, 227; relations with Prince Bismarck (after accession to throne), 230-1, 245-6; visit of Queen Victoria (1888), 231, 240; tribute to devotion of, 235; death of her husband, 246-9, 359-60; and Emperor William II after his accession to throne, 248, 255, 267, 271-2, 274, 277-8, 280, 318-9; and Prince Bismarck after death of her husband, 248, 253, 258, 262, 273, 276; and Friedrichskron, 244, 248-9, 252, 268, 285, 295, 304; tribute to her husband, 249-50, 257; and Emperor Frederick's War Diary, 268, 270; on Emperor William II's journeys, 268; estimate of Emperor William II, 272, 277-9, 284, 286, 292, 309, 311, 313-5, 322, 327-31, 341, 344; and Sir Morell Mackenzie's book, 272; visit to England (1888), 280; hostility to memoirs of Duke of Saxe-Coburg-Gotha, 282; and visit of Emperor William II to England (1889), 282; and death of Archduke Rudolf of Austria, 284-5; on colonial policy of Germany, 287, 340; causes of aggravation of breach between Emperor William II and, 287-8; memories of Emperor Frederick, 290; influence of Queen Victoria over, 291; opinion of Count von Waldersee, 300; on prospect of Prince Bismarck's retirement or death, 300, 315; at marriage of Princess Sophie, 301; on death of Empress Augusta, 305; refused headship of Red Cross societies, 306; on proposed Labour Conference (1890), 310, 349; on Bismarck's protectionist policy, 311; on Empress Augusta Victoria, 314, 322; effect of Bismarck's fall on position of, 317, 318; retirement to house at Cronberg, 318; and proposed monument to husband in Berlin, 319; silence on foreign policy (1888-90), 320-1; comments on birth of Emperor William II's fourth son, 322-3; resemblance to Queen Victoria, 323; semi-official visit to Paris (1891), 323-5; visit to England (1891), 324 ; opinion of *La Marseillaise*, 325; changed attitude to Bismarck after his fall, 326, 336-8, 341; on Emperor William II's Erfurt speech, 326-7; on efforts to reconcile Emperor William II and Bismarck, 328-9, 332; on riots in Germany (1892), 330; on Emperor William II's visit to Italy (1893), 336; visit to Sophie, Crown Princess of Greece, 336; on affairs in Germany (1893), 336-8; on Queen Elizabeth of Roumania, 339; on Bismarck and German colonial policy, 340-1; on Emperor William II's naval policy, 341; on General von Caprivi, 342; on Prince von Hohenlohe, 342, 344-6; on rumour of Mr Gladstone's visit to Bismarck, 345; on Bulgarian affairs (1895), 346-7; on Anglo-German relations (1897), 347-8; on Russian proposals for conference on disarmament, 348; on Nicholas II, Emperor of Russia, 349-50; accident to, 350-1; illness of, 350, 354-

7; on Egyptian War (1898), 350; last visit to England (1898), 351; on Queen Victoria's eightieth birthday, 352; interest in South African War, 352-6; on Emperor William II's 'Kruger telegram', 353; visits British battleship, 355; on President Kruger, 356; last visits of Prince of Wales to, 357, and death of Queen Victoria, 357; death of, 357; character of, 357-61; Emperor William II's description of, 358; causes of her unpopularity, 358-9; Liberal principles of, 358; survey of her career, 360-1

Frederick VII, King of Denmark, 48
Frederick, Duke of Schleswig-Holstein-Sonderburg-Augustenburg (Fritz Augustenburg), 48, 53, 139, 297, 303
Frederick, Grand Duke of Baden, 120, 227, 252, 253, 271, 279
Frederick, Prince, of Denmark, afterwards King Frederick VIII, 300
Frederick, Prince, of the Netherlands, 36
Frederick Augustus, Prince (of Oldenburg), 133
Frederick Charles, Prince, of Prussia ('the Red Prince'), 68, 82-3, 85, 90, 95-6, 133, 135, 260-1
Frederick Charles, Princess, of Hesse (Margaret, daughter of Empress Frederick), 257
Frederick William III, King of Prussia, 103
Frederick William IV, King of Prussia, 18, 24, 32, 329
Freiligrath, Ferdinand, 71, 74
Freytag, Gustav, 43, 302-45
Friedberg, 273, 286, 295

Gambetta, Leon, 82, 85, 100
Geffcken, Professor H, 265, 269-72, 274-5, 283, 296-8, 303, 339, 360
Geissel, Cardinal, 36
Genoa, Duke of, 64
George I, King of Greece, 321, 322
George, Duke of Cambridge ('Uncle George'), 60, 216
George, Prince, of Greece, 300
George V, King of Hanover, 48, 53, 60, 61
Gerhardt, Professor, 181-2, 185-90, 192, 202, 209, 242-3, 254, 258-60, 276, 290, 293, 295
Gerlach, General von, 21
Giers, M. de, Russian Chancellor, 160, 172
Gladstone, William Ewart 67, 102, 114, 124, 131, 147, 148, 150-5
Gloucester, Duchess of, 16
Goltz, Marie, 72, 76
Gordon-Cumming, R.G., 316
Gortchakoff, Prince, 121, 131, 160
Goschen, Viscount, 148, 154
Gramont, Duc de, 64, 74, 75, 77
Granville, Lord, 26, 64, 70-1, 74, 84, 93, 103, 106, 147, 151
Gregory, Sir William, 216
Grey, General, 42, 43

Hahn, Dr, 259-60
Hamilton, Duchess of, 83
Hardenberg, Karl August von, Prince, 79
Harmening, Dr, 304-5
Harrington, Lord, 153, 154
Hartington, Lord 216
Hatzfeldt (-Wildenburg), Count Paul von, 214, 234, 297-9, 301, 315, 325, 341
Hatzfeldt, Helene, Princess Max of Hohenlohe, 297, 301
Helena, Princess ('Lenchen', afterwards Princess Christian), 53, 54, 58, 69, 98, 139, 166, 254, 282
Henry, Prince, of Battenberg, 157, 231, 233
Henry, Prince, of Prussia, son of Empress Frederick, 40, 59, 61, 108, 110, 133, 167, 197, 207-10, 213, 217, 242, 259, 267, 331
Heyden, Geheimrath von, 310, 311
Hintzpeter, Dr, 108, 110, 294, 309, 310, 311
Hohenlohe, Prince Chlodwig von, 214, 248, 315, 341, 342, 344-6
Hohenlohe-Oehringen, Prince Max von, 297
Hohenthal, Lothar von, 78
Hohenthal, Walburga, Countess von (Walburga, Lady Paget), 22, 29
Hovell, Dr Mark, 193, 198, 200, 201, 206, 208-9, 213, 215, 217, 224, 241-4, 254, 258, 263-4

Ignatieff, General, 119, 121
Ihne, Herr, 318
Irene, Princess, of Hesse, 244
Isabella, Queen of Spain, 63, 79

Jasmund, Herr von, 75
Jenner, Sir W., 160, 185, 210
Joinville, Prince de, 77
Joubert, General, 355

Kalnoky, Count, 164
Karolyi, Count, 147, 164
Kaulbars, General, 161-2, 166
Keller, Herr von, 345-6
Kent, Duchess of, 16, 34
Kessel, G. von, 279, 290, 293, 295
Kirchbach, General, 92
Kitchener, Lord, 385
Koch, General Arzt, 80
Krause, Dr, 200, 202-3, 208-9, 213, 217, 219-20, 241, 254
Kruger, President, 353-6
Kuper, Admiral, 50
Küssmaul, Professor, 218-20

Landgraf, Dr, 192, 202, 243, 254, 259

Langenbeck, Dr, 62, 75, 243, 250
Lauer, Dr, 182, 186
Lavalaye, M de, 311
Layard, Sir Austen Henry, 119-20, 215-6
Leboeuf, Edmond, 74-5
Lenthold, Dr, 202
Leopold I, King of the Belgians, 16, 17, 20, 28, 54, 87, 3, 6, 9, 19, 20, 52, 58, 104
Leopold II, King of the Belgians, 135, 163
Leopold, Prince, Duke of Albany, 28, 83, 149, 212
Leopold, Prince, of Hohenzollern-Sigmaringen, 63-5
Leroy-Beaulieu, Anatole, 311
Lobanoff, Prince, 161, 347
Loe, General W. von, 288, 296, 298
Loftus, Lord Augustus, 84, 103-4, 106, 127
Louis, Grand Duke of Hesse-Darmstadt, 74, 78, 136, 217, 332
Louis, Prince, of Baden, 253
Louis, Prince, of Battenberg, 157
Louise, Grand Duchess of Baden, 17, 35, 67, 120, 1§24, 169, 227, 253, 254, 271, 306
Louise, Duchess of Argyll, 59, 69
Louise Margaret, Princess, of Prussia, Duchess of Connaught, 135, 137
Ludwig, Emil, 158, 183, 184, 222-4, 248
Ludwig II, King of Bavaria, 87, 88, 91, 95
Luitpold, Prince, of Bavaria, 36
Luiz, King of Portugal, 158
Lyncker, Herr von, 279, 299
Lyttelton, Sarah, Lady, 21, 30

Mackenzie, Dr. (later Sir) Morell, 183-93, 195-7, 199-203, 205-7, 209-11, 213, 215-6, 218-9, 222-4, 226, 241-2, 254, 257-8, 260, 264, 271-2, 274, 290, 295, 298
MacMahon, Marshal, 72, 74, 76
Malet, Sir Edward, 151, 184-5, 232-4, 236-8, 241, 251-2, 264, 278, 298, 332
Mallet, Sir Louis, 311-2
Malmesbury, Lord, 17
Manchester, Duchess of, 27
Manning, Cardinal, 310
Manteuffel, Marshal, 116
Margaret, Princess, of Prussia, Princess Frederick Charles of Hesse, 257, 323
Marie Alexandrovna, Empress of Russia, 142, 145
Marie, Grand Duchess, of Russia, Duchess of Edinburgh, 140, 142, 145
Marie, Princess, of Edinburgh, Crown Princess of Roumania, 335
Marie, Queen of the Belgians, 135
Martin, Sir Theodore, 74, 264, 269
Mary, Duchess of Gloucester, 16
Mecklenburg, Grand Dukes of, 60
Mecklenburg-Strelitz, Grand Duchess of, 29
Methuen, Lord, 356

Milan, King of Serbia, 286, 336
Milne, Sir Alexander, 348
Mischke, General, 270
Moltke, Count von, 78, 93, 101, 102, 107, 121, 383
Montpensier, Duchess of, 211-2
Morier, Sir Robert, 30, 47, 66, 115, 151, 160, 172-3, 296
Morley, John, 152-3
Motley, John Lothrop, 40
Moulton, Charles, 297
Münster, Count, 127, 129, 279, 324
Murad, Sultan, 117
Muravieff, Count, 348-9

Napier, Lord, 116
Napoleon I, Emperor of the French, 113, 125, 292, 339
Napoleon III, Emperor of the French, 17, 63-5, 75, 79, 81, 99, 103, 121, 310, 327
Natzmer, Major von, 248
Nicholas I, Tsar of Russia, 49
Nicholas II, Tsar of Russia, 301, 349
Nicholas, Grand Duke, 36

O'Danne, Lieutenant, 72
Oldenburg, Grand Duke of, 36, 133-4
Ollivier, Olivier Emile, 64, 74, 77
Osborne, Bernal, 50
Osman Pasha, 123-4

Paget, Sir Augustus, 22, 62, 164
Palikao, General, 78
Palmerston, Lord, 18, 26, 49
Parnell, Charles Stewart, 153-4
Perglas, Baron, 75
Perpignan, Mlle de, 210, 212, 302
Phipps, the Hon. Harriet, 231
**Pius IX, Pope**, 111, 120
Ponsonby, Mary, Lady, 150-1, 158-9, 196, 210, 212-6, 220, 254, 287
Ponsonby, Sir Henry, 201, 210, 213, 231-5, 237, 239, 252, 280, 292
Prim, Marshal, 63-4
Puttkamer, Robert von, 244-5, 293-5

Radolin - Radolinsky, Count, 130-1, 193-4, 196, 198, 204, 215, 217-8, 242, 286, 293, 297
Radoslavoff, Vasil, 161
Rasputin, Grigori, 359
Redigher, Colonel, 158
Regnault, Henri, 324
Reid, Sir James, 183-4, 197, 213, 215, 234

Reischach, Baron von, 274, 336, 347, 350
Reiss, Mr, 318
Renvers, Professor, 355
Reuss, Prince, 284-5
Rhodes, Cecil, 353
Richelieu, Cardinal, 339
Rilésef, General, 142
Roberts, Lord, 355-6
Rodd, Sir Rennell, 184-5
Roder, General von, 295
Roggenbach, Baron von, 191, 194, 210, 213, 274, 283, 296-8, 339, 360
Roon, A.T.E., Count von, 68, 85
Rosebery, Lord, 153-4, 160-1, 301, 333-4, 341, 351
Rudolf, Archduke, Crown Prince of Austria, 164-5, 186, 284-5, 287
Russell, Lady Emily, 107
Russell, Lord John, 42, 49-50
Russell, Lord Arthur, 151
Russell, Odo (afterwards Lord Ampthill), 106-7, 116, 119, 122, 144, 151
Rutland, Duke of, 239, 241

Sadullah Bey, 127
Salisbury, Lord, 117-8, 128-9, 131, 147, 153-5, 160, 163-4, 217, 232-4, 236, 238, 240, 277, 301, 347
Saxony, Albert, Crown Prince, later King, 36, 201
Schaffgotsch, Count, 108
Schillbach, Professor, 80, 91
Schmidt, Dr Moritz, 200, 202-4, 242
Schnabele, M, French Commissary, 169
Schrader, Dr, 182, 186, 193, 217, 264-5
Schröder, Dr, 200-2, 213
Schrötter, Professor von, 200-2, 218, 271
Schulenburg, Countess, 35
Schuvaloff, Count, 127, 131
Schweinitz, General, 72, 142, 340-1
Seckendorff, Count von, 68-9, 135, 150-1, 194, 210-2, 273, 306
Sedlnitsky, Countess Perponcher, 273
Semon, Dr Henry, and Sir Felix, 183
Senff, Major, 72
Sigismund, Prince, of Prussia, 55-7. 69, 110, 249, 360
Simmons, Sir J. Lintorn, 148
Sophie, Princess, of Prussia, Duchess of Sparta (later Queen of Greece), 64, 69-70, 73, 257, 290, 301-2, 321-2, 359
Spencer, Lord, 51, 153
Stambouloff, Stefan, 346
Steibel, Dr, 318
Stein, Heinrich F.K., Baron von, 79
Stephanie, Princess, of Belgium, 163

Stockmar, Baron, 16, 18, 30, 44, 87; Ernest von, 30, 38-9, 210, 299; Frau von, 237, 249, 275
Stosch, General von, 270, 296
Strachey, Sir G, 239
Straus, Hof Prediger, 29
Swaine, Colonel Leopold, 151, 201, 235-6, 252, 280
Symons, Sir William, 353
Szechenyi, Count, Austrian Ambassador, 285

Thiers, Louis Adolphe, 85
Tisza, Kalman, 161
Tobold, Professor, 183, 186, 189, 202, 209
Trautmann, Dr, 156
Treitschke, H.G. von, 293
Trochu, General, 83

Umberto, King of Italy, 321, 336

Vacaresco, Mlle., 335-6
Verne, Jules, 316
Victor Emanuel II, King of Italy, 121
Victoria, Princess, of Hesse, 157
Victoria, Princess, of Prussia, 59, 70, 156, 157, 212, 216, 231, 233-6, 238, 250, 257
Victoria, Princess, of Wales, daughter of King Edward VII, 302
Victoria, Queen of Great Britain and Ireland, Empress of India, 16; entertains Prince Frederick William of Prussia during Great Exhibition, 17; visits Emperor Napoleon III, 17; consents to engagement of Princess Royal, 18; chaperons Princess Royal, 20; opposes marriage in Berlin, 20; on departure of Princess Frederick for Berlin, 21; character of her court, 25; visits Princess Frederick at Babelsberg, 26; early attitude to Prince William (Emperor William II), 31, 100; at Coburg, 30, 47, 54; attitude to Schleswig-Holstein problem, 48; neutral attitude during Danish War (1864), 49; and Bismarck (1865), 53; and Prince Christian of Schleswig-Holstein, 53-4; engagement of Princess Helena, 54; endeavours to avert war between Prussia and Austria, 55; advice on Hohenzollern candidature, 63-4; sympathies during Franco-Prussian War, 66; and Crown Princess's appeal for hospital supplies, 69, 71; difficulty over Empress Eugénie's screen, 92-3; speech from the throne (1871), 100; on duties of princes towards their subjects, 101; accusations of breach of neutrality during Franco-Prussian War, 102; visit of Crown Prince and Princess Frederick (1871), 104; reconciles Crown Princess Frederick and Prince of Wales, 104; efforts for European peace, 111-3; opinion of Bismarck, 113, 115, 233, 236; on suggested British occupation of Egypt, 121-2; confers Order of the Garter on Prince William (Emperor William II), 138; on Prussian alliance with Austria, 147; and engagement of Princess Victoria of Prussia, 157, 233, 236-7; letter to Prince Alexander of Battenberg, 163; and illness of Crown Prince Frederick, 224, 259; visit to Emperor and Empress Frederick (1888), 231; and Crown Prince William (Emperor William II), 233-4, 237-9; relations with Prince Bismarck (1888), 236-

9; German visit (1888), 237-41; affection of Emperor Frederick III for, 250; and Emperor William II, 252; endeavours to reconcile Prince of Wales, Emperor William II and Empress Frederick, 278; invites Emperor William II to England, 282; influence over Empress Frederick, 291; as Colonel of German Dragoons, 294; efforts at reconciliation, 294; and proposed monument to Emperor Frederick III in Berlin, 319; invites Empress Frederick to England (1890), 319-20; visit of Empress Frederick to (1898), 351; eightieth birthday of, 352; death of, 357; see also 37, 42, 74, 90, 140, 153, 172, 230, 232, 259, 287, 314

Virchow, Professor R. von, 186-90, 192, 218-20, 224, 254

Voltaire, 140

Wagner, Richard, 316
Waldeger, Professor, 220
Waldemar, Prince, of Prussia, 70, 110, 137, 167, 271, 360
Waldemar, Prince, of Denmark, 149
Waldersee, General Count von, 280-1, 294, 299-300, 346, 359
Wales, Albert Edward, Prince of. *See* Edward VII., King
Wales, Alexandra, Princess of. *See* Alexandra, Queen
Wegner, Surgeon-General, 28, 69, 181-3, 185-7, 189, 191-2, 241, 243, 258, 306
Weimar, Grand Duke and Duchess of, 36
Wellington, Duke of, 16
Werder, General von, 96, 118, 142
Westminster, Duke of, 154
White, Sir George, 354
White, Sir William, 165, 171
William I, King of Prussia and German Emperor, 17, 25, 35, 38, 41, 43, 46-7, 64, 86-7, 95, 111, 130, 139, 182-3, 187
William II, German Emperor (Prince William of Prussia and Crown Prince): birth of, 27-8; physical disability of, 28, 61-2, 98, 222; christening of, 28; early attitude of Queen Victoria to, 31, 100; education of, 61; parental cares for, 97-8; character as a boy, 108, 133, 138; confirmation of, 109-10; influence of Emperor William I on, 110; and Empress Frederick (before his accession to throne), 138-9, 141, 143-4, 161, 190, 193, 203-6, 214, 220, 231, 243-4, 314; comes of age, 138; receives Order of the Garter, 138; character in early manhood, 138-9, 166; his opinion of his father, 139; secret engagement of, 139-40; visit to England (1880), 143; marriage of, 144, 156-7; estrangement between Crown Princess Frederick and, 156-8, 166, 223; presence at Gastein Conference, 161; question of presence at Queen Victoria's Jubilee, 190; influence in Berlin, 195; visits father and mother at Baveno, 197; at San Remo, 201, 203; prospect of his accession, 201, 231; attitude to his mother, 204, 220, 253; and operation on Crown Prince, 204, 259; imperial authority delegated to, 207; activities during father's reign, 231, 233, 237, 243, 245; and Queen Victoria, 233, 237-9, 252; and Dr Bergmann, 242; unfilial attitude after death of Emperor Frederick III, 248-9, 251, 271; and Empress Frederick (after his accession to throne), 249, 251, 255, 267, 271-5, 277-280, 318, 321, 347, 359-60; policy on accession, 251, 253, 260; references to Prince of Wales (King Edward VII), 260-2; and Emperor Frederick's War Diary, 265-7; journeys of, 268; Empress Frederick's opinion of,

272, 277-81, 292, 311, 313-5, 322, 326-8, 330-2, 342, 344; influence of Prince Bismarck on, 276-7, 309; visit to England (1889), 282-96; attitude of Prince Bismarck to, 286; breach with Prince Bismarck, 289, 297, 333; and Westphalian miners, 289-90; influence of Count von Waldersee on, 294; state visit to England (1889), 294; fails to deny Freytag's slanders, 303; refuses Empress Frederick headship of Red Cross societies, 306-7; conflict with Prince Bismarck over Socialist Law, 308-9; proposes Labour Conference, 310; forbids monument to Emperor Frederick III, 319; and Sophie, Duchess of Sparta, 322; birth of fourth son, 322; and Empress Frederick's Paris visit (1891), 323; Erfurt speech of (September 1891), 326-7; provocative acts and speeches of, 327-30, 344, 356; rapprochement between Bismarck and, 328-9, 332, 339, 345; attends silver wedding of King and Queen of Italy, 336; colonial policy of, 340; and German navy, 341; presents Bismarck with sword of honour, 345; and the 'Kruger telegram', 353; and last days of Empress Frederick, 357; description of Empress Frederick, 358
Williams, Montague, 259
Winter, Burgomaster von, 41
Winterfeldt, General von, 252, 290, 293
Wrangel, Field-Marshal, 26, 27, 49
Wurtemberg, Crown Prince of, 36
Wurtemberg, King of, 69

Zedlitz, Count, 436

# Also available

## FREDERICK, CROWN PRINCE AND EMPEROR, Rennell Rodd

Frederick III, second German Emperor, reigned for only three months, from March to June 1888. Having been Crown Prince for twenty-seven years, he was stricken with cancer of the larynx, and by the time he succeeded his elderly father on the throne he was unable to speak above a whisper. Married to Victoria, Princess Royal of Great Britain, he was the hope of liberals throughout Germany and Europe. Had he ruled for longer in good health, the war of 1914-18 would almost certainly have been avoided. Rodd's brief biographical essay, first published in November 1888, was the first life of him to appear. This new edition contains the original text, with a foreword by John Van der Kiste which includes the background to the writing of the book and a note on the life of the author, and additional illustrations.

153pp, paperback

ISBN 10: 151765923X
ISBN 13: 978-1517659233

# Also available

## ALEXANDER III, TSAR OF RUSSIA, Charles Lowe

Alexander III, Tsar of Russia, reigned from 1881 to 1894. Having succeeded to the throne on the assassination of his father, Alexander II, he rejected the latter's plans for constitutional reform. A firm autocrat, he made no concessions to liberalism and his reign was noted for political repression and persecution of the Jews, as well as a loosening of the alliance with Germany and a new understanding with France. Lowe's biography was first published in 1895, and though it appeared within a year of the subject's death, it remains an invaluable record of his life and times. This new illustrated edition contains an introduction by John Van der Kiste. Charles Lowe (1848-1931) was a foreign correspondent with The Times. His life of Tsar Alexander III remains his best-known and most important work.

240pp, paperback

ISBN 10: 1522840729
ISBN 13: 978-1522840725

Printed in Great Britain
by Amazon